POLICE and POLICING

POLICE and POLICING
Contemporary Issues

Second Edition

Edited by
Dennis Jay Kenney
and Robert P. McNamara

Westport, Connecticut
London

Library of Congress Cataloging-in-Publication Data

Police and policing : contemporary issues / edited by Dennis Jay
   Kenney and Robert P. McNamara. — 2nd ed.
      p.   cm.
   Includes bibliographical references and index.
   ISBN 0–275–95498–6 (alk. paper). — ISBN 0–275–95499–4 (pbk. :
alk. paper)
   1. Police professionalization—United States.   2. Police
administration—United States.   3. Law enforcement—United States.
4. Criminal investigation.   I. Kenney, Dennis Jay.   II. McNamara,
Robert P.
   HV8141.P56   1999
   363.2′0973—dc21   98–33609

British Library Cataloguing in Publication Data is available.

Library of Congress Catalog Card Number: 98–33609
ISBN: 0–275–95498–6
        0–275–95499–4 (pbk.)

First published in 1999

Praeger Publishers, 88 Post Road West, Westport, CT 06881
An imprint of Greenwood Publishing Group, Inc.

Printed in the United States of America

The paper used in this book complies with the
Permanent Paper Standard issued by the National
Information Standards Organization (Z39.48–1984).

10   9   8   7   6   5   4   3   2   1

Contents

Introduction:
Twenty Years of Change in Policing

Robert P. McNamara

In the first edition of this text, Samuel Walker described some of the most significant changes that had taken place in policing since the 1960s. In his review of the literature, he framed these changes in three main areas. The first revolved around attempts to change the officers. That is, policing in the future was going to require a different breed of officer and one of the most significant set of reforms evolved around recruiting and training in a vastly different way than in previous eras. Included in this discussion was the additional number of training hours, improved supervision, control of corruption, as well as efforts to make law enforcement more professional by attracting college-educated officers. While the research did not and does not convincingly demonstrate that a college education makes for a "better" police officer, efforts to professionalize policing in this way continue (Sherman 1978; Hoover 1983; Carter, Sapp, and Stephens 1989). In fact, many police departments are now requiring a minimum of two years of college as part of the criteria for entry into the profession (Gaines, Kappeler, and Vaughn 1994).

The second wave of reforms focuses more on the organizational characteristics of policing. While law enforcement has its share of traditions and ritualistic practices, these tended to give way during the 1980s to a more open approach by police departments. That is, many agencies attempted to restructure in an attempt to become more effective at fighting crime while enhancing organizational objectives. Community-oriented policing, for example, emphasizes improved police–community relations in hopes that that will assist in solving many problems in particular neighborhoods (Dunham and Alpert 1993).

Finally, Walker describes reforms as attempts to change the environment of policing. While this is related to the first two types of reforms in that it attempts to fundamentally change the types of services provided to the community and the individuals providing them, a large part of this effort focused on the role of the police. For instance, in contrast to the traditional model of policing, a new philosophy, broadly called *community policing*, became a common feature in the law-enforcement landscape. While there remain many definitional problems concerning what community policing is (a philosophical change versus a strategy within the existing organization), the development of this model was considered groundbreaking in terms of what was expected of police officers (Trojanowicz and Bucqueroux 1990). In sum, Walker's contribution greatly enhances our understanding of the nature of reforms in law enforcement.

Since the publication of this first edition in 1989, the amount of research being conducted on the police, as well as discussions of the issues surrounding the role of law enforcement, has grown considerably. With that has come a greater emphasis on empirical support for programs as well as a greater willingness on the part of police agencies to allow researchers access to the organizations and their personnel. Many police executives see the value of research, both in terms of a broader understanding of the issues as well as the practical benefits quality research can provide a police department. It is indeed a time of change in the study of policing.

While we are witnessing perhaps more research on the police than at any time in history, and while we have become much more sophisticated in our understanding of the role of law enforcement in society, a great many questions are left unanswered. As such, researchers, policy makers, and law-enforcement officials continue to wrestle with a host of complex issues. In addition, as with most social phenomena, as society changes it brings new challenges to existing problems. In short, we are learning a lot about the realities of policing, but the issues are extremely complex and our understanding is affected by the dynamic nature of society.

An additional problem occurs when we embrace progress only to resist change when programs or strategies are ineffective. While policing, like many professions, is bound with its traditions and customs, many times those very practices prevent us from seeing the larger picture. Part of the reason for this is our continual search for a single solution to a particular problem. James Finckenauer (1982) aptly describes this process as *the panacea phenomenon*. This process begins with the introduction of a new program or strategy which has some initial success. This is typically followed by a wave of enthusiasm, which increases its number of advocates. A bandwagon effect then results in exaggerated claims of the overall impact of the program, which is then followed by an expansion of the possibilities—it becomes the next cure-all to our problems. Finally, an objective evaluation of the program occurs, and this usually shows that the strategy is not nearly as successful, nor can it ever possibly have the kind of impact its makers suggest. This usually leads to frustration, which leads many people to take on the cynical attitude that "nothing works." This occurs, of course, until the next panacea is offered and the process begins anew.

Still, there is reason to be optimistic. While the risks of the effects of the panacea phenomenon are always a constant possibility, some of the reforms in policing are providing the tools to become more effective. Among the most significant changes in the last twenty years has been to reorient our thinking about what exactly law enforcement should do. The traditional approach suggests a crime-fighting, socially distant, calculating, rational model of policing. Police departments were organized as paramilitary bureaucracies, with clear lines of authority where each individual within the organization was designated with specific tasks.

The most recent changes in law enforcement have attempted to depart from this model in favor of a more liberal interpretation of policing. As several of the chapters in this book clearly demonstrate, there is evidence to suggest that expanding the police officer's role and allowing him or her to identify the problems in a particular area and to explore the ways in which to solve them have been effective. The broad term most often used to describe this approach is *problem-oriented policing*. Goldstein (1979) argued that the police must transcend their focus of addressing the immediate problem and recognize that many of their activities or incidents are connected rather than episodic events. In addition, Goldstein argued that police officers need to devise workable solutions to the problems in their particular areas of concern.

While there are problems with problem-oriented policing (as Michael Buerger explores in Chapter 15), most of them do not negate the viability of the approach. Rather, the problems are typically logistical ones of how to solve the problem. Thus, there has been increasing optimism for this approach to policing.

A second trend that can be identified in policing is a greater understanding of the issues and problems individual officers experience as members of the profession. Over the past few decades, the effects of police socialization and the influence of the subculture of policing (Westley 1970; Rokeach, Miller, and Snyder 1971; Kirkham 1976; Bittner 1970; Rubenstein 1973; Van Maanen 1973; Alpert and Dunham 1992; Neiderhoffer 1963), as well as the impacts of police stress (Gaines,

Kappeler, and Vaughn 1993; Territo and Vetter 1981), have been well documented. And while there have always been attempts to evaluate the performance of police officers, one of the more important trends that has emerged of late is a concern for the deleterious effects the job has on individuals. Recent studies have focused on common problems, although few have been empirically examined.

These issues and others are important to the discussion, not only of what law enforcement officers should be doing, but how well they perform these tasks. To some, it appears that the study of policing has taken on a more sensitive turn: Police departments have become more introspective as to what they are doing, how they are doing it, and, in the process, have come to recognize the synergistic relationship they have with the community in solving crime-related problems. At the same time, there is increased attention focusing on the more subtle yet important issues relating to the occupation. Both areas have a solid sociological foundation as well as a long tradition in research, where the value of building cohesion within a group or a society has a host of benefits for its members (Durkheim 1847). As it applies to policing, it not only makes for a more effective police officer, but society benefits in terms of the product that is provided by the department.

On the other hand, while there is a great deal of excitement and optimism, a litany of questions remains that we struggle to comprehend. On some issues, in fact, we seem as puzzled now as we were twenty years ago. For example, while the study of police corruption has provided researchers with basic ideas for solutions, we have not made significant strides toward solving this problem. As evidence, the recent Mollen Commission in New York City found systematic corruption within the New York City Police Department similar to what the Knapp Commission discovered nearly a quarter century earlier. In Chapter 13, Bob Leuci contends that much of what we have learned about police corruption has not, in fact, made much of a difference. In many instances, he suggests, the very nature of police work makes the elimination of corruption impossible.

Finally, there are those programs giving the appearance of success that are, in reality, not. The most recent illustration of this is the DARE program. Started in 1983 by the Los Angeles Police Department and the Los Angeles School District, this anti-drug and anti-alcohol program has quickly become the nation's standard for dealing with substance abuse through education for children. This is a well-financed and popular program: By one estimate the program will receive at least $750 million in 1997. Moreover, the program boasts that police officers working with DARE now lecture in more than 70 percent of the nation's school districts (Glass 1997).

Despite the extensive marketing and claims of success, however, a number of evaluative studies show different results. Aniskiewicz and Wysong found, among students in Kokomo, Indiana, that the level of drug use among kids who had gone through DARE was virtually identical to the level among kids who had not (Glass 1997). Clayton (1996) surveyed students in Lexington, Kentucky, where schools were randomly assigned to receive the DARE curriculum. Testing students before they received the DARE program, immediately afterward, and again each year through the spring of 1992, Clayton found that any results from DARE were extremely short-lived. Other studies focusing on the DARE program, although differing methodologically, have consistently found that DARE does not have long-term effects on drug use.

Given what we do know, it is important that we ask where are we headed and what we can expect as we move into the twenty-first century. As this book will show, we may be beginning to experience the effects of the reorientation of the role of law enforcement; allowing the problem-oriented approach to operate seems to be working, at least so far and in some places. At the same time, while we do not know for certain if community policing will be the standard for the twenty-first century, we need to remain flexible in the face of a changing society. In doing so, we should expect that the officer we select today will be different from those hired twenty years ago.

Finally, as Finckenauer (1982) cautioned us, we should remain realistic about the potential impact of such changes on crime. It is far too easy to envision sweeping, wholesale changes to a system and a phenomenon when incremental or retail changes are more appropriate. As Walker wrote in 1989, while we may be better informed today than we were twenty-five years ago, we should remember that with understanding comes a precautionary and sensible approach to the solutions that result.

BIBLIOGRAPHY

Adorno, T. W. (1950). *The Authoritarian Personality*. New York: Harper and Brothers.

Alpert, G. P., and R. G. Dunham. (1992). *Critical Issues in Policing*. Prospect Heights, Ill.: Waveland Press.

Bittner, E. (1970). *The Functions of Police in Modern Society*. Chevy Chase, Md.: National Clearinghouse for Mental Health.

Carter, D.; A. Sapp; and D. Stephens. (1989). Higher Education as a Bonafide Occupational Qualification for Police: A Blueprint. *American Journal of Police* 7 (2): 1–28.

Clayton, D. (1996). *Intervening with Drug Involved Youth*. Washington, D.C.: National Institute of Justice.

Dunham, R., and G. P. Alpert. (1993). *Critical Issues in Policing*. Prospect Heights, Ill.: Waveland Press.

Durkheim, E. (1847). *The Division of Labor in Society*. New York: The Free Press.

Finckenauer, J. (1982). *Scared Straight and the Panacea Phenomenon*. Englewood Cliffs, N.J.: Prentice-Hall.

Gaines, L.; V. Kappeler; and J. Vaughn. (1994). *Policing in America*. Cincinnati, Ohio: Anderson.

Gaines, L. K.; V. E. Kappeler; and J. B. Vaughn. (1993). *Policing in America*. Cincinnati, Ohio: Anderson.

Glass, S. (1997). Don't You DARE. *The New Republic*, 3 March, 18.

Goldstein, H. (1979). Improving Policing: A Problem-Oriented Approach. *Crime and Delinquency* 25: 236–258.

Hoover, L. (1983). The Educational Criteria: Dilemmas and Debate. In *The Police Personnel System*, edited by C. Swank and J. Cosner. New York: John Wiley.

Kirkham, G. (1976). *Signal Zero*. New York: Ballentine.

Neiderhoffer, A. (1963). *Behind the Shield: The Police in Urban Society*. Garden City, N.Y.: Doubleday.

Rokeach, M.; M. Miller; and H. Snyder. (1971). The Value Gap between Police and Policed. *Journal of Social Issues* 27: 155–171.

Rubenstein, J. (1973). *City Police*. New York: Farrar, Strauss, and Giroux.

Sherman, L. (1978). *The Quality of Police Education*. San Francisco, Calif.: Jossey-Bass.

Territo, L., and H. J. Vetter. (1981). *Stress and Police Personnel*. Boston, Mass.: Allyn and Bacon.

Trojanowicz, R., and B. Bucqueroux. (1990). *Community Policing*. Cincinnati, Ohio: Anderson.

Van Maanen, J. (1973). Observations on the Making of a Policeman. *Human Organization* 32 (4): 407–418.

Walker, S. (1989). Conclusion: Paths to Police Reform—Reflections on 25 Years of Change. In *Police and Policing*, edited by Dennis Jay Kenney, 271–284. Westport, Conn.: Praeger.

Westley, W. (1970). *Violence and the Police: A Sociological Study of Law, Custom, and Morality*. Cambridge: MIT Press.

1

The Socialization of the Police

Robert P. McNamara

The concept of socialization has been subjected to extensive analysis, with the definitions of the concept varying widely. Generally speaking, we can say the term *socialization* is used to describe the ways in which people learn to conform to their society's norms, values, and roles. Many sociologists contend that people develop their own unique personalities as a result of the learning they gain from parents, siblings, relatives, teachers, and all the other people who influence them throughout their lives (Elkin and Handel 1989). What is important about socialization, then, is that people learn to behave according to the expectations of their culture and transmit that way of life from one generation to the next. In this way, the culture of a society is reproduced (see, for instance, Parsons and Bales 1955; Danziger 1971).

It is also important to note that socialization occurs throughout an individual's life as he or she learns the norms of new groups in new situations. Generally speaking, there are three categories of socialization: *primary*, which involves the ways in which the child becomes a part of society; *secondary*, where the influence of others outside the family become important; and *adult* socialization, when the person learns the expectations of adult roles and statuses in society. This last type of socialization includes learning the standards set by one's occupation.

THE SOCIALIZATION PROCESS IN OCCUPATIONS

Of the many roles that a person is called on to perform, few surpass the importance of possessing the skills and attitudes necessary for one's occupation. This is especially true in modern society, where occupation has a central place in the life of the vast majority of adults. In fact, occupation is challenged only by the family and the peer group as the major determinant of behavior and attitudes (Moore 1969). To the degree that adequate socialization occurs to permit one to adequately perform in an occupation, an individual's worldview, attitudes toward others, and general well-being are influenced.

Interestingly, occupational socialization has not elicited the kind of scholarly interest that one might expect. While there are many studies on this topic, academic interest in socialization traditionally focused on infancy and childhood. It has only been since the 1960s that researchers have become keenly interested in occupational socialization, or what is sometimes referred to as the *sociology of work* (see Erikson and Vallas 1995). The topics seem to focus on the normative dimensions of occupations; that is, the rules relating to the proper conduct and attitudes of an individual in a particular job or career.

For instance, in a classic study of socialization into an occupation, Becker et al. (1961) examined the process by which medical students are socialized into their profession. At the University of Kansas Medical School, Becker found that lower-class medical students, by virtue of their undergraduate education and commitment to becoming successful physicians, had clearly assimilated middle-class norms and values. Becker also found that first-year medical students had idealistic reasons for becoming a physician: Helping people was more important than making money. In the beginning of their profession, then, there was a strong sense of idealism with many students feeling that medical school would give them the opportunity to develop the skills needed to further that goal.

As they proceeded through their medical training, however, Becker et al. (1961) found that the process caused many of the students to alter their views. Early on, they adapted to the expectations of medical school and developed a strong appreciation of clinical experience (working with patients rather than studying disease in the laboratory), learning to view death and disease as medical problems, rather than as emotional issues. Despite this initial idealism, however, many students soon realized that success in the program required refocusing their effort on the most economical methods of learning. Thus, during the course of their medical training idealism was replaced with a concern for getting through the program. Becker observed that medical students may in fact become cynical while in school, but he pointed out that these attitudes were often situational. As graduation approached, idealism seemed to return once the students were no longer under the intense pressure to "perform" (the immediate problem of completing their studies had passed). From this he concluded that when isolated in an institutional setting, the students adjusted to immediate demands. Once "released" from that setting, their attitudes changed to again conform to their new surroundings.

The broader implications of the work of Becker and colleagues (1961) are that individuals are socialized to meet the expectations that important institutions or organizations place on them. Attitudes, values, and beliefs become centered around fulfilling those expectations. In the case of physicians, where considerable autonomy exists, the original ideological concerns reemerge at the end of training largely because each individual has the ability to determine the circumstances under which he or she will practice medicine. In those professions where there is an intense training period, less autonomy, and greater internal control by the organization, the individual is greatly influenced by the members of that organization. In other words, where greater freedom to practice one's profession exists, there is less of an impact in terms of the socialization process. However, in those professions where the individual is constrained by organizational rules and regulations, other members will exert more influence on the thoughts and actions of the individual. This is exacerbated in professions that actively promote a sense of camaraderie and solidarity among members.

RESOCIALIZATION

Perhaps the most significant aspect of the socialization process is that members within an organization (or, more broadly, within a society) internalize a set of norms that dictate appropriate behavior. When this fails to occur, the organization is forced to employ corrective methods to ensure conformity. Examples include deviants or criminals. Others, however, are resocialized because of a decision to join a new group. A good example of this occurs when an individual selects a particular career, such as soldier or police officer. It is here that the work of Erving Goffman (1961) plays a significant part in our understanding. In his now classic *Asylums*, Goffman contends that the resocialization of individuals often occurs in *total institutions*. These are places where the individual's physical and social freedom are constrained and channeled in a certain direction. Goffman describes resocialization as a two-step process. First, there is what he calls the *mortification of the self*, where the attitudes, worldviews, and behavior patterns of the individual are stripped away:

The recruit comes into the establishment with a conception of himself made possible by certain stable social arrangements in his home world. Upon entrance, he is immediately stripped of the support provided by these arrangements. In the accurate language of some of our oldest total institutions, he begins a series of abasements, degradations, humiliations, and profanations of self. His self is systematically, if often unintentionally, mortified. He begins to radical shifts in his moral career, a career composed of the progressive changes that occur in the beliefs that he has concerning himself and significant others. The process by which a person's self is mortified are fairly standard in total institutions; analysis of these processes can help us to see the arrangements that ordinary establishments must guarantee if members are to preserve their civilian selves. (pp. 14–20)

This paves the way for the second step in resocialization, where a new set of attitudes, values, and beliefs are provided:

Once the inmate is stripped of his possessions, at least some replacements must be made by the establishment, but these take the form of standard issue, uniform in character and uniformly distributed. These substitute possessions are clearly marked as really belonging to the institution and in some cases are recalled at regular intervals to be, as it were, disinfected of identifications. . . . While the process of mortification goes on, the inmate begins to receive formal and informal instruction in what will here be called the privilege system. In so far as the inmate's attachment to his civilian self has been shaken by the stripping process of the institution, it is largely the privilege system that provides a framework for personal reorganization. (pp. 20–29)

In the case of the military, the new recruit or civilian is brought to a "boot" camp and stripped of any individual characteristics: Clothes are taken away, haircuts are given, and rules on every aspect of life in the institution are explained. It is during this process that the sense of self gives way and the individual becomes a cog in a much larger machine. Only after this process is complete can the organization implement the second part of the resocialization process. Upon completion of boot camp, the recruit has a different sense of self along with a new set of attitudes and behavior patterns.

A similar process occurs in law enforcement. After selection, the police academy (also considered to be a type of total institution), represents the first overt process of socialization. In addition to the skills and techniques needed to become an effective police officer, recruits are indoctrinated and exposed to the vernacular used by the profession, the cultural norms dictating acceptable and unacceptable behavior, as well as the worldview from the law-enforcement perspective. In addition, these values, attitudes, and beliefs are reinforced informally as new officers interact with more experienced ones outside of the classroom. The "war stories" told by more seasoned officers reinforce the points made by formal classroom lessons. Over time, recruits develop attitudes and behaviors that provide a consistent framework in which to understand the role of the police and the individual officer (see, for instance, Radelet 1986).

This process continues after the academy, when the officer is usually assigned some sort of field training. The time spent in this phase of training varies by department, but can be up to six months. The field training officer (FTO) is responsible for teaching the new officer how to apply lessons from the academy to the tasks on the street. There is also an evaluative component to the process, in that the FTO is charting the progress (or lack thereof) of the recruit. The style of the FTO, as well as the way in which the FTO interacts with citizens, will tend to be reflected in the recruit's behavior. In this way, FTO training is a part of the socialization process, even though it may not be a conscious process (Radelet 1986).

After FTO training, the officer remains on probation for a period of time, usually one year. During this time a supervisor evaluates the officer in terms of progress and overall performance in the job. As described by Becker and colleagues (1961), most recruits will admit that part of the learning process involves knowing the unique expectations their supervisor–teacher has for them. When this is learned, the officer will modify his or her behavior to conform with that of the supervisor (see also Radelet 1986). If, for instance, the officer learns that the sergeant places a great deal of emphasis on police–community relations, the officer will, in turn, have more community contacts. These learned behaviors are part of what Goffman (1961) refers to as *working the system*. More important, these behaviors are the essence of occupational socialization.

For the most part, this is a normal part of the learning process. In order to be an effective police officer, the rookie officer must first learn the tricks of the trade and the most knowledgeable officers should impart their wisdom on their less learned colleagues. However, there is also the potential for various forms of misconduct to be taught along with the proper procedures and attitudes.

NATURE VERSUS NURTURE IN POLICING

In 1991, Los Angeles police officers shocked the American public with the beating of Rodney King. In 1996, a South Carolina state trooper assaulted a motorist while she attempted to exit her vehicle after a traffic stop. Also in 1996, Los Angeles area officers were again accused of assaulting Hispanic motorists after a prolonged pursuit. Incidents like these raise many questions concerning the attitudes, values, and behavior of police officers around the country. Social scientists have offered differing and sometimes conflicting explanations for police use of authority and misconduct.

Some observers contend that the police personality is different than that found in other occupations. Others maintain that there is a cultural distinction that separates law enforcement from other occupations. Since a third group disputes both of these assumptions, it is probably safe to say that no single perspective provides a complete understanding of the varieties of police behavior. What can be said with some confidence, however, is that the roles and functions of the police set officers apart from other members of society (Radelet 1986).

The Socialization Argument

A number of researchers argue that personality is not fixed and rigid and is subject to change based on different personal experiences and socialization. This school of thought focuses on the role of the police in society and how professionalization, training, and socialization influence an individual's personality and behavior. Researchers operating from this paradigm study how the work environment, peers, and academy training shape and affect a police officer's personality and behavior. Many of these researchers, such as Adlam (1982), still focus attention on an individual's unique experiences and the development of individual personalities.

A somewhat different approach contends that socialization occurs, but it is more of a group experience than an individual one (Stoddard 1968; Van Maanen 1978). For example, Van Maanen disagrees with the idea that police officers have certain personality characteristics, such as authoritarianism. He argues instead for a perspective based on both group socialization and professionalism. The latter is the process by which norms and values are internalized as an individual begins his or her new occupation. In this way, just as attorneys and physicians learn the values endemic to their profession, so too do police officers.

This perspective assumes that police officers learn their "social" personality from training and through exposure to the demands of police work. It follows then that if police officers become cynical or rigid, it is not because of their existing personality or individual experience, but because of the demands of the job and the shared experiences of others. Some research supports this idea. For instance, Bennett (1984) found that while probationary officers' values are affected by the training process, little evidence that personalities were shaped by their peers in the department was available. Part of this explanation involves the legitimacy of newly hired officers, who do not become "real" police officers until they are accepted as a member in standing of the police subculture.

Other studies, such as that of Putti, Aryee, and Kang (1988), find that there may be a temporal factor at work in the socialization of police officers. That is, socialization into the subculture of police may occur at different points in the officers' careers. There is little evidence concerning the extent to which reference groups affect the personality of older officers, but it seems that in the beginning of his or her career the officer's occupational values are shaped during the training and probationary process.

Still another model is offered by Kappeler, Blumberg, and Potter (1993), who contend that there is an acculturation process whereby the beliefs and values of police work are transmitted from one generation of officers to the next. In effect, the group socializes the individual officer into ways of acceptable and unacceptable behavior. This perspective draws heavily from an anthropological point of view and introduces the concept of the police subculture more concretely.

The Authoritarian Personality

Many researchers adopting this perspective feel that personality is fixed and does not really change by choice of occupation or experience. In other words, each person has a fixed personality that does not vary during the course of his or her life (Adlam 1982). This does not imply that personality is inviolate or does not have some degree of malleability, but generally speaking it stays the same. As it applies to the police, most of the research in this area focuses on the personality characteristics of people who choose to become police officers. This perspective assumes that people with certain types of personalities enter law enforcement as an occupation and behave in certain ways.

One of the most influential scholars in this area is Milton Rokeach. In comparing the values of police officers in Michigan with those of a national sample of private citizens, Rokeach, Miller, and Snyder (1971) found that police officers seemed more oriented toward self-control and obedience than the average citizen. Further, he observed that officers were more interested in personal goals, such as "an exciting life," but less interested in larger social goals, such as "a world at peace." Rokeach also found evidence that experiences as police officers did not significantly influence their personalities. He concludes that most officers probably have a unique value orientation and personality when they embark upon their careers in policing.

In a similar study, Teevan and Dolnick (1973) compared values of officers in the Cook County, Illinois Sheriff Department with those Rokeach encountered in Lansing, Michigan. The findings suggest that the values of police officers in a large urban department are also far removed from those of the general public. Some of the reasons, according to Teevan and Dolnick, are that officers are isolated within society, they are required to enforce unpopular laws, and there is a sense of self-imposed segregation as officers think of themselves as a last bastion of middle-class morality.

In describing the authoritarian personality, Adorno (1950) characterizes it, in part, as aggressive, cynical, and rigid behavior. People with these characteristics are said to have a myopic view of the world where issues, people, and behavior are seen as clearly defined: good or bad, right or wrong, friends or enemies. They also tend to be very conservative in their political orientation (see also Neiderhoffer 1967; Bayley and Mendelsohn 1969). Levy (1967) proposes that certain personality traits established early in life are clues to whether a person would be more likely to find policing attractive as a profession:

We find that the appointees most likely to remain in law enforcement are probably those who are more unresponsive to the environmental stresses introduced when they become an officer of the law than are their fellow-appointees. These stresses include becoming a member of a "minority" (occupationally speaking) group, need to adhere to semi-military regimen, community expectation of incongruous roles and the assumption of a position of authority complete with the trappings of uniform, badge, holster, and gun, and all these imply. The officers who remain in law enforcement may well be the sons of fathers who imposed a rigid code of behavior to which their children learned to adhere, and who do not feel a strong need to defy or rebel against authority. (p. 275)

On the other hand, some researchers have pointed to a few positive aspects of this type of personality in police officers. Carpenter and Raza (1987), for example, have found that police applicants as a group are less depressed and more assertive in making and maintaining social contacts. Further, they suggest that police are a more homogeneous group than others, which may result from their similar interests in becoming police officers as well as their sharing of similar personality traits and worldviews.

Ultimately, many develop an occupational or working personality characterized by authoritarianism, suspicion, and cynicism (Rubenstein 1973; Van Maanen 1978; Alpert and Dunham 1994; Neiderhoffer 1967). Skolnick (1994) provides perhaps the best description of the police personality:

The policeman's role contains two principal variables, danger and authority, which should be interpreted in the light of a "constant" pressure to appear efficient. The element of danger seems to make the policeman especially attentive to signs indicating a potential for violence and lawbreaking. As a result, the policeman is generally a "suspicious" person. Furthermore, the character of the policeman's work makes him less desirable as a friend, since norms of friendship implicate others in his work. Accordingly, the element of danger isolates the policeman socially from that segment of the citizenry which he regards as symbolically dangerous and also from the conventional citizenry with whom he identifies. (p. 43)

Some have suggested that an integral part of the police personality is cynicism: the notion that all people are motivated by evil and selfishness. Police cynicism develops among many officers through the nature of police work. Most police officers feel they are set apart from the rest of society because they have the power to regulate the lives of others. Moreover, by constantly dealing with crime and the more unsavory aspects of social life their faith in humanity seems to diminish.

Probably the most well-known study of police personality was conducted by Arthur Neiderhoffer (1967). In *Behind the Shield*, Neiderhoffer builds on the work of William Westley (1970) that most officers develop into cynics as a function of their daily routines. Westley had maintained that being constantly faced with keeping people in line and believing that most people intend to break the law or cause harm to the officer leads officers to mistrust the people they are charged to protect. Neiderhoffer tested Westley's assumption by distributing a survey measuring attitudes and values to 220 New York City police officers. Among his most important findings were that police cynicism did increase with length of service, patrol officers with college educations became quite cynical if they were denied promotion, and military-like academy training caused recruits to become cynical about themselves, the department, and the community. As an illustration, Neiderhoffer found that nearly 80 percent of first-day recruits believed the department was an "efficient, smoothly operating organization." Two months later, less than one-third professed that belief. Similarly, half of the recruits believed that a supervisor was "very interested in the welfare of his subordinates," while two months later those still believing so dropped to 13 percent. Neiderhoffer states, "Cynicism is an ideological plank deeply entrenched in the ethos of the police world, and it serves equally well for attack or defense. For many reasons police are particularly vulnerable to cynicism. When they succumb, they lose faith in people, society, and eventually in themselves. In their Hobbesian view, the world becomes a jungle in which crime, corruption, and brutality are normal features of the terrain" (p. 9).

In sum, the police personality emerges as a result of the very nature of police work and of the socialization process which most police officers experience. To deal with the social isolation that is derived from their use of authority, some of it self-imposed, officers use other members of the profession to cope with social rejection. As a result, many, perhaps most, police officers become part of a closely knit subculture that is protective and supportive of its members while sharing similar attitudes, values, understandings, and views of the world.

THE SUBCULTURE OF POLICING

Occupational socialization creates occupational subcultures (Bennett 1984). The idea of the police being a subculture is not new and has been well documented (see, for instance, Westley 1970; Rokeach, Miller, and Snyder 1971; Kirkham 1976; Bittner 1970). For our purposes, subculture may be defined as the meanings, values, and behavior patterns unique to a particular group in a given society. Entry into this subculture begins with a process of socialization whereby recruits learn the values and behavior patterns characteristic of experienced officers.

The development and maintenance of negative attitudes and values by police officers has many implications. Regoli and Poole (1979) found evidence that an officer's feelings of cynicism intensifies the need to maintain respect and increase the desire to exert authority over others. This can easily lead to increased fear and mistrust of the police by the general public. This, in turn, can create feelings of hostility and resentment on the part of the officer, creating what is sometimes known as *police paranoia* (Regoli and Poole 1979, 43). Regoli and Poole also found that these negative attitudes result in conservative attitudes and a resistance to change among the officers.

As mentioned, the creation of the police subculture also stems from the unique police personality. However, despite the evidence, many researchers disagree with the notion of a police subculture. Balch (1972), in his study of the police personality, states, "It looks like policemen may be rather ordinary people, not greatly unlike other middle Americans. We cannot be sure there is such a thing as a police personality, however we loosely define it" (p. 117). Similarly, Tifft (1974) argues that, while the attitudes of officers may be influenced by their work environment, the idea that officers maintain uniform personality traits developed through socialization or innate drives is fallacious. Thus, he argues that the activities and responsibilities most officers engage in have a role to play in how they see the world, but in many ways this is symptomatic of many other occupations: "Task related values, attitudes and behavior are occupationally derived or created out of specialized roles rather than being primarily due to the selection factors of background or personality" (p. 268).

The debate over whether officers possess a distinct working personality, as well as whether the subculture of policing is pervasive, continues and no attempt will be made to resolve it here, especially in light of the recent community-oriented movement. What is important to remember is that the nature of police work remains complex and the issues surrounding law enforcement have not been completely understood. To that end, the purpose of this chapter is to shed light on a number of issues of importance to the study of policing.

BIBLIOGRAPHY

Adlam, K. (1982). The Police Personality: Psychological Consequences of Becoming a Police Officer. *Journal of Police Science and Administration* 10 (3): 347–348.

Adorno, T. W. (1950). *The Authoritarian Personality*. New York: Harper and Brothers.

Alpert, G., and R. Dunham. (1994). *Policing Urban America*. 2d ed. Prospect Heights, Ill.: Waveland Press.

Balch, R. (1972). The Police Personality: Fact or Fiction? *Journal of Criminal Law, Criminology, and Police Science* 63: 117.

Bayley, D., and H. Mendelsohn. (1969). *Minorities and the Police: Confrontation in America*. New York: The Free Press.

Becker, H.; B. Greer; E. Hughes; and A. Strauss. (1961). *Boys in White: Student Culture in Medical School*. Chicago, Ill.: University of Chicago Press.

Bennett, R. R. (1984). Becoming Blue: A Longitudinal Study of Police Recruit Occupational Socialization. *Journal of Police Science and Administration* 12 (1): 47–57.

Bittner, E. (1970). *The Functions of Police in Modern Society*. Chevy Chase, Md.: National Clearinghouse for Mental Health.

Carpenter, B., and S. Raza. (1987). Personality Characteristics of Police Applicants: Comparisons Across Subgroups and with Other Populations. *Journal of Police Science and Administration* 15 (1): 10–17.

Danziger, K. (1971). *Socialization*. Harmondsworth, England: Penguin.

Elkin, F., and G. Handel. (1989). *The Child and Society: The Process of Socialization*. 5th ed. New York: Random House.

Erikson, K., and P. Vallas, eds. (1995). *The Nature of Work: Sociological Perspectives*. Washington, D.C.: American Sociological Association.

Goffman, E. (1961). *Asylums*. New York: Anchor.

Kappeler, V.; M. Blumberg; and G. Potter. (1993). *The Mythology of Crime and Criminal Justice*. Prospect Heights, Ill.: Waveland Press.

Kirkham, G. (1976). *Signal Zero*. New York: Ballentine.

Levy, R. (1967). Predicting Police Failures. *Journal of Criminal Law, Criminology, and Police Science* 58 (2): 265–276.

Moore, W. (1969). Occupational Socialization. In *Handbook of Socialization Theory and Research*, edited by D. Goslin. New York: Rand McNally.

Neiderhoffer, A. (1967). *Behind the Shield: The Police in Urban Society*. Garden City, N.Y.: Doubleday.

Parsons, T., and R. Bales. (1955). *Family, Socialization, and Interaction Process*. New York: The Free Press.

Putti, J.; S. Aryee; and T. Kang. (1988). Personal Values of Recruits and Officers in a Law Enforcement Agency: An Exploratory Study. *Journal of Police Science and Administration* 16 (4): 245–249.

Radelet, L. (1986). *The Police and the Community*. 4th ed. New York: Macmillan.

Regoli, R., and E. Poole. (1979). Measurement of Police Cynicism: A Factor Scaling Approach. *Journal of Criminal Justice* 7: 37–52.

Rokeach, M.; M. Miller; and J. Snyder. (1971). The Value Gap between Police and Policed. *Journal of Social Issues* 27: 155–171.

Rubenstein, J. (1973). *City Police*. New York: Farrar, Strauss, and Giroux.

Skolnick, J. (1994). *Justice Without Trial: Law Enforcement in a Democratic Society*. 5th ed. New York: John Wiley and Sons.

Stoddard, E. (1968). The Informal Code of Police Deviancy: A Group Approach to Blue-Collar Crime. *Journal of Criminal Law, Criminology, and Police Science* 59 (2): 201–203.

Teevan, J., and B. Dolnick. (1973). The Values of the Police: A Reconsideration and Interpretation. *Journal of Police Science and Administration* 1: 366–369.

Tifft, L. (1974). The Cop Personality Reconsidered. *Journal of Police Science and Administration* 2: 268.

Van Maanen, J. (1978). On Becoming a Policeman. In *Policing: A View from the Street*, edited by P. Manning and J. Van Maanen. Santa Monica: Goodyear.

Westley, W. (1970). *Violence and the Police: A Sociological Study of Law, Custom, and Morality*. Cambridge: MIT Press.

I

Managing Police Personnel

2

Intelligence and the Selection of Police Recruits

Dennis Jay Kenney and T. Steuart Watson

It is by now well accepted that in the stressful unpredictable world of policing, officers must possess the emotional tools necessary to perform a variety of often difficult and taxing duties. Because of the demands which officers confront, most law-enforcement agencies have come to accept the need to screen police candidates in an effort to avoid hiring those persons with attributes or behaviors which might be detrimental to either the officer's well-being or the organization's mission. To accomplish this, programs of psychological testing have become almost commonplace.

While the need for psychological fitness is obvious, the role of today's police officer is becoming increasingly complex in other ways as well. As the more traditional methods of law enforcement are called into question (see, for example, Kelling et al. 1974; Chaiken, Greenwood, and Petersilia 1977; Spelman and Brown 1984; Burrows 1986) and experimental efforts are introduced, officers find that their skills in communication, counseling, information collection, analysis, interpretation, and consensus building are frequently more important than they had previously imagined possible. As more and more agencies adopt these newer methods—such as team policing, split-force and directed patrol, problem- and community-oriented policing, ROP (Repeat Offender Program), and RECAP (Repeat Call Address Policing)—this refocusing of police procedure will almost certainly be accelerated. Despite these obvious trends, few in either law enforcement or academe have given much notice to questions concerning the ability of today's officers to meet tomorrow's expectations. This chapter, which reports on a program of IQ testing of police recruits undertaken by a mid-sized southern city, is one such effort.

BACKGROUND

The use of intelligence tests as an element of police selection has a brief and fairly early history. Terman (1917), for example, used the Stanford Revision of the Binet-Simon Intelligence Scale and several pedagogical tests to select candidates for police and firefighter positions. From an applicant pool of thirty, he placed the median IQ at 84, with seven candidates falling below 78 and seven above 91. Terman concluded that "intelligence tests are likely to be found a valuable aid in the selection of applicants for certain types of positions" (p. 18). Further, he recommended a cutoff score of 80 on intelligence tests as a means to select eligible candidates.

Interest in identifying means to select more qualified police and fire candidates increased substantially between the late 1920s and mid-1960s (Thurstone 1922; Merrill 1926; Kates 1950; Dubois and Watson 1950; Frost 1955; Mullineaux 1955; Oglesby 1957; Sterne 1960; Chenoweth 1961). Matarazzo and colleagues (1964) conducted one of the first comprehensive psychological assessments of civil service employees in Portland, Oregon. At that time, successful applicants in Portland were screened with a combined process of a written examination, physical agility test, department interview, and a medical examination. To evaluate this process, Matarazzo and his colleagues at the University of Oregon Medical School administered the Wechsler Adult Intelligence Scale (WAIS), a complete battery of personality tests, and a psychiatric interview to a sample of 243 applicants. The Full Scale IQs of his sample ranged from 85 to 130. The most relevant finding was that only four of the 243 tested had IQs below 100. This is in sharp contrast to the general population, where 50 percent of such scores are expected. It was clear to these investigators that even without the aid of sophisticated psychological assessment practices the city of Portland was already hiring those applicants with above-average intelligence.

In 1972, Murphy examined current practices of psychological testing utilized by police agencies. Based on the responses (N = 203) to a questionnaire sent to state and local police, he discovered that 44 percent of local agencies and 13 percent of state agencies used psychological tests to aid in candidate selection. Where psychological testing was used, personality measures were, by far, the most commonly employed instruments. The Wechsler Adult Intelligence Scale was used in only 5 percent of the agencies, compared to the 49 percent using the Minnesota Multiphasic Personality Inventory (MMPI). Despite its widespread use, however, there has been no empirical research indicating the MMPI's validity as a screening measure for police. Murphy concluded that current testing practices of various police agencies were insufficient due to questionable validity and an absence of uniform procedures. Nonetheless, he advocated the use of psychological tests not only for selection, but in determining assignments and promotions as well.

In an effort to uphold the Minimum Standards Act in the state of Tennessee, Saccuzzo, Higgins, and Lewandowski (1974) attempted to develop procedures to select police applicants free of mental disorders. Here, 196 subjects were administered the MMPI, Otis–Lennon Ability Test–Form J, and the Kuder Preference Test–Vocational Form CH. Based on the –14 raw score algebraic sum of the F-K index on the MMPI, the authors concluded that the respondents were trying to cast themselves in a favorable light by "faking good." This, in turn, brought into question the validity of using such instruments to detect deviance in employment candidates. Saccuzzo and colleagues cite Cohen and Chaiken (1973), who found age and IQ to be the two most important variables related to police performance. In short, Cohen and Chaiken found age to be inversely related to disciplinary action and absenteeism and IQ directly related to the numbers of performance awards received by officers. From this, then, some have concluded that more emphasis should be placed on predicting performance and less emphasis on discovering deviancy or mental disorders.

At about the same time, Hogan (1971) administered the California Personality Inventory (CPI) to 183 male police officers at the Maryland State Police Academy. The respondents were first divided into four groups based on their training status. Pearson correlations for the four groups showed the Intellectual Efficiency Scale to be the most highly and consistently correlated with criterion scores for each group. As such, performance as a police officer was seen as being related to intelligence, self-confidence, and social ability. In a similar study, McDonough and Monahan (1976) concluded that if choosing those applicants who stand a good chance of being promoted is the primary concern, it is best to focus on correlates of general intelligence, such as IQ.

While there has been considerable research in the area of psychological testing of police, most efforts have been focused on identifying a "police personality" or the personality characteristics that differentiate police from non-police. One such attempt involved research conducted in New York City on patrol officers attending college, officers who had never taken a college course, non-police attending college, and civilians who had never been to college or served as police officers (Fenster, Wiedemann, and Locke 1977). Not surprising, college-educated officers obtained significantly higher IQ scores than noncollege-educated officers. And, consistent with some earlier findings, the IQs of average police officers were found to be higher than that of the general population.

While differences were found on measures of personality characteristics between the groups, many questions remain unanswered. For example, do officers who are more dogmatic tend to perform better than those less so? Is this generally so or are different personality characteristics more desirable in some policing situations and less in others? These and similar questions should be addressed more fully in future research before any meaning can be placed on the differences in personality as measured by traditional paper-and-pencil tests. Until then, it would seem that due to the varied nature of police work and the diverse demands placed upon officers there is no "ideal" police profile on which to pick and choose applicants. A review of the inadequacies of personality testing in police selection can be found in Crosby (1979).

More recent efforts (Roe and Roe 1982; Inwald 1985; Aylward 1985; Bennett 1987) have begun to recognize the need for establishing a statistical base in order to select applicants fairly and accurately. To do this, research must be undertaken that defines the many roles and job objectives of the police, the skills needed to carry out these functions, and the methods that best identify who might possess these skills and traits.

The goal of this chapter is to examine the scores obtained by police trainees on one of the more reliable intelligence exams, the Wechsler Adult Intelligence Scale–Revised (WAIS–R), in an effort to stimulate thought and research on these issues as well as to explore the usefulness of using this widely accepted instrument as one screening measure.

THE METHOD

The subjects of this research were newly hired recruits for the police department of a mid-sized southeastern city. Each of these new police officers was hired between November 1986 and May 1987 and began attending one of three classes at the regional police academy. It was during their academy assignment that each recruit was asked by the police department to take the WAIS–R on a voluntary basis. All the recruits hired during this period (36) agreed to participate in the research.

Overall, the participating officers were unmarried (67%), male (86%), and had educations consisting of high school (36%) or high school and a few college courses (39%). They ranged from twenty-one to thirty-seven years old and were almost evenly split racially: eighteen recruits (50%) were white, while sixteen (44%) were black. The remaining two officers were Hispanic. The median reported age was twenty-five years. A sizable majority (72%) of the participating recruits were still employed by the agency one year after entering the academy. Of the ten recruits no longer in service, one was dismissed for "unsatisfactory probation" and nine resigned citing personal reasons or for other employment opportunities.

The Procedure

The WAIS–R was administered individually to each participating recruit in a private setting at the academy. The battery of tests was scheduled in advance and administered by a research assistant who was trained and supervised by a clinical psychologist with a private practice in the community. In each case, the individual record forms were carefully reviewed and rescored by both the supervising psychologist and independently by one of the authors to insure scoring accuracy. All subjects were scored according to the overall norms as reported for the WAIS–R, as opposed to age-corrected norms, due to the narrow range of ages tested and the consistency of the ages with those used for the overall norms.

The Instrument

The WAIS–R is comprised of six verbal and five performance (nonverbal) subtests. From these subtests, a Verbal Scale IQ, a Performance Scale IQ, and a Full-Scale IQ are derived. For each scale, a score of 100 is considered the mean and represents the fiftieth percentile of a national sample of test takers. Average intelligence would be considered between the scores of 90 and 109, while 110 to 119 would indicate high average intelligence. Scores over 120 are considered superior. At the other end of the scale, scores from 80 to 89 are considered to be low average, 70 to 79 borderline, and 69 and below mentally retarded.

Early research (Silverstein 1969, 1982) concluded that the Verbal Scale IQ was the best measure of a person's verbal comprehension skills. Later factor analytic research (Gutkin, Reynolds, and Galvin 1984) found that four subtests—Information, Vocabulary, Comprehension, and Similarities—were actually a more accurate measure of verbal comprehension than the overall Verbal IQ. Collectively, these four subtests are referred to as the Verbal Comprehension Deviation Quotient (VCDQ). The formula for the VCDQ is equal to the sum of the scaled scores for the subtests times 1.4 plus 44. Its distribution has a mean of 100 and a standard deviation of 15 and can be interpreted in the same fashion as an IQ. The VCDQ is considered superior to the Verbal IQ because of its greater construct validity, reliabilities that exceed 0.90 at all age levels, and standard errors of measurement that range from 2.6 to 3.4.

Gutkin and colleagues (1984) also found a second factor on the WAIS–R, which they referred to as the Perceptual Organization factor or the Perceptual Organization Deviation Quotient (PODQ). Only the Block Design and Object Assembly subtests make up this factor. The PODQ does not have reliability that exceeds 0.90, nor that of the Performance Scale IQ, and has standard errors of measurement ranging from 5.0 to 6.5. The PODQ is computed by summing the scaled scores of the two subtests, multiplying the sum by 2.8, and adding 44. This final score has a mean of 100 and a standard deviation of 15 and is also interpreted as an IQ. Although it is not as reliable as the VCDQ, the PODQ may be routinely computed as a comparison measure with the Performance Scale IQ.

While it is not appropriate to interpret individual subtests for diagnostic purposes, there are several subtests whose specific variance falls in the high category and that are not included in the two factors mentioned, all of which renders them amenable to cautious interpretation for research studies. Digit Span (0.47) and Arithmetic (0.29) of the Verbal Scale and Picture Completion (0.30), Picture Arrangement (0.33), and Digit Symbol (0.46) of the Performance Scale, with their percentage of total specific variance in parentheses, may be interpreted according to the specific skill(s) they are purported to measure. It is also worth noting that none of these subtests' reliability exceeds 0.84.

Digit Span is reportedly a measure of auditory short-term memory, though other factors such as attention, concentration, and sequencing ability may play an important role in performing well on this subtest. The Arithmetic subtest is a measure of numerical reasoning using basic multiplication, division, addition, and subtraction. Advanced mathematical training is not required for this subtest.

As will be seen, the Performance Scale IQ will be used instead of the PODQ as the measure of perceptual organization. When doing so, it is inappropriate to interpret individual subtests from the Performance Scale. However, if the PODQ were used, the Picture Completion, Picture Arrangement, and Digit Symbol subtests could be interpreted individually with considerable caution.

Finally, the Full-Scale IQ is a combination of the Verbal Scale IQ and the Performance Scale IQ and is considered to be a robust measure of the general intelligence factor (g). This IQ score, however, is not interpreted in the same manner as the factor IQs or Scale IQs in that it is not a measure of specific skills or skill areas. Nonetheless, it is the most stable and reliable score on the WAIS–R.

It has been argued that candidates at either end of the Full-Scale IQ may be poorly suited for policing. Terman (1917) originally proposed that a minimum of low average ability (an IQ of 80 or above) be used as a cutoff point in selecting eligible candidates. Thurstone (1922), Levy

(1967), and others, however, have countered that officers who are too intelligent or too well educated may experience greater difficulty and more often be unsuccessful in adjusting to police department life than their less-skilled counterparts. Despite these arguments and the years of effort at identifying a single "correct" standard for police officers, it is our position that the skills and abilities required for police work vary greatly among different police assignments, different police agencies, and at different points in time for any given agency.

RESULTS

From the Full-Scale IQ results (Table 2.1), it quickly becomes obvious that the police officers tested in this project are a diverse group with widely differing skills. At the low end, three officers (8%) scored below 79 (Borderline) while eight (22%) had scores between 80 and 89 (Low Average). At the opposite extreme, five recruits (14%) scored in the High Average range (110 to 119) while only one officer scored above 120 (Superior). Another nineteen officers (53%) scored between 90 and 109, the range normally considered to be Average.

Though the scores obtained are, on average, somewhat lower than expected (67% of the officers scored below 100, the fiftieth percentile for the general population), what is perhaps most important about these results is their diversity. With scores ranging from 76 to 129, it should be apparent that no single group of characteristics will adequately describe the interests and abilities of these recruits. It should also be apparent that the differing intellectual skills found among these officers may leave some less prepared than others to perform the tasks that many of the more recent innovations in policing require.

While the WAIS–R is intended to measure an individual's general "intelligence," it does so by examining specific skills and abilities (see Table 2.2). Taken together, these components of intelligence comprise what Wechsler (1981) described as the individual's overall "potential for purposeful and useful behavior." However, since we believe that the specific skills being measured by the WAIS–R relate directly to the tasks of policing, each of the components and subtests described should be considered separately. Unfortunately, since the participating agency makes no effort to evaluate the performances of its officers, we can do no more than address the distribution of scores among the candidates while exploring the relationship of each to the outcome measures made available by the police academy. Nonetheless, we believe that the results raise several important questions that require further consideration by those interested in police selection, training, and the evaluation of police performance.

Table 2.1
Verbal, Performance, and Full-Scale Test Scores by Sex, Race, and Education Level

	Mean	N	t	p
FULL-SCALE SCORES				
SEX: Males	96	31	-1.60	0.12
Females	105	5		
RACE: White	104	18	4.34	0.00
Black	89	16		
EDUCATION:				
High School	92	13	-2.32	0.02
B.A. Degree	103	8		
VERBAL SCORES				
SEX: Males	97	31	-1.57	0.12
Females	106	5		
RACE: White	105	18	4.20	0.00
Black	90	16		
EDUCATION:				
High School	94	13	-2.13	0.04
B.A. Degree	104	8		
PERFORMANCE SCORES				
SEX: Males	95	31	-1.21	0.24
Females	102	5		
RACE: White	102	18	3.51	0.00
Black	88	16		
EDUCATION:				
High School	91	13	-1.80	0.07
B.A. Degree	100	8		

Verbal Comprehension Deviation Quotient

Twenty-two percent of the recruits tested scored below 90 on the VCDQ. Seventeen percent obtained scores above 110 and 61 percent scored in the average range (90–110). These results indicate that at least three-quarters of those tested have at least average verbal comprehension skills. On outcome measures used by the academy, the VCDQ correlated significantly ($p < 0.05$) with most tests (15 of 22), especially the written examinations, oral interview, and the overall applicant rating developed during the selection process (see Table 2.3).

Table 2.2
Subtest Scores by Sex, Race, and Educational Level

	Mean	*N*	*t*	*p*
INFORMATION				
SEX: Males	8.9	31	0.07	0.90
Females	8.8	5		
RACE: White	10.1	18	4.82	0.00
Black	7.4	16		
EDUCATION:				
High School	7.9	13	-2.63	0.01
B.A. Degree	10.2	8		
EMPLOYMENT:				
Employed	9.2	26	1.47	0.14
Not Employed	8.0	10		
PICTURE COMPLETION				
SEX: Males	9.3	31	-1.28	0.21
Females	10.8	5		
RACE: White	10.2	18	2.08	0.04
Black	8.5	16		
EDUCATION:				
High School	8.8	13	-1.44	0.16
B.A. Degree	10.4	8		
EMPLOYMENT:				
Employed	9.7	26	0.75	0.46
Not Employed	8.9	10		
PICTURE ARRANGEMENT				
SEX: Males	9.9	31	-0.25	0.79
Females	10.2	5		
RACE: White	10.3	18	0.70	0.50
Black	9.8	16		
EDUCATION:				
High School	8.9	13	-2.68	0.01
B.A. Degree	11.4	8		
EMPLOYMENT:				
Employed	9.9	29	-0.48	0.64
Not Employed	8.3	10		

This clearly indicates that those applicants who have average to above average verbal comprehension skills will score better than those less similarly skilled, both during the selection procedures and on most

Table 2.2 (*continued*)

	Mean	N	t	p
BLOCK DESIGN				
SEX: Males	9.4	31	- 0.37	0.71
Females	9.8	5		
RACE: White	10.6	18	3.78	0.00
Black	7.9	16		
EDUCATION:				
High School	9.2	13	0.20	0.82
B.A. Degree	9.0	8		
EMPLOYMENT:				
Employed	9.7	26	0.84	0.41
Not Employed	8.7	10		
OBJECT ASSEMBLY				
SEX: Males	9.6	31	-0.29	0.77
Females	10.0	5		
RACE: White	11.2	18	4.36	0.00
Black	7.6	16		
EDUCATION:				
High School	9.0	13	-0.94	0.36
B.A. Degree	10.2	8		
EMPLOYMENT:				
Employed	10.2	26	1.79	0.08
Not Employed	8.3	10		
DIGIT SYMBOL				
SEX: Males	8.8	31	-1.99	0.05
Females	10.8	5		
RACE: White	9.2	18	0.41	0.69
Black	8.9	16		
EDUCATION:				
High School	8.5	13	-1.23	0.23
B.A. Degree	9.8	8		
EMPLOYMENT:				
Employed	9.2	26	0.62	0.55
Not Employed	8.8	10		

academy measures. In addition, the evidence indicates that these officers will be more highly rated by their trainers than those with low verbal comprehension abilities.

Table 2.3
Correlations of WAIS–R Results to Selection Steps

	Written Exam	Oral Interview	Applicant Rating
Full Scale IQ	0.61*	0.54*	0.62*
Verbal IQ	0.51*	0.55*	0.58*
Performance IQ	0.58*	0.42*	0.53*
Verbal Comprehension Deviation Quotient	0.54*	0.58*	0.64*
Information	0.52*	0.38**	0.52*
Digit Span	0.29	0.33**	0.34**
Vocabulary	0.56*	0.62*	0.68*
Arithmetic	0.28	0.31	0.30
Comprehension	0.40**	0.55*	0.55*
Similarities	0.27	0.31	0.33
Picture Completion	0.46*	0.28	0.36**
Picture Arrangement	0.30	0.23	0.28
Block Design	0.57*	0.28	0.42**
Object Assembly	0.50*	0.28	0.42**
Digit Symbol	0.03	0.24	0.16

Key: $*p = 0.01$; $**p = 0.05$.

Perceptual Organization Deviation Quotient

Though the PODQ was computed for the subjects, it was not used as the indicator of perceptual organization skill due to its limited reliability, high standard error of measurement, and the fact that it consists of only two subtests. The distribution of PODQ scores among the recruits will be reported, however. Thirty-six percent of the subjects scored in the average (90–110) range, 35 percent were below average, and 29 percent scored above average.

Performance IQ

In looking at the distribution of scores from the Performance Scale IQ, 48 percent scored in the average range, 38 percent were below average, and 14 percent scored above average. The Performance IQ correlated significantly ($p < 0.05$) with thirteen of the twenty-two measures used by the agency's academy. Though perceptual skills may be less clearly linked to the performance of policing related tasks, they nonetheless account for a significant amount of the variance associated with performance on academy measures.

Full-Scale IQ

The distribution of scores on the Full-Scale IQ mirrored those of the VCDQ and Performance Scale IQ. Overall, 30 percent obtained below-average scores, 53 percent rated average, and 17 percent earned scores above average. As expected, the Full-Scale IQ correlated significantly ($p < 0.05$) with fifteen of the twenty-two academy measures. This finding would seem to indicate that with this agency's existing procedures general intelligence contributes to a recruit's likelihood of selection, performance in the academy, and ratings by trainers.

Digit Span

Scaled scores (mean = 10, SD = 3) ranged from 6 to 17. Nineteen percent of those tested obtained less than average scores, 64 percent earned average scores, and 17 percent scored above average. This subtest correlated significantly ($p < 0.05$) with nine of the measures used by the academy. However, since scores on the VCDQ and Digit Span are themselves closely correlated ($p < 0.05$), further interpretation of this subtest is unnecessary.

Arithmetic

Thirty-eight percent of the recruits scored below average on this subtest, which samples basic arithmetic skills. Forty-eight percent obtained average scores and 14 percent scored above average. This finding indicates that more than one-third of the recruits tested lack the ability to carry out simple arithmetic. When considering that all subjects have at least a high school education, it is surprising that they encounter such difficulty with basic mathematical operations. Interestingly, the only academy component significantly correlated ($p < 0.05$) with arithmetic skills was the examination that tests officer techniques during high-risk traffic stops.

SUMMARY OF FINDINGS

The distribution of scores obtained by recruits on the components of the WAIS–R are shown in Table 2.4. Readers will note that the results are consistent, except for the PODQ scores, where recruits were far more likely to receive above-average scores.

The verbal comprehension skills demonstrated by this group of recruits closely follow a normal distribution, suggesting that most have adequate verbal abilities to deal with the public and other consumers of their services. In general, higher scores received on these subtests would be suggestive of competency in some of the essential skills associated with problem solving and community-oriented duties. While recognizing that a test taker's early environment, particularly his or her educational environment, will influence performance on these test components (Feingold 1983), we nonetheless believe that the ability to tap communicative skills, especially the ability to understand, process, and express verbal information, makes them useful when combined with other measures.

As a group, our sample's perceptual organizational skills, as measured by the Performance Scale IQ, are somewhat lower than their verbal abilities. Higher scores here reflect the ability to accurately analyze and synthesize visually presented information and produce a timely motor response. Still, the differences found in our sample suggest that most recruits should experience few difficulties with those tasks requiring perceptual abilities.

General intelligence also appears to play an important role in the recruits' performance at this police academy. Correlating significantly with most academy measures, those officers with higher IQs overall tended to score higher on academy measures than did those with lower IQs. While this obviously does not mean that they will necessarily

Table 2.4
Grouped Scores of Recruits on WAIS–R Components (Percentages)

Test Component	Below Average	Average	Above Average
Full-Scale IQ	30	53	17
Performance IQ	38	48	14
Verbal IQ	19	67	14
VCDQ	22	61	17
Digit Span	19	64	17
Arithmetic	38	48	14

make better police officers, it does indicate an adaptive ability to conform to situational requirements.

DISCUSSION

Though the varieties of policing strategies presently under review or in experiment are many, virtually all have several important components in common. Each begins with some form of observation or scanning stage where officers interact with their environments in an effort to better understand the conditions and problems present in the neighborhoods they police. Once they are familiar with the community and its people and have identified problems appropriate for police attention, the officers then set about collecting data. While much of these data may come from crime and incident analysis, the more traditional police sources, it is expected that other sources of information will be tapped as well. Among these are informants, schools and other service agencies, and community surveys. With each program, it is stressed to officers that the more diverse the information, the more likely an effective solution will emerge. With all these new data at hand, the officers are then expected to undertake an analysis to reveal the true extent and nature of the issues identified as problems for the neighborhood or community involved. As anyone familiar with social science research will attest, the problems confronting the officers at this stage are considerable.

Following a thorough analysis, the officers must next formulate and introduce solutions. These solutions might involve a traditional police response, but might also include some other needed service. In one effort undertaken in Miami, officers became involved in efforts to build neighborhood cohesion among different ethnic groups. In some community and ombudsman programs, the officers involved in the process actually serve as neighborhood proponents in an effort to improve conditions. Regardless of the strategy, this stage asks for a considerable degree of creativity and conceptual skills from officers. Finally, once the problem solution has been undertaken, the officers assess the impact and take corrective action where necessary.

To say the least, each of these steps requires not only that the officer understand and be committed to the process, but that he or she possess the skills and abilities necessary to actually undertake each step. While some of the experimental efforts provide outside support for the officers (such as crime analysis), others do not. While some limit the innovative strategies to carefully selected teams of officers, others do not. In either case, each new method expects activities and requires skills from the officers which they often were not trained for and, in fact, may not be able to provide. If these new methods of policing are to survive beyond the experimental stage, it is important that agencies carefully assess the full range of actions and activities expected of officers and begin to evaluate and select candidates in terms of these required abilities. If intelligence exams are to be used to that end, we must first address the issues of discrimination and job relatedness.

The Issue of Bias

The question of bias in psychological testing, particularly IQ testing, has been debated since the 1970s. On one side are those who favor testing and argue that many tests are valuable tools to aid in understanding the abilities of the test takers. Others, however, oppose the use of most tests, in the belief that they are inherently biased against racial minorities. This bias, they contend, results from the fact that most tests were developed and standardized with predominately white, middle-class subjects (Williams 1971). In an effort to support the cultural-bias stance, these critics point out that most examiners are white, which may further depress the scores of ethnic minorities.

Psychologists and educators are not the only ones debating the cultural bias issue. Since 1967, the issue has also been a matter for the courts. Here too, however, the opinions have been mixed and real guidance has been slow to emerge. For example, in 1972 in the case of *Larry P. et al. v. Wilson Riles* (343 F. Supp. 1306 [N.D. Cal. 1972], aff'd, 502 F.2d 963 [9th Cir. 1974]), the California Supreme Court reasoned that the use of standardized IQ tests results in "grossly disproportionate" numbers of black California children being placed in classes for the mentally retarded. In a similar case, however, the Illinois courts held "that the WISC, WISC–R, and StanfordBinet tests . . . do not discriminate against black children in the Chicago public schools" (Bersoff 1982). Nor are schools the only venue where the use of intelligence tests has been challenged. In *Griggs et al. v. Duke Power Company* (401 U.S. 424 [1971]), the U.S. Supreme Court ruled that the general intelligence test (Wonderlic Personnel Test) used by Duke Power had rendered "ineligible a markedly disproportionate number of Negroes" (Jensen 1980). Further, the Court ruled that when the plaintiff can show racially disproportionate consequences from the procedures used for selection, "Congress has placed on the employer the burden of showing that any given requirement must have a manifest relationship to the employment in question." What is not clear, however, is what constitutes a "manifest relationship." Must the selection procedure have predictive validity, or must the items on the test be similar to tasks performed on the job? In *Washington v. Davis* (96 S. Ct. 2040 [1976]), the U.S. Supreme Court added to the confusion by ruling that disproportionate impact "is not the sole touchstone of an invidious racial discrimination forbidden by the Constitution." This case is particularly relevant, since it involved two blacks who, after applying for positions as police officers, charged that the District of Columbia police department had used a written personnel test that excluded a highly disproportionate number of black applicants. From these examples it would seem that the courts, like psychologists and educators, widely disagree about what is culturally biased in testing and practice.

But is the WAIS–R biased and does it produce unfair results? In standardizing the exam, Wechsler stratified his samples carefully according to age, sex, race, geographic region, and occupational group. Across each of these variables the proportion of whites and nonwhites in the sample was representative of that found in the population as a whole (Wechsler 1981). This directly refutes the claim that IQ tests, in particular the WAIS–R, are standardized on only white, middleclass subjects.

Those opposed to IQ testing further claim that blacks tested by whites perform worse than if they had been tested by a black examiner. However, in twenty-five of the twenty-nine published studies dealing with racial examiner effects on individual intelligence tests or other cognitive measures, no significant relationship was found between the race of the examiner and the examinee's scores (Sattler and Gwynne 1982; Sattler 1988). In fact, it was found that black children administered the Stanford Binet Form LM in black dialect (by a black examiner) scored no higher than when administered in standard English.

Finally, many writers mistakenly believe that a test is biased when it yields lower scores for one group than for another. However, as Thorndike (1971) explained, "The presence or absence of differences in mean score between groups, or of differences in variability, tells us nothing directly about fairness" (p. 64). Because of disparities among various groups in our nation with respect to socioeconomic status and other variables, it would be surprising if intelligence tests did not show mean differences in favor of some groups. While there are mean differences between whites and blacks in terms of Full Scale IQ (15 points), Verbal IQ (14 points), and Performance IQ (14 points), the differences are meaningless unless one partials out the effects of socioeconomic status and number of years of education. For example, using the WISC–R, IQs of seven-year-old black children were less than five points below those of white children when both groups came from the same socioeconomic level, lived in the same city, and whose mothers had gone to the same hospital for prenatal care (Nichols and Anderson 1973). This five-point difference is in great contrast to the often reported fifteen-point difference between blacks and whites in favor of the white children. While these differences do occur in IQ and other forms of testing, there is no indication of inferiority or superiority by any race.

Nor is such an indication present in the testing reported here. Although black officers consistently scored lower than their white counterparts, those differences may have more to do with the agency's recruitment and selection processes than with the test itself. An internal study conducted by the agency in 1986 just prior to the administration of the WAIS–R revealed that the department is struggling with a self-imposed goal of increased hiring of minorities. Thus, to maintain a roughly equal proportion of newly hired officers, the agency employs 71 percent of "qualified" black male applicants but only 32 percent of the white males. Recall from Table 2.3 that the WAIS–R results are significantly correlated with the existing selection procedures. This means, of course, that the agency is effectively limiting its selection to only the top third of the white candidates while hiring almost three of every four blacks who apply. It should hardly be surprising then that this well-selected group should score higher than its less carefully screened comparison group. Nor does the absence of testing eliminate this supposed form of bias, since the differences in the scores attained by white and black applicants on the agency's written exam, oral interview, and final rating are also statistically significant with blacks scoring considerably lower. And these figures represent only those candidates from the "qualified to hire" list. Of the fifty-nine black males who applied for employment during 1985, only twenty-one (36%) were rated as "qualified." Of the white males, however, forty-one (74%) of fifty-five received such a rating. Clearly then, if differential outcome is to be the standard for bias, the agency's existing selection procedures are at least as discriminatory as the results from the WAIS–R. In fact, when a comparison of the Full-Scale IQ scores is made between the white officers and the top seven black officers (32% of the "qualified" applicants), the differences all but disappear and are no longer significant.

The Issues of Job Relatedness

Questions concerning the suitability of not only standardized tests but physical fitness requirements and even the interview process are often raised in discussions of police officer selection. In each case, it is assumed that the procedure in question is only appropriate if it can be demonstrated to either predict employment performance or directly reflect the requirements of the job in question. Such standards, however, are almost always difficult to apply.

The difficulties of predicting employment performance are no less challenging than those of predicting future crimes. Using this standard, in order to properly validate a selection device in any given police agency it is first necessary to hire candidates who have done poorly on that procedure. However, since an agency can be held responsible (negligent) for hiring persons they suspect to be unsuitable, the administrator finds himself or herself in a rather difficult position (Inwald 1985). And, of course, there is the problem of deciding what constitutes unsuitable. As Inwald has explained, the process of determining how individual officers have performed on the job must be based on a performance-evaluation system developed from a job analysis. While many agencies evaluate their officers, few have based their evaluations on a complete analysis of their officers' work. Even worse, if no such analysis exists, it is equally difficult to determine which "requirements of the job" are most appropriate as selection criteria. As such, while it may be possible to challenge the use of the WAIS–R or similar tests from the standpoint of job relatedness, the same can be said of virtually every selection process currently in use.

CONCLUSIONS AND IMPLICATIONS

For many years, researchers have devoted considerable effort to the task of identifying one set of characteristics desired in all police officers. However, as Wilson (1968) and others have already shown, there are several "varieties" of police and policing, each demanding different skills and placing different expectations upon the individuals involved. Given the vast differences in officer skills observed in this project, we believe that it is quite proper to suggest that officers will vary substantially in their abilities to meet those expectations. If so, it is unlikely that any one officer can reasonably be expected to fit well into every police agency or policing environment. While by no means definitive, this observed variability in skills does suggest directions for the future and has both research and organizational implications.

Organizationally, the task confronting each manager should be to determine what the "personality" of his or her organization is to be. Traditional reactive policing appears to be less demanding of its personnel. If so, the more traditional agencies may find it sufficient, even preferable, as suggested by Thurstone (1922) and Levy (1967), to recruit and select personnel content to spend their workdays performing routine tasks repetitively. As the chief of the agency participating in this project stated while discussing this very issue, "Can you imagine what a mess this place would be if everyone were like [a bright, but questioning, employee]?" The point of his statement was that the added problems of directing such employees were not, in his mind, justified by the requirements of their jobs. At the other extreme, however, are agencies such as Houston, Texas, Madison, Wisconsin, and Portland, Oregon, where officers are asked to innovate, identify, and address community problems of all types and generally restructure the ways in which policing is performed in their respective communities. Surely these agencies need methods of recruiting and selecting self-confident employees rich with data-gathering skills, analytic and communications abilities, and creativity—all traits typically associated with IQ and identified by exams such as the WAIS–R. This does not argue, of course, that other less controversial methods might not be equally effective at identifying such candidates. The important point to remember is that it does agencies little good to carefully introduce innovative programs if their officers lack the basic skills necessary to implement them.

For researchers, much remains to be done as well. At a recent meeting of the Academy of Criminal Justice Sciences, one Texas researcher reported during his panel's discussions that we remain "light years" away from connecting selection steps to the specific skills required to match a given agency's methods and style (ACJS 1990). Others, however, have begun work in this direction by proposing to "profile" the successful community-oriented police officer using surveys administered to officers participating in existing community-based projects, peer nominations, and officer "focus" group discussions (Wycoff and Kenney 1990). The expected result is to identify the characteristics of such officers and the skills they find necessary to perform their responsibilities. Appropriate selection instruments tailored to those needs can then be adopted.

We have described the results of a program of candidate testing undertaken in a major southeastern police agency and have suggested that the varied results obtained will pose major problems to the problem-oriented policing strategies being considered by that agency. Even if implementation is careful and correct, we believe that the officers of this agency cannot uniformly perform the tasks that will be expected of them. As such, we have argued here that, in some organizations, tests that measure those traits frequently described as comprising "intelligence" may be appropriate.

NOTE

Reprinted from *American Journal of Police* 9 (4), with permission from MCB University Press.

BIBLIOGRAPHY

Academy of Criminal Justice Sciences (ACJS). (1990). Panel (#108) on Police Personnel: Selection and Testing. Annual meeting, Denver, Colo.
Aiken, L. (1987). *Assessment of Intellectual Functioning*. Newton, Mass.: Allyn and Bacon.

Aylward, J. (1985). Psychological Testing and Police Selection. *Journal of Police Science and Administration* 13 (3): 201–210.

Bennett, L. (1987). Psychological Assessment of Police Candidates: An Untapped Potential. Paper presented at the annual meeting of the American Society of Criminology, Montreal.

Bersoff, D. (1982). Larry P. and PASE: Judicial Report Cards on the Validity of Individual Intelligence Tests. In *Advances in School Psychology*, edited by T. Kratochwill. Vol. 2. Hillsdale, N.J.: Lawrence Erlbaum and Associates.

Burrows, J. (1986). *Investigating Burglary: The Measurement of Police Performance.* London: Her Britannic Majesty's Stationery Office.

Chaiken, J.; P. Greenwood; and J. Petersilia. (1977). The Criminal Investigation Process: A Summary Report. *Policy Analysis* 3 (2): 187–217.

Chenoweth, J. (1961). Situational Tests: A New Attempt at Assessing Police Candidates. *Journal of Criminal Law, Criminology, and Police Science* 52: 232–238.

Cohen, B., and J. Chaiken. (1973). *Police Background Characteristics and Performance.* Lexington, Mass.: D. C. Heath.

Cohen, J. (1957). A Factor-Analytically Based Rationale for the Wechsler Adult Intelligence Scale. *Journal of Consulting Psychology* 21: 451–457.

Crosby, A. (1979). The Psychological Examination in Police Selection. *Journal of Police Science and Administration* 7 (2): 215–229.

Davis, L.; I. Hamlett; and R. Reitan. (1966). Relationship of Conceptual Ability and Academic Achievement to Problem-Solving and Experiential Backgrounds of Retardates. *Perceptual Motor Skills* 22: 499–505.

DuBois, P., and R. Watson. (1950). The Selection of Patrolmen. *Journal of Applied Psychology* 34: 90–95.

Feingold, A. (1983). The Validity of the Information and Vocabulary Subtests of the WAIS for Predicting College Achievement. *Educational and Psychological Measurements* 43: 1127–1131.

Fenster, C.; C. Wiedemann; and B. Locke. (1977). Police Personality—Social Science Folklore and Psychological Measurement. In *Psychology and the Legal Process*, edited by B. Sales. Jamaica, N.Y.: Spectrum.

Frost, T. (1955). Selection Methods for Police Recruits. *Journal of Criminal Law and Criminology* 46: 135–145.

Gregory, R. (1987). *Adult Intellectual Assessment.* Boston: Allyn and Bacon.

Gutkin, T.; C. Reynolds; and G. Galvin. (1984). Factor Analysis of the Wechsler Adult Intelligence Scale–Revised (WAIS–R): An Examination of the Standardization Sample. *Journal of School Psychology* 22: 83–93.

Hogan, R. (1971). Personality Characteristics of Highly Rated Policemen. *Personnel Psychology* 24: 679–686.

Inwald, R. (1988). Personal correspondence with author, 17 March.

Inwald, R. (1985). Administrative, Legal, and Ethical Practices in the Psychological Testing of Law Enforcement Officers. *Journal of Criminal Justice* 13: 367–372.

Jensen, A. (1980). *Bias in Mental Testing.* New York: The Free Press.

Kates, S. (1950). Rorschach Responses, Strong Blank Scales, and Job Satisfaction. *Journal of Applied Psychology* 34: 249–254.

Kelling, G.; T. Pate; D. Dieckman; and C. Brown. (1974). *The Kansas City Preventive Patrol Experiment: A Technical Report*. Washington, D.C.: Police Foundation.

Levy, R. (1967). Predicting Police Failures. *Journal of Criminal Law, Criminology, and Police Science* 58: 265–276.

Matarazzo, J.; B. Allen; G. Saslow; and A. Wiens. (1964). Characteristics of Successful Policemen and Firemen Applicants. *Journal of Applied Psychology* 48 (2): 123–133.

McDonough, L., and J. Monahan. (1976). The Quality-Control of Community Care-Takers: A Study of Mental Health Screening in a Sheriff's Department. In *Community Mental Health and the Criminal Justice System*, edited by J. Monahan. New York: Pergamon Press.

Merrill, M. (1926). Intelligence of Policemen. *Journal of Personnel Research* 5: 511–515.

Mullineaux, J. (1955). An Evaluation of the Predictors Used to Select Patrolmen. *Public Policy Review* 16: 84–86.

Murphy, J. (1972). Current Practices in the Use of Psychological Testing by Police Agencies. *Journal of Criminal Law, Criminology, and Police Science* 63 (4): 570–576.

Nichols, P., and V. Andersen. (1973). Intellectual Performance, Race, and Socioeconomic Status. *Social Biology* 20: 367–374.

Oglesby, T. (1957). Use of Emotional Screening in the Selection of Police Recruits. *Public Personnel Review* 18: 228–231.

Roe, A., and N. Roe. (1982). *Police Selection: A Technical Summary of Validity Studies*. Orem, Utah: Diagnostic Specialists.

Saccuzzo, D.; G. Higgins; and D. Lewandowski. (1974). Program for Psychological Assessment of Law Enforcement Officers: Initial Evaluation. *Psychological Reports* 35: 651–654.

Sattler, J. (1988). *Assessment of Children*. San Diego: Jerome M. Sattler.

Sattler, J., and J. Gwynne. (1982). White Examiners Generally Do Not Impede the Intelligence Test Performance of Black Children: To Debunk a Myth. *Journal of Consulting and Clinical Psychology* 50: 196–208.

Silverstein, A. (1982). Factor Structure of the Wechsler Adult Intelligence Scale-Revised. *Journal of Consulting and Clinical Psychology* 50: 661–664.

Silverstein, A. (1969). An Alternative Factor Analytic Solution for Wechsler's Intelligence Scales. *Educational and Psychological Measurement* 29: 763–767.

Spelman, W., and D. Brown. (1984). *Calling the Police: Citizen Reporting of Serious Crime*. Washington, D.C.: National Institute of Justice.

Sterne, D. (1960). Use of the Kuder Preference Record, Personal, with Police Officers. *Journal of Applied Psychology* 44: 323–324.

Terman, L. (1917). A Trial of Mental and Pedagogical Tests in a Civil Service Examination for Policemen and Firemen. *Journal of Applied Psychology* 1: 17–29.

Thorndike, R. (1971). Concepts of Culture-Fairness. *Journal of Educational Measurement* 8: 63–70.

Thurstone, L. (1922). The Intelligence of Policemen. *Journal of Personnel Research* 1: 64–74.

Wechsler, D. (1981). *WAIS–R Manual.* Orlando, Fla.: Harcourt Brace Jovanovich.

Williams, R. (1971). Danger: Testing and Dehumanizing Black Children. *The School Psychologist* 25: 11–13.

Wilson, J. (1968). *Varieties of Police Behavior: The Management of Law and Order in Eight Communities.* New York: Atheneum Press.

Wycoff, M., and D. Kenney. (1990). *Facilitating Organizational Change from the Bottom: Democratic Planning in the Police Workplace.* Washington, D.C.: Police Foundation.

3

Supervising the Police

Kenneth J. Peak, Ronald W. Glensor,
and Larry K. Gaines

It is time for a new generation of leadership, to cope with new problems and new opportunities. For there is a new world to be won.
—John F. Kennedy

Uneasy lies the head that wears the crown.
—Shakespeare, *Henry IV*

Most of us have a pretty clear commonsense understanding of supervision. We recognize that it entails some degree of overseeing, guiding, and correcting. We probably also realize, either intuitively or from
experience, that the so-called first-line supervisor is often the most
important member of an organization (Brown 1992). The supervisor is
that member of the management team who is directly and regularly
in touch with those employees who actually do the work of the organization and interact with its customers and clients. If the supervisor
fails to make sure that employees perform correctly, the organization
will not be very successful.

Those of us who have ever had a job, unless we were self-employed
or started right out as the boss, had a supervisor to whom we reported.
That supervisor probably had a hand in showing us how to do our
work and certainly was responsible for making sure that we did it
properly. We have all probably experienced supervision in school, in
sports, or in other nonwork settings. Supervision is a crucial element
of almost any organized activity.

This chapter is specifically about police supervision. It is true that all supervisors, whether police sergeants, construction foremen, or office managers, share similar concerns and duties. It is also true that each and every organization is unique. However, police organizations are particularly unique for the simple reason that policing is significantly different from most other kinds of work.

This chapter begins with a review of the complexity of the police supervisor's role, and then addresses the issues of supervisory ethics, decision making, and values. Next we discuss supervisory liability and negligence, and then consider a companion issue, effective discipline of subordinates. Supervisory responsibilities and philosophy are then explored as they exist in agencies that have implemented the community-oriented policing and problem-solving strategy. The chapter concludes with a discussion of supervisors of the future.

THE SUPERVISORY ROLE

A Complex Position

The supervisory role is an extremely difficult one, as the supervisor deals with rank-and-file employees (labor) on the one hand and middle or upper management on the other. The concerns, expectations, and interests of labor and management are inevitably different and to some extent in conflict (Reuss-Ianni 1983). Labor and management are, respectively, at the bottom and the top of the organization; while it is management's job to squeeze as much productivity out of workers as possible, labor's motivation often seems to be to avoid work as much as possible. Supervisors find themselves right in the middle of this contest. Their subordinates expect them to be understanding, to protect them from management's unreasonable expectations and arbitrary decisions, and to represent their interests. Management, though, expects supervisors to keep employees in line and to represent management's and the overall organization's interests.

Complicating this situation even further is the fact that supervisors are generally in their first managerial position. New supervisors, especially those who are new and young, must go through a transition phase to learn how to exercise command and get cooperation from subordinates (Bock n.d.). They are no longer responsible solely for their own personal behavior, but also that of other employees. The step from worker to supervisor is a big step that calls for a new set of skills and knowledge largely separate from that learned at lower levels in the organization.

Even more complexity is created when, as is true in most police agencies, the new supervisor is promoted from within the ranks and placed in charge of friends and peers. Long-standing relationships are put under stress when one party suddenly has official authority over former equals. Expectations of leniency or preferential treatment may have to be dealt with. When new supervisors attempt to correct deficient behavior, their own previous performance may be recalled as a means of challenging the reasonableness or legitimacy of their supervisory action. Supervisors with any skeletons in their closets can expect to hear those skeletons rattling as they begin to use their new-found authority.

The supervisor's role, put simply, is to get one's subordinates to do their very best. This task involves a host of actions, including communicating, motivating, leading, team building, training, developing, appraising, counseling, and disciplining. Getting subordinates to "do their very best" includes figuring out the strengths and weaknesses of each, defining good and bad performance, measuring performance, providing feedback, and making sure that subordinates' efforts coincide with the organization's mission, values, goals, and objectives.

The Human Element

Supervising a group of subordinates is tough, in part because of what might be termed the "human element." People are complex and sometimes unpredictable. Rules and principles for communicating, leading, and similar supervisory tasks are rarely hard and fast because different people react differently. What works for a supervisor in one situation may not work for that supervisor in another situation, much less for some other supervisor. Thus, supervisors have to learn to "read" subordinates and diagnose situations before choosing how to respond. Supervisors have to become students of human behavior and of such behavioral science disciplines as psychology and sociology. Unfortunately, these are inexact sciences.

Effective supervision is also tough because the job is dynamic, not static. Even without any turnover of personnel, one's subordinates change over time as they age, grow, mature, and experience satisfaction and dissatisfaction in their personal and work lives. In addition, turnover is common, so that new subordinates come under the supervisor's wing; the supervisor must learn the best way to handle these new subordinates and also be attuned to a new person's effect on other subordinates and on the work group as a whole.

It is not only one's subordinates that change; the organization and its environment change over time. History is replete with organizations—even police agencies with corrupt employees from the chief executive down to the officers on the street—that, because of poor leadership, became pathological or catastrophic. Effective supervision over the long haul requires continuous monitoring and adaptation. The organization's rules and expectations may change. Clients and customers may make new demands. Societal values evolve and change. Certainly, new technologies come and go these days in the blink of an eye. Supervisors must be aware of these changing conditions if they are to be successful over time in getting their subordinates to do their very best. The organization expects the supervisor to keep up with such changes in order to keep subordinates on track; subordinates expect the supervisor to help them interpret and adapt successfully to such changes.

Supervision: The Bottom Line

Supervision, without question, is a difficult task, but it must be done and it must be done effectively. Supervisors serve as the linking pin (Likert 1961) between administration and those who perform the work. To this extent, supervisors delegate or assign responsibilities to subordinates, and they must ensure that they are accomplished. This perspective connotes that a large part of the supervisor's job is control and accountability.

The need for accountability may seem odd during a time when many police managers, as a result of community policing, are calling for the empowerment of line officers and first-line supervisors. Supervisory systems must be developed which provide officers with the latitude and discretion to do their jobs, but, at the same time, supervisors are responsible for ensuring that the job is done. This is the heart and soul of supervision, no matter what type of management structure is deployed.

A MATTER OF ETHICS

Ethical Decision Making

Fair and Pilcher (1991) argued that one of the primary purposes of ethics is to guide decision making. Ethics provide more comprehensive guidelines than law and police operational procedures and answer questions which may otherwise go unanswered. When in doubt, police officers should be able to consider the ethical consequences of their actions or potential actions to evaluate how they should act or proceed. It is impossible for a police department to formulate procedures that address every possible situation an officer may encounter. Therefore, other behavioral guidelines must be in place to assist officers when making operational decisions.

Some police officers, however, too often strictly adhere to the law and departmental policies to guide their behavior. They may also take the attitude that if a particular behavior is not prohibited by law or policy, it is permissible. If actions are not mandated, they merely represent an option. Such an attitude points to a general failure of police ethics. When police officers draw the line that separates the acceptable from unacceptable, they do so with the intention of performing at a level that is less than desirable. Their actions should be guided by what is "right" for the situation and individuals involved, not what is required or prohibited.

Police supervisors obviously play a key role in police ethics. Of course, they must first uphold ethical standards themselves. The following are two examples of incidents where sergeants failed to maintain ethical behavior (*Law Enforcement News* 1997, 2, 3):

Former New York City Sergeant Kevin Nannery was given one to three years in prison in June 1997 for perjury. Nannery, the highest ranking officer in the scandal, led a group that became known as "Nannery's Raiders," for their practice of breaking into apartments, stealing drugs and cash and taking payoffs. Atlanta Police Sergeant Randy Meyers, age forty-four, was suspended for thirty days without pay after being videotaped beating a man who drove through a police roadblock. Meyers and other officers surrounded a twenty-seven-year-old man, pummeled him with a baton, and doused him with pepper spray.

Obviously, police supervisors must be above reproach themselves if they are to guide and instruct officers in the ethical conduct of police business.

Maintaining Values

Supervisory values are just as important as line-officer values. A supervisor's values affect how the supervisor manages subordinates and situations. Von der Embse (1987, 66) has identified several areas in which supervisory values affect work and workers:

1. Supervisory perceptions of individuals and groups.
2. Supervisory perceptions of specific problems and their solutions.
3. A supervisor's ethics relative to the job.
4. The correctness of decisions and judgments of others.
5. A supervisor's appraisal of success or failure.

It is apparent that one's personal value system must be consistent with the department's if the supervisor is going to effectively assist the department to pursue its mission.

The importance of ethics and values cannot be overemphasized, and supervisors must understand that they are the organization's primary tool for ensuring that officers adhere to the department's ethics and values. If officers' behavior strays from ethical and departmental standards into inappropriate values, the department will experience difficulties.

THE IMPACT OF LIABILITY

Legal Consequences of Failure

Supervision is about behavior, for it is the direct responsibility of supervisors to monitor and regulate officers behavior and, when necessary, take disciplinary action to ensure that negligent or illegal behavior does not recur in the future. Next, we explore some of the legal consequences when police supervisors fail to control officers' behavior.

Liability can be imposed by state or federal courts. Most claims of supervisory liability are state tort cases or Section 1983 cases at the federal level. Section 1983 cases are civil rights cases which emanate from Title 42 of the United States Code. If a police officer acting in an official capacity violates a citizen's constitutional or other federally guaranteed rights, the citizen can seek redress under Section 1983.

Supervisors incur direct liability in a number of ways (del Carmen 1989):

1. They authorize the act. They give officers permission to do something that ultimately results in liability.
2. They participate in the act. They engage in activities with other officers which ultimately results in liability.
3. They direct others to perform the act. They order officers to do something which ultimately results in liability.
4. They ratify the act. Once the act is completed, they fail to admonish or take corrective action when it comes to their attention.
5. They are present when an act for which liability results occurs. They stand by and watch an act occur which results in liability and fail to take corrective action.

Supervisors must be mindful that a certain level of liability is attached to the job when they fail to supervise correctly. Furthermore, plaintiffs generally attempt to include as many officers, supervisors, and administrators in the lawsuit as possible to enhance the probability that the award will be greater and the defendants will have the ability to pay it. This is commonly referred to as the "deep pockets" approach.

Negligence

One of the most commonly litigated areas of liability is supervisory negligence, where a supervisor fails to provide the degree of care and vigilance required for a situation. *Gross negligence* is a deliberate indifference to life or property; *simple negligence* is where the supervisor failed to exhibit great care. Generally, the courts require gross negligence to hold a supervisor liable.

As a result of case law, there are seven areas where supervisors have been found liable as a result of negligence: negligent failure to train, negligent hiring, negligent assignment, negligent failure to supervise, negligent failure to direct, negligent entrustment, and negligent failure to investigate or discipline (del Carmen 1991, 227). The hiring and training of police officers is generally outside the responsibilities of the supervisor, but the remaining five areas of liability fall squarely with the supervisor and are discussed in the following section.

Negligent assignment occurs when the supervisor assigns a task to a subordinate without first determining that the subordinate is properly trained or capable of performing the required work. Negligent assignment also occurs when a supervisor determines that an employee is unfit or not qualified for a position but fails to relieve the employee of the assignment. An example of negligent assignment is when a supervisor allows a person to assume the duties of a police officer without receiving firearms training. If the officer subsequently negligently shot a citizen, the supervisor as well as the officer would be liable.

Negligent failure to supervise is when the supervisor fails to properly oversee subordinates' activities. The court, in *Lenard v. Argento* (699 F.2d 874 [7th Cir. 1983]), held that at a minimum a plaintiff must demonstrate that the supervisory official authorized (implicitly or explicitly), approved, or knowingly acquiesced in the illegal conduct. For example, if a supervisor knows that an officer on a number of occasions has used more force than was necessary to effect an arrest and fails to take corrective action, the supervisor can be held liable for failure to supervise in a subsequent action. Thus, any time a supervisor becomes aware of a problem, action must be taken to rectify the problem.

Negligent failure to direct occurs when supervisors fail to advise subordinates of the specific requirements and limits of the job. For example, if a police department fails to provide officers with the limits of when they can use deadly force and officers subsequently use deadly force inappropriately, the responsible supervisors can be held liable.

Negligent entrustment occurs when supervisors entrust officers with equipment and facilities, fail to properly supervise the officers' care and use of the equipment, and subsequently the officers commit an act using the equipment which leads to a violation of a citizen's federally protected rights. The government in these cases must show that the officer in question was incompetent and the supervisor knew of the incompetence. A supervisor's defense in negligent entrustment is that the employee was competent to use the equipment and was properly supervised.

Finally, supervisors must investigate complaints and work activities and take proper disciplinary actions when required. If a supervisor or department covers up or is inattentive to complaints of police misconduct, the department and supervisor are liable. Too often supervisors attempt to stall, discourage, or disregard complainants when they attempt to protest police officer actions. Such actions can ultimately lead to charges of negligent failure to investigate or discipline.

EFFECTIVE DISCIPLINE

Subordinates' Self-Discipline

The real purpose of discipline is to proactively get employees to voluntarily comply with departmental rules and regulations, work together as a team, respect each other, and perform to the best of their ability. In this sense, self-discipline provides the foundation for successful management. Without self-discipline, the organization is sure to face significant problems. Black (1986) provides the following checklist to assist supervisors in developing self-discipline within the work force:

1. Understand your disciplinary responsibilities. The road to success as a supervisor entails much more than simply being liked by subordinates. Judgement, fairness, and knowledge of the job provide the foundation upon which a supervisor earns respect. These traits provide the best means of ensuring the self-discipline of employees.
2. Make sure employees receive sound instruction. The employee who is half-taught is half-disciplined. Discipline means knowledge. Employees expect supervisors to provide them with the information, guidance, and coaching needed to increase their opportunities for improvement and advancement.
3. Insist on high standards of performance. The employee who is allowed to perform at a mediocre level has little incentive to improve.
4. Maintain effective communication. Effective communication begins the first day a supervisor and subordinate work together. Start by making sure that the subordinate understands all departmental rules and regulations and reasons behind them. Recognize accomplishments early and remember that two-way communication breeds respect and is the hallmark of constructive discipline.
5. Enforce discipline fairly. Do not ignore any discipline. A capable supervisor sees that all rules apply equally to all people. There should be no favorites.
6. Set the pace for discipline. Discipline begins with the supervisor. You cannot expect discipline from others if you are not disciplined yourself. The disciplined supervisor plans ahead and is organized. There is no lost motion or indecision.

Methods of Monitoring Behavior

One of the best means by which supervisors and other police leaders can monitor the behavior of their officers is through an early warning system (EWS). Such a system helps police agencies to proactively deal with repeated minor or unsubstantiated complaints that may lead to more serious problems. With an EWS, the supervisor can intervene with early prevention methods such as counseling or training. The importance of EWS was illustrated by an example in Kansas City, Missouri, where a task force investigated use-of-force complaints against police officers. It was discovered that twenty-nine officers were involved in nearly 50 percent of the 756 complaints filed (KCPD 1991). The department might have avoided more serious complaints had they developed a system of early detection (Ross 1992).

It is the supervisor's responsibility to intervene in any situation that may result in a violation of departmental policy or law. However, much of what an officer does during a shift may not be known by the supervisor; it is impossible for a supervisor to have first-hand knowledge of every call and activity of each officer during a shift. Therefore, supervisors must rely on a variety of other means to monitor officer performance and conduct, including review of reports, periodic field observation of calls, citizen commendations and complaints, conversations with the officers, and listening to what other officers and supervisors are saying about the officer.

Once the supervisor is informed of a problem, a plan must be developed to address it. In some cases the problem may be as obvious as the officer's being involved in three traffic accidents within a three-month period of time. In such a case, potential actions may include the recommendation of a driver's school or even having the officer's eyes checked. But what should be done with the officer who has no previous disciplinary record but has received four unsustained citizen complaints of being rude? How might a supervisor deal with this situation? Initial counseling may reveal that this officer has a family or personal substance abuse problem that is affecting his or her conduct. Is this a disciplinary issue or something the supervisor should refer to professional counseling?

The Need for Negotiation

An area that is related to the discipline of subordinates is negotiation by police supervisors. Police supervisors must constantly negotiate with their subordinates to be able to ensure their maximum compliance with orders, directives, and assignments. Although the sergeant can "order" his or her subordinates to perform certain tasks, it is generally more effective if a consensus is reached, and a consensus can normally be reached only through negotiations. A supervisor is better able to induce voluntary compliance when he or she is able to negotiate effectively. Supervisors must frequently convince subordinates that their compliance with a request is in the best interests of the unit and the individual, especially when the task that is involved is viewed as being less than desirable.

Police supervisors must also often negotiate with their superiors. They must argue their case when there are personnel shortages or when members of the unit are given too many responsibilities. Conflict between units over assignments sometimes occur, resulting in the supervisor having to negotiate with peers about working conditions.

So it is evident that negotiation becomes particularly problematic when we consider the nature of police work. Police officers are often called upon to engage in activities that are perceived as being less important or not as prestigious as other tasks. For example, most police officers would rather investigate a homicide or robbery than direct traffic after a high school football game. Directing traffic is not as interesting, nor will it reap the same amount of prestige or publicity that a successful homicide investigation might bring to the officer. Nonetheless, directing traffic is a vital function to be performed by the police department. Indeed, there are many more mundane tasks for officers than there are exciting ones. Yet all these tasks must be performed and be performed well.

COMMUNITY-ORIENTED POLICING
AND PROBLEM SOLVING

Community-oriented policing and problem solving (COPPS) is discussed in Chapter 4; thus, we will not elaborate on the concept here except as it involves the key philosophical support and responsibilities of supervisory personnel. We preface this discussion with a view of total quality management, a concept that is virtually a requisite for the successful implementation of COPPS.

A Shift to Customer-Oriented Government

One of the ways in which community problem solving can be accommodated is by "reengineering government," at present the hottest term in public management. This is accomplished through total quality management (TQM). Herman Goldstein (1993), commonly viewed as the originator of the modern problem-oriented policing movement, explained how police agencies have often resisted accepting the problem-solving role, and how TQM can assist in this endeavor:

It is troubling to find that a department's investment in the reorientation of management and supervisory personnel often consisted of no more than "a day at the academy"—and sometimes not even that. How much of the frustration in eliciting support from management and supervision stems from the fact that agencies simply have not invested enough in engaging senior officers, in explaining why change is necessary, and in giving these supervisors and managers the freedom required for them to act in their new role. The adoption of Total Quality Management . . . in policing has demonstrated very positive results and holds much promise. We can learn important lessons from TQM. (p. 12)

Indeed, supervisors must learn to emphasize to their officers the important role of persons working with other government agencies. The police do not function in a vacuum; representatives from other agencies must be mobilized in the problem-solving endeavor. The number of examples is rapidly growing across the country, where police use housing, fire, health, street, planning, social services, and other justice agencies to solve neighborhood problems.

TQM is now an increasingly dominant practice, and is a concept that can assist a COPPS initiative in several ways. As demands mount for less bureaucratic red tape and better services, police supervisors must mentally shift to a customer focus, which means realizing that the customer or client is the most important ingredient in the feedback loop of all organizational processes. They must also bear in mind the two primary concepts that are at the foundation of TQM: participative management and total involvement.

An aspect of TQM that is also central to community problem solving is decentralization and less bureaucracy. Under TQM, supervisors and other police leaders listen closely to the voices of their subordinates, including dissenters, and are always open to ideas for improvement from all sources. Managers also push power and decision making in the organization downward by delegating authority and encouraging problem solving at the lowest appropriate levels.

TQM, like COPPS, involves the complete rethinking and redesigning of the way a job is performed or a service is rendered, with the goal of improving the process. Proponents believe that both concepts begin with two things: a list of desired outcomes and a clean sheet of paper (Martin 1993).

What Constitutes a Good Problem-Oriented Supervisor?

Until recently, the traditional police first-line supervisor has been largely unprepared by training or experience for the COPPS strategy. The command and control model of policing during the past fifty years measured supervisors' success in statistical accomplishments of their unit. Arrests, citations, calls for service, response time, and case closings were all counted in this quantitative approach. Good line officers followed orders and stayed out of trouble, filled out forms and reports correctly, and did not abuse citizens. Orders came down from the top. Sergeants checked the accuracy and compliance of paperwork going up and down the chain of command, doing more and more of the lieutenant's administrative work and spending less and less time on the street. As a result, the sergeant saw his officers only once during the shift, during roll call (Robinette 1993).

The COPPS strategy requires a new type of supervisor, one who should be taught the "Characteristics of a Good Problem Oriented Supervisor" (Police Executive Research Forum 1990), which are shown in the following list:

1. Allowing subordinates freedom to experiment with new approaches.
2. Insisting on good, accurate analyses of problems.
3. Granting flexibility in work schedules when requests are proper.
4. Allowing subordinates to make most contacts directly and paving the way when they are having trouble getting cooperation.
5. Protecting subordinates from pressures within the department to revert to traditional methods.
6. Running interference for subordinates to secure resources, protect from criticism, and so on.
7. Knowing what problems subordinates are working on and whether the problems are real.
8. Knowing subordinates' beats and important citizens in them, and expecting subordinates to know them even better.
9. Coaching subordinates through the process, giving advice, helping them manage their time.
10. Monitoring subordinates' progress and, as necessary, prodding them along or slowing them down.
11. Supporting subordinates, even if their strategies fail, as long as something useful is learned in the process and the process was well thought through.
12. Managing problem-solving efforts over a long period of time; not allowing efforts to die just because they get sidetracked by competing demands for time and attention.
13. Giving credit to subordinates and letting others know about their good work.
14. Allowing subordinates to talk with visitors or at conferences about their work.
15. Identifying new resources and contacts for subordinates and making them check them out.
16. Stressing cooperation, coordination, and communication within the unit and outside it.
17. Coordinating efforts across shifts, beats, and outside units and agencies.

18. Realizing that this style of policing cannot simply be ordered; officers and detectives must come to believe in it. (Copyright by Police Executive Research Forum. Used with permission.)

Views Toward Problem Solving

A major departure of problem-oriented policing from the conventional style lies with the view of the line officer, who is given much more discretion and decision-making ability and is trusted with a much broader array of responsibilities. First and foremost, supervisors must have a working knowledge of the problem-solving process, known as SARA (scanning, analysis, response, and assessment). Of these four steps in the process, supervisors must be acutely knowledgeable about analysis, the heart of the problem-solving process. Here, officers gather as much information as possible from sources inside and outside their agency about the scope and nature of the problem and factors contributing to their underlying conditions.

Problem-oriented policing values "thinking" officers, urging that they take the initiative in trying to deal more effectively with problems in the areas they serve. This concept more effectively uses the potential of college-educated officers, "who have been smothered in the atmosphere of traditional policing" (Goldstein 1987, 17). It also gives officers a new sense of identity and self-respect; they are more challenged and have opportunities to follow through on individual cases—analyze and solve problems—which will give them greater job satisfaction. Using patrol officers in this manner also allows the agency to provide sufficient challenges for the better educated officers and a challenge for those who remain unpromoted patrol officers throughout their entire careers. We ought to be recruiting as police officers people who can "serve as mediators, as dispensers of information, and as community organizers" (Goldstein 1987, 21).

Under problem solving, officers continue to handle calls, but they also do much more. They use the information gathered in their responses to incidents together with information obtained from other sources to get a clearer picture of the problem. They then address the underlying conditions. If they are successful in ameliorating these conditions, fewer incidents may occur and those that do occur may be less serious. The incidents may even cease. At the very least, information about the problem can help police to design more effective ways of responding to each incident.

Unquestionably, the successful implementation of the COPPS strategy requires the support of supervisors. However, one of the most difficult hurdles for supervisors to overcome is the idea that giving officers the opportunity to be creative and take risks does not diminish the role or authority of the supervisor. Risk taking and innovation require mutual trust between supervisors and line officers. This requires a change from being a controller primarily concerned with rules to being a facilitator and coach for officers involved in problem solving. Supervisors must learn to encourage innovation and risk taking among their officers. A supervisor must also be prepared to intercede and remove any roadblocks to officers' problem-solving efforts.

Supervisors must also be prepared to answer the following questions for officers who are confused or resistant to the implementation of COPPS:

- What are the advantages and disadvantages of the traditional form of police supervision?
- What are officers' complaints about management?
- What are officers' complaints about their work?
- What kinds of objections do you anticipate from officers and detectives when they are told about COPPS?
- How will you respond to such statements as, "This is social work and we're not social workers," "We don't have the skills or training to do all this," or "Other cops won't see us as real cops?"

Supervisors should also understand that not all patrol officers or detectives will enjoy this kind of work or be good at it. However, at the other end of the continuum, some officers will work on their own unpaid time in their neighborhoods to solve problems. Furthermore, subordinates will occasionally want to work on problems that really should not be police business and do not deserve a high priority. Supervisors also need to be informed that they must avoid isolating the problem-solving function from the rest of the department. This could create the illusion that problem solving is composed of "privileged prima donnas" who get benefits that other officers do not. Also, supervisors should not contribute to the COPPS initiative becoming a mere public-relations campaign; the emphasis is always upon results (Police Executive Research Forum 1990).

Capitalizing on Officers' Motivation

There is one very important positive aspect of considering whether or not to implement a COPPS philosophy, one that all supervisors should remember: It encourages many of the activities that patrol officers would like to do. When asked why they originally wanted to join police forces, police officers consistently say they joined in order to help people (Sparrow 1988). By emphasizing work that addresses people's concerns, and giving officers the discretion to develop a solution, COPPS helps to make police work more rewarding.

Furthermore, many if not most police officers are natural problem solvers, and it is probably true that an observer can find problem-solving officers active in most police agencies. Police work by its very nature requires that problems be solved. While it is true that officers have always had to solve problems, in the past they had little guidance as to how to go about it. In some agencies officers have attempted to address problems in secret, fearful that their actions will be criticized by their supervisors and colleagues.

It is therefore essential that supervisors understand, accept, and communicate to rank-and-file officers the belief that COPPS is department-wide in scope, and that they encourage and guide all officers to engage in problem solving. To get the whole agency involved, the supervisor must adopt four practices as part of the implementation plan:

1. Communicate to all officers the vital role of COPPS in serving the public. They must describe why handling problems is more effective than just handling incidents.
2. Provide incentives to officers who engage in COPPS. This includes a new and different personnel evaluation and reward system, as well as positive encouragement.
3. Reduce the barriers to COPPS that can occur. Procedures, time allocation, and policies all need to be closely examined.
4. Officers must be shown how to address problems. Training is a key element of COPPS implementation (Eck and Spelman 1987).

Changing the Police Culture

It is widely held that the most challenging aspect of changing the culture of a police agency lies in changing first-line supervisors. The influence of first-line supervisors is so strong that their role warrants special attention. The primary contact of street officers with their organization is through their sergeant, who can be extremely reluctant to change. Herman Goldstein (1990) stated the following:

Changing the operating philosophy of rank-and-file officers is easier than altering a first-line supervisor's perspective of his or her job, because the work of a sergeant is greatly simplified by the traditional form of policing. The more routinized the work, the easier it is for the sergeant to check. The more emphasis placed on rank and the symbols of position, the easier it is for the sergeant to rely on authority—rather than intellect and personal skills—to carry out their duties. Sergeants are usually appalled by descriptions of the freedom and independence suggested in problem oriented policing for rank-and-file officers. The concept can be very threatening to them. This . . . can create an enormous block to implementation. (p. 29)

Goldstein maintains that currently the most effective means we have of altering the attitudes of first-line supervisors is to convince them that adopting a different style of supervision makes good sense in today's environment.

Furthermore, the adoption of the COPPS strategy has fostered the need for greater examination, flexibility, and modification of personnel deployment. Once the COPPS philosophy is adopted, the task falls to the supervisor to see that the personnel are deployed in keeping with the needs of that strategy and are given the necessary time to engage in COPPS activities. Conducting workload analyses and finding the time for officers to solve problems and engage with the community is an important aspect of supervision. The time between calls is the key element of the argument on whether officers have time for problem solving.

FUTURE CONSIDERATIONS

Supervisors, like futurists and other police leaders, need to focus on the future. Futurists think in terms of time frames of five years and beyond. However, police leaders tend to focus on the immediate future—from the present to two years ahead—dealing with problems that need resolution, trying to "stay on top of things," and "putting out fires." Future outcomes can be influenced by decisions of today. This axiom is critical for police leaders to understand because the choices that are made today will definitely affect their agencies in the next century.

A Changing Society

We are rapidly becoming a more diverse, elderly, and bifurcated society. By 2010, one in every four Americans will be fifty-five or older. The elderly are more likely to suffer the more harmful consequences of victimization, such as sustaining injury or requiring medical care.

The minority population is also increasing rapidly: By 2000 an estimated 34 percent of American children will be Hispanic, black, or Asian (Peak 1996). America now accepts nearly one million newcomers each year. In less than 100 years we can expect the white majority in the United States to end as the growing number of blacks, Hispanics, and Asians together become the new majority. And when these various minority groups are forced to compete for increasingly scarce, low-paying service jobs, intergroup relations sour and can even become combative, as has occurred recently in several major American cities. The gap between the "haves" and "have nots" is widening. An underclass of people who are chronically poor and live outside of society's rules is growing (Peak 1996).

We also live in a violent country. There are about 43 million personal- and property-crime victimizations in the country per year, with about 14 million serious crimes being reported to the police (Maguire and Pastore 1996).

The nature of crime is also changing rapidly in America, due in great measure to the advent of high technology in our society, including software piracy, industrial espionage, bank-card counterfeiting, and embezzlement by computer. These crimes will compel the development of new investigative techniques, specialized training for police investigators, and the employment of individuals with specialized, highly technological backgrounds. The distribution and use of narcotics, which is spreading in numbers and throughout various social classes, will also continue.

Adapting to Greater Diversity

As our society becomes more diverse in the future, so must the supervisory ranks of policing become more diverse. The proportion of women in state and local police agencies has risen to about 9.6 percent (4.8% of all state, 8.1% of municipal, and 15.4% of sheriff's employees) (U.S. Department of Justice, Bureau of Justice Statistics Bulletin 1996). Generally, the larger the city, the larger the percentage of female officers (McDowell 1992). Women are a growing presence in the police field. Minorities, like females, are slowly but steadily increasing their representation in state and local police agencies. For example, in local police departments, from 1987 to 1990, the percentage of African Americans increased from 9.3 to 10.5 percent, while the percentage of Hispanics went from 4.5 to 5.2 percent (U.S. Department of Justice 1990, 5, 11).

As the work of contemporary policing becomes more oriented toward COPPS, the growing presence of women may help improve the tarnished image of policing, improve community relations, and foster a more flexible and less violent approach to keeping the peace. Increasing the number of women in supervisory levels could influence police policy and create role models for younger female officers.

African-American police officers face problems similar to those of women who attempt to enter and prosper in police work. Until more African-American officers are promoted and can affect police policy and serve as role models, they are likely to be treated unequally and have difficulty being promoted, a classic catch-22 situation.

Community-Oriented Policing and Problem Solving

Much of the future of supervision centers on work with the ever-expanding COPPS strategy, which requires a different leadership methodology. In departments with the COPPS strategy, supervisors will have more freedom to intervene, innovate, reallocate resources, and task personnel. They will need to set clear, achievable goals and define outcomes, recognize and accommodate differences, and provide recognition, visibility, celebration, and rewards for team accomplishment. The new supervisor will be in the neighborhood talking to people, taking reports, and meeting with policing team members regularly (Robinette 1993). Supervisors in the COPPS strategy of policing will have to demonstrate and teach the new values of high-performance policing as values, quality of life, and consensus will become more important than traditional order giving and statistical measurements of productivity.

High Technology

It is not surprising that most of today's technological developments may be adopted by the police, given the nature of their work, tools, and crime problems. Indeed, as will be seen in this section, several exciting developments already exist in policing due to computer technology. Supervisors are certainly implicated in these advances. Local area networks (LANs) will so affect organizational communications that supervisors of the twenty-first century will need specific training and hands-on experience with the technology in the same way as with firearms and defensive tactics.

In terms of organization and operations, other noted speculators, such as former Madison, Wisconsin, police chief David Couper (1990), see policing in the twenty-first century as being more demilitarized and decentralized in its organization, with officers identifying citizens as "customers" and working as "neighborhood police specialists." These officers will be assigned to a specific neighborhood within their districts and provide a full range of police services. Couper also sees a training emphasis on community organization and conflict management. Supervisors will be "area coordinators" who are interested in their subordinates' ability to foster teamwork in their neighborhoods; the supervisors provide coaching, support, and necessary resources in order for their officers to perform COPPS work in a quality way. The organizational hierarchy is flatter, allowing for greater employee input and communication. Officers wear blazers instead of the military-style uniforms, and are not troubled (as in the past) with their "social work" orientation instead of the crime-fighter bent of the past. Officers see themselves as community workers and organizers, and have a variety of tools and resources (including arrest) at their disposal. They serve as mediators, negotiating settlements in all kinds of community problems, ranging from pollution to marital property disputes (Couper 1990).

SUMMARY

This chapter has reviewed the complex role of the police supervisor, addressing the issues of ethics, decision making, values, liability and negligence, discipline of subordinates, supervision as it relates to community-oriented policing and problem solving, and future challenges. It is clear more than ever that the police supervisor must be well trained and educated in order to cope with the various challenges of the day and the twenty-first century. The position of first-line supervisor is simply too rife with trials and tribulations for one's success or failure to revolve around on-the-job training. The guidance and treatment of subordinates and public alike require the best people we can "create" to occupy this position, lest the organization be visited with an unhappy community at the least and lawsuits and other problems at worst.

BIBLIOGRAPHY

Black, J. (1986). *The Real Meaning of Discipline*. Gaithersburg, Md.: International Association of Chiefs of Police.

Bock, W. (n.d.). Briefing Memo: On the Transition to Sergeant. Oakland, Calif.: mimeographed.

Brown, M. (1992). The Sergeant's Role in a Modern Law Enforcement Agency. *The Police Chief*, May, 18–22.

Couper, D. (1990). Comparing Two Positions on the Future of American Policing. *American Journal of Police* 9 (3): 161–169.

del Carmen, R. (1991). *Civil Liabilities in American Policing*. Englewood Cliffs, N.J.: Brady.

del Carmen, R. (1989). Civil Liabilities of Police Supervisors. *American Journal of Police* 8 (1): 107–136.

Eck, J., and W. Spelman. (1987). *Problem-Solving: Problem-Oriented Policing in Newport News*. Washington, D.C.: Police Executive Research Forum.

Fair, F., and W. Pilcher. (1991). Morality on the Line: The Role of Ethics in Police Decision-Making. *American Journal of Police* 10 (2): 23–38.

Goldstein, H. (1993). The New Policing: Confronting Complexity. Paper presented at the Conference on Community Policing, 24 August, U.S. Department of Justice, National Institute of Justice, Washington, D.C.

Goldstein, H. (1990). *Problem-Oriented Policing*. New York: McGraw-Hill.

Goldstein, H. (1987). Toward Community-Oriented Policing: Potential, Basic Requirements, and Threshold Questions. *Crime and Delinquency* 33: 17.

Kansas City, Missouri, Police Department (KCPD). (1991). Recommendation of the Task Force on the Use of Force. (January).

Law Enforcement News. (1997). July/August, 2, 3.

Likert, R. (1961). *New Patterns of Management*. New York: McGraw-Hill.

Maguire, K., and A. Pastore. (1996). *Sourcebook of Criminal Justice Statistics— 1995*. Washington, D.C.: U.S. Government Printing Office.

Martin, J. (1993). Reengineering Government. *Governing*, March, 27–30.

McDowell, J. (1992). Are Women Better Cops? *Time*, 17 February, 71.

Peak, K. (1996). *Policing America: Methods, Issues, Challenges.* 2d ed. Upper Saddle River, N.J.: Prentice Hall.

Police Executive Research Forum. (1990). Supervising Problem-Solving. Washington, D.C.: Author.

Reuss-Ianni, E. (1983). *Two Cultures of Policing: Street Cops and Management Cops.* New Brunswick, N.J.: Transaction Books.

Robinette, H. (1993). Supervising Tomorrow. *Virginia Police Chief*, Spring, 10.

Ross, R. (1992). Citizen Complaint Policy. *FBI Law Enforcement Bulletin*, March, 21–22.

Sparrow, M. (1988). Implementing Community Policing. Washington, D.C.: National Institute of Justice.

U.S. Department of Justice, Bureau of Justice Statistics Bulletin. (1996). *Local Police Departments, 1993.* Washington, D.C.: U.S. Government Printing Office.

U.S. Department of Justice, Bureau of Justice Statistics Bulletin. (1990). *State and Local Police Departments, 1990.* Washington, D.C.: U.S. Government Printing Office.

Von der Embse, T. (1987). *Supervision: Managerial Skills for a New Era.* New York: Macmillan.

4

Personnel Performance Evaluations in the Community-Policing Context

Timothy N. Oettmeier and Mary Ann Wycoff

Most performance evaluations currently in use by police agencies do not reflect the work officers do. Evaluations typically consist of compliance audits, statistical comparisons, or descriptive summaries of events. Mastrofski (1996) notes, "A contemporary police department's system of performance measurement remains substantively rooted in the perspective of the reform wave that was gathering force in the 1930s under the leadership of August Vollmer, J. Edgar Hoover, the Wickersham Commission, and others. More effort is put into recording UCR data (e.g., arrests, clearances, reported crime, etc.) than any other indicators" (pp. 209–210).

According to Whitaker and colleagues (1982), these measures have a number of well-documented technical weaknesses and an even more compelling limitation at the policy level. Because they do not reflect the work officers do and are seldom used for the purpose of making individual career decisions, it is not surprising that police personnel tend to perceive evaluations as academic exercises that neither have relevance for them nor utility for their departments. There is nothing simple about constructing a valid and reliable evaluation process and few individual agencies are staffed for the task. Many agencies lack basic planning and research units, and those that do have such units seldom have the resources to hire staff with this kind of expertise. And these units are not typically expected to do this kind of work. They more commonly function as an administrative arm of the executive. They may be used to develop new programs and initiatives, conduct phone or mail surveys, or generate statistical reports. They seldom serve as a repository of significant police-related research findings that could influence managerial decision making, and they seldom are used to conduct empirical evaluations that could guide policy decisions. While the thinking about performance evaluations will be advanced by some individual agencies, the largest gains are likely to result from the combined efforts of departments to trade ideas and information. That exchange can be enhanced by a common framework for thinking and talking about evaluation and related issues. For the purpose of this chapter, we focus our attention on redesigning performance measurement systems to more effectively evaluate officer performance. The focus of the evaluation should center on measuring differences in individual knowledge, skills, and attitudes; the nature of the effort; and the attainment of results.

A MODEL OF PERFORMANCE ANALYSIS

An evaluation process requires an initial definition of concepts and a model that links them. For the purpose of this chapter, we use the term "performance analysis" to refer to the collection of activities or analyses that constitute the identification and evaluation of purposive work. Purposive work assumes an objective to be accomplished. In the case of policing, that purpose might be to have an officer available to respond to calls in a specified area for a specified period of time, to close a drug house, to reduce the probability that citizens will become victims, to increase community structure in a given neighborhood, or the like.

Role definition refers to identifying types of tasks to be undertaken by the police. Before any evaluation instrument is designed, consensus must be attained among citizens, officers, supervisors, and managers as to the scope of work responsibilities. Failure to attain consensus will lead to confusion over who is responsible for which work assignments. This aggravates the ability to conduct valid and reliable performance evaluations.

Inputs are any resources that contribute to the delivery of police service. In most instances, inputs include different types of support mechanisms within the organization or community that facilitate the attainment of results through work efforts. Examples of this support include crime pattern identification through crime analysis; modifying standard operating procedures; training and education received; availability of personnel to implement an action plan, strategy, or tactic; time; equipment; and so on.

Outputs are the activities or strategies used and the efforts that are made to do the work that is done. The outputs of a performance can be analyzed in terms of content, quantity, quality, and motivation. The content (what is done) is the act or set of acts performed or strategies implemented. Quantity (how much is done) refers to the number of specified acts within a given period of time. Quality (how well the act is done) is a function of the competence with which actions are performed and the style in which they are performed. Competence depends on knowing what needs to be done and how to do that which is required. The style of the performance refers to the personal manner of the person(s) conducting it. Motivation refers to the reason why the act is performed.

Outcomes are the results, effects, or consequences of the work that is done. The outcome that is assessed will be determined by the purpose of the work. For the examples given, appropriate outcomes could include the number of calls for service answered during the shift, the fact that the targeted drug house was closed, a reduction in the victimization rate in a neighborhood, or action taken by neighborhood residents who worked with the police through organized community meeting in a given neighborhood.

At each stage of the model, the process of analysis requires both documentation and enumeration and evaluation. In the case of inputs, one asks what the inputs were (enumeration) and whether they were the right ones and in sufficient quantity (evaluation). For role definition, the question is whether a decision has been made about how to address an issue. For outputs, the questions are what actions were taken (enumeration) and what the quality of the actions was (evaluation). For outcomes, the question is whether the actions taken accomplished the objective (evaluation) and whether the nature and magnitude of the results merited the combination of inputs and outputs required to achieve them (cost/benefit analysis).

The model can be applied to any unit of organizational analysis; it can be used to conceptualize the performance of an organization, a unit or team, or (as most commonly applied) individual employees. An organization committed to accountability to a governing body meeting the needs of customers and its employees, showing efficient management of resources, and pursuing the continual improvement of the organization's ability to keep the first four commitments will create and regularly employ performance analysis of each type outlined for all divisions and levels within a respective system.

THE CHALLENGE OF PERFORMANCE MEASUREMENT

What is measured and how it is measured should depend on the reasons for collecting the data. Mastrofski and Wadman (1991, 364) identify three principal reasons for measuring employee performance:

1. Administration, to help managers make decisions about promotion, demotion, reward, discipline, training needs, salary, job assignment, retention, and termination.
2. Guidance and counseling, to help supervisors provide feedback to subordinates and assist them in career planning and preparation and to improve employee motivation.
3. Research, to validate selection and screening tests and training evaluations and to assess the effectiveness of interventions designed to improve individual performance.

From research conducted within the Houston Police Department on performance evaluation under the context of community policing (Wycoff and Oettmeier 1993b), three more reasons are added:

4. Socialization, to convey expectations to personnel about both the content and style of their performance and to reinforce other means of organizational communication about the mission and values of the department.
5. Documentation, to record the types of problems and situations officers are addressing in their neighborhoods and the approaches they take to them. Such documentation provides for data-based analysis of the types of resources and other managerial support needed to address problems and allows officers the opportunity to have their efforts recognized.
6. System improvement, to identify organizational conditions that may impede improved performance and to solicit ideas for changing the conditions.

In an organization that is undertaking a shift in its philosophy about service delivery, these last three functions of performance measurement are especially important. A philosophy that is articulated and reinforced through the types of activities or performances that are measured should be more readily understood by personnel than one simply espoused by (perhaps) remote managers.

A department may be interested in designing a new performance-measurement system to accomplish any or all of these purposes. However, multiple purposes are not always easy to accommodate with the same process. For example, it is not easy to design a system that meets administrative needs while providing guidance for the officer, and the conflict between these two objectives can be stressful for the evaluator. McGregor (1957) feels managers are uncomfortable with the performance-appraisal processes, not because they dislike change or the techniques they must use or because they lack skill, but because they are put in a position of "playing God." He feels the modern emphasis on the manager as a leader who strives to help his subordinates achieve both their own and the company's objectives is inconsistent with the judicial role demanded by most appraisal plans. A manager's role, he claims, is to help the person analyze performance in terms of targets and plan future work that is related to organizational objectives and realities. Rather than a focus on weaknesses, the employee needs a better means of identifying strengths and accomplishments.

Since the purpose will determine the nature of the evaluation, it will be essential for managers to identify the organizational purposes of the evaluation before the redesign process is undertaken.

Content of the Evaluation

Decisions also must be made about what is to be measured. Traditional assessments frequently report what might be called officers' administrative behaviors (times late for work, accuracy and completeness of reports, etc.). Most, however, have relatively little to say about the nature of the officer's work behaviors, a fact that Levinson (1976) argues causes most performance-appraisal systems to be unrealistic. An analysis of behavior could include documentation and evaluation of the content of work done, the amount of work done, its appropriateness, the style with which it is done, and the results of the effort. The issue of style or the way in which the work is done concerns Levinson, who claims a crucial part of any manager's job and the source of most failures is informing subordinates "how" work is to be done.

Consideration of content raises the question of whether all employees should be evaluated with the same criteria and, specifically, whether a given employee should be evaluated with the same criteria across the span of his or her career. It is a reasonable expectation that as an employee's tenure lengthens, individual competency should increase. Early in a career, it is important to determine whether the employee has the requisite knowledge, skills, and attitudes (KSAs), ability, and willingness to do the job. We want to determine if the employee has the capacity to do police work. Once this is established, performance assessment might more reasonably focus on whether the employee effectively uses these KSAs in the field. Evaluation is used to determine whether the officer is consistently doing things correctly. At some advanced stage of the career, assessment could focus on whether the officer does the right thing; in other words, whether the officer is able to select the correct response to fit the service needs of the area for which he or she is responsible.

Over the course of a career, assessment moves from an initial focus on ability to a focus on effort and, finally, to a focus on judgment and the results of an officer's efforts. Each of these stages would require using different performance criteria, instrumentation, and assessment processes.

Requirements for Performance Evaluations

In addition to this wide range of decisions managers need to make about performance evaluations, there are at least five standards that an employee performance measurement process should meet: (1) validity, (2) reliability, (3) equity, (4) legality, and (5) utility (Mastrofski and Wadman 1991). If the process is valid, it accurately reflects the content of the job an employee is expected to perform, as well as the expected quality of the job performance. The validity of an evaluation process is tied to job task analyses for the positions in question. The purpose of a job task analysis is to determine what specific tasks are performed by employees. They are asked to provide feedback regarding the frequency and criticality of tasks associated with their respective assignments. The tasks are prioritized followed by the identification of associated KSAs. Performance criteria are then developed to represent those KSAs which should be evaluated.

The Achilles heel of a job task analysis in the context of organizational change is that it describes a position as it currently exists, and not as it is planned for the future. An evaluation process that is to be used to promote and sustain change of the police role has to be designed to reflect the desired behavior while still reflecting current performance. As organizations modify responsibilities to reflect community policing, new performance criteria need to be developed. This is one reason why a performance evaluation process should not be a fixed process; it is one that should change as often as necessary to reflect the changing nature of the job.

A reliable process is one that will result in the same performance being given the same evaluation across evaluators and across repetitions of that performance. Any time one person is designated to evaluate the performance of another, subjectivity will be a factor. The challenge, irrespective of the type of evaluation used, is to minimize the subjectivity factor. According to Lawler (1971), the more subjective the rating system, the higher the degree of trust is required to make it work. Oberg (1972) suggests management identify appraisal techniques designed to achieve a particular organizational objective; such "results focused" appraisals would be less vulnerable to subjective influences. There probably is no way to guarantee full objectivity of performance assessment; objectivity is best maximized by good training for the evaluators.

An equitable process is one that will allow employees doing the same or similar work to receive equal evaluations. This is especially critical in an organization where performance evaluations are used to determine pay, transfers, or promotions. In such organizations, it is not uncommon for one evaluation point or even a fraction of a point to separate the rewarded from the unrewarded employee. This is a difficult issue for policing, because the nature and frequency of performance occur, to a large degree, in response to external conditions that vary by temporal and geographic variables. This element is accentuated under community policing because of the need to provide customized services within a wide array of different neighborhoods.

Legality is a significant issue in departments for which certain requirements of the evaluation process are established by law, either state law, city ordinance, or civil service code. It is also an issue for those agencies using performance evaluations to determine rewards and punishments for employees. Legality and validity are usually interwoven. People challenge performance-evaluation systems that are invalid because they result in management decisions that are inherently unfair to employees deserving equal treatment and consideration.

Utility refers simply to the purpose for the evaluation. If nothing is done with it, if employees see no benefit from the evaluation for either the organization or themselves personally, the process will be less than useless; it will breed contempt for management among employees.

It is beyond the scope of this chapter to instruct the reader in the various means of meeting each of these standards. These issues are discussed extensively in Whitaker and colleagues (1982) and by Mastrofski and Wadman (1991), whose work provides technical reference of value to agencies struggling with these topics.

The need for assessment procedures to be valid, reliable, equitable, and useful is the same, regardless of an organization's philosophy. Meeting these requirements is a difficult task given the high probability of conflicts among them. The goal of equity, for example, may conflict with the goal of validity. When jobs are dissimilar within patrols because of geographical assignment or duty time, the need for equity may reduce the evaluated job dimensions to the most common elements of the role. This could result in an evaluation that fails to reflect any officer's actual job responsibilities.

Concerns for both legality and reliability have pushed departments toward quantifiable performance indicators. The increased emphasis administrators placed on crime-fighting aspects of the police role in previous decades (Kelling and Moore 1988) also created pressure for quantifiable measures. The indicators most readily available were those associated (even if spuriously) with crime fighting (e.g., rapid response, numbers of arrests, etc.) and with administrative regulations (e.g., tardiness, sick time taken, accidents, etc.; see Kelling [1992]). When important behaviors or activities cannot be counted, then the ones that are counted tend to become those that are considered important (Wycoff 1982b).

PERFORMANCE MEASUREMENT IN THE
COMMUNITY-POLICING CONTEXT

Revision of performance-measurement systems to reflect the diverse responsibilities of an ever-broadening police role is something many executives still need to accomplish in the 1990s, regardless of whether they have any interest in changing their organization's current approach to policing. Changes in policing philosophies only make more apparent the need for managers to acknowledge and support activities effective officers have conducted but which have gone officially unrecognized.

The record of researchers is no better in this respect than the record of police managers. Despite their disclaimers about the validity and reliability of such indicators, researchers continue to use recorded crime data, arrest data, and administrative data as indicators of performance and outcome, because other indicators are unavailable or are too costly or time consuming to create. This fact led to Kelling's (1978) call for "a modest moratorium on the application of crime related productivity measures" until the full range of the police role could be documented and decisions made about how to measure a much wider range of police activity (and results).

Community policing draws attention to other issues about employee performance evaluation:

1. The means by which supervisors and managers can hold officers accountable for the greater discretion they are permitted.
2. The inclusion of the community in the evaluation process.
3. The evaluation of team, unit, or organization as distinct from the evaluation of the individual officer.

Weisburd, McElroy, and Hardyman (1989) suggest that the paramilitary model of policing facilitates close supervision of the officers' traditional role but is inappropriate for the broader, more discretionary role associated with community policing (see also Goldstein 1979; Bittner 1972). While it is debatable how many sergeants effectively "supervise" their officers in departments that restrict what officers are allowed to do, it is clear community policing will require a reformulation of the sergeant's role that corresponds with changes in officers' roles.

Official expansion of the officer's role will require sergeants, for example, to support the use of and to hold officers accountable for the greater discretion they are permitted. To support the work of officers, sergeants will need to become more efficient managers, team builders, and group facilitators. Sergeants should develop the capacity to build resource capabilities for their officers. They should be active participants in devising more global approaches to addressing problems of crime and disorder. Of critical importance is their ability to sense and interpret local opportunities for and hindrances to action being taken by officers.

To accomplish this, sergeants, like officers, will need to seek more effective means of getting information from the community. Generally, the only "significant" form of feedback from the citizenry has been in the form of complaints about improper police activity. Notwithstanding the importance of attending to citizen complaints, departments need to collect data about services citizens want and about whether citizens believe their service needs are being met.

There is also the issue addressed by Trojanowicz and Bucqueroux (1992), Wadman and Olson (1990), and others of the need to correspond to the problems officers are trying to solve in communities. For example, the use of discretion by an officer for how, when, and where is not a new issue for supervisors. It has always been an issue for rural police departments and sheriffs' agencies in which officers and supervisors may never have occasion to meet after roll call (and, sometimes, not even at roll call).

A number of strategies have been advocated for accomplishing this. Numerous departments have used community meetings as a forum for eliciting service needs and preferences (e.g., Houston's Positive Interaction Program). Some have employed door-to-door surveys conducted by officers (e.g., Grand Rapids, Michigan, and Newark, New Jersey). A few departments with substantial resources have conducted scientific community surveys. The Madison, Wisconsin, Police Department has surveyed, by mail, a sample of all citizens who have received service from the department in an effort to measure satisfaction and to collect information about ways of improving service.

In addition to recognizing the value of community feedback, community policing has also caused some administrators to question the appropriateness of individual employee evaluations. Some departments are emphasizing a focus on the team or workgroup rather than on the individual. Those retaining individual evaluations may abandon them as a means of differentiating among employees for the purpose of rewards and, instead, use them as a means of helping individual employees identify and meet their own career goals (Gabor 1992).

The appropriate role of employee performance evaluations in a community-policing context (or perhaps any policing context) is an issue that is being explored. The answers for each department may ultimately depend on the uses the agency wishes to make of the evaluations. Perhaps, as agencies embracing the Deming's philosophy of management argue (Scholtes 1987), there is no reason to "grade" individuals relative to each other. However, evaluations might still be a means of informing governing bodies about the work of the organization's accountability that will become ever more critical in the face of shrinking resources, determining the nature of problems in various neighborhoods and the strategies that are more and less effective in dealing with them, permitting officers to record and "exhibit" the work they are doing, and determining career objectives and progress for individual employees.

Some organizations may improve individual evaluations to better serve these purposes, and others may design alternative means of accomplishing these ends. One of the valuable consequences of the current interest in community policing should be the creation of a variety of new approaches to performance measurement.

THE PROCESS OF REDESIGNING
THE EVALUATION SYSTEM

There are many ways in which an organization could approach the redesign of their performance-evaluation system. For illustration, this section briefly describes the process used in Houston in the late 1980s. This section also examines issues that will be germane to any agency undertaking redesign, regardless of the specific process used.

The Houston Experience

The redesign of performance measurement in Houston was undertaken in conjunction with the development of Neighborhood Oriented Policing (NOP) and its implementation at Westside, Houston's first decentralized police facility. The project was directed by an Internal Advisory Committee which consisted of a project director, a representative from the Chief's office, the Deputy Chief from Westside, and the Westside Operations Captain.

An early meeting with sergeants at Westside led the committee to conclude that patrol officer activities under the NOP concept were still not sufficiently well articulated to support the redesign. Consequently, a task force of eleven patrol officers, one investigator, and two sergeants was created. The group met eight times over a six-month period to discuss the nature of activities being conducted by patrol officers who were attempting to implement the NOP philosophy and the challenges of measuring these activities. Representatives of the committee visited four other agencies (in New York City; Baltimore County, Maryland; Newport News, Virginia; and Madison, Wisconsin) to observe and discuss other approaches to performance measurement.

The committee developed a list of tasks, roles, and skills they felt would be essential to the role of officers working in the NOP context. The project manager developed a data-collection instrument designed to capture detailed information about the actions of police officers, sergeants, and lieutenants at Westside. Eight members of the task force were trained as facilitators, each of whom was to identify six other officers to complete the instrument. Data from these forms were then analyzed to identify attitudes and activities that were considered important for officers implementing NOP.

This process was supported by a two-day meeting with an External Advisory Committee. Eight individuals representing other police departments, police professional organizations, the National Institute of Justice, and private corporations spent two days in a seminar setting with the task force, the project's Internal Advisory Committee, and other selected department personnel discussing the nature of performance evaluation, its purposes, and the various forms it could take. Following this meeting, the task force designed performance-evaluation instruments that were then field tested and revised based on the results of feedback from the test.

Some aspects of this process (the trips to other cities and the work of the External Advisory Committee) were financially feasible because of a grant from the National Institute of Justice in support of the redesign effort. The other parts of the process, however, should be possible for most agencies without additional funding. It may be necessary to provide overtime pay for task-force members, and it should be anticipated this is not an undertaking that can be accomplished quickly. It is estimated that in Houston each task-force member contributed approximately two months of time (spread out over a six-month time period).

The role of the project director was also critical. The project director did a great deal of work between task-force meetings that would be difficult for a task force of officers to accomplish without this type of organizational support. The amount of time the process takes will concern managers who are watching budgets and implementation time tables, but this is a process that will undergird other implementation efforts and is one that should not be rushed. This is a difficult assignment and discussion about it will lead task-force members into critical discussions about other systems in the organization that are related to (or should be related to) the performance-evaluation system. An effort should be made to capture and utilize information from these discussions for the sake of rethinking and redesigning other systems.

Observations and evaluation of the Houston experience and of similar experiences of other departments that have been undertaking performance measurement redesign have led to the identification of several issues that will need to be addressed in the course of the process.

Adopt New Assumptions. Management has an obligation to provide structure and guidance in developing the performance capabilities of employees. Typically, this structure is provided using multiple formats: training, education, job enrichment, disciplinary action, rewards, incentives, and performance evaluation. To be effective, each of these management tools must be flexible in design and application. Each of these tools should be governed by a set of assumptions. In the case of performance evaluations, many of the baseline assumptions governing how it should be done have not been changed in years, if not decades:

- All personnel performance will be assessed at least once (or twice) a year.
- All personnel will be assessed using the same performance criteria.
- All personnel will use the same performance-evaluation instrumentation.
- The results of one's performance evaluation may (or may not) be used to help determine promotability.

These assumptions are not necessarily improper or incorrect. In many agencies, they are legal requirements set forth by state statutes, local ordinances, or civil service codes. However, this does not preclude executives from reexamining them to determine what flexibility, if any, they have to make adjustments.

The manner in which performance is assessed should be dynamic. As performance expectations change, so should the methodology and criteria used to measure effectiveness change. The following should be kept in mind:

1. Employee competency is expected to improve as a result of experience.
2. Performance-evaluation criteria should vary in accordance with an employee's assignment, tenure, and competency.
3. The relationship between the number and type of performance criteria and individual competency is not linear. People learn at different rates.
4. Performance can be assessed in phases consistent with individual development.
5. Employees should be allowed to voluntarily progress through an evaluation system at varying speeds.

Define Purposes of Evaluations. In many organizations, performance evaluation is an annual ritual people try to administer routinely and consistently. Executives and employees alike view it as an administrative duty. However, as this chapter has suggested, performance evaluations can have much more meaningful objectives. In organizations seeking to become community based, performance-measurement systems can be used as a management tool to accomplish the following:

1. Enhance officers' and supervisors' knowledge of community policing.
2. Clarify officers' and supervisors' perceptions of their respective behavior under community policing.
3. Redefine productivity requirements to include changes in the type, amount, and quality of work to be performed.
4. Build consensus between and among officers and supervisors regarding each other's work responsibilities.
5. Improve officers' levels of job satisfaction with department operations.
6. Measure citizens' perceptions of the way in which police deliver service to the community.

These objectives allow executives to recast performance-evaluation systems, but they require us to think differently about the nature of performance criteria, the design of instrumentation, and the participants in the process.

As a process, performance evaluation must be more than just a means of obtaining information about how well employees improve their KSAs. It should help management gauge, from different perspectives, how well employees are using their KSAs, what results they are attaining, and how susceptible they are to accepting and implementing other organizational changes. This information is critical because it helps management decide the pace at which organizational change can occur. Without this knowledge, managers will develop inaccurate expectations as to what is occurring in the workplace.

These inaccurate expectations will cause decisions to be made that will heighten resistance among employees. This resistance will be based on the employees' perception that management is out of touch with reality. When this happens, it will become more difficult for managers to gain support from employees for any initiatives, let alone those associated with improving the overall performance of the organization.

Identify New Performance Criteria. Determining what should be measured is heavily dependent on the work demands associated with an officer's work assignment and management's expectations regarding results. Earlier in this chapter, the various functions performed by an officer in a community-policing context were classified as reactive, proactive, or coactive. The addition of the coactive function means that criteria need to be developed that reflect this function. And, as suggested, many departments still need to make an effort to develop criteria that accurately reflect reactive and proactive work.

Even within these three functional categories, the career model of performance evaluation argues that different criteria need to be developed for application at different times in an officer's career. Again, this does not mean completely abandoning traditional criteria. It will still be important, for example, to measure the attainment of knowledge, skills, and attitudes in the early stages of an officer's career; such information will provide officers with information about their self-development, but it can tell us little about what an officer does to impact crime and problems in a neighborhood. At some point, criteria must be developed that tell us what is being done to improve the neighborhood that can be used in addition to those that tell us what is done (or needs to be done) to improve the officer.

In response to this concern, Stephens (1996) has identified the following performance inputs and outcomes for which executives who are implementing community policing and problem solving are attempting to develop indicators:

- Problem solving.
- Citizen satisfaction.
- Repeat business.
- Displacement.
- Neighborhood indicants (e.g., truancy rates, traffic patterns, occupancy rates, presence and actions taken by neighborhood groups, etc.).

The Houston task force (Wycoff and Oettmeier 1993b) based the creation of new performance criteria on tasks and activities officers performed within their neighborhoods. This information was collected from a representative sample of officers who kept records of their actual work during their shifts.

Measure the Effects of Officer Performance. Goldstein (1990) has contended that traditional management postures have required officers to emphasize "means over ends." For example, traffic enforcement is measured in terms of the number of tickets issued for moving violations (e.g., improper turns, running red lights, speeding, etc.). The association is seldom made between the need to issue speeding tickets and the need to reduce minor accidents or fatalities at a particular location. Police managers are only beginning to address the need to evaluate performance in relation to specific problems.

According to Goldstein (1990), evaluating police response to any problem requires the following:

- A clear understanding of the problem.
- Agreement over the specific interest(s) to be served in dealing with the problem, and their order of importance.
- Agreement on the method to be used to determine the extent to which these interests (or goals) are reached and a realistic assessment of what might be expected of the police (e.g., solving the problem versus improving the quality of the police management of it).

- Determination of the relative importance of short-term versus long-term impact.
- A clear understanding of the legality and fairness of the response (recognizing that reducing a problem through improper use of authority is not only wrong, but likely to be counterproductive because of its effects on other aspects of police operations).

Goldstein cautions against defining success as problem eradication, since many problems by their very nature are intractable or unmanageable because of their magnitude. Despite this limitation, there are a sufficient number of problems well within the boundaries of police control that merit attention.

In order to differentiate types of outcomes officers might achieve in problem-solving, Spelman and Eck (1987) developed five degrees of effectiveness:

1. total elimination.
2. reducing the number of incidents it creates.
3. reducing the seriousness of the incidents it creates.
4. designing methods for better handling of the incidents.
5. removing the problem from police consideration (assuming it is dealt with more effectively by some other entity than the police).

In this context, Goldstein claims that for much of police business the most realistic goal is to reduce the number of incidents a problem creates and to reduce the seriousness of these incidents. Correspondingly, he suggests it is helpful to characterize the police role more realistically as "managing deviance" and then concentrate on equipping the police to carry out this role with greater effectiveness. Officers should be involved in identifying the measurable conditions they would expect to see change before they undertake a problem-solving effort, and they should be allowed to identify factors not under an officer's control that can affect outcomes.

Strengthen the Verification Process. One of the most difficult aspects of conducting evaluations for supervisors is verification of performance. Technically, the assessment of officer performance is dependent upon the ability of supervisors to observe what occurred. Unfortunately, the verification of performance does not always occur, for a number of legitimate reasons. For example, the span of control can make it very difficult for a supervisor to consistently view officer performance. Too many officers going in too many directions makes it hard for a supervisor to observe performance. Another variable is the type and amount of work officers perform. Officers who constantly respond to calls for service, write numerous reports, or patrol indiscriminately do not provide their supervisor with a wide array of settings from which different types of performances can be observed.

Supervisors may not be motivated to observe officer behavior. It is not surprising that supervisors do not always hold performance evaluation as a priority duty. Many are apt to say it requires too much work and it interferes with "my other responsibilities." "Besides," they go on to say, "officers don't really care and it doesn't mean that much to them anyway." In actuality, it means a lot to them; many officers want feedback, they want their performance to be noticed, and they want to be recognized for what they have accomplished. If anything, officers are inclined to feel they do not receive enough credit for all the things they do during their tours of duty.

The St. Petersburg Police Department (1994) identified a number of different sources to verify officer performance, among them reviewing reports, responding to crime scenes, reading complimentary letters from citizens, reviewing internal affairs files, reviewing productivity statistics, monitoring radio communications, monitoring rumors, conducting street inspections, reviewing training records, monitoring community involvement, monitoring sick time, and so on. One way of addressing this conflict is to alter one of the traditional assumptions governing who participates in the evaluation process. Should performance evaluations be limited to just the observations of an officer's immediate supervisor? Not necessarily. Granted, the supervisor should have a major impact on determining how well an officer has performed, but not to the extent of ignoring input from citizens, investigators, or officers themselves.

As officers increase the amount of time working directly with citizens on neighborhood crime and disorder problems, citizens will form certain opinions about different aspects of their performance. Community leaders, civic club or association personnel, business association personnel, even apartment managers are all capable of providing input to a sergeant about an officer's performance. They can provide feedback in the following areas: communication skills, the nature of their relationship, and collaborative problem-solving efforts.

Investigators provide another potential source of verification for supervisors. Investigators working in the same neighborhoods as officers often end up conducting a follow-up investigation based on an officer's preliminary investigation. Investigators are able to provide information regarding the officer's written communication skills, procedural knowledge, legal knowledge, and, in instances when they are actually working together on a case, feedback on their ability to get along and their initiative in pursuing a case to its logical conclusion.

Officers should have the opportunity to provide input into their own evaluations. This should not be limited to just agreeing or disagreeing with the supervisor's observations. In addition to providing their supervisors with examples of successful work products, officers should be invited to identify efforts that may not have been known by the supervisor. They should be encouraged to discuss any failure, including why it occurred and what was learned from the experience. Should officers be allowed to assess each other's performance? Many Houston officers said "no" for a number of reasons, including the idea that officers will use it to "snitch-off" other officers, that it will cause conflicts among officers, that officers are not competent to evaluate KSAs, and that it will create role confusion. In addition, verification of officer performance is difficult. One rule of thumb is to make sure the source of feedback is capable of providing current, reliable, and practical information about an officer's performance. If there is any doubt as to the integrity of the information, do not use it.

Develop New Instrumentation. The nature of a new evaluation form should be determined by the expectations that are to be communicated about officer performance. It should be purposeful and consistent with supporting an officer's career development throughout his or her tenure within the agency. From an administrative standpoint, management should be concerned about a number of items. For instance, should one form be used by all officers, or should forms be developed to support an officer's assignment (e.g., patrol versus investigative versus support assignments)? How many copies of the form are needed? Will the supervisors be required to complete them by hand or will they be automated? If additional forms are created, where will each copy and/or form be filed and for how long? Will it be necessary to provide each supervisor with an instructional booklet? Is training necessary to acquaint supervisors with the new form(s) and, if so, how long will the sessions last and who will do the training? A rule of thumb to follow when developing new instrumentation is to make sure the forms capture information that adequately reflects what officers are capable of doing and what management expects them to accomplish within their respective neighborhoods.

Solicit Officer Feedback about the Sergeant. Officers cannot perform a full evaluation of their supervisors because they experience only one part of a supervisor's responsibilities. However, they can provide significant feedback in a number of areas, including the nature of their relationship, how well they get along, how responsive they are, whether they act as a leader or coach, the clarity of communications, and so on. The process should be designed so that the feedback is couched in constructive terms, otherwise sergeants may have difficulty "hearing" it. And the process could be designed to be anonymous, otherwise officers may not be inclined to provide this information for fear of retaliation.

Revise Rating Scales. Most performance-measurement systems contain rating scales. In time, the criteria used describe scale points can become dated and should be reexamined periodically. Determining the type of scale to be used depends on the distinction one wants to make with a person's performance. If the interest is in distinguishing between acceptable versus unacceptable behavior, a pass–fail scale is appropriate. In most cases, supervisors want more discretion in determining how well their officers are performing. The Likert scaling technique, involving a five- or seven-point scale, is a popular format used by many agencies. Seven-point scales tend to include detailed descriptions of a few anchor points (i.e., 1, 4, and 7), while five-point scales are apt to describe each point in detail. The fewer descriptions of anchor points, the greater the discretion for supervisors and, hence, the higher the probability for subjectivity and error. The greater the number of scale points, the less subjectivity, but the more difficult it becomes to describe behavioral differences between them.

All scale points for each performance criterion should be clearly defined. Definitions should be specific and not global. The reason most definitions are global is because departments use one form for all personnel, regardless of rank or assignment. In constructing scale-point definitions, make sure the descriptive criteria is consistent from one scale point to the next. For example, if five different descriptive criteria are used to define what "unacceptable" means, make sure those criteria are addressed in each of the succeeding scale-point descriptions. Do not use different descriptive criteria from one scale point to the next. This will skew the reliability of the evaluation tremendously.

If possible, develop instrumentation unique to both assignment and rank. Even if legally mandated to use a generic evaluation form, develop worksheets that feed into the primary instrument.

CONCLUSION

A performance-measurement system is an important management and leadership tool for police agencies. It should be designed to support individual professional development and to support behavioral changes. If the decision is made to revise an organization's current performance-measurement system, these points are worth bearing in mind:

1. Performance evaluations are not bad in and of themselves. Frustration sets in with how the process is administered and with the lack of suitable performance criteria.

2. Officers want feedback and a permanent record of their accomplishments and performance.

3. Officers feel they are doing more than they are receiving credit for given the typical narrow design of their evaluation instrumentation and performance criteria.

4. The goals and structure of the organization should be decided before new performance measurement is developed. Form follows function.

5. There should be separate forms for different assignments (unless law prohibits).

6. Administrative convenience should not be a primary criteria in the redesign. The goal of the performance evaluation should dictate the way in which it is conducted.

7. Any significant alteration of past practices is likely to cause some dissatisfaction among supervisors. It is likely that this, too, shall pass as the new becomes familiar.

8. Performance evaluation should be reprioritized as a critical supervisory responsibility. Without overreacting to sergeants' concerns, be responsive. Remove meaningless administrative duties from sergeants so they can spend more time verifying officer performance. In time, what was once considered drastic will become routine, provided it is perceived as having practical value to the sergeant.

9. Citizen involvement is central to performance evaluation. Citizens can be a good source of information about an officer's style, adequacy of effort, and community satisfaction with results. They also can provide valuable feedback about the status of neighborhood conditions. They should not be put in a position of judging the appropriateness of an officer's decisions.

10. The process should be as simple as reasonably possible. This will increase both acceptance and the probability that the information actually will be utilized.

Finally, performance-measurement systems are critical to facilitating change within personnel and throughout the organization. Executives who accept the challenge of modifying their system will discover an effective management tool to attain results within neighborhoods and their organization.

NOTE

Reprinted from *Personnel Performance Evaluations in the Community Policing Context* by T. Oettmeier and M. Wycoff with permission from the Police Executive Research Forum. Copyright by Police Executive Research Forum.

BIBLIOGRAPHY

Bittner, E. (1972). *The Functions of the Police in Modern Society*. Rockville, Md.: National Institute of Mental Health.

Community Policing Consortium. (1994). *Understanding Community Policing: A Framework for Action*. Washington, D.C.: Bureau of Justice Assistance.

Gabor, A. (1992). Take This Job and Love It. *New York Times*, 26 January.

Goldstein, H. (1990). *Problem-Oriented Policing*. New York: McGraw-Hill.

Goldstein, H. (1979). Improving Policing: A Problem-Oriented Approach. *Crime and Delinquency* 25.

Kelling, G. (1992). Measuring What Matters: A New Way of Thinking about Crime and Public Order. *The City Journal*, Spring.

Kelling, G. (1978). The Role of Research in Maximizing Productivity. In *Report of the Proceedings, Workshop on Police Productivity and Performance*, edited by P. Engstad and M. Lioy. Ottawa: Ministry of the Solicitor General of Canada.

Kelling, G., and M. Moore. (1988). The Evolving Strategy of Policing. Washington, D.C.: National Institute of Justice.

Lawler, E. (1971). *Pay and Organizational Effectiveness: A Psychological View*. New York: McGraw-Hill.

Levinson, H. (1976). Appraisal of What Performance. *Harvard Business Review* (July–August).

Mastrofski, S. (1996). Measuring Police Performance in Public Encounters. In *Quantifying Quality in Policing*, edited by L. Hoover. Washington, D.C.: Police Executive Research Forum.

Mastrofski, S., and R. Wadman. (1991). Personnel and Agency Performance Measurement. In *Local Government Police Management*, edited by W. Geller. Washington, D.C.: International City Managers Association.

McGregor, D. (1957). An Uneasy Look at Performance Appraisal. *Harvard Business Review* (May–June).

Meyer, C. (1993). How the Right Measures Help Teams Excel. *Harvard Business Review* (May–June).

Oberg, W. (1972). Make Performance Appraisal Relevant. *Harvard Business Review* (January–February).

Oettmeier, T. (1993). Counterpoint: The FTO Rating-Scale Debate. In *The Trainer*, edited by Frank Webb. Fall–Winter.

Oettmeier, T. (1992). Matching Structure to Objectives. In *Police Management: Issues and Perspectives*, edited by Larry T. Hoover. Washington, D.C.: Police Executive Research Forum.

Oettmeier, T., and M. Wycoff. (1994). Police Performance in the Nineties: Practitioner Perspectives. *American Journal of Police* 13 (2).

Schay, B. (1993). In Search of the Holy Grail: Lessons In Performance Management. *Public Personnel Management* 22 (4).

Scholtes, P. (1987). A New View of Performance Evaluation. Paper presented to the William G. Hunter Conference on Quality, Madison, Wisconsin.

Spelman, W., and J. Eck. (1987). Newport News Tests Problem-Oriented Policing. *NIJ Reports*, January–February, 2–8.

St. Petersburg Police Department. (1994). St. Petersburg Police Department Performance Evaluation Workshop: Summary of Workgroup Comments. October, St. Petersburg, Florida.

Stephens, D. (1996). Community Problem-Oriented Policing: Measuring Impacts. In *Quantifying Quality in Policing*, edited by L. Hoover. Washington, D.C.: Police Executive Research Forum.

Trojanowicz, R., and B. Bucqueroux. (1992). *Toward the Development of Meaningful and Effective Performance Evaluations*. East Lansing: National Center for Community Policing, Michigan State University.

Wadman, R., and R. Olson. (1990). *Community Wellness: A New Theory of Policing*. Washington, D.C.: Police Executive Research Forum.

Weisburd, D.; J. McElroy; and P. Hardyman. (1989). Maintaining Control in Community-Oriented Policing. In *Police and Policing: Contemporary Issues*, edited by D. Kenney. New York: Praeger.

Whitaker, G.; S. Mastrofski; E. Ostrom; R. Parks; and S. Percy. (1982). *Basic Issues in Police Performance*. Washington, D.C.: U.S. Department of Justice.

Wycoff, M. (1982a). Improving Police Performance Measurement: One More Voice. *The Urban Interest*, Spring, 8–16.

Wycoff, M. (1982b). *The Role of Municipal Police: Research As Prelude to Changing It*. Washington, D.C.: Police Foundation.

Wycoff, M. (1994). *Community Policing Strategies*. Washington, D.C.: Police Foundation.

Wycoff, M., and T. Oettmeier. (1993a). *Evaluating Patrol Officer Performance under Community Policing: The Houston Experience Research in Brief*. Washington, D.C.: Police Foundation.

Wycoff, M., and T. Oettmeier. (1993b). *Evaluating Patrol Officer Performance under Community Policing: The Houston Experience Technical Report*. Washington, D.C.: Police Foundation.

5 _____

Police Work Hours, Fatigue, and Officer Performance

Bryan Vila and Erik Y. Taiji

This chapter examines a number of possible connections between administratively controllable causes of fatigue and problems associated with police officer performance, health, and safety. Each year police accidents, injuries, and misconduct extract a heavy human and economic cost. Empirical research and practical experience with other occupational groups indicate that fatigue associated with the pattern and length of work hours may be expected to contribute to these problems. Fatigue arising from sleep loss, circadian disruption, and other factors worsens mood and may be expected to increase the probability that officers will be involved in official misconduct and to worsen relations between them and their families and the community. Fatigue may also be expected to increase the probability that police officers will be involved in accidents, because it decreases alertness and impairs performance.

   Despite the possibility of deleterious effects such as these, there are no work-hour standards for police and almost no data are available regarding the widely divergent work-hour practices of U.S. policing agencies. In preparation for a test of hypothesized links between fatigue and police performance, we collected information regarding extreme police work-hour practices from news-media accounts in California, Massachusetts, and Florida. We also examined annual time-keeping records from a medium-sized California police department.

FATIGUE AND POLICE PERFORMANCE

The effects of fatigue on human behavior, performance, and physiology are well understood and widely known. Excess fatigue arising from sleep loss, circadian disruption, and other factors tend to decrease alertness, impair performance, and worsen mood. It therefore may be expected to influence the performance, health, and safety of patrol officers and adversely affect police–community relations. Recently, in reviewing the topic, Vila (1996) argued that much of the fatigue experienced by patrol officers could be controlled administratively, just as we control the working hours of many other occupational groups. He also contended that the social and economic construction of police work in the United States tended to obscure links between fatigue and officer performance and discourages efforts to regulate police work hours.

Fatigue is widespread in police work. Psychologists, health care professionals, researchers, and practitioners all acknowledge fatigue as a fundamental source of stress in the police environment (e.g., Brown and Campbell 1994; Burke 1994; Kroes 1985, 32–36; Tang and Hammontree 1992; Violanti and Aron 1993; Violanti, Vena, and Marshal 1986; Yarmey 1990). Perceiving fatigue as part of the police environment, however, has made it easy to ignore the possibility that it could be controlled, and it has obscured possible links between fatigue and a number of intractable police problems. We control the work hours of truck drivers, train engineers, pilots, power-plant operators, and medical interns. Why have we tended to ignore the obvious dangers associated with tired cops?

One reason for ignoring fatigue may be that we often have unrealistic physical and emotional expectations of police officers, especially patrol officers. Though work-hours-related fatigue undoubtedly affects officers in investigatory and other assignments, in this chapter we focus primarily on patrol officers because there are many more of them in most agencies and because patrol is the backbone of policing. Patrol officers often have to help people resolve complicated, emotionally charged, and threatening situations. They also must stay alert during long periods of crushing boredom and are often required to perform their duties while exhausted from job-related activities that result in chronic lack of sleep and irregular sleep patterns (e.g., overtime assignments, sleep disruption associated with off-duty court appearances, and shift changes). Many of these activities could be modified by administrative and regulatory action. Yet not only do we generally fail to regulate the hours police officers work, we collect very little data on important administratively controllable sources of fatigue, such as overtime. When we do, overtime usually is treated as an economic issue rather than a performance, health, or safety concern.

SOURCES AND PERVASIVENESS OF FATIGUE

Fatigue and its antecedents, such as overwork, irregular and disrupted sleep patterns, and other well-known stressors, are often perceived as "normal" aspects of the police environment. Though there has been almost no attempt to measure fatigue among police officers directly, perceptions about the general pervasiveness of fatigue are supported by a substantial body of evidence from research findings and official statistics as well as anecdotal sources. Results from a preliminary telephone survey conducted to obtain more detailed information about overtime practices (Vila 1996) and recent reports by investigative journalists (Armstrong 1996; Grad and Schoch 1995; Schoettler 1996a) also confirm this conception of police work.

Common Sources of Fatigue

Patrol work is, at times, both physically and emotionally challenging. At other times, it is excruciatingly boring. Both boredom and the physically and emotionally challenging nature of patrol work contribute to the fatigue officers experience. The effects of these kinds of occupational stressors can be thought of as providing a baseline level of fatigue for patrol officers. By baseline level, we refer to the amount of fatigue that truly is an unavoidable part of police work.

Beyond this baseline, a number of other factors that are more or less amenable to change also contribute to officer fatigue. It is common for patrol officers to work double shifts in order to fill in for other officers who call in sick or to meet other demands for service such as those that community-oriented policing programs sometimes require. Research currently being conducted by Bayley and Worden of SUNY Albany will provide the first solid data on the amount of overtime associated with community-oriented policing programs that receive federal support. Though probably relatively rare, even triple shifts are sometimes worked (Bayley 1994, 68). Overtime work adds to fatigue, both by increasing the amount of work performed beyond normal levels and by disrupting sleep patterns. Other job-related sources of fatigue include off-duty court appearances (Boorstin 1986; Duggan 1993; Harriston 1993; Kroes 1985), shift changes (O'Neill and Cushing 1991; Pierce and Dunham 1992; Scott 1990), and attending college.

It is important to remember that combinations of stressors in the police patrol environment produce cumulative and synergistic effects. For example, overwork, loss of sleep, irregular sleep patterns, boredom, or high anxiety can each increase fatigue and the rate at which it accumulates. Furthermore, the net effect of interactions between these kinds of stressors can be more than additive. Chronic exposure tends to magnify their effects even more, in part because people tend to develop maladaptations. Another problem associated with chronic exposure to these kinds of problems is that their aftereffects tend to spill over into leisure time, perhaps for several weeks. This can make recuperation all but impossible (Gardell 1987, 65–66). The result is a vicious cycle in which fatigue diminishes an individual's ability to cope with many other job stressors in a healthy manner; they, in turn, increase fatigue (Hockey 1986; Mitler et al. 1988; Monk 1990). Over time, this process can be expected to lead to a downward spiral in which the erosion of an officer's ability to function effectively accelerates to crisis proportions.

Research Findings and Official Statistics

Three major sources of nationwide comparative data on police salaries and expenditures can be used to develop information about police work hours, but all of them are too highly aggregated to assess work-hour patterns. One is an annual survey about police personnel and expenditures conducted by the International City Manager's Association (ICMA annual). The other two are conducted by the U.S. Bureau of Justice Statistics under the Law Enforcement Management and Administrative Statistics (LEMAS) program (Reaves 1992a, 1992b; Reaves and Smith 1995) and the Survey of Criminal Justice Expenditure and Employment series (U.S. Department of Justice, Bureau of Justice Statistics 1991a, 1991b). ICMA reports on standard duty hours per week, but not the number of hours actually worked. LEMAS collects data on overtime expenditures, but they are reported as the total overtime expenditure per agency and per full-time officer within each agency. Recently, however, the Bureau of Justice Statistics has agreed to include questions regarding overtime and hours-worked policies in the next Law Enforcement Management and Administrative Statistics survey.

Unfortunately, there is no way to accurately estimate from these data how many hours of overtime are worked on average per officer per year. Neither is it possible to estimate the range of overtime worked by different officers or by officers in different assignments. Perhaps more important, there is also no way to estimate hours worked per day, week, or month. Data such as these are particularly important for identifying the kinds of practices likely to result in extreme short-term fatigue and chronic fatigue. The best conclusion about the pervasiveness of fatigue that can be made from official data is that officers in most law-enforcement agencies work overtime, and overtime expenditures tend to constitute a substantial proportion of overall operating expenditures. There is no information about how that overtime is distributed among officers or the extent to which overtime contributes to excess fatigue.

Overtime is a central topic in the discussion that follows for three reasons:

1. Preliminary research indicates that patrol officers in many police departments often work substantial amounts of overtime.
2. Research by physicians, psychologists, physiologists, and human-factors engineers demonstrates a strong link between substantial amounts of overtime work, especially erratic overtime, and fatigue associated with both overwork and sleep disruption.
3. Little attention has been given to deleterious links between overtime and police fatigue.

Pervasiveness of Fatigue

A recent preliminary survey of ten of the largest U.S. police agencies indicates that formal policies limiting hours worked are rare, patrol officers in high-crime urban precincts work a substantial amount of overtime, and some officers, some of the time, work large amounts of overtime (Vila 1996). Table 5.1 summarizes the results of that survey.

The potential detrimental effects of overtime-induced fatigue may be especially problematic for departments that are attempting to institute community-oriented policing programs because managers so often rely on overtime to meet the additional demands that these programs place on personnel resources (Worden 1995).

The view that officers in some agencies work extreme hours is supported by several recent reports by investigative journalists. For example, in a report on the highest-paid city employees in Orange County, California, Grad and Schoch (1995) found that because of overtime many of the highest-paid city employees were police officers. In one Orange County city, twenty-two of the twenty-five highest-paid employees were police or fire employees, and in several cities police officers made tens of thousands of dollars each year in overtime alone. Reports of high overtime among police officers motivated other cities in the county, such as Costa Mesa, to curtail police overtime because of fears of officer burnout or on-the-job injuries.

Armstrong's (1996) review of time-keeping records for Massachusetts state troopers assigned to the Massachusetts Turnpike provides a more dramatic and detailed example. He found that during a one-year period (in 1995) sixteen officers averaged over eighty total work hours per week (including regular and overtime hours). This was enough to double or triple their base pay. Two officers worked an av-

Table 5.1
Summary of Supervising Patrol Sergeants' Estimates of Overtime Worked by Patrol Officers in High-Crime-Rate Precincts in Ten of the Twelve Largest U.S. Police Departments

Department or Shift	*n* Sgts. Reporting	Average/ Month/ Officer	Highest in a Month	Highest in a Week	Court Related (Percentage)
A	2	25	80	30	50
B	3	23	74	25	77
C	1	20	120	35	unk
D	2	21	60	22	11
E	2	18	47	13	56
F	2	28	64	22	78
G	3	18	70	33	75
H	2	28	70	30	66
I	1	23	50	15	25
J	2	23	60	26	12
Means[a]	2	22.8	68.3	25.2	54.2
Ranges[b]	1-3	15-40	40-120	13-40	10-90
Graveyard Shifts	5	20	59	21	44
Day Shifts	7	22	66	28	60
Evening Shifts	8	25	76	26	57

Note: Estimates are averaged among sergeants reporting in each department. Shift estimates are averaged among departments reporting.

[a]Calculated from original data, rather than averaged from within-department data.

[b]Reported by all watch sergeants, not as averaged within departments.

erage of more than 100 hours per week during 1995, tripling their base salaries. Another officer worked 130 hours in a single week, averaging less than six hours off each day. Much of the overtime in these extreme cases resulted from a Massachusetts law requiring that a uniformed police officer be present at all times to direct traffic when roadways are blocked for construction or repair. In order to avoid conflicts with more pressing demands for police services, these duties normally are filled by off-duty officers whose overtime is paid for from highway construction funds.[1] At present, we are unsure about how widespread this practice is. At least one other state, Florida, has similar requirements, but there, off-duty officers are hired by road contractors rather than by other government agencies.

Moonlighting

Moonlighting (secondary employment) is another potentially important—and administratively controllable—source of fatigue. Moonlighting is quite common in many departments and has received substantial attention from researchers and managers (Arcuri, Gunn, and Lester 1987; Bayley 1994, 67; Reiss 1988). All but 4 percent of U.S. local law-enforcement agencies with 100 or more officers have written policies pertaining to off-duty employment (Reaves and Smith 1995). Still, recent reports from Jacksonville, Florida, indicate that each year some police officers average as many as 100 moonlighting hours *per week*.

In a series of articles, the *Florida Times Union* (Police Limit Moonlighting 1996; Schoettler 1996a, 1996b) reported that the majority of Jacksonville's 1,360 police officers supplement their annual incomes with part-time jobs. Though most of the officers who moonlight work less than ten off-duty hours per week, some were found to work over sixty off-duty hours per week. One lieutenant averaged sixty-two off-duty hours per week, for a total average workweek of 102 hours in off-duty and on-duty assignments. He earned $117,666 during 1995. He and other officers who worked similar amounts were able to work such hours because Jacksonville has no policies against moonlighting hours, something which newly elected Sheriff Glover reportedly planned to change. Glover argues that excessive off-duty hours might increase fatigue and decrease officer performance, as supported by the poor driving records and accidents of Jacksonville's officers. Sheriff Glover has assigned a committee to study the possible effects of fatigue on officer performance and, in spite of substantial resistance from the officers' collective bargaining unit, plans to restrict off-duty hours to twenty to forty hours per week.

Shift Work

Shift work, which has been a central aspect of modern policing since Sir Robert Peel founded the London Metropolitan Police in 1829 (New Police Instructions 1829), can also be an important administratively controllable source of fatigue. There is a solid body of research on problems associated with shift work and how it may be dealt with (e.g., Lewis 1985a, 1985b; Monk 1990; Pierce and Dunham 1992). Though a number of important empirical issues regarding compressed work schedules remain unresolved, the importance of properly managing shift-work problems in police organizations has been recognized by managers and employee organizations (O'Neill and Cushing 1991).

Along with two other researchers, we are currently evaluating a number of novel "compressed-shift" scheduling arrangements that proponents claim will reduce fatigue, overtime, or both (detractors claim they will do just the opposite). For example, one compressed-shift arrangement used by a medium-sized California police department alternates twelve hours on and off for three consecutive days followed by three days off, then alternates twelve-hour shifts for another four days, after which officers receive four days off. Under this scheduling scheme, officers and supervisors patrolling this relatively high-crime-rate city were assigned to one of six platoons that worked a fixed schedule for a year: either 0600–1800, 1400–0200, or 1800–0600. Opportunities to change platoons were limited to one per year. Under many other types of scheduling arrangements, officers are supervised by different sergeants and lieutenants every few days. By contrast, this form of compressed work schedule put the same officers and supervisors together each workday for a year at a time, an arrangement intended to improve the quality and consistency of supervision.

This rather unusual schedule was worked out by managers and the officers' collective bargaining unit as a means of improving supervision, diminishing the time officers spent commuting (a significant factor in many urban areas), and providing officers with larger blocks of time to spend in family and recreational pursuits. It also had the effect of seriously limiting the amount of overtime officers worked. Our analysis of summary work-hour data for all 144 nonsupervisory patrol officers on the schedule revealed that overtime was very limited—even the officer with over four times the mean overtime averaged less than fourteen hours per week. Department managers attribute this to improved supervision, lowered likelihood of late reports and arrests, and less need for off-duty court appearances.

Table 5.2 compares the sixteen officers from this department who worked the most overtime during 1995 with the high officers from both Massachusetts and Florida reported by Armstrong (1996) and by Schoettler (1996a). Though it obviously is not appropriate to make assumptions about the desirability of the type of compressed shift utilized by the California department, this approach does indicate that the amount of overtime worked by officers is amenable to administrative control.

Work Hours and Fatigue

Based on the limited information available, it seems reasonable to assert that police officers often work long hours or tend to have erratic work hours. But how much do overtime and other administratively controllable activities contribute to excess police fatigue? One way to address this question is to compare police hours-worked practices with usual and accepted practice in other occupations where, as in police

Table 5.2
Comparing Extreme Overtime and Moonlighting Reported by Media with Study Department Using a Compressed Work Schedule, 1995

Massachusetts Officer's Name	Average Overtime Hrs/Week	Florida Officer's Name	Average Moonlight Hrs/Week	California Officer Number*	Average Overtime Hrs/Week
Mahoney	60.6	Looney	62	74	13.4
Lynch	60.2	Johnson	60	20	11.8
Brock	54.7	Tyson	47	83	10.3
Berghaus	54.6	Moore	35	14	9.8
Decouto	54.5	Tyrell	30	142	9.1
Kenney	48.6	Vanaman	25	39	8.1
Bachelder	46.6	Hayes	24	121	7.8
Shea	45.6	Rolack	22	78	7.2
Mooza	45.1	Matthews	22	15	7.1
Lewis	44.1	Peaden	22	79	7.0
Macphee	43.4			66	6.6
Yee	42.9			100	6.5
Mullen	42.6			40	6.5
Adams	42.3			140	5.9
Douthwright	41.8			114	5.7
McCarthy	41.2			61	5.2
Mean	*48.05*	*Mean*	*34.9*	*Mean*	*8*

Source: Massachusetts data from D. Armstrong (1996), "Troopers' Extra Hours Spur Worry: Overtime, Details on Pike Pile Up Despite Regulations." *Boston Globe*, 3 September, A9; Florida data from J. Schoettler (1996a). "Sun Setting on Cop Moonlighting?" *Florida Times Union* 31 March, A1.

*Anonymous tracking numbers are used in the study to protect officer privacy.

work, an employee's performance has important public safety implications. If the standards set for the occupations listed in Table 5.3 are reasonable approximations of limits beyond which work can be expected to cause excess fatigue, it would appear that the levels of overtime worked by police officers may often be sufficient to cause excess fatigue.

Though no standards for maximum hours of work have been set for law-enforcement officers, it may be argued that officers, especially those working patrol assignments, generally would be more vulnerable to accidents, injuries, and making poor decisions due to fatigue than people working in the occupations covered by Table 5.3. While the risk of being injured or causing injury to others is a constant in all of these occupations, police patrol officers' jobs combine many of the worst aspects of them all. From the standpoint of performance, safety, and accident prevention, officers work in highly unstructured and

Table 5.3
Recommendations and Standards Limiting Hours of Work in Several Occupations Where Employee Performance Has Important Public Safety Implications

Period	Total Hours/Total Overtime Hours[a]			
	Nuclear Power Plant Operators[b]	Commercial Aviation	Air Force	Interstate Trucking
1 day	12/4	8/0	12/4	10/2
2 days	24/8			
7 days	60/20	30/0		60/20
28 days[c]	192/32	100/0	125/0	
1 quarter		300/0	330/0	
1 year	2,260/180	1,000/0		

Source: Adapted from P. Lewis (1985a). *Recommendations for NRC Policy on Shift Scheduling and Overtime at Nuclear Power Plants* (NUREG/CR-4248, PNL-5435). Washington, D.C.: U.S. Nuclear Regulatory Commission.

[a]Overtime is calculated as consecutive hours worked in excess of eight per day, forty per week, etc.

[b]This is the standard recommended by the Nuclear Regulatory Commission, the current legal standard is more limited in scope and more permissive at the one- and seven-day period and does not cover longer time periods. "A limit of 16 h is sometimes allowed in the event of a problem during operation, but no individual should be approved to work more than one 16-h day in a 7-day period or more than two 16-h days in a 28-day period" (Baker et al. 1994, 250).

[c]Commercial aviation and the U.S. Air Force use thirty days as the base for this period.

unpredictable environments with little direct supervision. They face the constant possibility of both accidental and malicious injury, and they have little control over their schedules because, for example, of the vagaries of court appearances. At a minimum, then, it would appear that officers working the kinds of exceptional hours reported for Florida and Massachusetts are differentially exposed to fatigue-related hazards than peers in departments that control work hours more strictly.

Based on the foregoing discussion, three propositions appear likely to be true and thus should be tested:

1. Police patrol officers sometimes work overtime and moonlight in excess of standards for other occupations where employee performance has important public safety implications and for which empirically based standards are enforced in order to avoid accidents and injuries caused by the detrimental effects of fatigue on worker performance.

2. On average, police are at least as vulnerable to fatigue as a result of over-work and chronic sleep disruption as members of other occupational groups whose hours of work are regulated as a matter of public safety, because the physiological, psychological, and cognitive demands of po-lice work on officers in the patrol environment often equal or exceed the occupational demands placed on those groups.

3. The potential social, economic, and human costs of fatigue-related impair-ment to police performance are equal to or greater than those for occupa-tional groups whose hours of work are regulated as a matter of public safety.

RESEARCH ISSUES AND QUESTIONS

We need to better understand both the extent of fatigue and its ef-fects on police officers, particularly those in patrol assignments. If there are relationships between fatigue and problems such as diminished performance, accidents, and illness, we need to develop policy guide-lines that enable law-enforcement managers and policy makers to minimize these threats to the health and safety of officers and the com-munities they serve. We think that this can be accomplished by an-swering the following research questions.

Prevalence of Fatigue

- What, if any, relationship exists between fatigue and the number, type, and pattern of hours worked per day, week, month, and year by patrol officers?
- What do patrol officers report about the subjective effects of fatigue and their strategies for managing it?
- What are officers' attitudes toward fatigue in themselves and their peers?
- What do the families of police officers report about the prevalence of seri-ous fatigue among officers and its effects on officers and their families?

Effects of Fatigue

- Is there a significant correlation between administratively controllable sources of fatigue and diminished performance measured by such things as frequency of citizen complaints, formal disciplinary action, on-duty acci-dents, or injuries?
- What are the work-hour characteristics of the career histories of officers who receive early medical retirements for cardiac or stress-related condi-tions, are chronic disciplinary problems, or are terminated for cause?
- Are there links between fatigue and officer fatalities on or off the job?
- How does excess fatigue affect the families of police officers in terms of problems such as marital difficulties and family violence that have been targeted by Law Enforcement Family Support legislation under §210201 of the 1994 Crime Act?

- Are there age, gender, attitude, or experience-based differences in the way patrol officers are affected by and respond to fatigue and fatigue inducers?
- What are the human and fiscal costs of administratively controllable fatigue and how do the costs and benefits of overtime assignments balance against overtime-related fatigue?

Measuring Fatigue

- How feasible is the use of objective, noninvasive eye reaction (Corfitsen 1993, 1994) and computer-based tests of readiness for duty?

Controlling Fatigue

- Is there a link between fatigue and unscheduled absenteeism that, in turn, can necessitate having others work overtime?
- What role do internal policies play in differences in overtime requirements between similar departments? That is, how much control do different policies provide managers regarding demand for overtime?
- How might implementation of compressed work schedules (Pierce and Dunham 1992) influence officer fatigue in different kinds of policing environments?
- To what extent could technological changes that improve officer efficiency (e.g., laptop computers to speed report writing, streamlined internal procedures, providing pagers to limit court-related overtime) lower fatigue by decreasing demand for overtime?

Ongoing Research

We currently are involved in a large research project being conducted by the Police Executive Research Forum (PERF) and funded by the National Institute of Justice (NIJ) that is attempting to assess the relationships between management and administrative policies and procedures and the prevalence and possible consequences of excess work-hour-related fatigue among patrol officers. In order to maximize convergent validity, three complementary research strategies are being applied at each of the four study sites (medium-sized police agencies in different geographical regions of the United States).

Analysis of Departmental Data. Departmental records on police work hours, accidents, injuries, illnesses, and misconduct as well as commendations and citizen complaints are being analyzed in order to determine if there are statistically significant relationships between these phenomena and the quantity and pattern of hours worked by patrol officers and the types of activities in which they are involved.

Assessments of Subjective Effects of Fatigue. Self-report surveys are being administered to police patrol officers in order to gather information on their subjective experience of fatigue and impressions about its effects on their professional performance, physical and emotional well-being, and personal lives. These surveys are complemented by focus groups in which researchers discuss fatigue, work hours, and overtime-related issues with the families of police officers.

Objective Tests of Fatigue Levels. Noninvasive eye-reaction tests that have been validated with other occupational groups are being used to test the hypothesized connection between the length and pattern of work hours and fatigue. These tests are taken by patrol officers at each test site in an attempt to assess the relative level of fatigue they are experiencing. At the time the tests are administered, a subsample of officers is asked questions about such things as how tired they feel, their official and off-duty activities in recent days, and sleep patterns in recent months. The reliability of these subjective accounts is assessed by comparing accounts of work hours with departmental time sheets. This makes it possible to test the relationship between objective measures of fatigue and independent variables associated with length and pattern of work hours as well as other factors that are less amenable to administrative control.

In each instance, the subject population is full-time, nonsupervisory, police officers assigned to patrol and/or community-policing activities. In keeping with the discussion, we chose this population because they are the largest subgroup within each department, have the most contact with members of the community, and are most likely to have to deal unexpectedly with hazardous situations.

SUMMARY AND POLICY IMPLICATIONS

Though we regulate the working hours of truck drivers, pilots, power-plant operators, and medical interns, the need to control police fatigue has been ignored. Research on people in other occupational groups indicates that fatigue tends to decrease alertness, impair performance, and worsen mood, and that sleep loss and circadian disruption are the two principal physiological sources of fatigue. Official statistics, anecdotal evidence, and our research to date indicate that excess fatigue may be very prevalent in some—perhaps many—police departments.

This problem seems especially important given the current emphasis on community-oriented policing, which places additional demands on personnel resources, demands that are often met by increasing the amount of overtime officers work. Since it seems likely that excess fatigue can have adverse effects on police–community relations and public safety, it is important to identify how many hours police officers are working, and in what patterns. It is also important to determine how work patterns may contribute to fatigue, and how that fatigue affects officers' performance and their family lives.

NOTES

An earlier version of this paper was presented at the 1996 meeting of the American Society of Criminology in Chicago, Illinois on November 20–23, 1996.

1. After this issue was raised by Armstrong, the State Police Association of Massachusetts (the trooper collective bargaining unit) reportedly began revamping the outdated 1974 work restriction that allows troopers to work such extraordinary hours. This restriction states that troopers cannot schedule themselves for more than sixteen consecutive work hours. However, if someone else (e.g., a supervisor) schedules a trooper for overtime, or if a scheduled detail goes beyond regular work hours, then the trooper is not in violation of the sixteen-hour limit. The State Police Association hopes to limit the total number of hours a trooper can work per month and penalize those who exceed this limit (Armstrong 1996).

BIBLIOGRAPHY

Arcuri, A.; M. Gunn; and D. Lester. (1987). Moonlighting by Police Officers: A Way of Life. *Psychological Reports* 60: 210.

Armstrong, D. (1996). Troopers' Extra Hours Spur Worry: Overtime, Details on Pike Pile Up Despite Regulations. *Boston Globe*, 3 September, A1, A9.

Baker, K.; J. Olson; and D. Morisseau. (1994). Work Practices, Fatigue, and Nuclear Power Plant Safety Performance. *Human Factors* 36: 244–257.

Bayley, D. (1994). *Police for the Future*. New York: Oxford.

Boorstin, R. (1986). Port Agency Police Overtime Up 24%. *New York Times*, 5 November, 5:B3L.

Brown, J., and E. Campbell. (1994). *Stress and Policing: Sources and Strategies*. Chichester, England: Wiley & Sons.

Burke R. (1994). Stressful Events, Work–Family Conflict, Coping, Psychological Burnout, and Well-Being among Police Officers. *Psychological Reports* 75: 787–800.

Corfitsen, M. (1994). Tiredness and Visual Reaction Time among Young Male Nighttime Drivers: A Roadside Survey. *Accident Analysis and Prevention* 26: 617–624.

Corfitsen, M. (1993). Tiredness and Visual Reaction Time among Nighttime Cab Drivers: A Roadside Survey. *Accident Analysis and Prevention* 25: 667–673.

Duggan, P. (1993). D.C. Losing in Overtime: Officers Wait to Testify—at $30 an Hour. *Washington Post*, 5 April, A1.

Gardell, B. (1987). Efficiency and Health Hazards in Mechanized Work. In *Work Stress: Health Care Systems in the Workplace*, edited by J. Quick, R. Bhagat, and J. Dalton. New York: Praeger.

Grad, S., and D. Schoch. (1995). Cities' Top 25 Lists Show Employees Generously Paid. *Los Angeles Times*, 9 September, B1.

Harriston, K. (1993). Kelly Calls for Clampdown on Police: Those Who Abuse Overtime Should Expect Harsher Penalty, She Says. *Washington Post*, 2 March, B3.

Hockey, G. (1986). Changes in Operator Efficiency as a Function of Environmental Stress, Fatigue, and Circadian Rhythms. In *Handbook of Percep-*

tion and Human Performance. Vol. 2, *Cognitive Process and Performance*, edited by K. Boff, L. Kaufman, and J. Thomas. New York: John Wiley.

International City Managers Association (ICMA). (annual). *The Municipal Year Book*. Washington, D.C.: ICMA.

Kroes, W. (1985). *Society's Victims—The Police: An Analysis of Job Stress in Policing*. 2d ed. Springfield, Ill.: Thomas.

Lewis, P. (1985a). *Recommendations for NRC Policy on Shift Scheduling and Overtime at Nuclear Power Plants* (NUREG/CR-4248, PNL-5435). Washington, D.C.: U.S. Nuclear Regulatory Commission.

Lewis, P. (1985b). *Technical Evaluation Report: Shift Scheduling and Overtime—A Critical Review of the Literature*. Richland, Wash.: Pacific Northwest Laboratory.

Mitler, M.; M. Carskadon; C. Czeisler; and W. Dement. (1988). Catastrophes, Sleep and Public Policy: Consensus Report. *Sleep* 11: 100–109.

Monk, T. (1990). Shiftworker Performance. *Occupational Medicine: State of the Art Reviews* 5: 183–198.

New Police Instructions. (1829). *London Times*, 25 September, 3.

O'Neill, J., and M. Cushing. (1991). *The Impact of Shift Work on Police Officers*. Washington, D.C.: Police Executive Research Forum.

Pierce, J., and R. Dunham. (1992). The 12-Hour Work-Day: A 48-Hour, Eight-Day Week. *Academy of Management Journal* 35: 1086–1098.

Police Limit Moonlighting. (1996). *Florida Times Union*, 12 April, A10.

Reaves, B. (1992a). *Law Enforcement Management and Administrative Statistics, 1990: Data for Individual State and Local Agencies with 100 or More Officers* (NCJ-134436). Washington, D.C.: U.S. Government Printing Office.

Reaves, B. (1992b). *State and Local Police Departments, 1990* (NCJ-133284). Washington, D.C.: U.S. Government Printing Office.

Reaves, B., and P. Smith. (1995). *Law Enforcement Management and Administrative Statistics, 1993: Data for Individual State and Local Agencies with 100 or More Officers* (NCJ-148825). Washington, D.C.: U.S. Government Printing Office.

Reiss, A. (1988). *Private Employment of Public Police* (NCJ-105192). Washington, D.C.: U.S. Government Printing Office.

Schoettler, J. (1996a). Sun Setting on Cop Moonlighting? *Florida Times Union*, 31 March, A1.

Schoettler, J. (1996b). Committee to Study Police Moonlighting. *Florida Times Union*, 10 April, A1.

Scott, A., ed. (1990). *Occupational Medicine: Shiftwork*. Vol. 5:2. Philadelphia: Hanley and Belfus.

Tang, T. L-P., and M. Hammontree. (1992). The Effects of Hardiness, Police Stress, and Life Stress on Police Officers' Illness and Absenteeism. *Public Personnel Management* 21: 493–510.

U.S. Department of Justice, Bureau of Justice Statistics. (1991a). *Justice Expenditure and Employment Extracts: 1984, 1985, and 1986—Data from the Annual General Finance and Employment Surveys* (NCJ-124139). Washington, D.C.: U.S. Government Printing Office.

U.S. Department of Justice, Bureau of Justice Statistics. (1991b). *Justice Expenditure and Employment in the U.S., 1988* (NCJ-125619). Washington, D.C.: U.S. Government Printing Office.

Vila, B. (1996). Tired Cops: Probable Connections between Fatigue and the Performance, Health, and Safety of Patrol Officers. *American Journal of Police* 15: 51–92.

Violanti, J., and F. Aron. (1993). Sources of Police Stressors, Job Attitudes, and Psychological Distress. *Psychological Reports* 72: 899–904.

Violanti, J.; J. Vena; and J. Marshal. (1986). Disease Risk and Mortality among Police Officers: New Evidence and Contributing Factors. *Journal of Police Science and Administration* 14: 17–23.

Worden, R. (1995). Telephone conversation with author, 30 November.

Yarmey, A. (1990). *Understanding Police and Police Work: Psychosocial Issues.* New York: New York University Press.

6 —————————————————————————

Police Suicide

Steven Stack and Thomas Kelley

The research on suicide among police officers is characterized by inconsistency and a number of shortcomings. First, almost all of the previous work is based on local data and, therefore, often few suicides (e.g., Danto 1978; Dash and Reiser 1978; Heiman 1975a). Chance fluctuations given small samples, as well as local and regional variations in suicide can affect the rates of police suicide and thus contribute to the inconsistent results (Bedeian 1982, 214). Josephson and Reiser (1990, 238) call for more comprehensive research across geographic lines. They note that without more global research, it is difficult to draw reliable conclusions about police suicide. Second, the only American national estimates of police suicide rates are for the year 1950, forty-four years ago (Labovitz and Hagedorn 1971). These estimates need to be replicated for police suicide in today's world. Third, in their estimates of the police suicide rate per se, previous research has often failed to use appropriate comparison groups (e.g., age relevant and gender matched). Hence, these studies often report either overinflated or underinflated estimates of police suicide (e.g., Danto 1978; Dash and Reiser 1978; James 1993). Finally, none of the previous studies employs multivariate analytic techniques for predicting the probability of police deaths from suicide. The covariates of police officer status, such as race or gender, tend not to be controlled for in estimating the risk of police suicide. This can result in both underestimates and overestimates of the impact of the police profession on suicide. Furthermore, any relationship between police officer status and risk of suicide may be spurious without statistical controls for covariates of police officer status.

This chapter extends the previous work by correcting for several of these shortcomings. Following the call by Josephson and Reiser (1990) for more global analyses, it analyzes data on police suicide from sixteen reporting states, a sample representing all regions of the nation. Second, these data are relatively recent and will provide an updated estimate of the national incidence of police suicide. Third, police suicide is appropriately compared to the suicide rate of adult males of working age. Fourth, through a multivariate logistic regression analysis this chapter explores the odds of death from suicide versus natural causes for police officers relative to the rest of the general population with alternative predictors of suicide controlled.

THEORIES AND RESEARCH ON POLICE SUICIDE

Work on police suicide has been based on an informal consensus that suicide among police officers is substantially greater than that for other occupations (Neiderhoffer 1967; Bedeian 1982, 213; Loo 1986). It is widely held that policing is one of the most stressful occupations in the labor force (Coleman 1986, 197–203). In fact, policing has been rated among the top ten stress-producing jobs by both the National Institute on Workers Compensation (Miller 1988, 43) and the American Institute of Stress (Schmalleger 1991, 201). Perceived high levels of divorce, alcoholism, and suicide are said to be connected to this stress. The media have also often presumed that the police have a high incidence of suicide (Josephson and Reiser 1990).

Little systematic evidence is available, however, to evaluate these presumptions and assertions. While there is a widespread belief in the association of police stress and suicidal behavior, there is little systematic data available to support or refute it (Hill and Clawson 1988, 243). Furthermore, given this assumption of high police stress and suicide, most theoretical work has formulated explanations of a presumed high police suicide problem. Two major types of explanations have been advanced: sociological and psychodynamic and psychological theories.

Nelson and Smith (1970), for example, formulated a general sociological explanation of high suicide risk among police officers, emphasizing suicidogenic conditions faced by police, including working conditions, opportunity factors, and police–community relations. First, the prevalence of alternating shift work in policing can contribute to suicide by creating difficulties in marital relationships, maintaining and developing friendships, and participating in community organizations. Second, officers often experience considerable apathy from the public and occasional antipolice sentiments, which can create negative definitions of the police role and foster alienation from work. Third, working with the other units of the "fragmented" criminal justice system is often demoralizing, given perceived injustices, contradictions, and unfair decisions of the courts and corrections establishment. Fourth, the constant danger of death, both to oneself and others, can lead to generalized psychological consequences contributing to suicide potential. Fifth, since police officers carry firearms the opportunity or means for suicide is unusually high. Sixth, police officers are overwhelmingly male, and males in U.S. culture have a suicide rate that is three to four times that of females.

A seventh risk factor for police involves the indirect effect of alcohol abuse on suicide. Suicide has been linked to alcohol abuse (e.g., Lester 1992; Stack and Wasserman 1993). Occupational stress may cause individuals to abuse alcohol and levels of alcoholism vary by occupation (Wasserman 1992, 527). Research based on Chicago indicates that 60 percent of the police suicide victims were alcohol abusers (Wagner and Brzeczek 1983). Alcohol may be a key contributing factor to the incidence of police suicide (Lester 1978; Stratton 1984; Josephson and Reiser 1990).

A second approach to explaining high police suicide stresses psychological and psychodynamic factors. According to the psychological explanation, police suicide is the end result of officers' inability to effectively cope with stress due to individual factors such as dysfunctional personality traits, distorted cognitive functioning, conditioning from the past, and so on. Maslach and Jackson (1984, 134), for example, point out that stressful working conditions can lead to police burnout, defined as "a syndrome of emotional exhaustion, depersonalization, and reduced personal accomplishment that can occur among individuals who work with people in some capacity." Emotional exhaustion reflects the feelings of police who have become emotionally overextended and "drained" by contact with the public. Depersonalization may take the form of officers becoming calloused or insensitive in their response to other people, or what Zimbardo (1970) calls "dehumanization in self-defense." Reduced personal accomplishment is manifested in a decrease in officers' feelings of competence in working with people (Maslach and Jackson 1984). In their study of police officers and their families, Jackson and Maslach (1982) point out that instead of focusing on the situational stressors that caused their burnout, police officers often focus on their own failings and the presumed failings of their spouse and other intimate family members. In this way, burnout can spill over from police work to police marriages. According to a study done in 1988, when police derive their sense of meaning from both work and love and they burnout in both areas, their physical, emotional, and mental exhaustion can become so all-encompassing that they may become completely immobilized and helpless. This is the state that supposedly leads officers to thoughts of suicide.

Psychodyanmic theories focus on unconscious personality dynamics to explain high police suicide rates. Friedman (1968), for example, posits that high police suicide rates are essentially a displacement of the police officers' homicidal impulses. Heiman (1977) extends a similar view that police suicide reflects two of Herbert Hendlin's (1963) concepts of suicide: retroflexed murder and a possible narcissistic injury with death as a process that in an affective sense has already taken place. The homicidal impulses turned inward in the form of suicide in Friedman's (1968) conceptual scheme are essentially the same causal mechanisms as retroflexed suicide in Heiman's (1977) scheme.

For aggressive police officers who commit suicide, Bonifacio (1991) suggests that the id has overwhelmed the ego's capacity to maintain a balance between external reality, the id, and the superego. Suicide is thus a desperate attempt to restore the officer's self-concept as a moral and decent individual after having given in completely to the bad pleasures of the street. Another psychodynamic explanation by Hendlin (1963) views suicide as the officer's attempt to retaliate for feeling abandoned by loved ones, a motive supported by the conclusion of both Friedman's (1968) and Danto's (1978) research that marital troubles were the precipitating factor in the majority of suicide cases they studied.

The psychodynamic view is not mutually exclusive from the sociological perspective. For example, the homicidal impulses that are displaced in suicide may themselves emanate from the negativistic working conditions outlined in the sociological view. Poor police–community relations and the danger of death in everyday work can contribute to narcissistic injuries.

Research on the actual incidence of police suicide has often been based on local samples and incorporated widely different time frames. As a result, findings have been mixed. Some studies report high rates of police suicide, while others report average or low rates. A review of the literature through the mid-1970s concluded that police do, in fact, have a high suicide rate (Lester 1978). In contrast, a review of the 1980s literature proposed the need for more global research before any reliable conclusion can be drawn (Josephson and Reiser 1990).

Eleven studies have reported relatively high rates of police suicide. During the 1930s, high rates were reported for New York City, Chicago, and San Francisco (Heiman 1975b). High rates were also reported in New York City from 1960 to 1973 (Heiman 1975a) and Chicago from 1977 to 1979, where twenty police suicides translated to a rate of 43 per 100 thousand (Wagner and Brzeczek 1983). More recently, James (1993) reported a high incidence of police suicide for New York City during the period from 1983 to 1992, a rate "double" the "national average." However, James's data translate to a rate of approximately 21 per 100 thousand per year (63 suicides over ten years for a police force of approximately 30,000 officers). This rate is lower than the national suicide rate for adult males of working age. Danto's (1978) often cited work implies an excessive rate for Detroit officers, but fails to provide any reference to the size of the population at risk or to give the actual rate of police suicide. Data from three state studies indicate an elevated risk of suicide for police: the state of Wyoming from 1960 to 1968 (Nelson and Smith 1970; Davidson and Veno 1978), the state of Tennessee (Richard and Fell 1975; Fell, Richard, and Wallace 1980), where the rate was 69.1 per 100 thousand from 1972 to 1974, and Washington state, where forty police suicides from 1950 to 1971 resulted in police suicide being 13 percent higher than suicide of white males in general (Hill and Clawson 1988).

Three national studies suggest a high incidence of police suicide. Labovitz and Hagedorn (1971) report a 1950 U.S. rate of 47.6 per 100 thousand, the second highest rate of suicide for the thirty-eight occupations covered by their national database. Though widely cited, these data are quite old, and may not reflect the changes in suicidogenic conditions impacting police work some four decades later. Using the same national data for 1950, similar conclusions were drawn by Guralnick (1963), who expanded the analysis to 148 occupations. Data from Northern Ireland indicate a doubling of the rate of police suicide between the 1970s and 1980s, from 12 to 33 per 100 thousand (Curran, Finlay, and McGarry 1988).

Three studies using urban samples have reported average rates of police suicide. In the 1930s, average rates were reported for both St. Louis (Heiman 1975b) and Buffalo (Vena, Violanti, and Marshall 1986), and for Buffalo again from 1950 to 1979 (Violanti, Vena, and Marshall 1986). Based on eleven police suicides over a thirty-year period, the latter study found that the standardized mortality ratio for police in Buffalo was 94 percent that of the U.S. male population.

Four studies have found low rates of police suicide. Low rates have been reported for Denver in the 1930s (Heiman 1975b). A rate of 8.1 per 100 thousand was found for Los Angeles between 1970 and 1976 (Dash and Reiser 1978). This rate, lower than the county, state, and national suicide rate for adults (Dash and Reiser 1978), was attributed to the rigorous screening and training of police recruits. A twelve-year follow-up study for Los Angeles (1977 to 1988) uncovered nine police suicides, which yielded an annual rate of 12 per 100 thousand. Again, this rate was lower than the county, state, and national suicide rates for adults, but the gap was much smaller than that in the first study. This narrowing of the gap was attributed to a presumed growth in the problems of police alcohol abuse and marital discord (Josephson and Reiser 1990).

A recent study of police suicide in Canada found that the elite Royal Canadian Mounted Police had a suicide rate half that of their age-matched male peers (Loo 1986). The low rate of suicide is partially explained by Loo in economic terms. The RCMP have higher salaries and much better fringe benefits than regular police (Aussant 1984), a package which includes funds for psychological counseling, a key suicide-preventive mechanism.

In summary, a majority of available studies have found that police are presumably at higher than average risk of suicide. However, seven studies claim that police have an average or low rate of suicide. These findings are clearly inconsistent and thus inconclusive. Furthermore, most of this work should be interpreted with caution, since the numbers of police suicides are generally low, such as the four cases cited in the Dash and Reiser study in 1978. As noted by Josephson and Reiser (1990), large databases are clearly needed to obtain reliable estimates of the incidence of police suicide. While two analyses of a large U.S. database found a high rate of police suicide, neither analysis rigorously controlled for possible covariates of police status, such as marital discord. Also, these data are now over forty-four years old. The present study was designed to correct for these and other methodological shortcomings of the past work.

METHODOLOGY

Data on suicide were extracted from the 1985 National Mortality Detail File computer tapes (U.S. Public Health Service 1988). These data are the product of the first coordinated effort at collecting a national database on occupation and suicide in over thirty-five years. Data were collected for all sixteen states that reported occupational status of the deceased to Washington following the standard federal occupational classification system code (U.S. Bureau of the Census 1980). These states are Colorado, Georgia, Kansas, Kentucky, Maine, Missouri, Nebraska, Nevada, New Hampshire, Ohio, Oklahoma, Rhode Island, South Carolina, Tennessee, Utah, and Wisconsin.

Police in the public sector are defined as standard occupation code number 418: police and detectives, public service. Also included are persons in occupational category 423: sheriffs and other law enforcement officers. Excluded are persons in private policing or category 426: guards and police except in public service. Police suicides, then, include the suicides from 12 thousand municipal police agencies, over 3 thousand sheriffs' departments, forty-nine state police agencies (except Hawaii), and various federal law-enforcement agencies, such as the boarder patrol.

Suicides are defined in terms of the Ninth International Classification of Disease (ICD) codes (codes E950–E959). There were a total of thirty-three police officers (24 in category 418 and 9 in category 423) who died from suicide in the sixteen reporting states in 1985.

Some caution needs to be exercised in interpreting the results of the present study, since it is based on official suicide statistics. Some undercounting of suicide may exist due to variation in such factors as the quality in the work at certification of the causes of death by local coroners. However, the measurement errors involved are not large enough to preclude meaningful analysis. In fact, even with controls introduced for variation in the professionalization of certification of death, research has shown that the relationships between sociological variables and suicide remain largely the same (Pescosolido and Mendelsohn 1986).

In calculating suicide rates for police officers, national data on the population of police were used (U.S. Bureau of the Census 1984, 123). In 1985, there were 409,293 police officers and detectives and 58,795 sheriffs and other law-enforcement personnel, a total of 468,088 offic-ers. This amounts to 0.485 percent of the U.S. labor force. The sixteen states in the present study had a labor force of 26,522,000 in 1985 (U.S. Bureau of the Census 1987, 377). Therefore, it was estimated that there were 128,738 police in public agencies in the sixteen state reporting areas in 1985 (26,522,000 × 0.00485). This is the population figure that was used to calculate a rate of police suicide. The rates of suicide refer to the number of suicides by officers per 100 thousand officers.

The suicide rates of police officers were compared to male age-matched controls. Data on the male suicide rate for five age divisions ranging from fifteen to sixty-four years were obtained from the U.S. Bureau of the Census (1989, 820). These suicide rates ranged from a low of 20.5 for fifteen to twenty-four-year-olds to a high of 27.2 for fifty-five to sixty-four-year-olds. The average of these rates was used as a comparison figure.

In order to more rigorously assess the extent to which being a police officer contributes to risk of suicide, a multivariate regression analysis was utilized. In this way, it could be determined whether or not any bivariate association between being a police officer and suicide was spurious. Also, this method helps determine the importance of being a police officer compared to other possible predictors of police sui-cide. For the regression analysis, the dependent variable is measured as a binary variable where 1 equals death by suicide and 0 equals death from natural causes. Natural causes are measured as deaths from mis-cellaneous and other malignant neoplasms of lymphatic and hemato-poietic tissues, or causes of death numbers 200–203 in the Ninth Revision of the International Classification of Diseases (U.S. Public

Health Service 1992). These cancer deaths follow gender and race mortality patterns that are similar to suicide mortality patterns by gender and race. Complete data were available on 1,903 cases of cancer deaths. Complete data were available for 5,418 cases of suicide. In results not reported here, natural deaths were measured as deaths from urinary cancer (i.e., malignant neoplasms of the urinary organs, or causes of death 188–189). The results were essentially the same. Heart disease deaths were not selected as controls since such deaths can be stress related; cancer deaths are, in contrast, more "natural" in the sense that there is less of a stress-related component.

This analysis strategy, based on a binary variable from which the odds of dying of suicide versus natural causes is the analytic plan, is similar to the recent work of Burnett, Boxer, and Swanson (1992). These researchers studied the odds of death from suicides versus deaths from natural causes across a sample of occupations. The analysis plan is also similar to that of Maris (1981), who employed a similar strategy in a study of suicides versus nonsuicides in Chicago.

Police officer status is measured in relation to a series of binary variables tapping into labor-force activity or lack thereof. Being a police officer is coded as a binary variable, where 1 equals police officer and 0 equals all others. Homemakers, mostly women, are coded as 1, and 0 equals all others. Other persons not in the labor force (e.g., unemployed, students, and so on) are coded as 1, and 0 equals all others. In this way, police officers are compared to the omitted category of all other labor-force participants.

In order to rigorously assess any link between police officer status and suicide, controls for other predictors of suicide are introduced. The risk of suicide is related to marital dissolution (e.g., Stack 1982; Stack and Wasserman 1993), and police are often said to have a high degree of marital conflict (Stratton 1975). Marital ties or "integration" are measured as a series of binary variables representing the status categories of divorced, single, and widowed, with married being the omitted category. That is, the status of divorced equals 1, and 0 equals all others, single equals 1 and 0 equals all others, and widowed equals 1 and 0 equals all others. This is a standard way of measuring categorical variables in regression analysis (Lewis-Beck 1980).

Controls are introduced for age, gender, and race. The probability of death by suicide relative to natural causes tends to go down with age. The overwhelming majority of people die of natural causes such as cancer and coronary heart disease, and as age increases, the probability of death from these two leading causes of mortality increases (Manton, Blazer, and Woodbury 1987). Age is measured in years, and it is anticipated that the higher the age the lower the probability of death from suicide relative to natural causes. Males are considerably more likely to die from suicide than females. This is true of both blacks and whites (U.S. Public Health Service 1992). Ninety-three percent of sworn police officers in 1985 were male (FBI 1986, 248). Gender is measured as a binary variable, where 1 equals male and 0 equals female. Whites are more likely than persons of other races to die by suicide (e.g., Stack 1982; Stack and Wasserman 1993). Race is measured as a binary variable, where 1 equals white and 0 equals all others.

RESULTS

Table 6.1 provides the estimates of suicide rates for the police and the controls. For police, the suicide rate is 25.6 per 100 thousand officers. This is slightly above the rate for the age-matched controls (23.8 per 100 thousand). The proportional mortality ratio of the police suicide rate to their expected rate is 1.08. It is also true, however, that the rate of police suicide is "double the national average," the latter being 12.3 (U.S. Public Health Service 1987). However, this is misleading, since the national average includes females who have a rate of only 5.1, as well as persons below age fifteen, who have a rate of near zero. Neither of the two groups is well-represented within the ranks of the police.

As a check on the interpretation of the crude suicide rate in Table 6.1, a multivariate analysis was performed. This controls for covariates of police officer status such as gender. Given that the dependent variable is a binary variable, ordinary least squares regression analysis

Table 6.1
Suicide Rates of Police Officers and Controls, 1985 (Sixteen Reporting States)

Group:	Suicides Rate (per 100,000)
(A) Police Officers	25.60
(B) Males 15-64	23.80
Proportional Mortality Ratio for Police (A/B)	1.08
All Males	19.90
All Females	5.10
All Persons	12.30
Whites	13.40
All Others Races	6.60
African Americans	6.20

Source: U.S. Public Health Service. 1987. Advance Report of Final Mortality Statistics, 1985. *Monthly Vital Statistics Report* 36 (5): Supplement.

cannot be applied, but logistic regression techniques are appropriate (Morgan and Teachman 1988).

Table 6.2 presents the results of the logistic regression results. Controlling for the other independent variables, police officers do not have significantly different odds of dying from suicide than other persons in the labor force. The logistic coefficient is only 0.23 times its standard error. The probability that we would be wrong in rejecting the null hypothesis is 0.81, considerably higher than the standard of 0.05.

Turning to the control variables, being a homemaker increases the odds of suicide, but being out of the labor force in other ways decreases it. All three marital status variables increase the odds of suicide compared to those of being married. The coefficient of divorce, for example, is 11 times its standard error. Being divorced increases the odds of suicide by 2.94 times, as indicated by the variable's odds ratio. Being single and being widowed also increase the odds of suicide.

As predicted, age decreases the odds of suicide. Each year or unit change in age decreases the odds of suicide 0.92 times, as indicated by

Table 6.2
The Effect of Police Officer Status and Control Variables on the Odds of Dying by Suicide versus Natural Causes (Logistic Regression Results, Sixteen Reporting States, 1985, Ages 18–64, n = 7,321 Deaths)

Variable	Logistic	Standard Error	Chi Square	Probability Level	Odds Ratio
Intercept	5.11*	0.17	316.61	0.000	---
Labor Force Status:					
Police Officer	0.11	0.47	0.06	0.81	1.11
Homemaker	0.24*	0.11	4.85	0.027	1.27
Other, Out of Labor Force	-0.57*	0.10	32.43	0.000	0.56
Marital Status Controls:					
Divorced	1.08*	0.10	127.35	0.000	2.94
Widowed	0.75*	0.13	31.73	0.000	2.12
Single	0.32*	0.10	10.07	0.0015	1.38
Demographic Controls:					
Age	-0.08*	0.003	875.65	0.000	0.92
White	0.84*	0.11	60.29	0.0000	2.32
Male	0.94*	0.08	146.56	0.0000	2.56

Model Chi Square: 1806.57; 9 d.f.; p = 0.00; Contingency C: 0.81; *p < 0.05.

the variable's odds ratio. Being white increases the odds of suicide 2.32 times. Finally, being a male increases the odds of suicide 2.56 times. The Contingency C coefficient for the association between the predicted and actual values of the dependent variable is 0.81. That indicates that the model provides a relatively good fit to the data at hand.

CONCLUSION

The present investigation employs recent national data in estimating the incidence of suicide among the police. It finds that police in public agencies have a suicide rate slightly higher than their age-matched male peers. However, the results of a logistic regression analysis find that once controls are introduced for socioeconomic variables, being a police officer is not significantly associated with the odds of death by suicide. The results question the dominant assumption in the field that police have a high suicide rate (e.g., Lester 1978; Bedeian 1982). Previous research on police in public agencies has often been based on local samples, and results have been inconsistent as a result. The present estimates, being based on a national sample, offer more systematic estimates.

These results need to be taken with caution for a number of reasons. First, many contend that police suicides are underreported primarily because police departments want to protect the image of their officers and fellow officers want to protect the reputation of their "dead brother officer" and "his" insurance benefits or family (Krocs 1976). To an extent, this is true—even national data will underestimate actual suicide rates—however, such can also be the case for persons in other occupations. Second, these results say nothing about the other possible consequences on police from job-related stress. That is, while these data suggest that job stress does not significantly affect police suicide, it may exacerbate other social problems, such as marital conflict, alcoholism, and heart disease. Further research is needed in these areas, preferably using national samples and controlling for race, gender, and so on.

Third, much of the theorizing on why police should have a high suicide rate is premised on a model of street-oriented or dangerous police work. In reality, most police officers work in less dangerous roles or confront danger very infrequently. Therefore, it is possible, in spite of the present findings, that the subgroup of police who fit the daily street work "danger" profile may, in fact, have an elevated incidence of suicide. Unfortunately, the relevant data needed to test this hypothesis were not available in the present or past investigations.

This is the first national study of the incidence of police suicide since the reporting of the 1950 data in Labovitz and Hagedorn (1971). Results revealed that the suicide rate for police in public agencies has declined from 46 to 26 per 100 thousand over the last thirty-five years. This finding deserves further explanation. One possibility might be a change in economic conditions faced by police. For example, by 1980 the mean annual income of police officers was approaching that of male pharmacists ($21,282) and already surpassed that of male registered nurses ($16,764) (U.S. Bureau of the Census 1984). To the extent that economic pressures contribute to suicide, the alleviation of such pressures ought to decrease suicide risk (Stack 1982). Also, improved economic packages often provide expanded medical fringe benefits, which include counseling and psychotherapy, an important factor in suicide prevention. Furthermore, by 1985 many departments had implemented training programs to help officers and their spouses better understand and cope with job stress and to assist administrators in recognizing and responding to early warning signs of chronic stress and burnout. Some departments had even hired full-time mental health personnel to help in selecting healthier officers and to aid police in handling the pressures of work.

NOTES

Reprinted from *American Journal of Police* 13 (4), with permission from MCB University Press.

Data on suicide were provided by the ICPSR at the University of Michigan.

BIBLIOGRAPHY

Aussant, G. (1984). Police Suicide. *International Criminal Police Review* 39: 179–188.

Bedeian, A. (1982). Suicide and Occupation: A Review. *Journal of Vocational Behavior* 21: 206–223.

Bonifacio, P. (1991). *The Psychological Effects of Police Work: A Psychoanalytic Approach*. New York: Plenum Press.

Burnett, C.; P. Boxer; and N. Swanson. (1992). *Suicide and Occupation: Is There a Relationship?* Cincinnati: National Institute for Occupational Safety and Health.

Coleman, S. (1986). *Street Cops*. Salem, Wisc.: Sheffield.

Curran, P.; R. Finlay; and P. McGarry. (1988). Trends in Suicide. *Irish Journal of Psychological Medicine* 5: 98–102.

Danto, B. (1978). Police Suicide. *Police Stress* 1: 32–36.

Dash, J., and M. Reiser. (1978). Suicide among Police in Urban Law Enforcement Agencies. *Journal of Police Science and Administration* 6: 18–21.

Davidson, M., and A. Veno. (1978). Police Stress: A Multicultural Interdisciplinary Review and Perspective, Part I. *Abstracts on Police Science* (July–August): 190–191.

Federal Bureau of Investigation (FBI). (1986). *Crime in the U.S.: 1985*. Washington, D.C.: U.S. Government Printing Office.

Fell, R.; W. Richard; and W. Wallace. (1980). Psychological Job Stress and the Police Officer. *Journal of Police Science and Administration* 8: 139–144.

Friedman, P. (1968). Suicide among Police. In *Essays in Self-Destruction*, edited by E. Shneidman. New York: Human Sciences Press.

Gaines, L.; M. Southerland; and J. Angell. (1991). *Police Administration*. New York: McGraw-Hill.

Guralnick, L. (1963). *Mortality by Occupation and Cause of Death among Men 20–64 Years of Age* (Vital Statistics Special Reports 53 [3]). Bethesda, Md.: U.S. Department of Health, Education, and Welfare.

Heiman, M. (1977). Suicide among Police. *American Journal of Psychiatry* 134: 1286–1290.

Heiman, M. (1975a). The Police Suicide. *Journal of Police Science and Administration* 3: 267–273.

Heiman, M. (1975b). Police Suicide Revisited. *Suicide* 5: 5–20.

Hendlin, H. (1963). The Psychodynamics of Suicide. *Journal of Nervous and Mental Disorders* 136: 236–244.

Hill, K., and M. Clawson. (1988). The Hazards of Street Level Bureaucracy: Mortality among the Police. *Journal of Police Science and Administration* 16: 243–248.

Jackson, J., and C. Maslach. (1982). After-Effects of Job-Related Stress: Families as Victims. *Journal of Occupational Behavior* 3: 63–77.

James, G. (1993). Police Detective Commits Suicide. *New York Times*, 15 November, B15.

Josephson, R., and M. Reiser. (1990). Officer Suicide in the Los Angeles P.D.: A 12 Year Follow Up. *Journal of Police Science and Administration* 17: 227–229.

Kendall, R. (1983). Alcohol and Suicide. *Substance and Alcohol Actions/Misuse* 4: 121–127.

Krocs, W. (1976). *Society's Victim—The Policeman: An Analysis of Job Stress in Policing*. Springfield, Ill.: Charles Thomas.

Labovitz, S., and R. Hagedorn. (1971). An Analysis of Suicide Rates among Occupational Categories. *Sociological Inquiry* 41: 67–72.

Lester, D. (1992). Alcoholism and Drug Abuse. In *Assessment and Prediction of Suicide*, edited by R. Maris. New York: Guilford Press.

Lester, D. (1978). Suicides in Police Officers. *Police Chief* 45: 17.

Lewis-Beck, M. (1980). *Applied Regression Analysis*. Beverly Hills: Sage.

Loo, R. (1986). Suicide among Police in a Federal Force. *Suicide and Life Threatening Behavior* 16: 379–388.

Manton, K.; D. Blazer; and M. Woodbury. (1987). Suicide in the Middle Age and Later Life: Sex and Race Specific Table and Cohort Analysis. *Journal of Gerontology* 42: 219–227.

Maris, R. (1981). *Pathways to Suicide*. Baltimore: Johns Hopkins University Press.

Maslach, C., and S. Jackson. (1984). Burnout in Organizational Settings. In *Applied Social Psychology Annual*, edited by J. Oskamp. Newbury Park, Calif.: Sage.

Miller, A. (1988). Stress on the Job. *Newsweek* (March 17) 40–45.

Morgan, S., and J. Teachman. (1988.) Logistic Regression: Description, Examples, and Comparisons. *Journal of Marriage and the Family* 50: 929–936.

Neiderhoffer, A. (1967). *Behind the Shield*. Garden City, N.Y.: Doubleday.

Nelson, Z., and W. Smith. (1970). Law Enforcement Profession: An Incident of High Suicide. *Omega* 1: 293–299.

Pescosolido, B., and R. Mendelsohn. (1986). Social Causation or Social Construction of Suicide? *American Sociological Review* 51: 80–100.

Pincs, A., and E. Drowson. (1988). *Career Burnout: Causes & Cures*. New York: Macmillan.

Richard, W., and R. Fell. (1975). Health Factors in Police Job Stress. In *Job Stress and the Police Officer*, edited by W. Kroes and J. Hurrell. Washington, D.C.: NIOSH.

Schmalleger, F. (1991). *Criminal Justice Today*. Englewood Cliffs, N.J.: Prentice Hall.

Stack, S. (1982). Suicide: A Decade Review of the Sociological Literature. *Deviant Behavior* 4: 41–66.

Stack, S., and I. Wasserman. (1993). Marital Status, Alcohol Consumption, and Suicide: An Analysis of National Data. *Journal of Marriage and the Family* 55: 1018–1024.

Stratton, J. (1984). *Police Passages*. Manhattan Beach, Calif.: Glennon.

Stratton, J. (1975). Pressures in Law Enforcement Marriages: Some Considerations. *Police Chief* November: 44–47.

U.S. Bureau of the Census. (1989). *Statistical Abstract of the U.S., 1989*. Washington, D.C.: U.S. Government Printing Office.

U.S. Bureau of the Census. (1987). *Statistical Abstract of the U.S., 1987*. Washington, D.C.: U.S. Government Printing Office.

U.S. Bureau of the Census. (1984). *1980 Census of the Population: Subject Reports: Earnings by Occupation and Education*. Washington, D.C.: U.S. Government Printing Office.

U.S. Bureau of the Census. (1980). *1980 Census of the Population: Classified Index of Industries and Occupations*. Washington, D.C.: U.S. Government Printing Office.

U.S. Public Health Service. (1992). Advance Report of Final Mortality Statistics, 1989. *Monthly Vital Statistics Report* 40 (8): Supplement 2.

U.S. Public Health Service. (1988). *Mortality Detail Files, 1988: Codebook*. Washington, D.C.: U.S. Government Printing Office.

U.S. Public Health Service. (1987). Advance Report of Final Mortality Statistics, 1985. *Monthly Vital Statistics Report* 36 (5): Supplement.

Vena, J.; J. Violanti; and J. Marshall. (1986). Mortality of a Municipal Worker Cohort. *American Journal of Industrial Medicine* 10: 383–397.

Violanti, J.; J. Vena; and J. Marshall. (1986). Disease Risk and Mortality among Police Officers: New Evidence and Contributing Factors. *Journal of Police Science and Administration* 14: 17–23.

Wagner, M., and R. Brzeczek. (1983). Alcoholism and Suicide. *FBI Law Enforcement Bulletin* 52: 8–17.

Wasserman, I. (1992). Economy, Work, Occupation, and Suicide. In *Assessment and Prediction of Suicide*, edited by R. Maris. New York: Guilford Press.

Zimbardo, P. (1970). The Human Choice: Individuation, Reason, and Order versus Deindividuation, Impulse, and Chaos. In *Negrosra Symposium on Motivation*, edited by W. Arnold and D. Levine. Lincoln: University of Nebraska Press.

7

Can I Get a Witness:
The Role of Religion in Policing

Robert P. McNamara and Maria Tempenis

At first glance, one might not think that religion plays an important role in the criminal justice system. However, some research has been devoted to this relationship (see, for instance, Goldsmith 1989; Cochran 1994, 1989; Clear et al. 1992; Johnson 1987a; Day 1987). Johnson (1987b), for example, using data gathered from prison inmates, has found that religiosity makes little difference in terms of whether they will violate institutional rules. On the other hand, however, Clear and colleagues (1992) found that religious participation helps inmates overcome the depression and guilt associated with incarceration and avoid the constant threats and dangers of prison life, and makes inmates less likely to violate institutional rules and regulations.

Thus, while there is a growing body of literature on religiosity with some conflicting results, one agency within the criminal justice system that has been omitted has been the police. This is interesting given the influence of the police subculture on officers' behavior and attitudes. It would seem that the subculture and its social influence would be problematic for devoutly religious officers, especially since the subculture often tolerates and even promotes unacceptable conduct (Seigel 1995; Livingston 1992; Roberg and Kuykendall 1993; Alpert and Dunham 1992). It is on these differences that we would like to focus our attention. Specifically, we seek to assess the problems devoutly religious officers encounter in the performance of their duties as well as when their spiritual beliefs conflict with the subcultural standards. For example, highly religious officers amend or suspend their spiritual concerns in order to accomplish a difficult task, strictly adhere to one value system over another, or simply decide to leave law enforcement altogether rather than wrestle with these issues.

In addition to problems relating to professional conduct, officers must contend with an array of job-related issues of a more personal nature, such as family problems, suicide, and the use of alcohol and drugs (Gaines 1993; Territo and Vetter 1981; Alpert and Dunham 1992). How well the officers resolve these dilemmas may be explained in part by their religious beliefs. It could be argued, for example, that religious officers have a greater sensitivity to the variety of personal issues that are commonly found in law enforcement, and through faith and fellowship are better equipped to effectively manage them.

This project consists of two parts. First, we examine the role religion plays in the socialization process of police officers as well as how it impacts on their perceptions with regard to issues such as the use of deadly force, job stress, and family life. Second, we examine the negative consequences, if any, that devoutly religious officers experience as a result of their spiritual ideology. Building upon the framework used by Leinen (1994) to examine the lives of homosexual police officers, we examine the stigmatization that these officers experience, especially those who make their views known to others.

The Subculture of Policing

The idea of the police being a subculture is not new and has been well documented (see, for instance, Westley 1970; Rokeach, Miller, and Snyder 1971; Kirkham 1976; Bittner 1970). Entry into this subculture begins with a process of socialization whereby recruits learn the values and behavior patterns characteristic of experienced officers. Ultimately, many develop an occupational or working personality characterized by authoritarianism, suspicion, and cynicism (Rubenstein 1973; Van Maanen 1973; Alpert and Dunham 1992; Neiderhoffer 1967). Skolnick (1994) provides perhaps the best description of the police personality:

The policeman's role contains two principal variables, danger and authority, which should be interpreted in the light of a "constant" pressure to appear efficient. The element of danger seems to make the policeman especially attentive to signs indicating a potential for violence and lawbreaking. As a result, the policeman is generally a "suspicious" person. Furthermore, the character of the policeman's work makes him less desirable as a friend, since norms of friendship implicate others in his work. Accordingly, the element of danger isolates the policeman socially from that segment of the citizenry which he regards as symbolically dangerous and also from the conventional citizenry with whom he identifies. (p. 43)

An integral part of the police personality is cynicism, the notion that all people are motivated by evil and selfishness. Police cynicism develops among many officers through the nature of police work. Most police officers feel they are set apart from the rest of society because they have the power to regulate the lives of others. Moreover, by constantly dealing with crime and the more unsavory aspects of social life, their faith in humanity seems to diminish. As Neiderhoffer (1967) has said, "Cynicism is an ideologicall plank deeply entrenched in the ethos of the police world, and it serves equally well for attack or defense. For many reasons police are particularly vulnerable to cynicism. When they succumb, they lose faith in people, society, and eventually in themselves. In their Hobbesian view, the world becomes a jungle in which crime, corruption, and brutality are normal features of the terrain" (p. 9).

In sum, the police personality emerges as a result of the very nature of police work and the socialization process which most police officers experience. To deal with the social isolation that is derived from their use of authority, some of it self-imposed, officers use other members of the profession to cope with social rejection. As a result, many, perhaps most, police officers become part of a closely knit subculture that is protective and supportive of its members, and shares similar attitudes, values, understandings, and views of the world.

Occupational Hazards and the Subculture of Policing

If social solidarity is an important element of the police subculture, then camaraderie and its manifestations should be expected as a coping mechanism for many of the occupational stressors that exist. Not only does it allow the officer to manage the problems of facing most of life's dangerous events and characters, it also plays an important role when officers engage in illegitimate activities as well—activities such as corruption, drug abuse, brutality, and other forms of misconduct. This is especially important since camaraderie and social support are part of what attract many to law enforcement to begin with. How then do individuals with strong faiths manage these problems? Perhaps even more important, how do they perceive themselves in terms of their status in the police community and how do other officers perceive them?

METHODS

To begin answering these questions, this project sought out a group of devoutly Christian police officers so that a sample could be surveyed to identify their primary issues of occupational concern. The questions in this survey were of three types: individual attitudes, social cohesion, and organizational issues.

Individual Attitudes

This included a self-report measure of religiosity, along with statements about the level of difficulty experienced as Christian officers. Among the areas of concern were coworker's use of profanity, marital infidelity, sexual promiscuity, drug and alcohol abuse, and minor forms of graft. Other issues included the use of deadly force in the line of duty, arrests of abortion demonstrators, and various forms of lying related to undercover work as well as those types of activities involved in suspect interrogations. All responses were on a scale of one to five, with five being the highest level of concern.

Social Cohesion

The second type of questions targeted levels of inclusion into the community. Respondents were asked whether or not they felt a part of the police community, if other officers looked down on them or showed them a lack of respect because of their Christianity, or if they felt set apart from other officers because of their beliefs. In addition, if they had encountered such problems, did it cause them to consider resigning from the profession? These questions were also scaled from one to five.

To get a better sense of how accurate officers' perceptions were, we also asked them how often they socialized with other officers, both Christian and non-Christian. The logic, of course, was that if they did not socialize with other officers, this could be taken as an indication that they did not feel a part of the subculture or did not feel as though they were members in good standing. Similarly, if they only socialized with other Christian officers, this could be interpreted as a form of self-segregation within their occupation.

Organizational Issues

Finally, respondents were asked about how their organization responded to their beliefs. Had the department ever sanctioned them or attempted to curtail the expression of their beliefs in any way, or had they been denied promotions or choice assignments because of their beliefs? As mentioned, this first phase was used as an outer marker of the role of religion in law enforcement.

The Sample

With approximately 3,500 members and over one thousand chapters nationwide, the Fellowship of Christian Peace Officers (FCPO) represents perhaps one of the largest groups of religious police officers in the country. Formed in 1971 when a group of Christian officers in the Los Angeles Police Department felt they were charged with the task of sharing Christ with their "lost" fellow officers, the FCPO emerged a year later with a mission to "unite Christian men and women in the criminal justice system using time-proven ministry methods and to strengthen members' faith and help them be more effective witnesses to those around them." FCPO members pray for the salvation of lost men and women around them in their daily encounters as well as in meetings among chapter members. Members are trained how to give a testimony of their conversion experience and how to lead others in the "sinner's prayer."

After conducting approximately fifteen in-depth telephone interviews with members of this organization, a survey was developed and administered to a random sample of 470 members. In an effort to maintain the anonymity of the officers, the surveys were mailed to the executive director, who in turn randomly selected individuals from the membership list and sent them a copy of the survey. When completed, they were then mailed back to the authors.

The Problem of Defining Religious Ideology

Because of the great deal of variability in defining terms and perspectives, and to avoid a seemingly endless theological debate, we chose to use a self-report measure of religion. This technique is very effective and well-grounded in the sociological literature on symbolic interactionism. Sociologists who use this perspective try to understand life from an insider's point of view. It attempts to identify the significance of events, behavior, and objects to the members of a group of people. In short, it tries to understand all aspects of the social life of a group of people, including the problems they encounter and the methods used to cope with them. A central assumption of the interactionist perspective can be summarized by this statement of William Thomas: "If people define situations as real they are real in their consequences" (Kornblum 1994). In other words, people act on the basis of their beliefs and perceptions about situations. In short, a self-report measure of religion simplifies the problems of defining a religion and has the added benefit of a long-standing tradition in sociological research.

The members of FCPO define themselves as evangelical and fundamentalist Christians. The overarching category is evangelicism, with born-again Christianity as one of its subsets. Authority of scripture and the belief in salvation by grace through faith characterize evangelical Christianity. The born-again movement asserts that sin and temptation no longer persist in the lives of those who are saved through repentence. According to basic born-again theology, one must undergo an internal conversion experience and proceed to externalize this experience through rigorous moral and spiritual discipline. Fundamentalism, in turn, is a subset of the born-again category. Like all Christians, fundamentalists believe that the incarnation of Christ constituted a divine revelation. They point out, however, that Christ is known only through scripture. The Bible, then, is the word of God and is an essential aspect of fundamentalist theology, and any subjective encounter with God must be authenticated by scripture (if it is not, the encounter should be rejected).

If one's eternal destiny depends on a right relationship with God, and if that God is reliably known only through the Bible, it follows that one must read and read correctly. Fundamentalism asserts the need for followers to model Christ in behavior, to obey the laws of the land, to give priority to marriage and family (second only to obedience to God), and to learn contentment in whatever the circumstance (Eitzen 1993). Furthermore, fundamentalist born-again Christians feel compelled by God to spread the Gospel to everyone; this belief in the Great Commission is held as a responsibility for all true Christians.

In an effort to understand their version of faith, one of the authors conducted an interview with the executive director of FCPO, who explained the following:

We believe a fundamentalist and evangelical Christian is someone who believes in biblical inerency. That it has no errors. So when it says you do, you do it and when it says you don't, you don't. Fundamentalists follow the teaching of the New Testament as amplified by the letters of Paul, James, Peter, and John and these have instructions on how to live the Christian way of life. Knowing what the Bible says about conducting one's self, with regard to job, families and to respect all authority, after all governments were established by God. We also believe in a literal heaven and hell and if you live your life according to the gospel, you will end up in heaven. And I want to talk to you about your Christianity since I don't want to see you end up in hell. I think the most important thing that happened in Evangelicism is what can be called "confrontational evangelicism." This is the "turn and burn" approach. These are the people who go around and aggressively try to get you to convert.

Today, people are attuned to what is called "lifestyle evangelicism," as read in Mathew chapters 5–8 and his sermon on the Mount. These are those who believe in practicing righteousness, they keep a low profile and try not to call attention to themselves because in doing so, they are calling attention away from God. And when we give money to charity, as well as in prayer, we do it in secret. We don't need to be ostentatious, we know what the Bible says: lead a good life and be a friend to man and when given the opportunity to show him the way, do it.

I guess the easiest way to understand this is to say that people are hopelessly religious—you find it in all aspects of life, even football. The Bible is saying

God created man and gave man a choice—the basic choice was evil and he didn't know it. And it got way out of hand. So much so that God had to sacrifice his son to reestablish the relationship he really wanted with us. All we need to do is to admit that he was sacrificed for our sins.

RESULTS

Of the 470 surveys sent by the FCPO (which included a cover letter by the researchers as well as by the executive director encouraging members to respond), only 106 were returned, a response rate of approximately 20 percent. A second plea for cooperation was subsequently sent out a few months later and completed surveys continue to arrive. The analysis presented here is only on the first wave of 106.

Profile of Christian Police Officers

The mean age of the respondents is 44.1, with ages ranging from twenty-five to seventy. Their tenure as Christians was rather lengthy, with a mean of 22.7 years; 75 percent of the officers had been a Christian for 30 years or more. The officers had also been involved in their chosen profession for a considerable length of time, with a mean of 18.67 years, and 60 percent had 20 or more years of service. The officers also remained with their current department for a considerable length of time, an average of 14.2 years, with 60 percent having served 15 or more years. This figure, coupled with their time in law enforcement, shows that they probably made one change during their careers and have essentially remained with their current department. This is somewhat reflected in their assignment within their department: 24 percent were detectives or investigators, 16 percent were in management positions, and 55 percent were involved in patrol.

On a personal level, 89 percent were married, 5 percent single, and 5 percent separated or divorced. The vast majority were also white (92%), with African Americans, Hispanics, and Native Americans each representing 2 percent. Like most people in law enforcement, the officers were predominantly male (91%). In terms of a profile, these officers are very similar, not only in terms of their religious ideology, but in terms of their physical characteristics and career paths in law enforcement.

Individual Attitudes: Profanity, Marital Infidelity, Promiscuity, Drugs, Corruption

All statements indicating these issues were a problem are based on scoring three or higher on a five-point scale. When it does not present a problem, the officers scored one or two. As Table 7.1 indicates with regard to the use of profanity among coworkers, 72 percent of the re-

Table 7.1
Individual Attitudes among Christian Officers

	Profanity	Infidelity	Promiscuity	Drugs	Graft
Problem	72%	56%	53%	43%	28%
	(76)	(59)	(56)	(46)	(30)
No Problem	28%	44%	47%	57%	72%
	(30)	(47)	(50)	(60)	(76)
Total	100%	100%	100%	100%	100%

sponding officers replied that this was problematic for them as police officers. Similarly, 56 percent stated that marital infidelity was a difficult issue for them in their work climate. Sexual promiscuity was problematic for approximately 53 percent of the officers. Drugs and alcohol were troubling for 43 percent. Officers had little difficulty with minor forms of corruption; nearly 72 percent stated that this did not pose difficulty for them as Christians. This is consistent with the fundamentalist philosophy concerning the prescribed behavior of Man, that he should live a model life according to the teachings in the Bible. This means presenting a public persona that serves as an example to others and includes avoiding the use of profanity and extramarital affairs, and not associating with others who abuse drugs and alcohol or engage in forms of corruption.

As Table 7.2 shows, for half of the officers arresting abortion demonstrators was a troubling experience. While this may be interpreted in a few different ways (like the other issues), this finding indicates that for some, ideological issues and religious dogma influences the performance of their duties. The other half commented that, despite what they might feel personally on the issue, professionalism dictates that they carry out their prescribed duties in an objective manner. For them, the issue was devoid of any extraneous factors and they simply arrested protestors as they would anyone else who violated the law. As one officer stated in an interview, "I try to be as objective as I possibly can about it. I mean, it's not like I try to shove my beliefs down anyone's throat. I have tried to explain the consequences of their actions to them, but overall it is their choice. I really don't have a problem with it. I think there are legal avenues for pro-life and pro-choice groups and they should pursue them. But if they violate the law, whatever my own feelings, I have to remain professional and make the arrest." In contrast, another officer stated, "I have a very hard time doing this. I mean, I really and truly believe in their cause and I sometimes think that I should be out there protesting with them. And while

Table 7.2
Related Issues: Abortion, Deadly Force, Undercover Work

	Abortion	Deadly Force	Undercover
Problem	50%	22%	43%
	(53)	(23)	(46)
No Problem	50%	78%	57%
	(53)	(83)	(60)
Total	100%	100%	100%

I understand it is illegal in some cases, it is the only way we can be heard sometimes. I try to tell them to get up and leave before they are arrested, but I feel like a hypocrite. And if they ever knew that I was a Christian officer, they probably would call me one."

Officers generally expressed few problems in taking the life of another in the line of duty. The vast majority, 78 percent, expressed little difficulty in using deadly force in the line of duty if called on to do so. The issues here may be clearer for many officers, especially since the gravity of the situation as well as the finality of their actions may allow them to see the issue in a more consistent and clear way. One officer stated, "To me, shooting someone gets an immediate acceptance. I wouldn't like it and would probably fall apart emotionally, but I could do it. The way I see it is that the person put me in this position and had choices to make. He or she chose to escalate it and I am obligated to respond: morally, ethically, and professionally." Another officer offered this comment: "When I became a Christian I gave some serious thought to leaving law enforcement because of that possibility. By studying scripture and through fellowship with other Christian officers, I have come to believe that we are keepers of the governed. I think there is a difference between violence and unreasonable force." Still another officer stated he never gave it much thought; however, "If my life was gravely threatened, I would react out of self-preservation and there is nothing biblically wrong with it. There is biblical support for that so I could do it with a clear conscience, not that I would be happy about it."

With regard to lying as a part of undercover work, there were very few officers who have participated in the past or are currently engaging in undercover operations who responded to the survey: Most were either in patrol or management-level positions. However, in those cases where officers had worked undercover operations, 43 percent stated that it was difficult for them to engage in the deceit and lying that makes for a successful undercover operation. Still, the majority, 57 percent, did not find this problematic. As one officer put it, "I use informants all the time and I essentially allow them to break the law. I think it is the lesser of two evils. I have been given the authority to make these types of decisions and feel responsible to continue collecting information which will ultimately lead me to solving a case. It promotes order and my mandate for society, even though I know the Bible says it is wrong and I should not do it. The way I have to look at it is it's needed to fulfill my greater mission." Another officer stated, "I think it is justifiable. After all, Moses sent spies into Jericho. I think this is part of God's work and I must believe that he knows what is best in these situations." Because they look upon their role as police officers as guardians of the public trust, the officers generally recognize the need to engage in deceit at some level. Similarly, few officers had problems with lying or other forms of deceit involved in suspect interrogations.

Cohesion and Fit into the Community

Recall that these questions focused on whether or not Christian officers felt they fit into the police community. As Table 7.3 shows, 80 percent of the officers scored a three or higher on the five-point index. Only 20 percent of the officers felt they did not fit into the police subculture. Similarly, a little less than half of the officers, 47 percent, felt as though their fellow officers looked down on them or showed a lack of respect because of their Christian beliefs, while 51 percent did not feel as though this was a problem in their experiences. However, two-thirds of the officers said they felt set apart or different from other officers because they were Christian. Again, part of this may be explained by the fact that Christian officers feel as though they live by different standards than other officers. This is especially true given that some of the values and attitudes surrounding the police subculture may not be very compatible with evangelical and fundamentalist beliefs.

In an effort to learn more about the social support networks Christian officers have in place, as well as to illustrate how closely they feel a part of the entire police community, officers were asked if they socialized with other police officers. Approximately 65 percent responded that they socialize with non-Christian officers. Approximately 14 percent said they did so every week, while 21 percent did so about once a month, and 19 percent once every two months. Collectively, 54 percent spent some time with other officers off-duty. Officers were also asked to estimate how many other Christian officers were members of their department. Almost 91 percent stated there were other Christian officers, and overall they represented approximately 10 percent of the

Table 7.3
Perceptions of Cohesion into the Police Subculture

	Fit into Subculture	Lack of Respect	Problems
Yes	80%	47%	51%
	(85)	(50)	(54)
No	20%	53%	49%
	(21)	(56)	(52)
Total	100%	100%	100%

population. In comparing the frequency of contact between Christian and non-Christian officers, 73 percent stated they socialized with other Christians and did so on average either once a week (19%), once a month (23%), or once every two months (18%).

In sum, in terms of contact, more Christian officers socialize with other Christians off-duty than with non-Christians (59% versus 54%), but the difference is relatively small and statistically insignificant. Officers may feel as though they are a part of the police community based on the frequency of their interaction with other officers, although they prefer to spend more time with other Christians. It also seems clear that these officers make a distinction between participating in an occupational subculture and seeing themselves as on its periphery. Thus, officers may feel as though they are respected, which may or may not be true, but many feel as though they are outsiders. Moreover, since very few (17%) expressed any interest in leaving the job because of the problems they experience, it seems that their beliefs may also be driving much of this attitude. In fact, since many view their role as police officers as a type of missionary work to which God has directed them, officers may be unwilling to change their career paths. Moreover, because a substantial proportion are in management positions, it may be impractical for some to make a change. Thus, it seems that the problems are looked upon by these officers as occupational stressors which can be minimized or reduced through fellowship and prayer.

Organizational Issues

In an attempt to understand how their faith affects their standing within the organization, officers were asked a series of questions regarding how their supervisors responded to their beliefs. As mentioned, a large contingent of responding officers were involved in law enforcement for a rather lengthy period of time and a sizable percentage were involved in management-level positions. Thus, it would seem at first glance that religion was not an obstacle to career advancement.

On the other hand, the largest cluster of Christian officers were assigned to patrol, with varying lengths of service time. As such, it is also possible to conclude, without a more detailed examination, that these officers remain in entry-level positions because of their faith. To look at this more closely, officers were asked if their department had ever tried to curtail expression of their beliefs, either through disciplinary action or informal sanctions by their supervisors. Obviously this calls for some subjectivity on the part of the officers, but it is important to note that their perceptions of persecutions, whether substantiated or not, affect their behavior. However, this does not appear to be a significant problem. Approximately 10 percent of the officers responded that they had experienced this type of incident, with another 8 percent admitting they did not know if any such treatment had occurred due to religion. One officer who did experience this type of treatment explained, "I wear an ID badge because I work at an airport and I have put crosses and I love Jesus pins on my badge. My Lieutenant asked me to take them off because of complaints that were made, but there were no such complaints." Another officer stated, "I confronted a training class that involved a film involving sexual activity between a man and child. I was told that there was a fine line between my morals and the activities we encounter." Still another officer offered this comment: "I was brought up on disciplinary action by a Jewish commanding officer who accused me of "proselytizing." I appealed to "Ceasar," demanded a trial/hearing, and he backed off and dropped the charges."

Similarly, 73 percent of the officers felt that they did not suffer setbacks in their careers, such as being passed over for promotions or choice assignments because of their faith. Of those that stated it did occur, the types of incidents that occurred include this officer's account: "My Christian beliefs and pro-family stance had alienated me from the 'good old boy' promotion/assignment network." Another officer stated, "I did not have any previous problems with promotions until I was promoted to Lieutenant. Now I am experiencing difficulty being promoted to Commander rank due to my Christian beliefs. I was told by an Assistant Chief that I am perceived as being 'too protective of women.' Also, I don't get fair consideration for some assignments because I am considered to be 'too good' or may make people uncomfortable by being too 'preachy.'"

DISCUSSION

As the data suggest, in many ways being a Christian police officer presents a host of difficulties. In some ways these officers are stigmatized by their colleagues. One officer stated that the biggest problem he encountered as a Christian was always feeling the need to be mindful of his behavior, lest his colleagues chide him for inconsistency: "I've got to be very careful all the time. I feel like I'm being watched every moment of the day. I can't get mad and go off on somebody or have moments of indiscretion like everyone else because of my beliefs. Sometimes that bothers me because I didn't take an opportunity to witness when I wanted to or should have." Another officer stated, "I think the hardest part of being a Christian officer is the professional ostracization. There is a lot of stress involved in this job but even more so sometimes when you don't fit in. I can't be as outspoken about things as I would like to be because my supervisors and politicians see my views as unworthy. So I always have to watch what I say, how I say it, and even then, a lot of guys will respect my skills as an officer, but not as a person. That is really hard sometimes."

It seems clear that at some level some degree of stigmatization does occur. As a result, some Christian officers tend to remain outside the social circles within the occupation and instead find comfort by spending time with families or members of their church. Still, on a day-to-day level this can easily be stressful and distracting. In short, within the subculture of policing, a group to which they all aspire to belong, they perceive themselves as labeled, to varying degrees, as outsiders.

The Labeling Perspective

The essence of the labeling perspective is that deviance does not exist independent of the negative reaction of people who condemn it. Behaviors are never weird, bad, sick, or deviant in themselves, they are deviant only because someone or some group responds to them in this fashion. According to the labeling perspective, the most crucial step in the development of a stable pattern of deviant behavior is usually the experience of being caught and publicly labeled deviant. Whether this happens to a person depends not so much on what the person does but on what other people do.

Once a person is stigmatized by being labeled a deviant, a self-fulfilling prophecy is initiated, with others perceiving and responding to the person as a deviant. Further, once people are publicly processed as deviants, they are typically forced into a deviant group. As Lemert (1951) contends, once this happens the deviant will face an audience that anticipates the worst and will take steps to protect itself, which will make it difficult for the person to reintegrate himself or herself into society.

Labeling theory also describes how deviance becomes a person's master status. While people have many statuses, the master status is the one that dominates and plays an important part in a person's social identity (Becker 1964). In our society, particularly for men, one's occupation usually serves as the master status. However, once people are labeled this changes and the stigma becomes their dominant status and they may encounter problems in dealing with other people.

In sum, the labeling perspective has focused its attention on the societal attributes of those who react and those who are reacted against in order to explain why certain persons and not others are labeled as deviant. Theorists argue that once a person has been labeled a deviant, and particularly if that person has passed through a "degradation ceremony" (Garfinkel 1956) and been forced to become a member of a deviant group, the person experiences a profound and often irreversible change. He or she has not only acquired an inferior status, but has also developed a deviant worldview and the knowledge and skills that go with it. And perhaps equally important, he or she has developed a deviant self-image based upon the evaluations of himself or herself received through the action of others.

As a result, the labeling process has profound consequences for individuals. Our society tends to be rather unforgiving in its treatment of deviants, irrespective of what they do to reintegrate themselves into society. And since we tend to be very quick to affix labels, it is easy to see how problematic this can become for certain segments of our society.

Despite a strong sense of solidarity among police officers, a clearly defined master status, and the pervasive influence of the norms and values surrounding the police subculture, there remain several groups who are clearly stigmatized in law-enforcement circles. These include officers whose religious beliefs run counter to standards and expectations of the law-enforcement population. While religious officers are not always labeled or stigmatized, those that consider themselves born-again or who espouse a fundamentalist ideology are particularly susceptible to problems of compatibility or fit within the community. As such, even within a subculture where brotherhood and camaraderie are considered occupational advantages, even necessities, there is a type of labeling that occurs. It also seems clear that while many Christian officers are able to transcend the influences of this subculture and have a higher calling which serves as a guide for living on many issues, about half struggle with the problems discussed in this chapter. Among them are the moral dilemmas of arresting abortion demonstrators, marital infidelity, and drug and alcohol abuse. On other issues, it is clear that the responding officers have few problems squaring their ideological and professional belief systems. There is relative consensus on the use of deadly force or avoiding minor forms of corruption. On a few other issues religious dogma wins out: The use of profanity is not in line with the criteria of being a good Christian and they cannot ignore it as easily as the other indiscretions. Further, in a profession that already sets them apart from the rest of society, many officers feel as though they are outsiders within the law-enforcement community, a kind of double stigma.

The issues raised in this study are far from clear and generate more questions than answers. For now it seems safe to assert that the battle between religious ideology and professional acceptance, as well as the influence of the police subculture, remains and continues to present problems for those officers who have a strong desire to fit into one community while at the same time remaining faithful servants of a different kind.

BIBLIOGRAPHY

Alpert, G., and R. Dunham. (1992). *Policing Urban America*. Prospect Heights, Ill.: Waveland.

Becker, H., ed. (1964). *The Other Side*. New York: The Free Press.

Bittner, E. (1970). *The Function of Police in Modern Society*. Cambridge, Mass.: Delgeschlager, Gunn and Hain.

Clear, T.; B. Stout; H. Dammer; L. Kelly; P. Hardyman; and C. Shapiro. (1992). Does Involvement in Religion Help Prisoners Adjust to Prison? *National Council on Crime and Delinquency*, November, 1–7.

Cochran, J. (1994). Religiosity and Juvenile Delinquency. *Journal of Research in Crime and Delinquency* 31: 92–123.

Cochran, J. (1989). Another Look at Delinquency and Religion. *Sociological Spectrum* 9: 147–162.

Conrad, P., and J. Schneider. (1980). *Deviance and Medicalization: From Madness to Sickness*. St. Louis: C. V. Mosby.

Day, J. (1987). *Crime, Values, and Religion*. Norwood, N.J.: Ablex.

Eitzen, S. (1993). *In Conflict and Order*. Boston: Allyn and Bacon.

Gaines, L. (1993). Coping with the Job: Police Stress. In *Critical Issues in Policing: Contemporary Readings*, edited by R. Dunham and G. Alpert. Prospect Heights, Ill.: Waveland.

Garfinkel, H. (1956). Conditions of Successful Degradation Ceremonies. *American Journal of Sociology* 61: 420–424.

Goldsmith, E. (1989). *Indians in Prison*. Lincoln: University of Nebraska Press.

Johnson, B. (1987a). Religion in Prisons. *Criminal Justice Review* 12: 21–30.

Johnson, B. (1987b). Religiosity and Institutional Deviance: The Impact of Religious Variables Upon Inmate Adjustment. *Criminal Justice Review* 12: 21–30.

Kirkham, J. (1976). *Signal Zero*. New York: Ballentine.

Kornblum, W. (1994). *Sociology in a Changing World*. New York: Harcourt Brace.

Leinen, S. (1994). *Gay Cops*. New York: New York University Press.

Lemert, E. (1951). *Social Pathology*. New York: McGraw-Hill.

Livingston, J. (1992). *Crime and Criminology*. Englewood Cliffs, N.J.: Prentice Hall.

Neiderhoffer, A. (1967). *Behind the Shield: The Police in Urban Society*. Garden City, N.Y.: Doubleday.

Roberg, R., and J. Kuykendall. (1993). *Police and Society*. Belmont, Calif.: Wadsworth.

Rokeach, M.; M. Miller; and J. Snyder. (1971). The Value Gap between Police and Policed. *Journal of Social Issues* 27: 155–171.

Rubenstein, J. (1973). *City Police*. New York: Ballantine.

Siegel, B. (1995). Anthropology and the Science of Race. *Furman Studies* 38: 1–22.

Seigel, L. (1992). *Criminology*. 4th ed. New York: West.

Skolnick, J. (1994). *Justice Without Trial*. 3d ed. New York: Macmillan.

Territo, L., and H. Vetter. (1981). *Stress and Police Personnel*. Boston: Allyn and Bacon.

Vander Zanden, J. (1993). *Sociology: The Core*. New York: McGraw-Hill.

Van Maanen, J. (1973). Observations on the Making of Policemen. *Human Organization* 32: 407–418.

Westley, W. (1970). *Violence and the Police*. Cambridge: MIT Press.

II

Managing Police Organizations

.

8

Tactical Patrol Evaluation

Gary W. Cordner and Dennis Jay Kenney

Doubts about the efficacy of routine preventive patrol began to increase in the 1970s among both police practitioners and researchers. Following the Kansas City Preventive Patrol Experiment (Kelling et al. 1974), which suggested that neither eliminating nor doubling patrol coverage had any significant effect on reported crime, fear, police responses, or citizen satisfaction, many administrators began seeking alternatives to their traditional reliance on random visibility and reactive handling of calls for service. More directed methods targeting specific problems became increasingly popular. Subsequent research and innovation have advanced the knowledge of what works in policing (see Cordner and Hale 1992). Those in the field are still a long way, though, from having authoritative knowledge about which specific tactics work best against which problems in which settings.

BACKGROUND

As much as tactical patrol now seems intuitively logical and just plain common sense, its development out of the ashes of routine preventive patrol was aided immensely by research studies and accumulated police experience. For example, during a study of field interrogations (FIs) in San Diego in the 1970s, perhaps the first major test of tactical patrol, researchers found that suppressible crime increased significantly (by 39%) in areas where field interrogations were discontinued. Once the FIs were resumed, suppressible crime returned to approximately its previous level (Boydstun 1975). Quite important, this apparent FI effect was not simply a mask for an arrest effect, since arrests in the no-FI area actually increased by about 25 percent during the experimental period. In other words, the level of suppressible crime appeared to have been affected by the use or avoidance of field interrogations, independent of the number of arrests made in the area.

During the same time period, the Police Foundation tested the ability of crime analysis to support directed and traditional patrol approaches to criminal apprehension in Kansas City, Missouri (Pate, Bowers, and Parks 1976). Two directed patrol (DP) programs were tested: Location-Oriented Patrol (LOP) and Perpetrator-Oriented Patrol (POP). As the names imply, the LOP strategy directed patrol officers to surveil areas with particularly high crime rates; POP officers, on the other hand, surveilled a selected group of suspected offenders. Both strategies were intended to increase arrests of suspects in the act of committing crimes, especially robberies and burglaries. A special Criminal Information Center (CIC) was created within the police department to develop and disseminate suspect information intended to guide the efforts of both the special units and a selected group of regular patrol officers.

When the three groups (LOP, POP, and regular patrol) were assessed, the evaluators concluded that the specialized units had outperformed the regular patrol officers on almost all comparisons. Results varied between LOP and POP, however. LOP officers were more efficient in terms of hours spent per arrest, they had a greater number of robbery arrests as a percentage of their arrest total, and they had more charges filed for prosecution per arrest. POP officers had a greater percentage of arrests resulting from officer-initiated activities, they arrested suspects with more extensive felony records, and they produced more information for CIC use and dissemination. POP officers also received fewer citizen complaints than their LOP counterparts. Considering all comparisons collectively, the Kansas City staff concluded that, in terms of apprehending suspects, the location-oriented strategy was slightly superior to the perpetrator-oriented strategy and substantially better than traditional patrol. The staff also found that providing CIC information to the comparison group of regular officers significantly increased their arrest rates as well.

In the late 1970s, Pontiac, Michigan, experimented with directed patrol as part of the federally funded Integrated Criminal Apprehension Program (Cordner 1981). Over a period of nearly eighteen months, directed patrol responsibilities were shifted from all patrol personnel to a special directed patrol unit, and then back to all personnel. The study concluded that target crimes could be decreased through the use of directed patrol based on crime analysis. Interestingly, the most significant impact was achieved during the initial time period, when directed patrol assignments were widely distributed among all patrol officers. Overly large investments of time in limited areas, however, appeared to offer no additional benefits, perhaps because of the relatively limited number of "opportunities" in any particular target area for aggressive patrol efforts.

Calling them "crackdowns," Sherman (1990) noted that efforts to direct patrol resources to specific problems became quite widespread during the 1980s. Drunk driving, public drug markets, streetwalking prostitutes, and even illegal parking each became targets for various directed patrol responses in programs throughout the country. In the 1990s, drug problems have remained a popular target of directed patrol activity (see Weisburd and Green 1995); and in addition, gun-related crime has been increasingly targeted (see Sherman, Shaw, and Rogan 1995). Still, Sherman notes that some observers remain skeptical about whether these tactical applications of patrol have any real effects; they argue that lasting impacts, especially deterrence, have not yet been demonstrated.

Sherman goes on to point out that the debates about tactical patrol fail to make an important distinction among the different kinds of deterrent effects possible. Specifically, most planners fail to separate the initial deterrence that might be achieved once a tactical operation is undertaken from the possible residual deterrence that may remain following its completion. In addition, the extent to which such impacts decay during or after the effort is seldom considered (Sherman 1990, 2). Determining these differential effects, he argues, might suggest new ways of maximizing tactical patrol's effectiveness. An example might help to explain these varying forms of deterrence.

In the 1987 Minneapolis Repeat Call Address Policing (RECAP) Experiment, patrol officers were given directed assignments that called for problem solving at locations that had been identified as requiring frequent police services. The idea was to solve the problems generating the repeat calls, thereby reducing the volume of activity at those addresses. The officers involved in the project were formed into special teams. Each team participated in the repeat call analysis for its location, in the design of tactics for reducing the volume of calls, and then in the implementation of the tactics. After six months, the RECAP officers had considerable successes to show—calls for service at their experimental addresses were reduced significantly. However, during the second six months officers increasingly found their targets resistant to further improvement. In fact, by the fourth quarter of the project all of the earlier results had disappeared.

To Sherman, the obvious conclusion was that an operational policy of short-term targeting might offer the best investment of police resources. Instead of trying to maintain a tactical response over a long period of time, as many departments do, police might "use their resources more effectively if crackdowns are seen as short-term efforts frequently shifted from area to area or problem to problem. By constantly changing crackdown targets, police may reduce crime more through residual deterrence than through initial deterrence. And by limiting the time period devoted to each target, police might also avoid wasting scarce resources on a decaying initial deterrent effect" (Sherman 1990, 3).

The Concept of Tactical Patrol

Obviously, any number of variations of tactical patrol are possible. Strategies focused on crime prevention might include directed assignments requiring officers to conduct security surveys, recommend housing repairs and self-protection steps, and encourage and work with citizen groups. Other programs focus more on crime deterrence. As suggested, short-term tactics intended to raise the perception of risk might be most effective (and efficient). Included might be saturation patrolling, field interrogations, increased traffic enforcement, and other "aggressive" patrol procedures causing increased or high visibility. Still other strategies might concentrate on criminal apprehensions by using covert and stakeout activities designed not only to deter but also to catch offenders while they are committing crimes. Regardless, in each instance virtually all tactical or directed patrol projects share four common characteristics (Warren, Forst, and Estrella 1979):

1. They are proactive and aggressive.
2. Officers use noncommitted time to engage in purposeful activity.
3. Officers have specific instructions directing their activities.
4. These instructions ("directions") are based on thorough analyses of crime data.

Aside from the support it receives from recent research, tactical patrol is attractive to police managers for at least two additional reasons. One is its directed nature; it is seemingly the very opposite of random patrol, the approach so often criticized for not working. The other is that the strategy is neither officer- nor community-directed, but rather information- and management-directed. Traditionally, calls for service have dictated the use of a substantial portion of patrol resources, and the use of the rest of patrol officer time has been left to individual discretion. Tactical patrol strategies are a means for police managers to regain some control over their most significant resource, patrol officers' time and activities. Careful implementation and evaluation are essential, though, if tactical patrol's goals are to be reached and its potential benefits realized.

Implementing the Concept

As each agency designs its own tactical patrol system, managers have two basic models they can follow. First, and probably most common, is a *geographically focused* approach, which tries to increase police presence in a specific area. Much like the LOP strategy in Kansas City, this approach requires agencies to first identify through analysis the areas experiencing particular problems of police interest. Of course, these may include areas with crime or accident problems, with frequent demands for police services, with order-maintenance problems, or where fear is especially high. The areas chosen could be as small as a single address or as large as a park, a section of road or highway, several square blocks, or even a patrol beat or sector. Once assigned, the officers responsible for these areas—either routinely or as part of some special unit—then implement tactics selected to match the concerns identified.

With an *offense-* or *event-specific* approach, the agency seeks to change how it responds to some specific type of crime or incident, regardless of where it may be occurring. Examples might include domestic abuse, traffic violations, or parking problems. Officers are provided with pattern and trend data and instructions to make arrests, issue tickets, or take other appropriate actions wherever the problem is encountered. Similarly, special units may be formed to help analyze a specific problem, say, robbery or burglary. The unit's officers may then conduct tactical operations based on that analysis. Reacting to public alarm, the police in Savannah, Georgia, for example, recently used this approach in response to a growing citywide problem of black-on-black crimes. Simultaneously, they implemented geographically focused efforts to address street robberies that analysis showed were occurring with regularity in the city's popular historic district.

An additional implementation question confronting the manager concerns whether tactical assignments should be given to routine or to specialized patrol units. In general, if the assigned tactic requires only short periods of dedicated time, it may be preferable to use regular patrol units. Field interrogations, vehicle checks, security surveys, and saturation patrols can usually be conducted by regular officers without serious disruptions to their ability to handle other calls for service. As the time needed to complete the directed activity increases, however, so does the desirability of developing specialized patrol capabilities. This would be a virtual necessity whenever the tactical assignment required an officer's full-time commitment, such as for covert surveillance, decoy operations, and stakeouts. Fearing conflicts in communication and grumbling about elite units, some departments have preferred to create this capacity by relieving regular patrol officers for a single tour of duty on special assignment. Others, however, have chosen to establish specialized units with their own structure, training, and deployment (Gay, Schell, and Schack 1977).

Beyond these basic options (geographic versus offense focus, regular patrol versus special unit) are a number of mundane but important implementation considerations. One concerns participation: It is vital that officers and supervisors who are expected to implement tactical patrol assignments be given every opportunity to participate in designing those assignments. Such involvement is likely to lead to better-designed tactics, and it will certainly lead to greater commitment to implementing them.

Another crucial consideration relates to information. It is utterly impossible to effectively design and target tactical patrols without accurate and up-to-date information on crimes, calls for service, and other problems. Departments that lack solid crime-analysis and operations-analysis capabilities may need to consider upgrading their analytical capabilities as a prerequisite to implementing full-fledged tactical patrol systems.

Finally, implementing any program, including tactical patrol, requires that attention be paid to such basic management considerations as resources, communication, authority, responsibility, and accountability. Depending on the nature of the tactical patrol program, personnel reassignments may be necessary, new policies and procedures may be demanded, and training may be required. Personnel throughout the organization should be notified of the new program. Systems should be put in place to ensure adequate supervision and reporting. Assuming that tactical patrol is a good idea, attention to implementation helps guarantee that the idea becomes reality.

EVALUATION

It is difficult, if not impossible, for a police department to know whether its use of tactical patrol is successful without a systematic evaluation. Unless an evaluation is conducted, how will the department know whether the program was implemented as intended, what individual tactics were implemented, and whether the program's goals were achieved? To what extent was success or failure the result of factors other than the tactical patrol project? To answer these questions, a two-stage approach to evaluation is recommended: first, a *process evaluation* to capture the early development and actual implementation of the program and tactics, and second, an *impact evaluation* designed to measure the program's effects and the extent of goal attainment.

Process Evaluation

An important aspect of any evaluation is documentation and analysis of program development and implementation. This process evaluation is directed at providing qualitative and quantitative measures of the program, its operation, and its immediate outputs. Assessments are made regarding whether services are provided in the manner the program plan specifies and whether expected program outputs are actually produced. The process evaluation is also necessary for appropriate interpretation of impact-evaluation data. Detailed knowledge about the intervention as it actually took place is invaluable for determining what worked and what did not. A thorough process evaluation should address the following areas:

1. The environment within which the program is designed and implemented.
2. The process by which the program is designed and implemented.
3. The continuous measurement of the program's operation over time to ensure compliance and to document any changes that occur.
4. The identification and description of intervening events that may affect implementation and program outcomes.

The process phase of the project's evaluation should begin as soon as the tactical patrol project gets under way (if not sooner, during the planning phase) and should continue until the tactical operations are completely in place. To complete the process study, two primary sources of data should be used.

The first includes official police, city, and census data. What crime and call-for-service patterns exist throughout the city and in the areas where the program is to focus? Are trends identifiable and, if so, are geographic patterns present? Once an area has been selected for tactical patrol, the ethnic and economic conditions, residents' ages, and composition of the buildings—residential or commercial, occupied or unoccupied—should be noted. Such data should be readily available and are essential if experimental areas are to be selected, program outcomes are to be generalized to other areas, and effective tactics are to be identified.

A second source of data should include observations of and interviews with program participants. The observations should begin with early developmental work and continue throughout the evaluation. Focusing on major planning and tactical activities, observers should note participation and interactions at each project stage. Does the process appear to go smoothly, or are relations and communications difficult and strained? Do participants work together to identify a range of tactical options, or do the organization's hierarchy and traditional methods assert themselves? These observations should focus on process as well as content, with observers being careful to note the decisions and events that contribute to program planning and implementation.

To complement observational data, interviews that focus on process issues should be conducted with key participants. The reactions of officers, staff, and supervisors to the program's development, the degree of participation, the tactics selected, and the difficulties in completing tactical assignments should all be noted and analyzed. Any problems that occur and the solutions attempted or suggested should be described. While the format for observations should probably remain open-ended so that observers are not limited in their focus, the protocol for interviews should be far more structured to ensure consistency and validity.

Impact Evaluation

To evaluate a program's impacts (results), any of four basic evaluation designs is appropriate. Each can produce useful information about a patrol tactic's effectiveness, but the authoritativeness of that information is greater for some designs than for others. Designs that "track" effects over extended periods (*time-series* designs) are generally superior to those that simply compare before and after periods (*pre–post* designs). *Comparison-group* designs are superior to those that lack any basis for comparison. Designs that use true control groups (*experimental* designs) are better.

There is no reason why evaluations of tactical patrol should not employ, at a minimum, pre–post designs, and preferably, longer time-series analysis and some kind of comparison or control groups. This is because data on the primary "pre" conditions of interest, reported crimes and arrests, are routinely gathered by police departments and are readily available. Even if the decision to evaluate a tactical patrol program is not made until after the program has started, it should be relatively easy to go back to the records and gather crime and arrest data for the period before the program started. Moreover, when a program targets a particular area, historical data can usually be gathered for both the targeted area and comparison areas.

Regardless of which evaluation designs are used to investigate tactical patrol's impact, a number of fundamental procedures should be followed. The most important of these are the following:

1. Careful specification of hypothesized effects.
2. Identification of plausible unintended effects.
3. Operationalized measures of effects.
4. Determination of appropriate time periods.
5. Monitoring of program implementation.

6. Systematic collection of data.
7. Analysis of data.
8. Replication.

Hypothesized Effects. Specification of hypothesized effects simply calls for a careful statement of the program's expected effects. In other words, if the program is correctly implemented, what should happen? The hypothesized effects are sometimes singular and direct, as in "saturation patrol will decrease street robberies." In other instances, there may be multiple expected effects, as in "saturation patrol will increase arrests, decrease street robberies, and decrease citizen fear," or the expected effects may occur in stages, as in "saturation patrol will increase car stops and field interrogations, which will decrease street robberies." Regardless of the simplicity or complexity of the expected effects, it is important to think them through and spell them out early in the evaluation.

Unintended Effects. Thinking about hypothesized effects should naturally lead to thinking about unintended effects. Most programs have potential dangers or costs associated with them. These should be identified so that the evaluation can determine whether they occur. An example of an unintended effect might be "saturation patrol will increase car stops and field interrogations, which will negatively affect citizens' attitudes toward the police." Other examples might be "saturation patrol will simply displace street robberies to adjoining areas," or "saturation patrol will result in less activity per officer (less productivity) and more officer boredom because of the extreme concentration of officers in small areas."

Operationalization. Spelling out the program, its hypothesized effects, and its plausible unintended effects pretty well identifies what will have to be measured in the evaluation. It is important, though, to explicitly operationalize these measures, to specify exactly what will be measured and how. For example, it would certainly be necessary to define "street robberies" to ensure consistent, reliable measurement. It would be even more critical to carefully operationalize such conditions as "fear of crime" and "attitudes toward police," since they are such vague and multidimensional concepts.

Time Periods. Determining appropriate time periods is essential, both to facilitate a meaningful evaluation and in terms of economy. Judgment must be used for such questions as "How long should the program be run in order to give it a fair opportunity to display its effects?" and "How far back in time should we go in collecting data to be sure that we have a good picture of things before the program's implementation?" Ideal time periods sometimes must be shortened for practical reasons, since data collection is costly and determinations of program success must sometimes be made sooner than evaluators would prefer.

Monitoring. Monitoring program implementation, which goes hand in hand with process evaluation, is required for several reasons. If difficulties are encountered in implementation, monitoring may provide the feedback that enables program managers to get things back on track. In situations where the program is never correctly implemented, evaluators cannot interpret results unless they are aware of what was and was not implemented. Monitoring in these situations may also lead to future improvements in program management that reduce such implementation failures.

Data Collection. The purpose of systematic data collection is simply to collect information on program implementation and on hypothesized and unintended effects. For tactical patrol, this typically involves such endeavors as gathering official records data on crimes and arrests and gathering officer activity information from dispatch records or individual activity reports. As with any kind of data collection, careful attention must be directed toward quality control so that the information collected is as accurate as possible. If more than one person is involved in data collection, pains must be taken to ensure that everyone follows the same rules and definitions. Similarly, if data collection extends over a long period of time it is important to ensure that the same rules and definitions are applied at the end as were used in the beginning.

A word about sampling is also in order. When evaluating tactical patrol, official records data on crimes, arrests, and other activities are of principal concern, and sampling is not usually required. That is, the evaluation will generally be based on information about *all* the reported crimes, arrests, and so on in the target area and in any control or comparison areas during the appropriate time periods. Occasionally, though, it may be necessary to measure such conditions as fear of crime or citizen satisfaction, in which case sampling of community residents probably will be required (unless the targeted area is so small that every resident can be surveyed). If sampling must be used, two considerations are paramount: (1) determining the size of the sample and (2) choosing the sample in such a way that everyone in the population group has an equal chance of being selected. Since sampling will not usually be necessary when evaluating tactical patrol, this chapter will not go into great detail on the subject, but the reader is advised to seek additional information if sampling becomes an issue in an evaluation.

Data Analysis. Data analysis involves manipulating of collected data to derive results and conclusions. Data analysis related to program implementation should produce a description of the program as implemented. Analysis related to hypothesized and unintended effects should provide clear information on what happened. If the research design was strong enough, analysis may be able to go beyond simply what happened and offer convincing explanations for why it happened. In particular, the analysis should present evidence that helps determine whether the program had its hypothesized and/or unintended effects.

In some situations, it may be useful to determine whether differences in effects between target and control groups are statistically significant. Statistical techniques such as t-tests and analysis of variance can be used to investigate whether observed differences are likely to have occurred merely by chance, or whether, instead, they are probably due to the program. Instructions on using these techniques can be found in any elementary statistics book. In most cases of tactical patrol evaluation, however, the statistical significance of a difference between target and control groups will be less important than its substantive significance (whether the program effect in the target area is large enough to really matter, and whether it represents enough benefit to outweigh the program's costs). These are practical judgments best left to police executives rather than to program evaluators or statisticians.

Replication. No matter how well an evaluation is conducted, no matter how strong the design, doubts about conclusions will linger at least until the study can be replicated. Replication is the surest hedge against the possibility that the documented effects of any particular program were a fluke, a chance occurrence, a lucky break, the result of unobserved intervening factors, limited strictly to one place, or limited to but one moment in time. Once a tactical patrol program has been found to have consistent effects in several applications, though, doubts can be allayed and the strategy can be confidently deployed with predictable results.

A Summary of the Issues

Any evaluation of tactical patrol should include a process evaluation that documents the setting in which the program was implemented, the program's design and implementation (including design flaws and implementation problems), any variations in the program during the study, and any intervening events that must be considered when interpreting the results of the impact evaluation. Beyond the process, however, the actual impact of the patrol effort should be determined as well. For that, four basic evaluation designs are available: experimental, comparison group, time-series, and simple pre–post designs. It should be noted that these four designs are not necessarily mutually exclusive—an experimental study can use extended time-series data, for example. A few general principles should guide the choice of designs for evaluating the impact of tactical patrol programs:

1. Always use at least a pre–post design.
2. Use extended time series data (rather than just before or after data) whenever possible.
3. Use comparison or control groups whenever possible.
4. Use randomization to select program and control groups whenever possible.
5. Regardless of design, give careful attention to hypothesized and unintended effects, measurement, time periods, implementation monitoring, data collection, and data analysis.
6. Whenever possible, replicate.

Carefully conducted process and impact evaluations of tactical patrol can produce information of tremendous value for police administrators and, ultimately, for society. As we learn more about the effects of different patrol tactics on various problems in various settings, we will be able to make better decisions that lead to enhanced public safety and security.

EXPERIMENTAL EVALUATION OF TACTICAL PATROL

The distinguishing feature of an experimental design is random assignment. The use of an experimental design generally puts the evaluator in the best position, if an effect is observed, to argue that it is neither a chance effect nor a result of bias, but rather a true program effect. This is one of the basic aims of evaluation design, to be able to rule out as many alternative explanations as possible and to be able to attribute observed effects, if any, to the program itself.

While the prospect of randomization may seem impractical or even dangerous in policing, it is, at times, often quite feasible. In the Kansas City Preventive Patrol Experiment, randomization was used to decide which of the fifteen patrol beats in the study got assigned to the proactive, control, and reactive categories. In the Minneapolis Domestic Violence Experiment, random chance determined whether those who had allegedly committed misdemeanor spousal assaults were arrested, counseled, or required to leave the premises.

Randomization makes one huge contribution to an evaluation: It ensures that mere chance determines who (or what neighborhood) receives the program and who, instead, serves as the control group. Without randomization, there is a greater likelihood that those who got the program were systematically different to begin with from those who did not get the program, or even worse, that those who got the program were in fact selected because they were likely to benefit from it. If this kind of selection bias is present at the outset, it becomes extremely difficult to later distinguish between the program's true effects and the confounding effects introduced through the biased assignment of subjects to groups.

It is highly unlikely, of course, that we would ever really allocate tactical patrols purely on the basis of random chance. After all, tactical patrols are almost always meant to be targeted against a particular problem; random assignment would seem more in tune with random patrol than with tactical patrol. But there is a more rational approach to random assignment that makes sense and might sometimes be feasible. That approach is to select an overabundance of candidate problems for targeting, and then to randomly decide which ones actually get targeted and which ones serve as controls for comparison.

For example, if a tactical patrol unit was to be assigned to work on a street-robbery problem, we could first identify the two locations with the most serious problem and then flip a coin to decide which one got the unit's attention. Similarly, if we had identified four areas with substantial rates of thefts from autos, we could randomly choose two to receive directed patrols and two to serve as control groups. Or, if we wanted to test the effects of different levels of field interrogation activity, we could select six beats and then randomly assign two each to no-FI, normal-FI, and high-FI groups.

The practical, ethical, and political issues involved in randomization must always be considered, but they are often manageable. The three examples cited share several characteristics that make randomization supportable: (1) Because of scarce resources, the "treatments" (tactical unit, directed patrol, high-FI) cannot be offered to everyone anyway, (2) those chosen to receive or not receive the treatments are equally deserving, (3) there is little or no authoritative evidence that "proves" that the treatments are beneficial (or harmful) to those who receive them, and (4) the information that could result from a randomized study would be of substantial value. Whenever these conditions are met, one should consider using randomization in the evaluation design.

Whenever randomization is used, though, it is wise to carefully monitor relevant indicators (such as reported crime) in treatment and control areas. In this way, any unexpected harmful effects of the treatment or its absence can be detected quickly, enabling informed decisions to be made and averting any extended inequitable conditions caused by the evaluation design. On occasion it may be necessary to call a halt to a study, even though the problem detected through monitoring (such as rapidly increasing crime in a control area) may be caused by an external factor not connected to the program being evaluated. The truth is that field experiments are difficult to conduct, and they are sometimes contaminated by unforeseeable changes in the community.

An Illustration: Directed Patrol

Suppose we wanted to evaluate the effects of directed patrol using an experimental design. To start, we could pick two areas suffering from roughly the same problem, say, thefts from autos, at roughly the same rate. We could then flip a coin to decide which would get the directed patrol treatment (the DP area) and which would serve as the control group (the no-DP area). Our principal hypothesis would simply be that target thefts will decline in the DP area but not in the no-DP area. Two plausible unintended effects might be that target thefts will increase in areas surrounding the DP area (spatial displacement), or that other property crimes will increase in the DP area (displacement to other crimes).

The hypothesis and the plausible unintended effects point to several conditions that would need to be measured: target thefts in both the DP and no-DP areas, target thefts in areas surrounding the DP area, and other property crimes in the study areas. These would need further definition. For example, "target thefts" should probably be defined as any thefts from autos or attempted thefts from autos (the latter is often a judgment call between attempted theft and vandalism; it would be important to use consistent rules in making this judgment). "Surrounding areas" would have to be defined in a way that made sense given the jurisdiction's particular geography. "Other property crimes" could be defined to include robberies, burglaries, thefts of autos, and all other thefts (with the possible exception of frauds and forgeries, if these were deemed unlikely to be taken up by those displaced from thefts from autos).

The determination of appropriate time periods is an important decision that should be based on information about the problem being addressed and the program being implemented. In this case, for purposes of discussion we might determine that target thefts in the study areas had been at a high level for three weeks, and that two weeks of directed patrol in the DP area ought to be sufficient to affect the problem. Thus, we would decide on a three-week "before" period and a two-week "during" period; in addition, we might decide on a ten-week "after" period throughout which we would continue to measure target thefts and other property crimes to see whether the effects, if any, persisted after directed patrol was withdrawn.

Because of these unequal time periods, it would be important to compute and use daily or weekly averages of target thefts and other property crimes for the before, during, and after periods. Otherwise, we would almost certainly find fewer target thefts in the two-week during period than in the longer before and after periods, and we might be led to erroneous conclusions.

While directed patrol was being carried out in the DP area and not in the no-DP area, it would be necessary to monitor program implementation. Through some means, we would need to determine that directed patrols actually were being carried out in the DP area, and that no such directed patrols were being surreptitiously or accidentally applied in the no-DP area. This could be accomplished through various means, including supervision, formal reporting, and review of dispatch-center data.

The amount of directed patrol devoted to the project should be measured as well. Ultimately, questions will arise over how much directed patrol is enough to achieve an effect: three hours a day, one hour, every other day? Immediate outputs should also be measured, such as arrests, tickets, car stops, and FIs. This is important in determining whether directed patrol has a relatively diffuse effect achieved primarily through visibility, or a more specific effect accomplished via aggressive patrol tactics.

Data gathering in this illustration would not be particularly difficult or burdensome. Reported crime data on target thefts and other property crimes for the DP, no-DP, and surrounding areas would be collected from routine department sources. Data on program implementation could also be collected from routine sources (such as officer activity sheets or communications logs), or from special directed patrol assignment forms. Since emergencies often arise in policing and interfere with planned directed activities, it would be very important to document actual directed patrol efforts rather than planned efforts.

The principal form of analysis would be simple comparison of averages and percentage changes. A cautionary note is appropriate, however, since the numbers do not always come out clearly. Interpreting results and drawing honest conclusions can be quite difficult; frequently, in fact, the results are unavoidably inconclusive. With an experimental design, though, you put yourself in the best possible position to identify positive program effects if they are there.

Conducting an Experimental Evaluation

This section outlines step-by-step instructions for conducting a basic experimental evaluation of a tactical patrol program. The instructions apply specifically to a tactical patrol program applied in one targeted area with a second area serving as a control. The same approach could be followed, with only modest adjustments, if multiple targeted areas and/or multiple control areas were to be used.

1. Carefully specify the form of tactical patrol (directed, saturation, etc.) to be used. Make any personnel assignments, develop any written

guidelines, and provide any training necessary to implement the tactical patrol.

2. Begin the process evaluation by gathering information, making observations, and conducting interviews in order to describe the program environment, program development, program operations, and intervening events.

3. Select two areas with the same kind and magnitude of problem that will be addressed by the tactical patrol. These two areas should be as similar as possible in other respects as well.

4. Randomly choose one of the two areas to receive the tactical patrol program and one to serve as control. This can be done by flipping a coin, rolling dice, picking a number out of a hat, or using any other random-chance process.

5. Carefully specify the program-specific hypothesized effects of the tactical patrol in the targeted area. These should be stated as clearly and as simply as possible.

6. Specify any important and plausible unintended effects of the program to be implemented. These should also be stated clearly and simply.

7. Develop and define operational measures of program implementation, hypothesized effects, and unintended effects. Decide exactly what you are going to measure to describe the program as implemented and what happened as a result of the program.

8. Determine what time periods will be used. This may involve two time periods (before and after), three time periods (before, during, and after), or more extended time-series periods. Make sure the time periods are sufficiently long to give the tactical patrol program a chance to show its effects.

9. If any of the operational measures require baseline data collection before program implementation (such as surveys of citizens, surveys of officer attitudes, or observations of officer behavior), gather the baseline data.

10. Implement the tactical program in the targeted area.

11. Monitor the implementation of the program in the targeted area and the maintenance of normal conditions in the control area.

12. Begin data collection if this did not precede program implementation. If extreme conditions develop in the targeted or control areas, consider ending the experiment.

13. Continue data collection throughout the program implementation and any appropriate after periods.

14. Conduct data analysis. Describe the program as implemented and specify any changes in measures of hypothesized and unintended effects. Use averages, percentages, statistical comparisons, and graphical presentations as appropriate to show any changes. Consider whether changes can be attributed to the program and whether they are substantial enough for the program to be judged a success or failure.

15. Prepare any written reports required. At a minimum, make a permanent record of the experiment and its results. Consider sharing your findings with other police professionals.

16. Look for opportunities to replicate the program and its evaluation. Replications should include similar programs implemented in similar settings. Exact duplication is never possible, but replication does require a fair degree of similarity (otherwise, it is not a replication, it is a new study). Take advantage of any such opportunities, since replication is the key to developing confidence in evaluation findings.

COMPARISON-GROUP EVALUATION OF TACTICAL PATROL

The directed patrol experiment illustrated included the use of surrounding areas to measure possible displacement effects. Those surrounding areas exemplified one type of comparison group, selected solely on the basis of geographic proximity. Ideally, in a comparison-group design (which does not have the benefit of a true control group) comparison groups can be found that are comparable in many other respects besides just proximity to the group receiving the treatment.

Suppose, in the thefts from autos illustration, randomization was not possible—instead, an area had already been selected to receive directed patrol. In that situation, it would make sense to seek out one or two other areas suffering from a similar problem. If such areas could be identified, they could serve as comparison groups. The more comparable the target and comparison areas, the more meaningful the eventual results. No matter how comparable the areas, however, two threats to validity that would be hard to dispel would be (1) the possibility that the target area was chosen because it was particularly amenable to directed patrol, or (2) that the problem in the area was about to decline naturally. Basically, without randomization the various forms of selection bias are difficult to dismiss.

Nevertheless, in the absence of a randomized control group, a comparison group is better than nothing, and several comparison groups are often better than one (assuming they are all in fact comparable). Some highly respected police evaluation studies have used comparison-group designs and produced worthwhile information.

An Illustration: Field Interrogations

As noted, during the 1970s a field-interrogation study was conducted in San Diego using three patrol beats selected for their comparability. These beats were located in the same part of the city (although they were not adjacent), and they were deemed comparable on a host of crime and demographic measures. For a nine-month period the levels of FI activity were manipulated: The no-FI beat had all FI activity eliminated, the control beat retained a normal level of FI activity (about twenty per month), and the special-FI beat received extra FI activity (almost fifty per month).

In every respect except random assignment of these beats to control and treatment groups, the San Diego study adhered to the design characteristics outlined. Hypothesized and unintended effects were carefully defined and measured, relevant time periods were specified, implementation was monitored, and data were systematically collected and analyzed. The overall results were as follows:

Part 1 Suppressible Crimes (Monthly Averages)

	Before	During	After
Control	40.9	42.9	38.6
Special-FI	57.7	60.2	56.6
No-FI	63.1	83.2	63.2

As long as we can assume that the three beats really were comparable, the conclusions are inescapable that (1) eliminating FI activity for nine months in the no-FI area led to a substantial increase in Part 1 suppressible crimes, (2) resuming FI activity in the no-FI area returned suppressible crime to its previous normal level, and (3) vastly increasing FI activity in the special-FI area for nine months had little or no effect on suppressible crime. But can we assume comparability? The no-FI beat had over 50 percent more Part 1 suppressible crime to start with than the control beat—maybe crime increased when FIs were eliminated because it was a "rough" beat. Maybe if FIs had been eliminated from the quieter control beat instead, nobody would have noticed. Still, the no-FI beat's experience differed dramatically from the special-FI beat's, despite the fact that these beats had similar levels of suppressible crime before the study began. So something must have happened. The question of comparability makes interpreting the results of the study more uncertain, yet using the comparison groups does strengthen our judgment that differing levels of FI activity had an effect on suppressible crime.

The principal unintended effect of concern in the San Diego study related to the possibility that increased FI activity would negatively affect police–community relations. The evaluators measured the number of FI-related citizen complaints coming from the three beats, and found no differences among the beats nor any increases due to the additional FI activity in the special-FI beat. They also conducted before and after community surveys in the three beats and found no negative effects on attitudes toward the police. Thus, they were able to rule out, in their case at least, the most worrisome of the plausible unintended effects of extensive use of field interrogations.

Conducting a Comparison-Group Evaluation

This section outlines step-by-step instructions for conducting a basic comparison-group evaluation of a tactical patrol program. The instructions apply specifically to a tactical patrol program applied in an already targeted area, with a second area chosen subsequently to serve as a comparison group. The same approach could be followed, with only modest adjustments, if multiple targeted areas and/or multiple comparison areas were to be used.

1. Carefully specify the form of tactical patrol (directed, saturation, etc.) to be used. Make any personnel assignments, develop any written guidelines, and provide any training necessary to implement the tactical patrol.

2. Begin the process evaluation by gathering information, making observations, and conducting interviews in order to describe the program environment, program development, program operations, and intervening events.

3. Identify as many comparison areas as possible with approximately the same kind and magnitude of problem as that to be addressed in the targeted area.

4. Carefully choose one comparison area that is most similar to the targeted area in other important respects, such as geography, demographics, and so on.

5. Carefully specify the program-specific hypothesized effects of the tactical patrol in the targeted area. These should be stated as clearly and as simply as possible.

6. Specify any important and plausible unintended effects of the program to be implemented. These should also be stated clearly and simply.

7. Develop and define operational measures of program implementation, hypothesized effects, and unintended effects. Decide exactly what you are going to measure to describe the program as implemented and what happened as a result of the program.

8. Determine what time periods will be used. This may involve two time periods (before and after), three time periods (before, during, and after), or more extended time-series periods. Make sure the time periods are sufficiently long to give the tactical patrol program a chance to show its effects.

9. If any of the operational measures require baseline data collection before program implementation (such as surveys of citizens, surveys of officer attitudes, or observations of officer behavior), gather the baseline data.

10. Implement the tactical program in the targeted area.

11. Monitor the implementation of the program in the targeted area and the maintenance of normal conditions in the comparison area.

12. Begin data collection if this did not precede program implementation. If extreme conditions develop in the targeted or comparison areas, consider ending the program or expanding it to the comparison area, as appropriate.

13. Continue data collection throughout the program implementation and any appropriate after periods.

14. Conduct data analysis. Describe the program as implemented and specify any changes in measures of hypothesized and unintended effects. Use averages, percentages, statistical comparisons, and graphical presentations as appropriate to show any changes. Consider whether changes can be attributed to the program and whether they are substantial enough for the program to be judged a success or failure.

15. Prepare any written reports required. At a minimum, make a permanent record of the evaluation and its results. Consider sharing your findings with other police professionals.

16. Look for opportunities to replicate the program and its evaluation. Replications should include similar programs implemented in similar settings. Exact duplication is never possible, but replication does require a fair degree of similarity (otherwise, it is not a replication, it is a new study). Take advantage of any such opportunities, since replication is the key to developing confidence in evaluation findings.

TIME-SERIES EVALUATION OF TACTICAL PATROL

Both of the illustrations—directed patrol (experimental evaluation) and field interrogation (comparison-group evaluation)—provided in the previous two sections relied on data representing three time periods: before, during, and after. The use of three time periods is fairly typical, often quite satisfactory, and generally preferable to a simple pre–post design that uses only two time periods. In some situations, though, it makes sense to gather and analyze information representing a larger number of time periods. Using such a time-series design is particularly helpful when the dependent variable (the condition the program hopes to affect) has trends or cycles in it. With time-series data, one can attempt to identify such trends and then determine whether the program interrupted the pattern of the dependent condition.

Time-series designs are particularly feasible for evaluating tactical patrol programs because much of the data of interest (reported crimes, arrests, calls for service, etc.) should be routinely available for extended periods before program implementation. Police departments with good computer-aided dispatching (CAD) and automated records systems should be able to produce at least the previous year's worth of weekly or monthly data for a targeted area. Even departments restricted to manual systems should have the paper records to similarly recreate time-series data for a targeted area.

Some conditions of interest for tactical patrol evaluation will not usually be susceptible to time-series analysis, however. In the San Diego FI study, for example, it might have been interesting to look at repeated measurements of citizen satisfaction with the police department in the three study beats. Since such data are not routinely collected, though, they would not be available for months or years back in time. Two measurements (before and after) are generally all that is feasible for conditions such as citizen satisfaction that are not subjected to routine data collection.

A time-series design could have been used in our directed patrol experiment discussed earlier. Instead of comparing average weekly target thefts in the before, during, and after periods, one could have charted the actual number of target thefts by week. A graph of the fifteen-week period (three weeks before implementing directed patrol, two weeks during, and ten weeks after) would presumably have shown that target thefts dropped substantially when directed patrol was begun and remained at a lower level throughout the after period. Similar graphs for the no-DP area and the three surrounding areas would probably have shown overall "flatter" lines throughout the fifteen-week period, though weekly fluctuations would certainly have been seen in all five areas (including the DP area). The graphs might also have revealed whether target thefts were already declining in the DP area when directed patrol was implemented, for example, or whether target thefts had begun to rise again in the DP area toward the end of the after period. These kinds of specific observations can be shrouded when data are averaged over long periods, but are sometimes quite apparent when time-series analysis is used.

An Illustration: Field Interrogations

For another illustration, one can look at some time-series data for the San Diego field-interrogation study discussed earlier. Instead of presenting average monthly Part 1 suppressible crime data, the actual number of Part 1 suppressible crimes for the twenty-one-month study period (seven months before, nine months during, and five months after) could have been used. In that case, the results would show that the no-FI beat experienced a higher level of Part 1 suppressible crime in the during period, when FIs were eliminated, than in either the before or after periods. It would appear that it took two or three months without FIs for this effect to set in, after which suppressible crime stayed at a high level for the six months until FIs were resumed.

The special-FI beat, in which the number of FIs was increased, had a more surprising experience, however. For the first six months of the during period, suppressible crime stayed at about the same levels despite the additional FI activity. Crime in the special-FI beat increased substantially in the last three months of the during period, however, to levels almost identical to those in the no-FI beat. Whether this rise in crime was caused by some external factors operating in the special-FI beat or by a diminishing return from the extra levels of FI activity in the beat cannot be determined from the data.

The fact that the amount of monthly suppressible crime in the control beat was more consistent offered further credence to the possibility that it was the elimination of FIs in the no-FI beat that caused that beat's increase in crime in the during period. When, four months into the during period, suppressible crime really jumped up in the no-FI beat in December 1973 and stayed very high in January 1974, crime levels stayed normal in both the control and special-FI beats. Then, for the next five months, while suppressible crime stayed high in the no-FI beat and crime in the special-FI beat also increased, still the line for the control beat stayed quite flat.

Conducting a Time-Series Evaluation

This section outlines step-by-step instructions for conducting a basic time-series evaluation of a tactical patrol program. The instructions apply specifically to a situation in which there is no comparison or control group. The same approach could be followed, with only modest adjustments, if time-series data were also available for one or more comparison or control groups.

1. Carefully specify the form of tactical patrol (directed, saturation, etc.) to be used. Make any personnel assignments, develop any written guidelines, and provide any training necessary to implement the tactical patrol.
2. Begin the process evaluation by gathering information, making observations, and conducting interviews in order to describe the program environment, program development, program operations, and intervening events.
3. Carefully specify the program-specific hypothesized effects of the tactical patrol in the targeted area (which could be jurisdictionwide). These should be stated as clearly and as simply as possible.
4. Specify any important and plausible unintended effects of the program to be implemented. These should also be stated clearly and simply.
5. Develop and define operational measures of program implementation, hypothesized effects, and unintended effects. Decide exactly what you are going to measure to describe the program as implemented and what happened as a result of the program.

6. Determine what time periods will be used. Make sure the periods are sufficiently long to identify preimplementation norms and trends and to give the tactical patrol program a chance to show its effects.

7. If any of the operational measures require baseline data collection before program implementation (such as surveys of citizens, surveys of officer attitudes, or observations of officer behavior), gather the baseline data. (Any such measures will not ordinarily be part of the main time-series analysis, which will usually stretch back much further. However, analysis of unintended effects or of officer acceptance of the program may adhere to a pre–post design while the main analysis of hypothesized effects follows a time-series design.)

8. Implement the tactical program in the targeted area.

9. Monitor the implementation of the program in the targeted area.

10. Begin data collection if this did not precede program implementation. If extreme conditions develop in the targeted area, consider ending the program.

11. Continue data collection throughout the program implementation and any appropriate after periods.

12. Conduct data analysis. Describe the program as implemented and specify any changes in measures of hypothesized and unintended effects. Use averages, percentages, statistical comparisons, and graphical presentations as appropriate to show any changes. Consider whether changes can be attributed to the program and whether they are substantial enough for the program to be judged a success or failure.

13. Prepare any written reports required. At a minimum, make a permanent record of the evaluation and its results. Consider sharing your findings with other police professionals.

14. Look for opportunities to replicate the program and its evaluation. Replications should include similar programs implemented in similar settings. Exact duplication is never possible, but replication does require a fair degree of similarity (otherwise, it is not a replication, it is a new study). Take advantage of any such opportunities, since replication is the key to developing confidence in evaluation findings.

PRE–POST EVALUATION OF TACTICAL PATROL

A simple pre–post design is one that has before and after measurements but no comparison or control groups. The pre–post measurements can indicate whether anything changed after the tactic or program was implemented, but the lack of a comparison or control group makes it much harder to know whether the program caused the change. If, in fact, the change happened everywhere, or at least in many other settings besides the program's, then the program probably did not cause it. But this would not be known in the absence of comparison or control groups, and hence a false claim of success would be likely. Similarly, if such a change occurred naturally and periodically in the program's setting but no time-series data were collected, a false causal interpretation would probably result.

When it is not possible to gather longer time-series data or to use control or comparison groups, a simple pre–post design should be used, and it can yield valuable information. Moreover, a number of techniques can be used to make this design more powerful:

1. If the program or tactic can be subjected to pre–post testing several times (replication), any consistent patterns in the results will lend them more credence.
2. If the timing of the program or tactic can be arranged such that the probability of other factors causing any changes is minimized, one can more confidently interpret the results.
3. If different levels of the program or tactic can be tested, differential results can shed light on the program's or tactic's effects, if any.

An Illustration: Directed Patrol

A study of directed patrol in Pontiac, Michigan, several years ago relied primarily on a pre–post design without the benefit of control or comparison groups. Each week for seventy-four weeks, several geographically based directed patrol assignments were created. Data were collected on the number of target crimes in the target areas during the week preceding the assignment and during the week the directed patrols were implemented. The primary statistic of interest was the "weekly change in target crimes in target areas." This could be a positive or negative number; negative numbers would indicate the hoped-for decreases in target crimes.

The weekly changes were almost always negative, and averaged –7.6 crimes. The pre–post design showed that target crimes per week in target areas decreased once directed patrol was implemented. But did directed patrol cause the target-crime decreases?

Two explanations were at least plausible. One was that crime was perhaps decreasing citywide throughout this period; the department's crime statistics refuted this possibility, though. Another explanation was that a phenomenon called "regression to the mean" had occurred. Any time one selects problems to target because they are at extreme levels, the possibility exists that they will begin to decline naturally, regardless of the program implemented. This is a recurring difficulty when evaluating any kind of targeted program such as tactical patrol; moreover, the better one is at choosing truly needy target areas, the greater the difficulty.

Two aspects of the Pontiac pre–post study help refute the likelihood that regression to the mean was responsible for the entire decline in target crimes. One is simply that so many pre–post comparisons were made (over 750 different directed patrol projects during the seventy-four weeks). It is not logical to think that each of these target areas, or even most of them, was selected at the precise time when its rate of target crimes was about to start dropping naturally. With all due respect to crime analysts, their powers of prognostication are not consistently that good.

In addition, three different levels of directed patrol were tested over the seventy-four-week period. Initially, the department devoted about 3,500 minutes of patrol time per week to directed assignments; this jumped to 17 thousand minutes per week during the middle period, and then dropped to 2,900 minutes per week. The amount of proactive work done during directed assignments (car stops, FIs, arrests) increased more or less proportionately from the first to the second period, but dropped off dramatically during the final period. The three levels of directed patrol implemented could thus be characterized as (1) moderate time and activity, (2) heavy time and activity, and (3) moderate time and low activity.

The following data were collected during the Pontiac directed patrol experiment:

	Period 1	Period 2	Period 3
DP Minutes Per Week	3,467	17,045	2,895
Car Stops and FIs per Week	13.4	60.6	3.8
Arrests per Week	1.8	4.4	0.4
Weekly Change in Target Crimes in Target Areas	–9.2	–9.1	–3.5

Average weekly changes in target crimes in target areas were almost identical for the first two time periods, but were much smaller during the final period. This suggests two things: The tremendous increase in directed patrol time and activity during the middle period had no additional effect over and above the baseline effect observed in period one, and the substantial decrease in directed patrol activity in the last period reduced the tactic's effects.

If chance or regression to the mean were completely responsible for the decreases in target crimes in target areas, one would expect about the same magnitudes of decrease in all three periods. Instead, the finding of differential effects for different levels of directed patrol strongly implies that directed patrol did have some effect on target crimes in target areas and that the crime decreases that were measured did not occur merely by chance or solely due to regression to the mean.

Conducting a Pre–Post Evaluation

This section outlines step-by-step instructions for conducting a basic pre–post evaluation of a tactical patrol program. The instructions apply specifically to a program applied in a targeted area (including jurisdictionwide), without benefit of a comparison or control group. The same approach could be followed, with only modest adjustments, if multiple targeted areas were to be used.

1. Carefully specify the form of tactical patrol (directed, saturation, etc.) to be used. Make any personnel assignments, develop any written guidelines, and provide any training necessary to implement the tactical patrol.

2. Begin the process evaluation by gathering information, making observations and conducting interviews in order to describe the program environment, program development, program operations, and intervening events.

3. Carefully specify the program-specific hypothesized effects of the tactical patrol in the targeted area. These should be stated as clearly and as simply as possible.

4. Specify any important and plausible unintended effects of the program to be implemented. These should also be stated clearly and simply.

5. Develop and define operational measures of program implementation, hypothesized effects, and unintended effects. Decide exactly what you are going to measure to describe the program as implemented and what happened as a result of the program.

6. Determine what time periods will be used. This may involve two periods (before and after) or three periods (before, during, and after). Make sure the periods are sufficiently long to give the tactical patrol program a chance to show its effects.

7. If any of the operational measures require baseline data collection before program implementation (such as surveys of citizens, surveys of officer attitudes, or observations of officer behavior), gather the baseline data.

8. Implement the tactical program in the targeted area.

9. Monitor the implementation of the program in the targeted area.

10. Begin data collection if this did not precede program implementation. If extreme conditions develop in the targeted area, consider ending the program.

11. Continue data collection throughout the program implementation and any appropriate after periods.

12. Conduct data analysis. Describe the program as implemented and specify any changes in measures of hypothesized and unintended effects. Use averages, percentages, statistical comparisons, and graphical presentations as appropriate to show any changes. Consider whether changes can be attributed to the program and whether they are substantial enough for the program to be judged a success or failure.

13. Prepare any written reports required. At a minimum, make a permanent record of the evaluation and its results. Consider sharing your findings with other police professionals.
14. Look for opportunities to replicate the program and its evaluation. Replications should include similar programs implemented in similar settings. Exact duplication is never possible, but replication does require a fair degree of similarity (otherwise, it is not a replication, it is a new study). Take advantage of any such opportunities, since replication is the key to developing confidence in evaluation findings.

NOTE

Reprinted from *Police Program Evaluation* with permission from the Police Executive Research Forum. Copyright by Police Executive Research Forum.

BIBLIOGRAPHY

Tactical Patrol

Bartch, F. (1978). Integrating Patrol Assignments: Directed Patrol in Kansas City. In *Review of Patrol Operations Analysis: Selected Readings from ICAP Cities*. Washington, D.C.: U.S. Department of Justice.

Boydstun, J. (1975). *San Diego Field Interrogation: Final Report*. Washington, D.C.: Police Foundation.

Burrows, J., and H. Lewis. (1988). *Directing Patrol Work: A Study of Uniformed Policing* (Home Office Research Study No. 99). London: Her Majesty's Stationery Office.

Cawley, D., and H. Miron. (1977). *Managing Patrol Operations: Manual*. Washington, D.C.: U.S. Government Printing Office.

Cordner, G. (1981). The Effects of Directed Patrol: A Natural Quasi-Experiment in Pontiac. In *Contemporary Issues in Law Enforcement*, edited by J. Fyfe. Beverly Hills: Sage.

Cordner, G.; L. Gaines; and V. Kappeler. (1996). *Police Operations: Analysis and Evaluation*. Cincinnati: Anderson.

Cordner, G., and D. Hale, eds. (1992). *What Works in Policing? Operations and Administration Examined*. Cincinnati: Anderson.

Gay, W.; T. Schell; and S. Schack. (1977). *Improving Patrol Productivity*. Vol. 1, *Routine Patrol*. Washington, D.C.: U.S. Government Printing Office.

Hoover, L. (1996). *Quantifying Quality in Policing*. Washington, D.C.: Police Executive Research Forum.

Kelling, G.; T. Pate; D. Dieckman; and C. Brown. (1974). *The Kansas City Preventive Patrol Experiment: A Summary Report*. Washington, D.C.: Police Foundation.

Kenney, D., ed. (1989). *Police and Policing: Contemporary Issues*. New York: Praeger.

Krajick, K. (1978). Does Patrol Prevent Crime? *Police Magazine*, September, 5–16.

Pate, T.; R. Bowers; and R. Parks. (1976). *Three Approaches to Criminal Apprehension in Kansas City: An Evaluation Report*. Washington, D.C.: Police Foundation.

Schack, S.; T. Schell; and W. Gay. (1977). *Improving Patrol Productivity*. Vol. 2, *Specialized Patrol*. Washington, D.C.: U.S. Government Printing Office.

Schnelle, J.; R. Kirchner; J. Casey; P. Uselton; and M. McNees. (1977). Patrol Evaluation Research: A Multiple-Baseline Analysis of Saturation Police Patrolling During Day and Night Hours. *Journal of Applied Behavior Analysis* 10: 33–39.

Sherman, L. (1990). Police Crackdowns: Initial and Residual Deterrence. In *Crime and Justice: A Review of Research*, edited by M. Tonry and N. Morris. Chicago: University of Chicago Press.

Sherman, L. (1986). Policing Communities: What Works? In *Communities and Crime*, edited by A. Reiss and M. Tonry. Chicago: University of Chicago Press.

Sherman, L.; J. Shaw; and D. Rogan. (1995). The Kansas City Gun Experiment. In *Research in Brief*. Washington, D.C.: National Institute of Justice.

Tien, J.; J. Simon; and R. Larson. (1977). *An Alternative Approach in Police Patrol: The Wilmington Split-Force Experiment*. Cambridge, Mass.: Public Systems Evaluation.

Warren, J.; M. Forst; and M. Estrella. (1979). Directed Patrol: An Experiment That Worked. *Police Chief*, May, 48, 49, 78.

Webb, K.; B. Sowder; A. Andrews; M. Burt; and E. Davis. (1977). *National Evaluation Program: Specialized Patrol Projects*. Washington, D.C.: U.S. Government Printing Office.

Weisburd, D., and L. Green. (1995). Policing Drug Hot Spots: The Jersey City Drug Market Analysis Experiment. *Justice Quarterly* 4: 711–735.

Wilson, J., and B. Boland. (1979). *The Effect of the Police on Crime*. Washington, D.C.: U.S. Government Printing Office.

Program Evaluation

Campbell, D., and J. Stanley. (1963). *Experimental and Quasi-Experimental Designs for Research*. Chicago: Rand McNally.

Cook, T., and D. Campbell. (1979). *Quasi-Experimentation: Design and Analysis Issues for Field Settings*. Chicago: Rand McNally.

Cook, T., and D. Campbell. (1976). The Design and Conduct of Quasi-Experiments and True Experiments in Field Settings. In *Handbook of Industrial and Organizational Psychology*, edited by M. Dunnette. Chicago: Rand McNally.

Eck, J. (1984). *Using Research: A Primer for Law Enforcement Managers*. Washington, D.C.: Police Executive Research Forum.

Fitzgerald, J., and S. Cox. (1987). *Research Methods in Criminal Justice: An Introduction*. Chicago: Nelson-Hall.

Fitz-Gibbon, C., and L. Morris. (1987a). *How to Analyze Data*. Newbury Park, Calif.: Sage.

Fitz-Gibbon, C., and L. Morris. (1987b). *How to Design a Program Evaluation*. Newbury Park, Calif.: Sage.

Hatry, H.; R. Winnie; and D. Fisk. (1973). *Practical Program Evaluation for State and Local Government Officials.* Washington, D.C.: The Urban Institute.

Herman, J.; L. Morris; and C. Fitz-Gibbon. (1987). *Evaluator's Handbook.* Newbury Park, Calif.: Sage.

King, J.; L. Morris; and C. Fitz-Gibbon. (1987). *How to Assess Program Implementation.* Newbury Park, Calif.: Sage.

Maltz, M. (1972). *Evaluation of Crime Control Programs.* Washington, D.C.: U.S. Government Printing Office.

Maxfield, M., and E. Babbie. (1995). *Research Methods for Criminal Justice and Criminology.* Belmont, Calif.: Wadsworth.

McCleary, R., and R. Hay, Jr. (1980). *Applied Time Series Analysis for the Social Sciences.* Beverly Hills, Calif.: Sage.

McDowall, D.; R. McCleary; E. Meidinger; and R. Hay, Jr. (1980). *Interrupted Time Series Analysis.* Quantitative Applications in the Social Sciences Series. Beverly Hills: Sage.

Rossi, P.; H. Freeman; and S. Wright. (1979). *Evaluation: A Systematic Approach.* Beverly Hills: Sage.

Spector, P. (1981). *Research Designs.* Quantitative Applications in the Social Sciences Series. Beverly Hills: Sage.

Vito, G., and E. Latessa. (1989). *Statistical Applications in Criminal Justice.* Newbury Park, Calif.: Sage.

Weiss, C. (1972). *Evaluation Research: Methods of Assessing Program Effectiveness.* Englewood Cliffs, N.J.: Prentice Hall.

9

A National Survey of Pursuits and the Use of Police Force: Data from Law-Enforcement Agencies

Dennis Jay Kenney and Geoffrey P. Alpert

Nationally, very little is known about police pursuit driving. The National Highway Traffic Safety Administration (NHTSA) maintains some statistics, but they are limited to pursuit-related deaths as captured by the Fatal Accident Reporting System (FARS). Prior to 1994, this system received information from local agencies only when a pursued vehicle or its driver was involved in a fatal crash. There were 347 pursuit-related deaths reported in 1993. In 1994, the reporting system was modified to include a driver-level factor, "in pursuit." While this modification will increase the number of fatal accidents that qualify for the "pursuit-related" category, other reporting problems remain. In fact, the *FARS Newsletter* reported that "These changes will maximize our ability to recognize fatalities on the file related to police pursuit; still, we won't be able to record all pursuits resulting in fatalities. Again, some do not qualify as 'accidents'; others may not be reported on the FAR as involving any pursuit" (FARS 1993, 2). In other words, some incidents do not fit into the FARS definition and the investigating agency may not report others properly. A possible consequence of the improved system was the increase to 388 pursuit-related deaths reported in 1994. Though the NHTSA is working diligently to improve data collection and retrieval, the number of pursuit-related deaths in the United States remains unknown. Certainly, the number of pursuits with outcomes other than a death is unclear and insufficient information exists to even estimate their totals. Likewise, nothing is known about other aspects of pursuits on a national basis.

Equally limiting as our lack of knowledge about pursuits is the absence of information about other areas of police force. For example, in discussing the use of firearms, Geller and Scott (1992) have described the current research:

More is known now about the nature and frequency of shootings in which police are involved, although we have nothing resembling a comprehensive, continuous national picture of these violent police–citizen encounters. Even police insight into the nature, extent, causes and prevention of police shootings tends to draw on anecdotal rather than systematic information, and insight is highly localized . . . This state of affairs poses a dilemma for public policy makers, who do not have the luxury of waiting for systematic data or tactical advances before making concrete decisions about how the police are supposed to conduct themselves. The atmosphere surrounding the "deadly force debate" is charged with emotion, fear entrenched assumptions, class- and race-based suspicions and virtually intractable value conflicts. (p. 1)

Beyond anecdotal impressions, the most comprehensive national look at use-of-force issues can be found in a recent survey conducted by Pate and Fridell (1993). From their research, they report that "despite the importance of these issues, relatively little is known about the extent to which police use force, the types of force used, the extent to which force results in citizen complaints . . . and the extent to which those complaints are determined by the departments to be justified" (p. 31).

Their survey, the authors contend, "provide[s] the first national data on these topics." Still, limited, however, they report that many agencies do not require reports for most types of force. They also show that training, number of incidents, rates of force, complaints about force, and the justification of those complaints vary significantly among agencies (Pate and Fridell 1993, 153). Since the survey reported here focused on many of these same questions, reference to responses concerning the use of force will be offered for comparison to pursuit.

Though what we know about police use of firearms and use of less-than-lethal force is limited, the quantity and quality of information concerning pursuits are at least a decade or so behind (Alpert and Fridell 1992). It is the purpose of this chapter to begin addressing these voids by describing the results from the first national survey on police pursuits and the use of police force.

What We Know Beyond Fatalities

In 1992, the Bureau of Justice Statistics published its Law Enforcement Management and Administrative Statistics for 1990. In its section for large agencies (more than 100 officers), each agency was asked if it maintained a pursuit policy. Ninety-nine percent of the agencies reported having one. Unfortunately, there was no indication of the nature or quality of the policy or when it was implemented. With one important exception, no other national-level data were found.

In an effort to address similar issues nearly twenty-five years ago, Fennessy and Joscelyn (1970) attempted a national survey of both state police and municipal departments serving cities with populations over 100 thousand. Unfortunately, after receiving only limited responses (40%) with information that was "inadequate, inconsistent, and sometimes suspicious," they concluded their effort to define "the national implications of hot pursuit with an historical data collection approach" to be unworkable. Specifically, the issues they encountered were summarized as follows:

- an absence of a consistent definition of "hot pursuit."
- a lack of a consistent standard for charging violators apprehended after a pursuit.
- police records systems that are not designed for such analysis.
- inconsistent reporting by officers of unsuccessful pursuits.
- records-keeping procedures intended primarily for officer and agency defense.

To replace their survey, the authors turned instead to a four-site field study using research staff to systematically collect data during a one-month time frame at each site. From that, they extrapolated to the nation as a whole. While more recent studies have provided other important perspectives on police pursuits (Nugent et al. 1989; Shuman and Kennedy 1989; Alpert and Fridell 1992; Kennedy, Homant, and Kennedy 1992; Homant and Kennedy 1994a; Falcone 1994; Payne and Corley 1994), none, so far, have overcome the obstacles found by Fennessy and Joscelyn (1970) to offer a national picture. We believe that the present work fills that gap by reporting information from a national sample of law-enforcement agencies.

METHODS

The national survey on pursuits and use of police force was conducted between October 1994 and May 1995. The purpose of the survey was to collect pursuit and use-of-force information from police agencies throughout the country. For consistency, we requested that each agency apply the standard definition adopted by the International Association of Chiefs of Police (1990) in its *Model Policy* for vehicular pursuits: "An active attempt by an officer in an authorized emergency vehicle to apprehend fleeing suspects who are attempting to avoid apprehension through evasive tactics." Specifically, the instrument asked about the following:

1. mandated vehicle pursuit policies, both local and statewide.
2. pursuit data collection and incident analysis.
3. incidents resulting in accidents, injuries, assaults on officers, or reports of officer misconduct.
4. policies governing pursuit actions, options, alternatives, and terminations.
5. training provided to pursuing officers.
6. procedures, if any, for pursuit reviews and/or investigations.
7. discipline and litigation resulting from pursuits.

Similar information on police uses of other forms of force was requested as well. In all, this eight-page instrument contained fifty items, though many included multiple parts and/or requested open-ended answers.

A sampling frame of 800 municipal and county police agencies was selected. Using a national mailing list compiled by the International City Managers Association, a randomly selected group consisting of 40 percent large agencies (N = 320) and 60 percent smaller jurisdictions (N = 480) was selected for an initial mailing. For our purposes, the point of division between large and small jurisdictions was placed at 100 thousand population.

Once selected, our survey group was examined for obvious duplications and inaccuracies before the initial mailing. From this review, twenty-six agencies were removed from the sampling frame. Included were agencies that no longer existed or had been merged or consolidated into larger jurisdictions or departments. Our remaining sample now consisted of 774 agencies. With our first wave of mailings, another thirty-six surveys were returned by the post office as undeliverable, although accurate addresses for eight of these were identified. Though many of the missing jurisdictions were unknown to project staff, our estimate is that all were from sparsely populated communities. In all, our first-wave survey sample consisted of 746 law-enforcement agencies.

Each survey in the initial wave was addressed to the responding agency's chief executive and included a requested return by the second week of November 1994. Our survey instructions requested that the chief executive designate the persons appropriate for the instrument's completion. With our instructions we acknowledged that the information requested was quite detailed and might require a longer time for some agencies to complete.

While a one-month completion date was requested, responses were returned regularly throughout the month of November. As such, project staff decided to postpone a second mailing for approximately one week until the returns from the first wave were exhausted. In fact, by the last week of November, 322 responses (43%) had been received. Following several days with no additional returns, a second wave mailing to the 424 nonresponding agencies was completed with additional instructions stressing the importance of the project. For this wave, a completion date of 20 December 1994 was requested to encourage departments to complete the instrument before the Christmas holidays. By the end of the year, an additional sixty-eight responses were received, bringing the response rate to more than 52 percent. During January 1995, PERF staff contacted the remaining 356 agencies by telephone.

From the telephone contacts, project staff located another nine agencies that no longer existed independently. This further reduced the sample total to 737. Many others reported a change in their chief executive and explained that they had not received the survey request since personalized mail was forwarded to the addressee. In those cases, the request for participation was repeated and a copy of the survey instrument was sent to the new executive by fax. Other agencies reported that they had simply failed to complete their questionnaires. Where it was still available, staff requested that they do so; where it was not, a third copy was faxed to them as well. From these requests, another forty-six instruments were received, raising the overall response rate to more than 59 percent. Of the remaining 301 nonresponding agencies, only seventeen (2%) reported a desire not to participate. The other 284 (38%) informed us that they could not supply the requested information because their agencies did not collect it. As such, we are reluctant to label this group nonrespondents.

In sum, contact was made with 737 agencies, of which 436 completed useable data, 284 reported they did not collect or maintain the information, and 17 refused to participate. It is important to recognize that 38 percent of the agencies reported that they could not provide the necessary information because it was not collected. This is a discouraging figure that reflects the generally poor state of record keeping as it relates to pursuit-driving information. It is encouraging that only seventeen agencies (2%) that may have had the requested information available refused to provide it.

In all, our respondent sample included 149 agencies (34%) employing 1 to 25 sworn officers, 97 agencies (22%) with 26 to 150 sworn officers, 100 agencies (23%) with 151 to 500 sworn officers, 49 agencies (11%) with more than 500 sworn officers, and 41 agencies (10%) that did not report their size.

THE NATIONAL SURVEY OF PURSUIT

Nearly all the agencies (91%) reported having written policies governing pursuit situations, though the dates that their current policies were implemented varied considerably from as early as 1970 to as recently as 1995. Most, however, had implemented their current pursuit policy since 1990 (57%) while a sizable group (42%) had done so since 1992. Further, nearly half (48%), reported having modified their pursuit policy within the past two years. Most of those (87%) noted that the modification had made the policy more restrictive than the earlier version. Similarly, most of the responding agencies (72%) had their pursuit policies reviewed by a legal authority prior to its adoption. Table 9.1 compares the availability of pursuit policies, policy modifications during the previous two years, and policies on the use of force by police by the type and size of agency responding.

Similarly, the data in Table 9.2 compare the availability of statistics and other data on pursuits and use-of-force incidents. From these data, municipal agencies and larger agencies are more likely to routinely collect such information, a difference that may be related to the frequency of occurrence for these events. In addition, those agencies that collect such data apparently do so voluntarily, since only 11 percent of our respondents reported that their data-collection programs for pursuits are state mandated. Interestingly, while respondents from ten states advised that they operated under a state requirement, in only two of those states (California and New Jersey) were the responding agencies in agreement. For example, in Minnesota, while eight departments reported a state-mandated pursuit data-collection program, three others apparently were not aware of such a requirement. In six other states, only one responding agency believed data collection was required. From this, it would appear that the value of pursuit and use-of-force data, and the issues and requirements of collection, have not yet been clearly defined at local departmental levels.

Analyzing Pursuit-Policy Elements

Recall that nearly one-half of the responding agencies reported modifying their pursuit policies within the past two years and that in nearly each instance the result was a more restrictive policy than the one in place before the modification. Even so, when the individual elements of each agency's policy are examined, interesting differences emerge. For example, while departments were evenly split over permitting pursuits for any offense (48%), some restricted officer chases to incidents involving violent felonies (16%). Most permitted only marked vehicles to conduct a pursuit (58%), and a few restricted pursuing speeds to a specific maximum over the speed limit (11%). Overwhelmingly, supervisors were assigned the responsibility of terminating a pursuit (79%), while most agencies also placed responsibility on the officers involved (69%). Many (40%) required that pursuits be terminated once a suspect's identity becomes known.

Table 9.1
Pursuit and Use-of-Force Policies by Agency Type

	Pursuit Policy		Policy Modified in Past Two Years		Use of Force Policy	
	Yes	No	Yes	No	Yes	No
Agency Type						
City	271 (95%)	14 (5%)	143 (51%)	138 (49%)	267 (93%)	19 (7%)
County	103 (87%)	15 (13%)	54 (46%)	63 (54%)	110 (92%)	9 (8%)
Unknown	21 (81%)	5 (19%)	12 (52%)	11 (48%)	20 (77%)	6 (23%)
Agency Size						
Below 100 Officers	203 (89%)	24 (11%)	95 (43%)	128 (57%)	208 (91%)	20 (9%)
101-500 Officers	114 (100%)	—	72 (63%)	42 (37%)	113 (99%)	1 (1%)
501-2,500 Officers	44 (98%)	1 (2%)	25 (56%)	20 (44%)	44 (96%)	2 (4%)
Over 2,501 Officers	3 (100%)	—	1 (33%)	2 (67%)	3 (100%)	—

Beyond these cumulative results, however, some agencies clearly had differing expectations. Municipal agencies, for example, were significantly more likely to restrict pursuits to felony incidents (19%) than were their county counterparts (11%). Similarly, municipal agencies restricted pursuits to marked vehicles (64% versus 53%) and imposed supervisory responsibility (85% versus 77%) far more often than did county departments.

Among those who had modified their policies within the past two years, the differences were even more remarkable. For example, 68 percent restricted pursuits to marked vehicles. Of those with unchanged policies, however, only 54 percent imposed a similar limit. At least 89 percent of those with revised policies gave the supervisor responsibility for deciding whether to terminate a chase, though fewer than 77 percent of those agencies whose policies that had not changed had a similar requirement. While significant for all types of responding agencies, the patterns of policy change were most pronounced between county and sheriff's departments. As such, among those who had recently modified their policies few significant differences between

Table 9.2
Availability of Pursuit and Use-of-Force Statistics

	Pursuit Data		**Use-of-Force Data**	
	Yes	*No*	*Yes*	*No*
Agency Type				
City	105 (37%)	180 (63%)	121 (44%)	152 (56%)
County	26 (22%)	91 (78%)	43 (38%)	71 (62%)
Unknown	4 (15%)	22 (85%)	11 (42%)	15 (58%)
Agency Size				
Below 100 Officers	46 (20%)	181 (80%)	69 (32%)	148 (68%)
101-500 Officers	56 (50%)	57 (50%)	62 (56%)	49 (44%)
501-2,500 Officers	25 (56%)	20 (44%)	28 (65%)	15 (35%)
Over 2,500 Officers	3 (100%)	---	3 (100%)	---

city and county policy were found. From those where recent modifications had not occurred, however, county officers were consistently less restricted on either their pursuit actions or supervision. Table 9.3 demonstrates these differences.

In addition to when they can pursue, recent policy modifications appear to have imposed changes on how officers pursue as well. When asked about alternatives allowed, nearly one-half (42%) reported that roadblocks were permitted, though more (47%) advised that pursuits should be terminated once the offender's license plate number was determined. Far fewer permitted vehicle immobilization techniques (5%), channelization efforts (20%), ramming (12%), or had portable barrier strips available (15%). While few differences based on agency size or type could be found, county officers were significantly more likely to be permitted to employ roadblocks (55% versus 43%), spinouts (10% versus 3%), or barrier strips (30% versus 10%) than officers from municipal departments. Similarly, mid-sized departments (501 to 2,500 officers) were significantly more likely to employ roadblocks (67%),

Table 9.3
Policy Differences by Agency Type

Agency Type	Restrictive	Discretionary	Discouragement
City	43%	52%	5%
County	39%	59%	1%

	Policy Modified			No Policy Change		
Agency Type	Marked Veh Only	Supv. Resp	End if Susp Id	Marked Veh Only	Supv. Resp	End if Susp Id
City	70%	91%	44%	57%	80%	42%
County	64%	89%	49%	44%	79%	36%

but less likely to have barrier strips available than were agencies of any other size.

A Review of the Incidents

Though only 135 (31%) of the agencies systematically maintain police-pursuit statistics or data, 308 (71%) could provide estimates of the numbers of pursuits their officers had engaged in during 1993, the last full year prior to the survey. The figures ranged from zero (N = 34) to 870 pursuits, with large agencies obviously experiencing greater numbers of incidents than smaller ones. When pursuit incidents per officer were examined, however, it was the smaller and municipal agencies that experienced the highest rates of pursuing. Despite this, the rate of pursuit-related accidents increased substantially with agency size. Table 9.4 presents pursuits and related accidents by agency type and size.

Pursuit Training and Accountability

Despite an awareness that pursuits do occur and the understanding that they can result in accidents or injuries, many departments acknowledged taking only limited steps to prepare their officers for pursuits. Similarly, there was a conspicuous lack of institutional review of pursuit incidents. As a result, a general absence of corrective measures should not be surprising. For example, although 60 percent of the agencies responding provide entry-level pursuit-driving training at the academy, the average time devoted to these skills was estimated at less than fourteen hours. The remaining 40 percent of the agencies reported no preservice pursuit training. Once in service, the agencies

Table 9.4
Pursuits and Pursuit-Related Accidents by Agency Type and Size

| | Pursuits per 1,000 Officers | Per 1,000 Pursuits | | | | |
		Accidents	Ofc. Injuries	Susp. Inj.	Other Inj.	Deaths
Agency Type						
City	112	324	25	70	19	2.4
County	105	198	27	82	24	8.6
Agency Size						
Below 100	181	164	22	72	20	4.1
101-500	109	297	26	71	18	5.7
501-2,500	124	394	46	129	30	3.2
Over 2,501	99	577	24	61	26	2.0

with training averaged just over three hours per year of additional training. In contrast, nearly 83 percent of these agencies required in-service training in the use of force which averaged more than eight hours per year. These differences exist despite the fact that 12 percent reported five or more incidents each during the previous year where vehicle pursuits ended with one or more suspects fleeing from officers on foot, nearly 16 percent had one or more pursuits result in assaults on officers, and almost 13 percent had at least one pursuit result in an intentional ramming of a police vehicle. Interestingly, the county agencies provided an average of nearly two additional hours of academy-based pursuit-driving training to entry-level officers although they have a pursuit-related accident rate nearly 40 percent below the municipal departments. The mid-sized departments (501 to 2,500 officers), on the other hand, have a pursuit-related accident rate more than twice that of the small departments (less than 100 officers), yet on average offer less than half the in-service training in pursuit driving. The agencies that have modified their pursuit policies within the past two years required from their officers both more hours of training in pursuit decision making (both entry and in-service) and practical exercises at a driving track or similar setting than agencies not having modified their policies recently.

Beyond training for such situations, our responding agencies reported important differences in their follow-up evaluations once an actual pursuit incident had occurred. While most (89%) routinely conducted some follow-up, for many that amounted to nothing more than an informal supervisory review (33%) or a report addressing the incident by the pursuing officer (47%). Others, however, require a formal supervisory review (46%), while a few (8%) initiate an internal investigation into all incidents. Internal investigations were more commonly used in response to pursuits resulting from inappropriate actions or that ended in an accident or injuries.

Disciplining Officers

Given their regularity, it is probably inevitable that officer error and misconduct will sometimes result from vehicle pursuits. In fact, slightly more than 12 percent of the agencies reported having to discipline officers at least once during 1993 for pursuit-related actions. The actual discipline offered ranged from simple counseling with an oral reprimand to the termination of two officers.

Beyond internal actions, nearly 16 percent of our sample of police agencies advised that during 1993 they had been involved in litigation resulting from pursuits (Table 9.5). Eighteen (2.5% of the sample; 26% of those involved in litigation) of those agencies either lost or settled the actions against them. Municipal agencies, agencies that had modified their pursuit policies within the past two years, and larger agencies were more likely to be involved in such actions, though only agency size was associated with significant differences in the legal outcomes. Unfortunately, we were unable to determine whether the previously reported pursuit-policy modifications were a result of the litigation during 1993.

Earlier we noted that training requirements and intensity were generally greater for use-of-force issues than for pursuits. While the risks to others posed by police chases may be greater, our results suggest that the responses (both internal and external) to force incidents are more serious. For example, while 12 percent of our respondent agencies administered discipline for pursuit-related actions, more than 18 percent employed discipline in response to a police use of force. Further, nearly 5 percent of our agencies reported disciplining officers five or more times during 1993, whereas fewer than 2 percent did so with such frequency in response to pursuit violations. In addition, the range of disciplinary action was more limited for pursuits than uses of force. Where disciplinary actions for pursuit-driving violations normally involved some form of a reprimand (82% of all actions taken), the actions taken for use-of-force violations included reprimands alone (7% of actions taken), reprimands with suspensions, demotions, or terminations (44%), suspensions alone (25%), additional training (10%), and termination or retirement (7%).

Finally, when combined, pursuits and the uses of force that result can be especially problematic. During 1993, 25 percent (109) of our

Table 9.5
Involvement in Pursuit-Related Litigation during 1993

	Involved		Lost or Settled	
	Yes	*No*	*Yes*	*No*
Agency Type				
City	53 (20%)	216 (80%)	13 (5%)	247 (95%)
County	11 (9%)	106 (91%)	3 (3%)	109 (97%)
Agency Size				
Below 100 Officers	10 (4%)	217 (96%)	2 (1%)	223 (99%)
101-500 Officers	31 (30%)	73 (70%)	6 (6%)	91 (94%)
501-2,500 Officers	20 (49%)	21 (51%)	5 (14%)	31 (86%)
Over 2,500 Officers	1 (100%)	----	1 (100%)	----
Policy Status				
Modified in Past Two Years	44 (22%)	154 (78%)	12 (6%)	180 (94%)
No Recent Modifications	25 (12%)	177 (88%)	6 (3%)	187 (97%)

sample departments experienced police pursuits that resulted in officers using force, in addition to the pursuit itself, to apprehend a suspect. In only a few of those incidents (24), however, were allegations filed that the force used was excessive or unreasonable. In twelve of those cases, those allegations were sustained. Fortunately, the trends for the future appear positive, as most (68%) of the participating agencies see either no change or a decrease in complaints of excessive pursuit-related force over the past two years.

CONCLUSION

The responses to our national survey revealed or reinforced several important trends. First, it is critical for law-enforcement agencies to create and maintain systems to collect information on pursuit driving. The inability of many to respond to our questions was discouraging. Second, the fact that most agencies had policies was favorable; however, the overall quality and direction of those policies was questionable, since some departments had instituted theirs as many as twenty years ago. More favorably, we note that many agencies have updated their policies and most who have made them more restrictive than those previously in effect. Third, the necessary training for pursuits needs rethinking. It is obviously unwise for our law-enforcement agencies to expect officers to make proper and appropriate decisions with minimal or no training. Similarly, the supervisory aspect of each agency's policies should be reviewed and enforced. Finally, the requirements that officers justify their actions or have a supervisor evaluate their pursuit (after-action reports) needs more attention. When actions are found to be inappropriate, officers often do not receive meaningful discipline for problem pursuits. Perhaps as a result, litigation in pursuit is a real and serious concern.

NOTES

Reprinted from *Journal of Criminal Justice*, Vol. 25, No. 4, D. Kenney and G. Alpert, "A National Survey of Pursuits and the Use of Police Force: Data from Law Enforcement Agencies," pp. 315–323, Copyright 1997, with permission from Elsevier Science Ltd, The Boulevard, Langford Lane, Kidlington 0X5 1GB, UK.

Support for this research has been provided, in part, by the National Institute of Justice Grant #93-IJ-CX-0061. Opinions stated in this paper are those of the author and do not necessarily represent the official position of the National Institute of Justice.

BIBLIOGRAPHY

Alpert, G., and L. Fridell. (1992). *Police Vehicles and Firearms*. Prospect Heights, Ill.: Waveland.
Bureau of Justice Statistics. (1992). *State and Local Police Departments—1990*. Washington, D.C.: Author.
Falcone, D. (1994). Police Pursuits and Officer Attitudes: Myths and Realities. *American Journal of Police* 13 (1): 143–155.
Fatal Accident Reporting System (FARS). (1993). Coding Focus. *FARS Newsletter*, September, 2.
Fennessy, E., Jr., and K. Joscelyn. (1970). A National Study of Hot Pursuit. *Denver Law Journal* 48: 389–403.
Geller, W., and M. Scott. (1992). *Deadly Force: What We Know*. Washington, D.C.: Police Executive Research Forum.
Geller, W., and H. Toch, eds. (1995). *And Justice for All*. Washington, D.C.: Police Executive Research Forum.

Homant, R., and D. Kennedy. (1994a). Citizen Preferences Concerning Police Pursuit Policies. *Journal of Criminal Justice* 22: 415–458.

Homant, R., and D. Kennedy. (1994b). The Effect of High-Speed Pursuit Policies on Officers' Tendencies to Pursue. *American Journal of Police* 13: 91–111.

International Association of Chiefs of Police. (1990). *Model Policy: Vehicular Pursuit*. Washington, D.C.: Author.

Kennedy, D.; R. Homant; and J. Kennedy. (1992). A Comparative Analysis of Police Vehicle Pursuit Policies. *Justice Quarterly* 9: 227–246.

Nugent, H.; E. Connors; J. T. McEwen; and L. Mayo. (1989). *Restrictive Policies for High-Speed Pursuit Pursuits*. Washington, D.C.: U.S. Government Printing Office.

Pate, A., and L. Fridell. (1993). *Police Use of Force: Official Reports, Citizen Complaints and Legal Consequences*. Washington, D.C.: Police Foundation.

Payne, D., and C. Corley. (1994). Police Pursuits: Correlates of the Failure to Report. *American Journal of Police* 13: 47–71.

Shuman, I. G., and T. Kennedy. (1989). Police Pursuit Policies: What Is Missing? *American Journal of Police* 10: 21–30.

Wells, L. E., and D. Falcone. (1992). Organizational Variations in Vehicle Pursuits by Police: The Impact of Policy on Practice. *Journal of Criminal Justice Policy Review* 6: 311–333.

10

Rethinking Detective Management: Why Investigative Reforms Are Seldom Permanent or Effective

John E. Eck

THE DETECTIVE CYCLE

Plainclothes detectives may be the oldest form of public police. The Bow Street Runners, created by Henry Fielding in London during the late eighteenth century, spent considerable time pursuing highwaymen (Fitzgerald 1888). A uniformed London Metropolitan Police did not appear until 1829. Yet the English parliamentary debates leading up to the creation of the London Metropolitan Police depict the conflict between uniformed and plainclothes policing that persists to this day and is likely to continue far into the future. That is, plainclothes officers can blend with the public and presumably get closer to the criminals they are pursuing. But the fact that they are not obviously police officers creates public suspicion that these agents may be engaged in dubious behaviors. These suspicions, often half by police administrators and sometimes exaggerated, are not misplaced.

Detectives' abuse of authority has a history as long as the history of the profession (Kuykendall 1986). A colorful example is Jonathan Wild. Wild was a private "thief taker" before the creation of any public police in England. To understand how Wild operated, one has to understand the nature of property theft in eighteenth-century England. The well-to-do owned many things, but most of their possessions were too bulky to be stolen easily. However, they did purchase from skilled artisans small objects made of precious metals and jewels, such as snuff boxes, jewelry, and other personal items. Because these items were not mass manufactured, each was distinctive. And each was valuable enough to attract the attention of thieves. In the absence of a public police, a gentleman whose wife's jewels were stolen would hire a thief taker like Jonathan Wild. The thief taker's primary job was to recover the stolen artifact for a reward. If possible, he would also capture the thief. Wild was particularly good at recovering stolen property and apprehending offenders. Because of his prowess, Wild was known as the "Thief Taker General" (Howson 1970).

The penalty for theft was death, and this was the secret of Wild's success. For as it turned out Wild not only recovered property and sent a few errant individuals to the gallows, he also organized the thieves and planned thefts from the start. Those thieves who did not cooperate with him were threatened with apprehension. A number of individuals were executed because they resisted Wild's attempts to organize the underworld. When Wild was discovered, he was sent to the gallows himself (Howson 1970).

Wild's familiarity with the thieves and his ability to use his intimate knowledge for corrupt purposes were lessons that were not lost on early police reformers. Also not lost were the lessons from using undercover officers in Napoleonic France to ferret out threats to the government (Forssell 1970; Critchley 1979). Concerns over corruption and political influence resulted in the London Metropolitan Police's focusing almost entirely on uniformed officers. But the advantages of having a few specialists out of uniform who could mix with offenders could not be ignored (Cobb 1957). Consequently, a small number of constables were assigned to plainclothes work. The number of these detectives increased as they were able to demonstrate some successes, and declined when they became involved in political or corruption scandals (Cobb 1957; Critchley 1979). After one particularly major scandal, a special inquiry was established to determine what should be done. Howard Vincent was asked to head the inquiry. Vincent had studied the French and other continental European police systems, and he recommended the establishment of a special detective bureau to investigate crime and to help combat Fenians (Irish rebels) who were terrorizing England. Thus, the outside threat overcame the inside threat and resulted in the creation of the detective force commonly referred to as Scotland Yard. It also resulted in the formation of the antiterrorism section then called the Irish Special Branch (Critchley 1979; Porter 1987).

We see in this sketch of the early history of detectives a cycle that continues to this day. First, plainclothes work is criticized for corruption, ineffectiveness, political interference, or any number of possible scandals associated with detectives. This leads to the marginalization of detective work and the reduction of its capacity to operate. After some period of time, the police agency confronts a serious problem that refocuses attention on the need for increased detective capacity. (In late nineteenth-century England, it was Irish terrorism. In late twentieth-century Washington, D.C., it was the historically high homicide rate.) This leads to the expansion of detective operations. This expansion eventually, if not initially, begins to conflict with the demands of other parts of the police agency, in particular uniformed patrol. Then, when the next scandal occurs—as it always does—a group interested in curtailing plainclothes operations surfaces within the police agency.

Detectives are particularly vulnerable to cycles of scandal and reform (Sherman 1978) for a number of reasons. First, as a distinct minority with relatively advantageous working conditions (out of uniform and with more discretion than patrol officers), they incur the jealousy of the majority of the police force. Second, detective work appears to be secretive even when it is not. Detectives are not known to share information routinely or often, and they have the same aura that surrounds spies, even when they are not conducting undercover work. Third, it is never clear what they are accomplishing. This puts detectives in a difficult position. Knowing that they are judged in part by their productivity, detectives often seek opportunities to enhance their records, even at the expense of others in the police service. Finally, detectives are invisible to their supervisors. Thus, there is uncertainty as to what they are really up to, and when a few detectives exploit this invisibility for personal gain, the discovery of malfeasance reinforces the suspicions. For all these reasons, specialized investigation sections are seldom popular, except with their members and the entertainment media.

At the beginning of the 1970s, the United States was entering the first step of this cycle. Corruption scandals, civil rights violations, and other problems put the police under a great deal of scrutiny at a time when crime was rising. Thus, when research began to question detectives' effectiveness, many police administrators were mentally prepared to cut back the number of plainclothes detectives.

INVESTIGATIONS RESEARCH

Over the last twenty-five years, the results of investigative research have been pessimistic for supporters of specialized plainclothes detective sections. For police officials who are skeptical of such units, it has been a breath of fresh air. Let us look briefly at this line of research.

Though observational studies of investigations had been published before 1970 (Skolnick 1966), and the President's Commission on Law Enforcement had used quantitative data to examine detectives' effectiveness (Issacs 1967), much of this went unnoticed by policing. But in 1970, the New York City RAND Corporation issued a damning report on follow-up investigations of burglaries and assaults in New York City. Though it found some evidence that investigations of assaults increased arrests, the report's authors claimed that the solution of burglary cases had virtually nothing to do with detective effort. Instead, the report stated, the solution of these cases was due solely to the evidence available to the patrol officers who first arrived at the scene. If patrol officers did not gather the relevant information, detectives were unlikely to collect it later. Further, the availability of information necessary to solve cases is random (Greenwood 1970). In short, there is little follow-up investigators can do to solve burglaries, except to process reports.

This conclusion was important for several reasons. First, it gave a coherent and empirically supported explanation for detective work that conflicted with the explanations detectives gave. By highlighting the important role of patrol officers, the study drew attention to a neglected aspect of investigation, an aspect that was hard to deny once attention was drawn to it. Though people could claim that patrol officers were not as thorough as detectives, they could not deny their importance. But the report went further. It claimed that, on average, detective work contributes little additional value to the case once it leaves the hands of a patrol officer. Second, the New York City RAND Corporation had the ear of decision makers at the highest level of the police department, and these people were not great fans of detectives (Daley 1971; Murphy and Pate 1977; Seedman and Hellman 1974). Finally, the researchers went on to conduct a study of investigations nationally that came to similar conclusions.

Five years later, another study by some of the same researchers examined solved cases from the Kansas City, Missouri, Police Department and came to the same conclusion. In particular, they found that the activities detectives engaged in to solve those crimes were common, everyday police work; they took no special actions. They also surveyed police agencies across the United States and found no relationships between various ways of organizing detective operations and clearance and arrest rates. This was the now-famous RAND report on detectives (Greenwood, Petersilia, and Chaiken 1977). This study nationalized the New York City conclusions and forced police officials across the United States to confront the possibility that their detectives might not be as useful as once thought.

Finally, from the early to late 1970s a series of studies in California (Greenberg, Yu, and Lang 1973), Minnesota (Johnson and Healy 1978), and nationally (Eck 1979) examined solved and unsolved burglary cases. These studies came to similar conclusions: Detectives solved few burglary cases; the information that led to arrests was collected by the first patrol officer at the scene, not by the follow-up investigator; this patrol information came from victims and witnesses, for the most part; and, absent this information, there was little that could be done to solve the case. These studies recommended that police managers use statistical tools to predict case outcomes and screen out cases that could not be solved. Thus, detectives should get only those cases that had the information needed to make an arrest. In short, the detective was viewed as a report processor, not a case solver.

The findings from all these studies, though never implemented to the extent that the researchers recommended, fell on fertile ground. Corruption scandals in New York and other places had tarnished the public image of detectives and reinforced the position of uniformed branch supporters. Civil libertarians had become more vocal about police abuses, and some of their concerns centered on the activities of plainclothes police. Finally, police managers trying to reform law-enforcement operations found that the detective branches were often quasi-independent power sources that resisted reform efforts. In academic circles, criticism of the police had greater support than support for the police. Thus, police practitioners, policy makers outside of police agencies, and academics gave the research findings far more credence than an objective view of the evidence would suggest.

These studies had several problems. First, none of them directly measured the level of detective effort that went into cases and compared this with case outcomes. Therefore, statements about the absence of a relationship between detective effort and case solution had no direct empirical support. Second, the RAND analysis of the Kansas City data only looked at solved cases. Consequently, it could not find differences between solved and unsolved cases that could be due to detective work, if such differences existed. Third, though studies showed that information patrol officers collected was critical to solutions, no study examined what information detectives collected. Thus, though these studies created a very plausible theory of how cases were solved, there were sufficient problems with the study designs that their conclusion and recommendations should not have been taken as "facts." But for many police officials and researchers, these findings were interpreted as having settled the question of detective effectiveness (Kuykendall 1986).

In 1980, the Police Executive Research Forum (PERF) began a study to overcome some of the limitations of the earlier work (Eck 1983). Unfortunately, this was the last major study of detective work and, consequently, research still cannot answer many questions. The PERF study was designed to overcome the main problems with earlier research. First, patrol and detective efforts were measured directly by having the police officials complete detailed logs of their activities, the time spent on each activity, and the information the activity produced. Second, solved and unsolved cases were examined so that comparisons between these types of cases could be made. Third, the logs allowed examination of the additional information detectives collected beyond that available to patrol officers. Finally, burglary and robbery investigations were examined at three sites: St. Petersburg, Florida; DeKalb County, Georgia; and Wichita, Kansas (Eck 1983).

Two theories of detective work were developed for comparison. The first theory, called the *Effort–Result Hypothesis*, claimed the cases were solved because of detectives' work. In short, the more effort by detectives, the better the results. The second theory, called the *Circumstance–Result Hypothesis*, was based on the RAND researchers' ideas. That is, the availability of information to the patrol officer depended on circumstances beyond the control of the police, and additional work by the detective did not help solve the case. In short, cases were solved through random factors.

In comparing the two hypotheses, it was found that both are right and both are wrong. Some cases were solved through circumstances beyond the police's control. Some cases could not be solved within the resource constraints the police agencies faced. And some cases were solved because of the additional efforts of detectives. In other words, detectives are neither heroes nor demons. Follow-up investigations of property crime will have low solution rates because offenders avoid being seen. Nevertheless, absent detective work, some of these offenders will not be arrested. Both hypotheses make exaggerated claims, but both contain more than a little truth.

WHY INVESTIGATE?

Up to this point, we have assumed that there is a need for investigators without clearly stating exactly what this need is. Addressing this question is of fundamental importance if police agencies are to manage investigations effectively. There are only three goals. The first two are often confused, and the third is seldom discussed. We will examine each.

Crime control through law enforcement is the first goal. It is achieved by apprehending offenders. Detective units attempt to achieve this goal by arresting offenders, but once offenders have been caught, at least one of three objectives must be met: deter other offenders by making them believe that if they commit the same offense, they too will be caught; incapacitate the apprehended offender so that he or she cannot commit another crime for some specified period of time; or rehabilitate the offender so that, when released, he or she does not continue to offend. The research about the criminal justice system's ability to accomplish any of these three objectives will not be reviewed here. It is sufficient to state that research does not suggest that any of them are remotely close to being the silver bullet for crime (Blumstein, Cohen, and Nagin 1978; Blumstein et al. 1986; Sechrest, White, and Brown 1979). Nevertheless, some people are rehabilitated; recidivism is not 100 percent. Clearly, a serial murderer in prison is not killing women on the street. And some people do stay away from crime because they are afraid of getting caught. Still, if detectives solved more crimes and arrested more offenders, would this translate into noticeable reductions in crime? Though there is no direct evidence that can answer this question, it does seem dubious, especially given the problems of courts and corrections.

There is a possibility of an alternative answer. The Washington, D.C., Metropolitan Police faced an increasing homicide rate with no increase in the number of homicide investigators. Recently, the number of homicide investigators was increased and supplemented with investigators from the FBI and other federal agencies, and there has been a decline in the number of homicides. Whether an increase in staffing caused the decline or whether it just happened to coincide with the decline is impossible to tell from the anecdotal evidence available.

The second goal, often confused with the first, is justice. From a pure justice perspective, it does not matter when crime declines as a result of apprehending offenders. One tries to catch offenders because they have done something bad and they should be punished. Because humans are fallible, the court system stands between the arrest and the punishment. From a justice perspective, what matters is that the public, through the courts, can examine the case and the offender and then determine the penalty, if appropriate. Detectives contribute to justice if they catch the right offenders and provide prosecutors with the relevant information. If this also happens to result in fewer crimes in the future, so much the better.

There is a third goal that is seldom discussed. This is crime prevention. Though one can call crime control crime prevention, we will make a distinction between the two goals, principally because crime prevention does not depend exclusively on apprehension of offenders. Crime prevention will be discussed more extensively when we examine problem-oriented policing and problem solving. Though neglected, this is an area that detectives should be more involved in and where they have special expertise that can be applied to this goal.

REACTIVE INVESTIGATION MANAGEMENT

Investigations are usually divided into two categories: reactive and proactive. The research described earlier examined reactive investigations; that is, investigations of crime events after they occur because a citizen initiates the investigation through a request. Proactive investigations are police initiated, sometimes before any crime has been committed.

The research on reactive investigations has been relatively pessimistic, in large part because these investigations begin after the crime has taken place. Nevertheless, research into the productivity of criminal investigations led to a national program to change the way investigations were managed. Throughout the latter half of the 1970s, the Managing Criminal Investigations (MCI) program produced seminars, sponsored training sessions, and published manuals for police officials (Cawley et al. 1977; Greenberg and Wasserman 1979). Among many elements, the MCI program emphasized four points:

1. Police officers need to collect as much information as possible during the first stages of an investigation. The difference between solvable and unsolvable cases is in large part, but not entirely, determined by the quality of patrol officers' work.
2. Investigative managers need to sort those case that cannot be solved from those that may be solved. Putting time into unsolvable cases wastes resources and diverts attention from cases that may be solved if more effort is put into them.
3. Of those cases that may be solved, some will, in essence, solve themselves, while others will require more effort. It is this last group that should receive the greatest attention.
4. Investigators should examine patterns of crime to link bits of information from several offenses. This point seems particularly obvious, but as we will see later, it has some implications beyond crime control.

The first point emphasizes one of the main conclusions from the research. It assumes that there is substantially more information to be gained at the earliest stage of the investigative process. Though there is evidence that this is the case for physical evidence (Peterson 1974), there is no scientific data that more witnesses can be found or that victims will recall more information if patrol officers make a more detailed initial investigation.

Case screening (Point 2) makes the best out of a bad thing. Though it diverts attention from unsolvable cases, by itself it does nothing to put resources to productive use. Often, case screening is just a mechanism for dealing with cutbacks in staffing or increases in caseload. In this sense, it prevents things from getting worse. To make improvements, attention must be shifted toward productive activities. Points 3 and 4 suggest ways of doing this. Another approach is to use the resources to target offenders proactively.

REFORM AND THREE LAWS OF INVESTIGATIONS

Though little research has been conducted on reactive investigations in the last decade, virtually no comparable work has been done on proactive investigations. The studies that have been conducted have focused on career criminals and narcotics investigations. These studies have found that targeting offenders is highly productive in generating arrests, but the costs of such efforts can be very high and there are many concerns about how offenders are selected for targeting (Martin and Sherman 1986; Sherman 1983).

Proactive investigations are very expensive because a great deal of investigative time must be spent watching people and places and waiting for something to happen (Pate, Bowers, and Parks 1976). Undercover work also requires a substantial resource investment. Adding to the expense are the extra personnel needed to ensure the safety of the undercover officers and to ensure that informant funds are not misallocated. Reactive investigations are relatively cheap because the victim or witness brings forth information, and the investigation can be curtailed if no useful information is found. Proactive investigations are expensive because one starts with the least information and detectives need to spend a great deal of time looking for it. Thus, there is a fundamental dilemma, which will be called the *first law of investigation*: relying on cheaply obtained information results in few solutions, but to get many solutions one must gather expensive information. Technology can help make the first law of investigations less onerous, but it cannot eliminate it.

Targeting offenders proactively presents a different problem. Investigators like to select targets, and they often do so based on the information at hand. If the investigation is proactive, then the information will have to come from people with direct contact with offenders, often criminal informants. So proactive investigations are likely to be informant driven. If the investigation is reactive, then the information will come from victims and witnesses. But in neither case are detectives in direct control over the direction of the investigation. In both circumstances, persistent and dedicated management practices can reduce the negative aspects of this—by case screening in reactive investigations and by careful informant control procedures for proactive investigations—but it cannot eliminate the problem. Thus, the *second law of investigations* is that the direction of all investigations is largely out of the investigator's control, and the more control that is desired, the more expensive the investigation will become.

Ideally, one would have some objective form of targeting based on explicit goals. One might want to target the most violent offenders of proactive investigations, for example. Then information, much of it from police records of prior offenses, would be used to rank-order potential targets. One could target the most active offenders, regardless of their propensity for violence, or one could target offenders who prey on special victims (children, for example). One could target offenders active in a specific neighborhood. Once a rank-order target list was prepared, additional information could be collected. This approach would target the worst offenders, not just the easiest-to-get offenders. The first and second laws of investigations assert, however, that this approach will be labor intensive and expensive.

Another standard reform is to rotate personnel through investigations sections. This may improve communications throughout the agency and decrease the isolation of investigative units. However, because it does little to address the difficulty of gathering information and does nothing to focus outcomes it does not get to the heart of the problem of detective work.

The third type of investigative reform includes decentralization and despecialization. These reforms have received considerable attention in the context of community policing (Skolnick and Bayley 1986), just as they did during the late 1960s, when community policing was being examined (Bloch and Bell 1976; Schwartz and Clarren 1977; Sherman, Milton, and Kelly 1973). Decentralization moves investigations from a central command location to area commands, from headquarters to precincts. It often involves disbanding or shrinking the separate investigations bureau and putting the decentralized detectives under the direct control of the area commander. Whatever centralized independent investigative bureau that remains focuses on the most serious and rarest crime, homicide, for example.

Despecialization reduces the number of special units within investigations. For example, the separate burglary, larceny, and auto-theft squads are combined to form a single property–crime unit. An extreme form of despecialization involves moving investigative functions into patrol and shrinking the investigative section. Decentralization almost always requires some form of despecialization. This is because when detectives are moved to area offices each detective must take on a more heterogeneous caseload, since there are seldom enough cases of each particular type to keep a specialist detective busy. Despecialization does not require decentralization, however. One could keep all of the detectives at headquarters while combining the specialty units.

Despecialization and decentralization are useful under some circumstances. To the extent that the investigation of each crime type requires distinctive skills and knowledge, specialization is defensible. If distinctive skills and knowledge are not required, then specialization is not justifiable. When the jurisdiction is very large and the areas within the jurisdiction are very different, decentralization makes a great deal of sense. In medium-size and smaller cities, it is not clear how much difference decentralization will make, but in jurisdictions with relatively few crimes, either because the jurisdiction is small or because it is relatively safe, despecialization may be very useful. Under such circumstances, there are too few crimes to justify having specialists. In large cities and other cities with large numbers of crimes, despecialization may not be warranted.

This leads us to the *third law of investigations*: The circumstances that call for specialization also call for decentralization, and the circumstances that require centralization require despecialization. Small cities and towns have few problems with this law: Everyone works out of the same building, patrol officers conduct the investigations, and, if there are any detectives, they handle all crimes. But in large cities the third law explains why investigative units are constantly being reorganized; there is no formula that simultaneously satisfies the needs of despecialization and decentralization. When a large department decentralizes its investigations, it also despecializes. Decentralization brings the detectives closer to the peculiarities of the areas, but the despecialization makes it more difficult to develop and mobilize expertise in particular crimes. Later, under different leadership, the department recentralizes and respecializes. This solves the problem of expertise but reduces the detectives' interaction with the areas. Bayley (1992) has noted that debates about centralization versus decentralization seem to have little impact on agency performance.

The three laws of investigations limit the effectiveness of the standard reforms police managers have attempted over the last fifteen years. Each attempt to manage investigations is a little useful. That is, each of these types of reforms can help under some circumstances, but each brings with it difficulties of its own. One should not throw out these approaches, but one should not expect too much from them, either. And none of these approaches provides permanent fixes. In fact, one could argue that there are no permanent fixes to the problems that the standard reforms are meant to address.

But whether one accepts or rejects these laws and their implications, there is a deeper criticism of the standard reforms. None of them does much to change the nature of investigations. Shifting from reactive to proactive investigation increases the amount of information, but at greater expense. Or one can invest considerable resources to exercise greater control over the direction of investigation. Or one can decentralize and despecialize. Still, none of these efforts will substantially increase the ability of investigations to achieve the goals of crime control and justice.

Thus, we need to rethink not only how we manage criminal investigations, but also the goals that we are trying to achieve. One cannot and should not abandon justice as a goal. The public has a right to demand that the police pursue the ends of justice, at least within the bounds of the resources available. We should downplay the goal of crime control through law enforcement, however, and substitute for it the goal of crime prevention. Simply put, investigators (and all others in police agencies) should work to keep crimes from occurring. When, despite these efforts, crimes do occur, the detective's job (shared with others in the agency) is to bring the offender to the prosecutor. More elaborately, we can suggest four guiding principles.

1. Abandon crime control through apprehension as a principle goal of investigations. There is little evidence that increase apprehensions by detectives make much of a difference in crime levels, except under special circumstances.

2. Detectives should focus on justice. Offenders should be arrested because they violated the law. Detectives should find out who the offenders are and bring their evidence forward.

3. The special circumstances mentioned in Point 1 are clear crime patterns. Obviously, arresting a repeat rapist or killer prevents crimes. And, as we will see in Point 4, focusing on patterns allows detectives to combine enforcement powers with many other techniques.

4. Crime prevention through problem solving should be emphasized. Detectives should look for patterns of crimes, determine why the patterns exist, and implement programs that stop the patterns. Criminal apprehension is one technique that may be useful, but there are many other techniques (some illustrated next) that can be used in conjunction or as substitutes.

THE PROBLEM-SOLVING DETECTIVE

Problem-oriented policing is a style of policing that is designed to make the police more effective. Many see problem-oriented policing as an aspect of community policing (Moore 1992), while others do not (Goldstein 1990). Community policing is such an ambiguous term that debating this point is not particularly productive. Though problem solving has been most often discussed with regard to patrol officers, there are many cases in which detectives have applied a problem-oriented approach. The principles of problem solving have been explained in other books and reports (Goldstein 1979; Goldstein 1990; Eck and Spelman 1987), and the basic approach can be easily adapted to detectives. In fact, because detectives are not tied to a radio and have more control over how they use their time, its possible that they would find it easier to address problems than would patrol officers. Rather than go over the details of problem-oriented policing, we will examine three examples of how detectives have addressed problems.

Domestic Homicides

One of the very first examples of how detectives used a problem-oriented approach occurred in Newport News, Virginia, during the first effort to use problem solving throughout an agency. One of the homicide detectives felt that as satisfying as it was to solve murders, it would be more satisfying to prevent them from occurring. He noted that half of the homicides the department had investigated in the previous year were related to domestic violence. Moreover, in half of these cases the police had been to the address in the past. This led him to consider the possibility of early intervention with the couples involved.

He brought together representatives from many public and private organizations: the prosecutor's office, the women's advocates, the hospitals, the local newspaper, the military, and many others. Together, they developed a program that forced the couples into mandatory counseling. Under very specific circumstances (e.g., serious injury, presence of a gun or knife, and so forth), arrests of the assaulter were mandatory. The prosecutor agreed to refuse to drop charges unless the abuser and the victim entered counseling. If they completed the counseling and if the victim allowed, the charges could be dropped. The goal was to reduce repeat domestic violence and domestic homicides while keeping families intact. No formal evaluation has been conducted, so it is impossible to be certain of the results. Nevertheless, the police department reports that domestic homicides and repeat domestic violence declined in the first years after implementation.

Gas Station Robberies

The Edmonton, Alberta, Police Service, as part of its community-policing reforms, has undertaken a variety of changes throughout the agency, including decentralization and despecialization of detectives. In addition, detectives are encouraged, like patrol constables, to address problems. Patrol constables and decentralized detectives are focused on geographically based communities (i.e., neighborhoods). The headquarters detectives are encouraged to look for nongeographic communities. For example, two detectives are members of the bankers association and attend its meetings.

One robbery detective noted that one chain of gas stations had a very high robbery rate. Because of the high cigarette tax in Canada, there is a thriving black market for cigarettes, and cigarette theft can be lucrative. The detective reviewed the crime reports and found that many of the robberies involved the theft of cigarettes and nothing else. He visited those stations and noted that the single attendant was in a small booth stocked with candy, cigarettes, and other small items. The detective worked with the managers of the gas station chain to identify a number of simple changes that could be made to the booth, cigarette displays, and attendant procedures. The gas station chain made the changes. The police service reports a major decline in the robberies of these gas stations.

Drug Houses

Cities throughout the United States have seen an increase in street drug sales over the last decade. More recently, some cities have seen a decline in open street sales. Trends in sales from indoor locations are more difficult to determine because these places are harder to detect. The San Diego Police Department's narcotics section noted that their investigators were repeatedly called back to the same apartment build-ings and rental houses. They asked the question: Is there something that can be done about repeat drug places? One approach was to go directly to property owners. Owners were told about the use of their rental property for drug dealing, and their cooperation was sought in evicting the dealers. Though landlords were rarely uncooperative, the police used civil law—nuisance abatement—in conjunction with crimi-nal law to close down drug houses. If after the police warned a land-lord about the drug dealing the dealing continued, and it was determined that the landlord had done nothing to curb the problem, the police asked the city attorney to file a civil suit in state court to seize the house as a public nuisance. This approach has not solved the drug problem in the city, but it has resulted in the elimination of a number of persistent drug locations. In combination with the abate-ment approach, San Diego detectives (like police officials in other cit-ies) put on training courses for landlords to help them manage their property better and keep out drug offenders.

Problem-Solving Typology

These examples were selected because they demonstrate the diverse nature of problems and solutions detectives have addressed. They also illustrate that problem solving can be an effective method of prevent-ing crime. And they show how strict enforcement can be used as part of a comprehensive prevention strategy. If detectives increase their overall arrest rate, chances of a reduction in crime are small, but if they target their efforts and use their powers of arrest along with other tactics, it is possible to have an impact on crime.

Problem solving requires the examination of crime patterns, a manage-ment reform consistently recommended by advocates of managing crimi-nal investigations. Three basic types of patterns can be examined. First, one can look for common offenders. This is the most common approach to applying crime analysis to investigations. Another approach is to look for common victims or targets. The Edmonton detective who noted that one chain of gas stations was suffering a high number of robberies illus-trates this example. By determining what is similar about the victims and targets and how they differ from nonvictims and nontargets, one can make some headway toward solutions. A third approach, illus-trated by the San Diego example, is to focus on repeat places and ask why crimes are occurring there instead of at other, similar places.

CONCLUSION

In this chapter we have examined some of the developments in in-vestigative reform. We have seen how plainclothes investigations have gone through cycles of popularity and decline. We have seen how, in the last twenty-five years, research has attempted to examine the productivity of detectives. We asked what the goals of investigations are. Then we examined the changes police officials have made in investigative operations, changes that have often been lumped together under the title of "managing criminal investigations." We noted how the reforms have severe limitations and summarized these limitations with three laws of investigations. Finally, we reviewed the proposal that detectives focus more on justice and crime prevention and focus less on crime control through law enforcement.

A recurring theme of this chapter is that managing criminal investigations involves conflicting difficulties. Addressing one almost necessarily ensures that the other will get worse, thus forcing change in another directions. We see cycles of expansion and contraction of specialized investigative units, movements from centralization to decentralization and back, enthusiasm for proactive tactics followed by focusing on reactive investigations, and so on. One of the reasons for this seeming lack of permanent unassailable management principles is that we try to force investigative units to do too much with too little.

Instead of recognizing that justice is an important goal in and of itself, some have emphasized the crime-control efficacy of investigations. Though there are some important exceptions, follow-up investigations are unlikely to have much influence on overall crime rates. If detectives focused on justice and crime prevention, then there would be some possibility that more progress could be made. If detective work were more than tracking down and arresting offenders, detectives would have to interact with communities. They would also have to work more with other sections of the police force and other public and private groups to achieve their objectives. Since most of this work would be open, there would be less likelihood of corruption and abuse of authority, perceived or otherwise. One must be careful about making greater claims for police reforms than can be delivered. Nevertheless, even modest improvements would be welcome.

NOTE

Reprinted from *Quantifying Quality* with permission from the Police Executive Research Forum. Copyright by Police Executive Research Forum.

BIBLIOGRAPHY

Bayley, D. (1992). Comparative Organization of the Police in English-Speaking Countries. In *Modern Policing, Crime and Justice*, Vol. 15, edited by M. Tonry and N. Morris. Chicago: University of Chicago Press.

Bloch, P., and J. Bell. (1976). *Managing Investigations: The Rochester System.* Washington, D.C.: Police Foundation.

Blumstein, A.; J. Cohen; and D. Nagin, eds. (1978). *Deterrence and Incapacitation: Estimating the Effects of Criminal Sanctions on Crime Rates.* Washington, D.C.: National Academy of Sciences.

Blumstein, A.; J. Cohen; J. Roth; and C. Visher, eds. (1986). *Criminal Careers and "Career Criminals."* Vol. 1. Washington, D.C.: National Academy of Sciences.

Cawley, D.; H. Miron; W. Araujo; R. Wasserman; T. Mannello; and Y. Huffman. (1977). *Managing Criminal Investigations: Manual.* Washington, D.C.: U.S. Department of Justice, Law Enforcement Assistance Administration.

Cobb, B. (1957). *The First Detectives.* London: Faber and Faber.

Critchley, T. (1979). *A History of Police in England and Wales.* London: Constable.

Daley, R. (1971). *Target Blue: An Insider's View of the NYPD.* New York: Delacorte Press.

Eck, J. (1983). *Solving Crimes: The Investigation of Burglary and Robbery.* Washington, D.C.: Police Executive Research Forum.

Eck, J. (1979). *Managing Case Assignments: The Burglary Investigation Decision Model Replication.* Washington, D.C.: Police Executive Research Forum.

Eck, J., and W. Spelman. (1987). *Problem Solving: Problem-Oriented Policing in Newport News.* Washington, D.C.: Police Executive Research Forum.

Fitzgerald, P. (1888). *Chronicles of Bow Street Police Office with an Account of the Magistrates, "Runner" and Police; and a Selection of the Most Interesting Cases.* Vol. 1. London: Chapman and Hall.

Forssell, N. (1970). *Fouche: The Man Napoleon Feared.* New York: AMS Press.

Goldstein, H. (1990). *Problem-Oriented Policing.* New York: McGraw-Hill.

Goldstein, H. (1979). Improving Policing: A Problem-Oriented Approach. *Crime and Delinquency* 25: 2.

Greenberg, B.; O. Yu; and K. Lang. (1973). *Enhancement of the Investigative Function.* Vol. 1, *Analysis and Conclusions.* Springfield, Va.: National Technical Information Service.

Greenberg, I., and R. Wasserman. (1979). *Managing Criminal Investigations.* Washington, D.C.: U.S. Department of Justice, Law Enforcement Assistance Administration.

Greenwood, P. (1970). *An Analysis of the Apprehension Activities of the New York City Police Department.* New York: Rand Institute.

Greenwood, P.; J. Petersilia; and J. Chaiken. (1977). *The Criminal Investigation Process.* Lexington, Mass.: D. C. Heath.

Howson, G. (1970). *Thief-Taker General: Jonathan Wild and the Emergence of Crime and Corruption as a Way of Life in Eighteenth-Century England.* New Brunswick, N.J.: Transaction.

Isaacs, H. (1967). A Study of Communications, Crimes and Arrests in a Metropolitan Police Department. In *Task Force Report: Science and Technology.* Washington, D.C.: U. S. Government Printing Office.

Johnson, N., and D. Healy. (1978). *Felony Investigation Decision Models.* St. Paul: Minnesota Statistical Analysis Center.

Kuykendall, J. (1986). The Municipal Police Detective: An Historical Analysis. *Criminology* 24: 175–201.

Martin, S., and L. Sherman. (1986). Selective Apprehension: A Police Strategy for Repeat Offenders. *Criminology* 24: 155–173.

Moore, M. (1992). Problem-Solving and Community Policing. In *Crime and Justice*. Vol. 15, edited by M. Tonry and N. Morris. Chicago: University of Chicago Press.

Murphy, P., and T. Pate. (1977). *Commissioner: A View from the Top of American Law Enforcement*. New York: Simon & Schuster.

Pate, T.; R. Bowers; and R. Parks. (1976). *Three Approaches to Criminal Apprehension in Kansas City: An Evaluation Report*. Washington, D.C.: Police Foundation.

Peterson, J. (1974). *The Utilization of Criminalistics Services by the Police: An Analysis of the Physical Evidence Recovery Process*. Washington, D.C.: U.S. Department of Justice, Law Enforcement Assistance Administration.

Porter, B. (1987). *The Origins of the Vigilante State: The London Metropolitan Police Special Branch before the First World War*. London: Weidenfeld and Nicolson.

Schwartz, A., and S. Clarren. (1977). *The Cincinnati Team Policing Experiment: A Summary Report*. Washington, D.C.: Police Foundation.

Sechrest, L.; S. White; and E. Brown, eds. (1979). *The Rehabilitation of Criminal Offenders: Problems and Prospects*. Washington, D.C.: National Academy of Sciences.

Seedman, A., and P. Hellman. (1974). *Chief*. New York: Arthur Fields Books.

Sherman, L. (1983). From Whodunit to Who Does It: Fairness and Target Selection in Deceptive Investigations. In *ABSCAM Ethics: Moral Issues and Deception in Law Enforcement*, edited by G. Caplan. Washington, D.C.: Police Foundation.

Sherman, L. (1978). *Scandal and Reform: Controlling Police Corruption*. Berkeley and Los Angeles: University of California Press.

Sherman, L.; C. Milton; and T. Kelly. (1973). *Team Policing: Seven Case Studies*. Washington, D.C.: Police Foundation.

Skolnick, J. (1966). *Justice without Trial: Law Enforcement in Democratic Society*. New York: John Wiley and Sons.

Skolnick, J., and D. Bayley. (1986). *The New Blue Line: Police Innovation in Six American Cities*. New York: The Free Press.

11

Affirmative Action, Diversity, and Law Enforcement

Samuel Walker and Tara O'Connor Shelley

How have affirmative action and diversity issues affected policing? Over the past twenty years the composition of American law-enforcement agencies have become increasingly diverse. Though most departments have not yet attained many of the goals of affirmative action, Walker (1989) reports that by 1988 African Americans composed 12.3 percent of all police positions. This was up from 6.5 percent in 1975. He reported that Hispanic officers represented an estimated 4.1 percent of all sworn officers in 1988. Today, in at least five departments in the fifty largest cities, white officers constitute the minority (Washington, D.C., Miami, Atlanta, Detroit, and El Paso).

The impact of the introduction of diversity into the traditional white male police subculture has gone largely unexplored, despite some evidence that changes have been accompanied by considerable conflict and turmoil. According to the Equal Employment Opportunity Commission (EEOC), from 1991 to 1996 over 11,165 discrimination complaints were filed. Further, in some departments the rank and file is polarized along racial and ethnic lines. Jacobs and Cohen (1978) indicate that neither the New York nor the Chicago police departments are homogenous and that they and other police departments struggle with interracial conflict. In most large city departments, African-American and Hispanic officers belong to separate fraternal organizations (the National Organization of Black Law Enforcement Executives, the National Black Police Officers Association, the Hispanic American Police Association, and various local organizations and chapters) and, in some cases, minority officers have withdrawn from local police unions, which they criticize as representing white officers at the expense of others. In fact, litigation over affirmative action often pits minority organizations (e.g., Black Guardians) against local police unions.

In some departments the racial and ethnic differences have culminated in actual violence. Anecdotal accounts of fights between different groups of officers in police station houses around the country (especially in Philadelphia, Miami, and Washington, D.C.) are common and widespread. In response, many agencies have tried sensitivity training and other cultural awareness programs, although, to date, the results from these efforts have offered little cause for optimism. Though no systematic or reliable data about the extent of the problem are available, the persistence of reports from knowledgeable and credible sources suggests that the problems are real. If so, the impacts on police and community relations are both numerous and considerable.

THE NEED FOR ATTENTION

Obtaining additional knowledge is critical because intergroup racial conflict imposes serious costs on police organizations. Managerially, it can damage morale, create divisions that interfere with the pursuit of departmental goals and employee performance, and distract the attention of upper and mid-level management from long-term department goals. In some instances, conflict may cause qualified personnel to resign from the agency or even leave policing as a profession. This, in turn, can impact recruitment and selection efforts as opinions about the police department as a workplace spread throughout the minority community. Finally, employment discrimination litigation is costly to the agency and the jurisdiction.

Such intergroup conflict is an operational issue as well. Taken together, the issues of intergroup conflict have implications for police effectiveness and the implementation and maintenance of quality community-policing programs. Community policing brings policing into a new era where strong community relationships, partnership building, and problem solving are essential. When properly implemented, community policing offers the potential to reduce civil disorder and crime, though this potential can only be realized if police agencies learn to manage their diverse environments, both internally and externally (Fisher-Stewart 1994). For those agencies experiencing internal racial conflict and tension, bridge building may be difficult and the solutions to community conflicts remain beyond their grasp. As such, agencies need to examine their organizational cultures and determine how those cultures affect the people they employ and the communities they serve (Fisher-Stewart 1994).

Because law-enforcement agencies influence the communities they serve, personnel practices and the images portrayed to the public are visible reminders of organizational values. Underrepresentation of minorities that aggravates tensions can become self-reinforcing as capable women and minorities come to consider law enforcement as hostile to their interests, leaving them to seek employment elsewhere. Further, while much has been written about the issues and difficulties in recruiting and selecting minorities, little emphasis has been given to employment issues after the initial stages of an officer's career.

Despite its importance, however, the law-enforcement community has generally failed to acknowledge and address the problem of intergroup racial conflict. As Captain Larry Plummer states, "Behavior motivated by bigotry and hate is endemic to the law enforcement profession. It persists not so much because we fall victim to basic 'human' shortcomings, but rather because we—police professionals—have not taken the very deliberate individual and collective actions required to eliminate, or at least control the problem" (Plummer 1995).

Nor has the academic community helped much. In the professional literature there are few articles and little research discussing the issues of intergroup conflict. Most of the literature on employment discrimination and affirmative action is legalistic in nature, interpreting the formal requirements of the law. The issues that arise for agencies complying with equal employment opportunity laws that significantly alter the composition of their work forces are virtually ignored. Research addressing the retention rates of minorities and females in comparison with white males, as well as an analysis of the causes and influences affecting such rates (Kuykendall and Burns 1980), is largely missing.

WHAT IS CURRENTLY KNOWN

Any investigation of diversity and affirmative action in policing should begin with an historical perspective. Kuykendall and Burns (1980), for example, report that, early on, African-American officers were hired almost exclusively by large cities. By the turn of the century, in fact, African Americans represented only 2.7 percent of the population of the nation's sworn force. By the middle of the century, a University of Pennsylvania study (1957) of employment data from the twenty largest police departments concluded that little had improved and that blacks continued to be substantially underrepresented among sworn officers. The population of Chicago, for example, was nearly 14 percent African American, yet the police force was only 3.9 percent black (ACLU of Southern California 1984).

Title VII of the 1964 Civil Rights Act (as amended in 1972) prohibits discrimination on the basis of race, color, sex, or national origin. Still, even since the adoption of Title VII, the representation of minorities among the police has improved only slowly. In addition, while increased employment of minority officers introduces diversity into police organizations, it does not by itself result in equality. For example, African Americans who were able to obtain positions in the few departments willing to open their ranks to minorities were initially denied desirable job assignments with regard to both position and location. In Miami, they were not permitted to drive departmental vehicles, so they patrolled their beats on foot or by bicycle (Mor 1992). As a consequence of unfair assignments, they were further discriminated against in evaluation for promotions (Leinen 1984), and when African-American officers did receive promotions, often their duties differed from those of white officers holding the same positions (Kuykendall and Burns 1980). These incidents of inequality contributed to the beginnings of intergroup racial conflict and tensions in law-enforcement agencies.

The 1967 Police Task Force of the President's Commission on Law Enforcement and Administration of Justice urged police departments in all communities with substantial minority populations to vigorously recruit minority officers. The Kerner Commission concurred with the President's commission recommendation after studying twenty-eight police departments and finding the median figure for the African-American population on these forces to be only 6 percent while the median figures for African Americans in the general population was approximately 24 percent. These commissions, the civil rights movement, and the creation of the Law Enforcement Assistance Administration (LEAA) and the Law Enforcement Education Program (LEEP) began the process of change within the law-enforcement community. As others have observed, however, law-enforcement agencies are known for resisting change (Guyot 1979). This resistance has likely contributed, and continues to contribute, to intergroup racial conflict. Nevertheless, some police agencies have begun to address prejudice and discrimination within their ranks and now voluntarily participate in affirmative action and diversity plans. Though the efforts and results of the civil rights movement, the formations of commissions, the LEAA, and the LEEP are noteworthy, problems with recruitment and diversity still exist and police agencies are unsure about how to respond.

How Diverse Are Today's Police Departments?

In 1983, 1988, and 1992, Walker surveyed police departments in the fifty largest cities to collect data on the employment of African-American and Hispanic officers in each department. With his results, he created an index to measure the percentage of minorities employed relative to the percentage of minorities in the local population (yielding an index of 0 to 1). The results of Walker's surveys revealed that police departments in the nation's fifty largest cities made only modest progress during the 1980s. Specifically, while nearly half of the large-city departments exhibited some progress in employing African-American officers, 17 percent reported a decline in the number of African-American officers employed (Walker 1989). For Hispanic officers, Walker (1989) explains that 42 percent of the departments reported increases in the percentages employed, while 11 percent reported a decline.

Walker and Turner (1992) surveyed the same departments to compare current employment with results from the 1983 survey. By 1992, they discovered that 38 percent of the departments surveyed had achieved an index of 0.74 or higher, compared with only 6 percent in 1983. The percentage of departments with an index of less than 0.50 dropped from 52 percent to 16 percent. With respect to Hispanic officers, the data indicate much less progress, with only 20 percent of the responding departments achieving the 0.74 index, compared to 16 percent in 1983. The percentage of departments with an index of less than 0.50 for Hispanic officers declined from 58 percent to 42 percent. It is important to note that Walker's research made no attempt to determine the causes of progress (or lack of progress) in individual departments (Walker and Turner 1992). However, previous research by Lewis (1989) and Martin (1989) attribute employment trends of minority officers to the presence of affirmative action plans (voluntary or court ordered).

Beyond just the presence of minorities in policing, the racial diversity of police supervisory positions is important as well. According to Kaufman and Gaiter (1995), for example, in New York City, where 28.7 percent of the population and 11.4 percent of police are African American, only 6.6 percent of police supervisors are black. Similarly, in Jacksonville, Florida, where 25.2 percent of the population and 22.3 percent of the force are black, only 4.8 percent of supervisors are black. Kaufman and Gaiter (1995) elaborate further and explain that, "Most major cities show similar disparities, which many blacks to lawsuits and other opposition from mostly white unions." Some blacks also report it is difficult to be assigned to elite units such as SWAT teams or to headquarters jobs that help lead to promotions (Kaufman and Gaiter 1995).

Minorities and Attitudinal Studies

It is often assumed that white officers are concerned that the added pressures of affirmative action to recruit minorities results in lowered selection standards and thus reduced professionalism of the police officer role (Felkenes 1990). Some white officers feel that minorities are given preferential treatment and perceive themselves as the real minority group. For example, in Los Angeles white supervisors and field training officers have claimed that the practices of graduating practically all minority recruits in order to meet quota requirements has had the effect of placing incompetent officers in the field—a claim not supported by data (Felkenes 1990). Nonetheless, Kaufman and Gaiter (1995) quote departmental observers who believe "There is a lot of feeling among white officers that they lowered the standards to bring in black officers." Recently, in Hartford, Connecticut, officers brought suit against the city alleging that promotions to sergeant fell victim to reverse discrimination. These officers contend that the department used unfair oral tests to promote a larger number of women and minority officers (Bosarge 1996). On the other hand, minority groups often feel that Caucasian officers receive preferential treatment, and are themselves taking legal action. In Chicago for example, Felkenes (1990) tells about members of the Afro-American Patrolmen League freezing the hiring and promotion of all officers in addition to tying up general revenue funds for the entire city.

Concerning officers' attitudes about policing, John Teahan (1975) conducted a longitudinal eighteen-month study on the attitudinal differences between black and white officers. After surveying ninety-seven white and twenty-four black officers, he found significant attitudinal shifts for both groups from the time they entered the police academy until they were assigned to patrol. In contrast to the belief that contact between groups enhances the acceptance of diversity and builds solidarity, his results found polarization instead. Attitude shifts for blacks reflected increased unity, increased negative evaluations of white officers, and a perception that preferential treatment was given to whites. White officers meanwhile developed a decreased interest in equality for minorities, an increase in prejudice toward blacks, and a perception that blacks received preferential treatment. Both groups experienced an increased desire for separate organizations based on race (Teahan 1975). Whether Teahan's findings are more generally felt by officers in other settings is, of course, not known.

Kuykendall and Burns (1980), however, do provide an historical perspective about discrimination toward blacks as police officers as well as strategies that have been used to attempt to decrease discrimination. These authors perceived that practices of overt organizational discrimination were transformed in the 1960s and were largely replaced with both overt and covert discrimination by individual officers. Leinen (1984) tracked patterns of discrimination against police officers by exploring the work relationships between whites and African Americans from the perspective of forty-six black New York City police officers. Using an interview procedure, his conclusions were as follows:

- fifty-two percent of the respondents felt that black officers were treated similarly to white officers. They reasoned this was the result of government intervention and civil rights activists.
- twenty-four percent perceived discrepancies between official departmental policy and practices of individual white superiors toward black officers.
- More than 19 percent were dissatisfied with the progress made in attempting to remove racial barriers to ensure full job equality and opportunities. This group indicated that discrimination existed, both at the individual level and in the operation of the department in its entirety.

Meanwhile, Carter's (1986) survey and interview data indicate that Hispanic officers perceive departmental discrimination as well. Carter concluded that minority officers continue to feel that they experience discrimination, even though 70 percent of the personnel in the organization he studied were of an ethnic minority. From this, he inferred that the perceptions of discrimination may be even more pervasive in departments where members of racial and ethnic groups are in a true numerical minority.

Other studies have investigated other possible indicators of inequality factors. Stein (1986) and Dye and Renick (1981) each noted that city size is an important factor in creating a hospitable environment for minorities. Stein (1986) reasoned that larger cities create a more hospitable environment for affirmative action because they offer more employment opportunities as well as better educated and civic-minded individuals more accepting of affirmative action. There are geographical, cultural, and economic indicators as well. According to Warner, Steel, and Lovrich (1990), "Both cultural and economic variation between regions have been suggested as important circumstantial factors in compliance with affirmative action." They defend this statement with evidence presented by Stein (1986), who found that "If a city is located within the Sunbelt, it may add seven percent to its minority work force component due to the more favorable economic conditions existing in that part of the country" (p. 702). Warner, Steel, and Lovrich (1990) also cite Riccucci (1986) who suggested that "Employer and private sector union discriminatory practices have long been ascribed to the south. . . . The employment progress of minorities is expected to be greater in cities outside the South" (p. 7). They also note that one of the most significant determinants of minority representation in municipalities is the number of minority residents. Stein (1986) adds that a significant concentration of minority residents translates into a potential labor pool and "the need for elected officials to recognize their minority constituents" (p. 699).

The Impacts of Diversity

In examining the institutionalized racism that continues to exist in society, it is logical to conclude that it influences the law-enforcement community as well, since it is a microcosm of society itself (Fisher-Stewart 1994). When examining the impacts of diversity, we should begin by exploring and investigating the kinds of effects diversity and affirmative action might be expected to have on the culture of law enforcement. An increase in minority officers hired may have various implications for individual police departments. It has potentially significant ramifications for the dynamics of the police culture, the role of the local police union, and the public perception of the department itself (Walker 1989). Conflicts, tensions, miscommunications, misunderstandings, prejudice, discrimination, and racism (intentional or unintentional) are also likely to occur. For example, Kaufman and Gaiter reported in 1995 that tensions exploded in Detroit the summer of 1975, when off-duty white officers protested a court ruling that allowed certain black officers exemption from layoffs. The protest resulted in the assault of a black officer and a two-hour standoff between white and black officers with guns drawn. Moreover, in St. Louis, one commander reported that, as a result of hostilities between officers of different races, he had to coax black police officers to ride with white partners (Kaufman and Gaiter 1995).

To begin an exploration of the possible impacts of affirmative action and diversity, it is important to define terminology. For purposes of this chapter, "conflict" is defined as a clash between opposing elements, ideas, or forces, while "tension" is defined as a state of strained relations; uneasiness due to hostility (Guralnik 1986). Carter (1986) defines prejudice as "an attitude; it is an integration of one's values, beliefs, and cultural norms as they are reflected in an individual's mental processes when assessing a person, place, or object." Discrimination is a behavior illustrated when one's attitudes are acted upon and produce inequitable treatment (Carter 1986). According to Carter, there are different forms of prejudice and discrimination that can interact with the policing function. He defines them as follows:

- *Homeostatic prejudice* is the desire to maintain attitudes and behavior in a manner consistent with one's social group standards. Those who do not conform with the defined status quo will experience discrimination which will increase the variance from the status quo.

- *Institutional discrimination* is where custom, law, or policy discriminates against individuals or groups. The prejudice becomes the convention of institutional behavior and occurs under the guise of legitimacy.
- *Circumstantial discrimination* is developed by the perceptions and relationships between two people which occur during some form of encounter. It is founded in one person's perception of another's values, attitudes, and beliefs. If the perceived characteristics conflict, then discrimination may occur.

Mor (1992) has a similar opinion that discrimination occurs at individual and organizational levels. He believes prejudice results from several factors, one of which is the process of contamination. In his opinion, we all are affected and influenced by those around us as we grow from children to adults. Family, friends, and others teach us how to how to treat others according to their racial, ethnic, and religious backgrounds. Another contributing factor is ethnocentrism—the natural tendency to view our own culture and customs as correct and superior and to judge others by those standards (Mor 1992).

An officer who experiences discrimination (or the perception of discrimination) within his or her organization could become cynical, alienated, and isolated. The stresses imposed by an organization that discriminates may contribute to officers acting in a more authoritative manner toward citizens. This is what Carter (1986) defines as "cumulative interactive stressors." Leinen (1984) suggests that officer performance may also be affected: "For blacks and other ethnic minorities, stereotypical 'myths' may affect their performance as police officers, due to persisting views in which race is the sole criteria used by white police officers in distinguishing the good guys from the bad." Peter Sarna, quoted in Kaufman and Gaiter (1995), agrees that "The tensions over affirmative action fester. At some point they bubble over in a reduced level of cooperation, in a lack of enthusiastic assistance. If people have lingering tension, it is going to affect their work." Felkenes (1990) points out that "Rulings and legislation can neither legislate against nor eliminate persisting negative attitudes, stereotypical ideologies and narrow concepts of equality and justice which continue to work to the disadvantage of these groups." Such attitudes may have a negative impact on both the performance and attrition of racial minorities (Felkenes 1990).

In addition, intergroup racial conflict may cause qualified personnel to voluntarily resign from police work. David Freed, a *Los Angeles Times* reporter, conducted a three-month journalistic study of the LAPD where he found that 1985–1986 minority academy graduates were either fired or resigned prior to finishing probationary periods at twice the rate as that of their white male counterparts. With respect to Caucasians, 5.5 percent failed to complete a probationary period, compared to 10.7 percent for Hispanics and 12.3 percent for blacks. Contrasting sharply, failure rates in the training academy are 2.6 percent for Blacks, 3.4 percent for Hispanics, and 13 percent for Caucasians. Freed inferred that minorities are more successful in training but less successful in probationary periods. The LAPD also speculate that the organizational culture influences the success rates of new minority recruits. Biases against women and minorities may work to the disadvantage of police departments in attracting and retaining qualified, competent individuals from both minority and majority groups.

Intergroup racial conflict may also lead minorities to establish their own professional organizations. Hispanic and black officers have created separate associations and support organizations for patrol and command-level officers. Examples include the National Black Police Officers Association, the National Organization of Black Law Enforcement Executives, the Hispanic American Police Association, and various other local organizations.

Similarly, "reverse discrimination" claims by white male officers are no longer unusual in many police agencies. Affirmative action often divides an agency internally between those that are helped by it and those who feel they are discriminated by it when implemented (Warner, Steel, and Lovrich 1990). When one's race, religion, gender, or ethnic identity is perceived as a factor in appointment, the issue of preferential treatment arises. This has led to resentment and actual increases in racial disharmony (Warner, Steel, and Lovrich 1990). In addition, some feel that the quality of police services suffers when less-qualified individuals are hired to meet quotas (see *San Francisco Police Officers Association v. San Francisco*; Lott 1997).

Do departments attempt to control, eliminate, or avoid these conflicts? For the most part, the internal police culture has difficulty admitting diversity problems may exist within police departments and most likely has difficulty in acknowledging that a single cultural focus does and can create conflict (Fisher-Stewart 1994). Fisher-Stewart further argues that "The police organizational culture, reinforced through policies, practices, and informal norms, can foster a bias against those who are different and can have serious ramifications in the treatment of minority and female segments of society, both within the police department and in the community."

It is easy to rationalize why law-enforcement agencies have ignored or covered up the problems of interracial conflict. To acknowledge intergroup racial conflict is to publicly admit that problems exist. That few departments will expose such politically sensitive and volatile information is hardly surprising, since experience tells us that most businesses and other organizations are reluctant to do so as well. Racial conflict is highly sensitive in nature and people often fear that open discussion will make things worse. Ignoring such problems, however, is most certainly detrimental to policing.

Some departments, in attempting to reduce discrimination, have created diversity, sensitivity, and human relations training to attempt to gain organizational control over intergroup conflict. The impact of these programs is problematic, because it is not known whether the content of such programs addresses the specific problems that exist in law enforcement. Many sensitivity and diversity training programs are generic in nature, designed to heighten knowledge and sensitivity about different racial and ethnic groups with no content specifically related to law enforcement. There are few, if any, published evaluations of the effectiveness of sensitivity and diversity training programs in law-enforcement agencies. It is also possible that police managers contract for such programs more for the sake of appearance and lip service to the community than with any assurance that they will be effective. Finally, according to Fisher, social habits and prejudice are so deeply rooted in one's personality that they are extremely difficult to change. Therefore, without strong leadership at national and local levels, the status quo will remain intact.

BIBLIOGRAPHY

American Civil Liberties Union of Southern California. (1984). *Of the Community and for the Community: Racial and Gender Integration in Southern California Police and Fire Departments.* Los Angeles: California Civil Liberties Union.

Bosarge, B. (1996). Hartford Police Sue Department, Allege Reverse Discrimination in Hiring. *Crime Control Digest* 30: 3.

Carter, D. (1986). Hispanic Officers' Perception of Discrimination. *Police Studies* 30: 204–210.

Decker, S., and R. Smith. (1980). Police Minority Recruitment: A Note on Its Effectiveness in Improving Black Evaluations of the Police. *Journal of Criminal Justice* 8: 166–183.

Dunham, R., and G. Alpert. (1993). *Critical Issues in Policing.* Prospect Heights, Ill.: Waveland.

Dye, T., and J. Renick. (1981). Political Power and City Jobs: Determinants of Minority Employment. *Social Science Quarterly* 62: 475–486.

Felkenes, G. (1990). *The Impact of Blake v. City of Los Angeles on the Selection, Recruitment, Training, Appointment, and Performance of Women and Minorities for the Los Angeles Police Department and the City of Los Angeles.* Claremont, Calif.: Claremont Graduate School.

Felkenes, G., and P. Unsinger. (n.d.). *Diversity, Affirmative Action and Law Enforcement.* Springfield, Ill.: Charles Thomas.

Fisher-Stewart, G. (1994). Multi-Cultural Training for Police. (ICMA MIS Report 26 [9]). Washington, D.C.: ICMA.

Guralnik, D. (1986). *Webster's New World Dictionary of the American Language.* New York: Prentice Hall.

Guyot, D. (1979). Bending Granite: Attempts to Change the Rank Structure of American Police Department. *Journal of Police Science and Administration* 7: 253–284.

Hochstedler, E. (1984). Impediments to Hiring Minorities in Public Police Agencies. *Journal of Police Science and Administration* 12: 227–240.

Hochstedler, E. (1982). *Analyses of Impediments to Hiring Minorities in Criminal Justice Agencies*. Washington, D.C.: National Institute of Justice.

Jacobs, J., and J. Cohen. (1978). The Impact of Racial Integration on the Police. *Journal of Police Science and Administration* 6: 168–183.

Kaufman, J., and D. Gaiter. (1995). Shades of Blue: Many Minority Police Doubt That the Force Is Really with Them: They Trail in Assignments, Promotions and Respect, Despite Integration Push. *Wall Street Journal*, 7 September.

Kenney, D., and S. Watson. (1997). Intelligence and the Selection of Police Recruits. *Managing Police Personnel*. Cincinnati: Anderson.

Kuykendall, J., and D. Burns. (1980). The Black Police Officers: An Historical Perspective. In *The Ambivalent Force: Perspectives on the Police*. 3d ed. New York: Holt, Reinhart, and Winston.

Lanam, M. (1993). *Achieving Ethnic Diversity in the Police Command Ranks by the Year 2001*. Sacramento: California Department of Justice, Commission on Peace Officer Standards and Training.

Leinen, S. (1984). *Black Police, White Society*. New York: New York University Press.

Lewis, W. (1989). Affirmative Action: Is It Just a Numbers Game? *Police Magazine* 5: 9–21.

Lott, J. (1997). *Does a Helping Hand Put Others at Risk? Affirmative Action, Police Departments, and Crime*. Chicago: University of Chicago School of Law.

Martin, S. (1991). *On the Move: The Status of Women in Policing*. Washington, D.C.: Police Foundation.

Martin, S. (1990). The Effectiveness of Affirmative Action: The Case of Women in Policing. *Women in Criminal Justice* 8: 490–504.

Martin, S. (1989). Women on the Move? A Report on the Status of Women in Policing. *Justice Quarterly* 10: 21–40.

Mor, H. (1992). Equality of Opportunity: Discrimination and its Resolution. In *Special Topics in Policing*. Cincinnati: Anderson.

Plummer, L. (1995). The Problem of Bigotry and Hate Requires a Collective, Intentional Response. In *Subject to Debate* 9 (10–11). Washington, D.C.: Police Executive Research Forum.

President's Commission on Law Enforcement and the Administration of Justice. (1967). *Task Force on the Police*. Washington, D.C.: U.S. Government Printing Office.

Reeves, B., and P. Smith. (1995). *Law Enforcement Management and Administrative Statistics, 1993: Data for Individual State and Local Agencies with 100 or More Officers*. Washington, D.C.: Bureau of Justice Statistics.

Riccucci, N. (1986). Female and Minority Employment in City Government: The Role of Unions. *Police Studies Journal* 15: 3–16.

Senaka, S. (1993). The Representation of Visible Minorities in Canadian Police: Employment Equity Beyond Rhetoric. *Police Studies* 16: 44–59.

Steel, B., and N. Lovrich. (1987). Equality and Efficiency Tradeoffs in Affirmative Action—Real or Imagined? The Case of Women in Policing. *Social Science Journal* 24: 121–134.

Stein, L. (1986). Representative Local Government: Minorities in the Municipal Work Force. *Journal of Politics* 48: 694–716.

Stewart, C. (1985). Multiple Claims under Rule 54(b): A Time for Reexamination? *Brigham Young University Law Review*, Spring, 2.

Stokes, L., and J. Scott. (1996). Affirmative Action and Selected Minority Groups in Law Enforcement. *Journal of Criminal Justice* 24: 29–38.

Stokes, L., and J. Scott. (1993). Affirmative Action Policy Standards and Employment of African Americans in Police Departments. *Western Journal of Black Studies* 17: 135–142.

Stroup, T. (1982). Affirmative Action and the Police. *Applied Psychology* 1: 1–19.

Teahan, J. (1975). A Longitudinal Study of Attitude Shifts among Black and White Police Officers. *Journal of Social Issues* 31: 47–56.

Walker, S. (1989). *Employment of Black and Hispanic Officers, 1983–1988: A Follow-Up Study*. Omaha: Center for Applied Urban Research.

Walker, S. (1985). Racial Minority and Female Employment in Policing: The Implications of Glacial Change. *Crime and Delinquency* 31: 555–573.

Walker, S., and K. Turner. (1992). *A Decade of Modest Progress: Employment of Black and Hispanic Officers, 1983–1992*. Omaha: University of Nebraska at Omaha, Department of Criminal Justice.

Warner, R.; B. Steel; and N. Lovrich. (1990). Economic, Political, and Institutional Determinants of Minority Employment in Municipal Police Departments. *American Journal of Police* 9: 41–61.

12

Citizen Complaints and the Community

Samuel Walker

The review of citizen complaints is an important and rapidly changing aspect of police oversight. Police officer misconduct results in public
dissatisfaction with police services, particularly when citizens who file
formal complaints believe that their charges are not investigated thor-
oughly. Problems associated with the complaint process have inhib-
ited positive relations between law-enforcement agencies and the
communities they serve. This issue is even more important today, as
American law enforcement moves into the era of community policing, with its emphasis on closer interaction between police departments and community residents.

Traditionally, police departments have reviewed citizen complaints
internally. Sworn officers assigned to the internal affairs or office of
professional standards unit investigate individual complaints and recommend a final disposition to the chief executive. But nationally, municipal law-enforcement agencies sustain an average of only 10 percent
of all citizen complaints reviewed internally (Pate and Fridell 1993,
113–120).

Because many citizens have been dissatisfied with the police's internal complaint review, community groups have long demanded some
form of external or citizen review. After many years of controversy
and conflict, external review has gained acceptance. By late 1994, there
were an estimated sixty-six external complaint-review bodies (Walker
and Wright 1995a). This represents a 400 percent increase over the thirteen that existed in 1980.

One index of the growth of external review was the creation in 1985 of a professional association for civilian review staff and board members, the International Association for Civilian Oversight of Law Enforcement (IACOLE). IACOLE publishes a newsletter, holds an annual meeting, and has published compendia describing external complaint-review procedures (IACOLE 1989). Many IACOLE members are from other countries. External review of police complaints is now found in almost all English-speaking countries (Goldsmith 1991).

A DEFINITION OF CITIZEN REVIEW

As a result of the rapid growth of external review, there is a wide variety of approaches used, differing with respect to organizational structure, role and mission, staffing, and operating procedures. No one term for external review has gained universal acceptance. "Citizen review," "civilian review," and "civilian oversight" are used interchangeably. This chapter uses the term "citizen review," as "civilian review" suggests a civilian–military dichotomy that is inappropriate for American policing.

For the purposes of this chapter, citizen review is defined as a procedure for handling citizen complaints about police officer misconduct that, at some point in the process, involves people who are not sworn officers. Several aspects of this definition merit explanation. First, the involvement of people who are not sworn officers is the crucial factor that gives a complaint review system its "external" or "citizen" character. Second, there are many different ways in which non-sworn people may participate in complaint review, which will be explained. Third, this definition does not use the term "review board." Many existing bodies involve an agency with a single director rather than a multimember board.

CHARACTERISTICS OF CITIZEN REVIEW

The Prevalence of Citizen Review

Citizen review is both a national and an international phenomenon. The majority of the big U.S. cities have adopted it, and medium-size and small cities are increasingly adopting it as well (Walker and Wright 1995a). As already mentioned, citizen review is almost universal in the other English-speaking countries (Goldsmith 1991).

No analyst has offered a conclusive explanation for the recent spread of citizen review. The concept was first proposed in 1935, and it was implemented in a few cities in the 1940s and 1950s. The procedures New York City and Philadelphia adopted were abolished in the 1960s, however. One factor contributing to the recent growth of citizen review has been the increase in African-American political activity, resulting in the election of mayors and city council members who consider police misconduct a major issue. It should be noted, however, that many cities with very small minority populations have also adopted citizen review. Opposition from police chiefs has declined significantly, as they increasingly recognize the importance of responding effectively to citizen complaints.

Types of Law-Enforcement Agencies

Most of the existing citizen review procedures apply to municipal police departments. By 1994, seven applied to county sheriff's departments. The Public Safety Review Commission in Denver handles complaints against both the municipal police department and the county sheriff's department. The Iowa Citizens' Aide/Ombudsman, meanwhile, is a state agency that handles complaints against any government agency in Iowa, including all city and county law-enforcement agencies.

City or County Size

Citizen review procedures are most common in the largest cities (e.g., New York City), but they are also increasingly common in medium-size cities (e.g., Dayton) and many small cities (e.g., Evanston, Dubuque). By 1994, 72 percent of the fifty largest cities had some form of citizen review, compared with only 26 percent of the fifty second-largest cities. Ten citizen review procedures were found in small cities. Seven additional procedures applied to county sheriffs' departments (Walker and Wright 1995a).

Citizen review procedures are most common in big cities because of the political dynamics affecting police misconduct. Since the 1950s, police misconduct has primarily been a civil rights issue. The African-American community has been the leading advocate of citizen review, and in most cities an incident involving an African American has precipitated the creation of some form of external review. Consequently, citizen review is most prevalent in those cities with large minority communities and/or effective local civil rights organizations.

Sources of Legal Authority

Citizen review bodies have been established in six different ways: by municipal ordinance, state statute, voter referendum, mayoral executive order, police chief administrative order, and memorandum of understanding. Municipal ordinances have established the vast majority. State statute created the Iowa Citizens' Aide/Ombudsman Office. A voter referendum authorized the San Diego Citizens' Review Board. A mayoral executive order established the Omaha Citizen Review Board. Police chiefs' administrative orders have authorized other citizen review bodies. Finally, the Community Advisory Panel in Dubuque, Iowa, was established by a memorandum of understanding between the city and the local National Association for the Advancement of Colored People (NAACP), as part of a settlement the U.S. Justice Department's Community Relations Service negotiated.

The various sources of legal authority reflect underlying differences in the nature of support for citizen review. The enactment of an ordinance indicates support by the majority of the elected representatives in that jurisdiction. From a historical perspective, it is worth noting that the two most important citizen review procedures in the 1950s and 1960s (in New York and Philadelphia) were created by mayoral executive order in the face of opposition from the cities' respective city councils. The lack of broad political support left both of them vulnerable to attack, and both were eventually abolished. The fact that ordinances have created most of the current procedures demonstrates the growing public support for citizen review.

The growing number of review procedures that police chiefs' administrative orders have created suggests increased support for citizen review within the law-enforcement profession. This represents a significant change in attitude from 1965, when the International Association of Chiefs of Police (IACP) adopted an official policy statement opposing citizen review. However, in recent years, the Police Executive Research Forum and the Commission on Accreditation for Law Enforcement Agencies (CALEA) have recognized the need for effective (although not necessarily external) procedures for reviewing citizen complaints.

ORGANIZATIONAL STRUCTURE

Board versus Agency

Citizen review takes many different organizational forms. Although the term "civilian review board" is still commonly used, it is inappropriate because many systems do not involve a multimember board. Of the sixty-six citizen review bodies that existed in 1995, fifty-four (82%) involved a multimember board, and eleven (17%) were agencies with a single director (Walker and Wright 1995b).

Boards are found in Minneapolis, San Francisco, Baltimore, and many other cities. Examples of agencies with a single administrator include the Office of Municipal Investigation in Cincinnati, the Office of Citizen Complaints in Kansas City, and the Flint, Michigan, Ombudsman.

The majority of citizen review bodies are separate municipal or county agencies, such as the Cincinnati Office of Municipal Investigation and the Kansas City Office of Citizen Complaints. Some, however, are essentially committees within the police department that include citizen members. Examples include Phoenix and Yonkers. Another variation exists in Evanston, Illinois, where one of the city council's standing committees is responsible for hearing complaints about the police.

There appears to be no clear explanation for why different forms of citizen review are found in various cities. Some are apparently borrowed from other cities, while other arrangements are unique. In the absence of any detailed comparative evaluations, it is impossible to say that any particular approach to citizen review is more appropriate for certain kinds of jurisdictions than others.

Employees Covered

Citizen review has traditionally applied only to complaints against police officers. Understandably, police officers have objected to being singled out for special scrutiny. In several cities, however, the citizen review agency is authorized to review complaints against other municipal employees as well. Nationally, 17 percent of the citizen review bodies in 1995 handled complaints against police officers and employees in other agencies (Walker and Wright 1995b). In Cincinnati, New Orleans, and Flint, the citizen review body handles complaints against any municipal employee. The Flint Ombudsman, for example, investigates complaints about the purchasing procedures of the city and the management of the cable television franchise.

The San Diego County Citizens Law Enforcement Review Board not only hears complaints against sheriff's deputies, custodial officers, and probation officers, but is also responsible for conducting an annual inspection of the county adult detention facilities. The Denver Public Safety Review Commission has jurisdiction over complaints involving both the Denver Police Department and the Denver County Sheriff's Department.

Policy Review

In addition to reviewing individual complaints, many citizen review bodies are authorized to review police department policies and procedures and to recommend changes where necessary. Almost two-thirds of all citizen review bodies (42 of 66) are authorized to review police policy (Walker and Wright 1995b). Examples of policy-review models include those in Dayton, Rochester, San Diego County, San Francisco, and Denver.

Seattle and San Jose have created auditor systems wherein the primary function is the review of police department policy. The auditors do not review individual complaints, in the sense of conducting the initial fact-finding. The San Diego County Citizens Law Enforcement Review Board is also responsible for conducting an annual inspection of the county adult detention facilities.

Policy review is meant to be a preventive measure to identify and correct problems that have either generated complaints or may cause complaints in the future. It is important to note that the policy-review function is advisory only. Citizen review bodies may recommend changes in law-enforcement policy but have no power to impose them.

Citizen review agencies have reviewed a variety of police department policies. The San Francisco Office of Citizen Complaints, for example, recommended that the police department develop written policies regarding the arrest of disabled people and specialized training for handling "[people] whose gender may not be immediately apparent." The Denver Public Safety Review Commission recommended changes in how the Denver Police Department compiled its gang list. The San Jose Independent Police Auditor recommended and secured changes in how internal affairs handled complaints, including changes in the system for classifying complaints and in how investigators maintained their notes.

The Nature of Citizen Input

The most important distinction among various citizen review procedures involves the nature of citizen input. Several different classification systems have been developed to categorize citizen review bodies in this regard (Walker and Bumphus 1991; Kerstetter 1985; Perez 1994; Goldsmith 1988). Despite some differences in terminology, the various classification systems are roughly similar. This chapter uses the classification system Walker and Bumphus (1991) developed.

Class I. The most independent citizen review bodies are those where people who are not sworn police officers handle complaints. A full-time professional investigator who is not a sworn officer conducts the initial fact-finding investigation of each complaint. Non-sworn personnel also review investigative reports and make recommendations to the law-enforcement chief executive. Complaint procedures of this type are found, for example, in New Orleans and Cincinnati.

Class II. In some jurisdictions sworn officers in the police department investigate citizen complaints. A non-sworn individual or a board that contains at least some non-sworn people reviews the officers' reports. The individual or board then recommends action to the chief law-enforcement executive. Examples are found in Kansas City, Portland, and Albuquerque. Because sworn officers conduct the initial fact-finding investigation, Class II systems are considered less independent of the police than Class I systems.

Class III. Citizens participate even less in Class III systems. In these systems, the police department investigates and reviews citizen complaints. Internal affairs then recommends action to the chief executive. If the complainant is not satisfied with the final disposition, however, he or she may appeal the decision to a board containing at least some non-sworn individuals. This board reviews the complaint and may recommend a different disposition to the chief executive. Omaha is an example of a Class III system.

Class IV. Two cities, Seattle and San Jose, have established auditors for citizen complaints; these cities have Class IV systems. The auditor does not investigate individual citizen complaints. Instead, the auditor reviews the police department's complaint procedure and recommends changes where necessary. The San Jose Independent Police Auditor, for example, reviews all force complaints and at least 20 percent of all complaints involving other allegations. It employs a call-back system, interviewing complainants to assess their satisfaction with the complaint process.

As Table 12.1 indicates, Class II systems are currently the most common form of citizen review; thirty-one of the sixty-six citizen review bodies (47%) that existed in early 1995 were Class II systems. Class I systems represent 33 percent (22 of 66) of the current citizen review procedures and Class III systems represent 17 percent of the existing procedures.

Board Composition

Eighty-three percent of the citizen review bodies in the United States involve multimember boards. These boards range in size from a high of twenty-four members to a low of three members (Walker and Wright 1995b). Among the boards cited in this text, the Rochester Civilian Review Board has three members, while the Baltimore Complaint Evaluation Board has twelve members. There does not appear to be any connection between the size of boards and the size of the jurisdictions they represent; large and small boards are found in cities of all sizes.

Police Officer Participation

Sworn police officers' participation as members of citizen review boards is a particularly controversial issue. Many citizen review advocates believe that police participation eliminates the independent

Table 12.1
Distribution of Citizen Review Procedures

Class	Fifty Largest Cities	Second Fifty Cities	Small Cities	County Sheriff's/ Police Departments	Total
I	17	0	3	2	22
II	13	10	4	4	31
III	4	3	3	1	11
IV	2	0	0	0	2
Total	36	13	10	7	66

or "citizen" character of external review. Nationally, 26 percent of citizen review boards have sworn officers as members (Walker and Wright 1995b). The number and percentage of these officers vary considerably. For example, the Baltimore Complaint Evaluation Board has twelve members, one of whom is a sworn police officer. The Yonkers Police Professional Standards Review Committee is evenly balanced with four sworn officers and four citizens. On the other hand, five of the seven members of the Phoenix Disciplinary Review Board are police officers. In Tucson, the police union has explicit authority to nominate two of the thirteen members of the complaint review board. In Omaha, the police union selects three of the Citizen Review Board's nine members.

There are different patterns with respect to public officials' participation on review boards. The citizen members of most boards are presumed to be people who do not hold public office. The Baltimore Complaint Evaluation Board, however, is dominated by high-ranking public officials (e.g., the state's attorney of the city of Baltimore, the attorney general of Maryland, the city solicitor of Baltimore, the police commissioner, the executive director of the Maryland Human Relations Commission, etc.).

Disciplinary Authority

Virtually all citizen review bodies in the United States only have the authority to recommend disciplinary action to the police chief executive. Local or state civil service law generally specifies the chief executive's responsibility regarding officer discipline. A few exceptions to the general rule exist. In Detroit, the Board of Police Commissioners has ultimate authority to "act as final authority in imposing or reviewing discipline of employees in the department." The Milwaukee Fire and Police Commission is also the final arbiter of police disciplinary cases.

MODELS OF CITIZEN REVIEW

With respect to the content of rules and procedures, some of the most important questions involve such issues as subpoena power and public hearings. A useful way to make sense of the variations that exist regarding these issues is to identify different models of the complaint process.

Some review bodies adopt a criminal trial model, in which the investigation of citizen complaints resembles the traditional criminal trial. These bodies tend to have subpoena power, public hearings, and strict rules of evidence, and they permit legal representation for police officers accused of misconduct. Other bodies, however, adopt an administrative review model, which resembles a traditional personnel disciplinary procedure. In this approach, the investigation of complaints is confidential, closed to the public, and without many of the other procedures associated with a criminal trial. Minneapolis follows the criminal trial model, while Cincinnati and New Orleans follow the administrative review model.

Subpoena Power

There has been much controversy over whether citizen review agencies should have the power to subpoena witnesses, including police officers. Citizen review advocates argue that subpoena power is necessary for the thorough investigation of complaints. Police officers, on the other hand, generally oppose granting citizen review bodies subpoena power. Nationally, almost 40 percent of review bodies (25 of 66) have subpoena power (Walker and Wright 1995b). Examples of such bodies include those in San Diego County and New Orleans.

Public Hearings

Some complaint review bodies conduct public hearings on individual complaints, while others keep hearings closed to the public. Nationally, almost half (46.2%) conduct public hearings (Walker and Wright 1995b). Even where public hearings are permitted, however, they are not necessarily mandatory. Most complaints are disposed of without a public hearing. Review bodies with public hearings include those in Minneapolis and San Diego County. Bodies that do not permit public hearings include those in Cincinnati and New Orleans.

Legal Representation

About one-third (21 of 66) of citizen review procedures specifically allow legal representation for the police officer, the citizen, or both

(Walker and Wright 1995b). Some citizen review bodies have adopted mediation or conciliation procedures to resolve citizen complaints. This approach is designed to be less costly and time consuming than the full criminal trial model, in addition to being satisfactory to both sides in the complaint. The Minneapolis Civilian Police Review Authority has a mediation procedure.

Subject Officer's Disciplinary Record

One of the most significant new developments regarding police officer misconduct has been the recognition that a small percentage of the officers in any department tend to generate a disproportionate share of citizen complaints (Christopher Commission 1991). Some departments have instituted special training sessions for such officers.

Existing citizen review bodies have different rules about the handling of an officer's disciplinary history. In San Diego County, the Citizens Law Enforcement Review Board may consider an officer's prior disciplinary record only after it has "sustained" a complaint against that officer. In Denver, the Public Safety Review Commission compiled a list of officers with three or more citizen complaints in the previous twenty-one months and reported that approximately 5 percent of all sworn officers were responsible for 43 percent of the complaints filed during that period. The Public Safety Review Commission discussed issues related to training, assignment, and policy development, based on these data. San Jose has a formal procedure for monitoring the number of complaints and requiring special training for officers with frequent complaints. Any San Jose police officer who is the subject of three or more formal complaints within a twelve-month period is required to receive intervention counseling. In Minneapolis, any officer who has participated in mediation for a serious misconduct allegation in the previous twelve months is not permitted to mediate a current complaint.

Information Dissemination

As public agencies, virtually all citizen review bodies publish information about their activities. There is considerable variety, however, in the nature of the information published and the manner of its release.

Annual Reports. Most civilian review bodies publish annual reports. The San Jose Independent Police Auditor also publishes quarterly reports. The Seattle Investigations Auditor is directed to publish reports twice a year. Annual reports generally provide a statistical summary of complaints and their disposition. Some reports, however, provide far more detailed data. The annual report of the New York City Civilian Complaint Investigative Bureau includes, for example, data on where complaints were filed, how complainants learned about the complaint process, what injuries were associated with use-of-force allegations, and how complaints were handled, in addition to summary information on officers who were the subjects of complaints. Such officer information includes length of service on the police force, place of residence, race, ethnicity, and gender. Data on the race of the officers are cross-tabulated with data on the race of the complainants. Generally, annual reports provide only summary data on complaints. Some of the reports of the Flint Ombudsman are unique in that they provide detailed descriptions of individual cases, including the name of the investigator who handled each case. The annual reports of some of the citizen review bodies in Canada and other countries contain the names of the complaining citizens.

Whether some or all of the data available to a citizen review body should be confidential is a matter of controversy involving a conflict between the public's right to information about a public agency and the complainants' and officers' rights to privacy. In particular jurisdictions, the confidentiality of data is governed by state statutes regarding public records and/or privacy, as well as police union contract provisions. The rules and procedures of complaint review bodies often include guidelines regarding confidentiality. For example, the administrative rules of the Minneapolis Civilian Police Review Authority and the New Orleans Office of Municipal Investigation specify which data are public and which are confidential in those jurisdictions.

Publicity.   Several cities have taken extra steps to publicize or otherwise facilitate the complaint process. Some cities have published information brochures or complaint forms in several languages. The San Francisco Office of Citizen Complaints, for example, has published a complaint form in four languages. Pittsburgh has published an employee's guide to the complaint process, including a statement of employee rights.

CONCLUSION

Citizen review of complaints against police officers is an important and rapidly changing aspect of American policing. Citizen review procedures have spread quickly in the last ten to fifteen years, and all indicators suggest that they will continue to spread in the near future. Because of this rapid growth, there is a wide variety of citizen review models. This chapter attempts to highlight the most important features of citizen review, but does not recommend any one model or ideal form of citizen review.

NOTE

Reprinted from *Citizen Review Resource Manual* with permission from the Police Executive Research Forum. Copyright by Police Executive Research Forum.

BIBLIOGRAPHY

Abbott, D.; L. Gold; and E. Rogowsky. (1969). *Police, Politics and Race: The New York City Referendum on Civilian Review*. New York: American Jewish Committee.

Adams, K. (1995). Measuring the Prevalence of Police Abuse of Force. In *And Justice For All: Understanding and Controlling Police Abuse of Force*, edited by W. Geller and H. Toch. Washington, D.C.: Police Executive Research Forum.

Administration of Complaints by Civilians against the Police. (1964). *Harvard Law Review* 77: 499–519.

American Civil Liberties Union (ACLU). (1992). *Fighting Police Abuse: A Community Action Manual*. New York: Author.

American Civil Liberties Union. (1966). *Police Power and Citizens' Rights: The Case for an Independent Police Review Board*. New York: Author.

American Civil Liberties Union. (1964). Civilian Review Boards (Policy no. 204). In *Policy Guide*. New York: Author.

American Civil Liberties Union of Northern California. (1992). *A Campaign of Deception: San Jose's Case against Civilian Review*. San Francisco: Author.

American Civil Liberties Union of Southern California. (1992). *The Call for Change Goes Unanswered*. Los Angeles: Author.

Americans for Effective Law Enforcement (AELE). (1982). Police Civilian Review Boards: Brief no. 82-3. *AELE Defense Manual*. San Francisco: Author.

Americans for Effective Law Enforcement. (1976). Brief no. 73-5 (1973). In *AELE Defense Manual*. Rev. ed. San Francisco: Author.

Barton, P. (1970). Civilian Review Boards and the Handling of Complaints against the Police. *University of Toronto Law Journal* 20: 448–469.

Bayley, D. (1992). Police Brutality and Civilian Oversight. In *Another Viewpoint*. No. 2. Evanston, Ill.: IACOLE.

Bellush, J., ed. (1971). *Race and Politics in New York City*. New York: Praeger.

Bray, R. (1962). Philadelphia's P.A.B.: A New Concept in Community Relations. *Villanova Law Review* 7: 656–673.

Brown, D. (1987). *The Police Complaints Procedure: A Survey of Complainants' Views* (Home Office research study no. 93). London: Her Majesty's Stationery Office.

Brown, D. (1983). *Civilian Review of Complaints against the Police: A Survey of the United States Literature* (Home Office research paper no. 19). London: Her Majesty's Stationery Office.

Brown, L. (1991). President's Message: The Civilian Review Board, Setting a Goal for Future Obsolescence. *Police Chief*, July, 6–7.

Caiden, G., and H. Hahn. (1979). Public Complaints against the Police. In *Evaluating Alternative Law-Enforcement Policies*, edited by R. Baker and F. Meyer, Jr. Lexington, Mass.: Lexington Books.

Carter, D. (1991). Police Disciplinary Procedures: A Review of Selected Police Departments. In *Police Deviance*. 2d ed., edited by T. Barker and D. Carter. Cincinnati: Anderson.

Chevigny, P. (1969a). *Police Complaints: A Handbook*. New York: ACLU.

Chevigny, P. (1969b). *Police Power: Police Abuses in New York City*. New York: Vintage Books.

Christopher Commission. (1991). *Report of the Independent Commission on the Los Angeles Police Department*. Los Angeles: City of Los Angeles.

Cohen, B. (1972). The Police Internal System of Justice in New York City. *Journal of Criminal Law, Criminology, and Police Science* 63: 54–67.

Cohen, B. (1970). *Police Internal Administration of Justice in New York City*. New York: Rand Institute.

Corbett, C. (1991). Complaints against the Police: The New Procedure of Informal Resolution. *Policing and Society* 2: 47–60.

Coxe, S. (1965). The Philadelphia Police Advisory Board. *Law in Transition* 2: 179–193.

Coxe, S. (1961). Police Advisory Board. *Connecticut Bar Journal* 35: 138–155.

Culver, J. (1975). Policing the Police: Problems and Perspectives. *Journal of Police Science and Administration* 3: 125–135.

Decker, S., and A. Wagner. (1982). Race and Citizen Complaints against the Police: An Analysis of Their Interaction. In *The Police and the Public*, edited by J. Greene. Beverly Hills: Sage.

Dugan, J., and D. Breda. (1991). Complaints about Police Officers: A Comparison among Types and Agencies. *Journal of Criminal Justice* 19: 165–171.

Epstein, D. (1992). The Complaint: Advisory Reflections to the Law Enforcement Agency Head. *Police Chief*, May, 58–61.

Fogel, D. (1987). The Investigation and Disciplining of Police Misconduct: A Comparative View—London, Paris, Chicago. *Police Studies* 10: 1–15.

Fyfe, J. (1985). Reviewing Citizens' Complaints against Police. In *Police Management Today*, edited by J. Fyfe. Washington, D.C.: ICMA.

Geller, W., and H. Toch. (1995). Improving Our Understanding and Control of Police Abuse of Force: Recommendations for Research and Action. In *And Justice For All: Understanding and Controlling Police Abuse of Force*, edited by W. Geller and H. Toch. Washington, D.C.: Police Executive Research Forum.

Gellhorn, W. (1969). *The Ombudsman and Others*. Cambridge: Harvard University Press.

Goldsmith, A. (1994). Recognizing Difference in Civilian Review: The Limits of Mono-Logical Thinking in a Polyphonic World. Paper presented at the IACOLE annual meeting.

Goldsmith, A. (1993). Necessary but Not Sufficient: The Role of Police Complaints Procedures in Police Accountability. In *Accountability in Criminal Justice*, edited by P. Stenning. Toronto: University of Toronto Press.

Goldsmith, A. (1991). External Review and Self-Regulation: Police Accountability and the Dialectic of Complaints Procedures. In *Complaints against the Police: The Trend to External Review*, edited by A. Goldsmith. Oxford: Clarendon Press.

Goldsmith, A. (1988). New Directions in Police Complaints Procedures: Some Conceptual and Comparative Departures. *Police Studies* 11: 60–71.

Goldstein, H. (1967). Administrative Problems in Controlling the Exercise of Police Authority. *Journal of Criminal Law, Criminology, and Police Science* 72: 160–172.

Grant, A. (1976). Complaints against the Police—The North American Experience. *Criminology Law Review* (June): 339–343.

Griswold, D. (1994). Complaints against the Police: Predicting Dispositions. *Journal of Criminal Justice* 22: 215–221.

Hudson, J. (1972). Organizational Aspects of Internal and External Review of the Police. *Journal of Criminal Law, Criminology, and Police Science* 63: 427–432.

Hudson, J. (1971). Police Review Boards and Police Accountability. *Law and Contemporary Problems* 36: 515–538.

Hudson, J. (1970). Police–Citizen Encounters That Lead to Citizen Complaints. *Social Problems* 18: 179–193.

Hudson, J. (1968). The Civilian Review Board Issues as Illuminated by the Philadelphia Experience. *Criminologica* 6: 16–29.

International Association for Civilian Oversight of Law Enforcement (IACOLE). (1989). *International Compendium of Civilian Oversight Agencies*. Chicago: Author.

International Association for Civilian Oversight of Law Enforcement (IACOLE). (1985). *Compendium of Civilian Oversight Agencies*. Chicago: Author.

International Association of Chiefs of Police. (1965). Position Statement of Police Review Boards. *Police Chief*, June, 1.

International Association of Chiefs of Police. (1964). Police Review Boards (critique of the Harvard study). *Police Chief*, February, 12–34.

International Association of Chiefs of Police. (1960). Resolution. 6 October.

International City Management Association. (1992). Police Review Systems. *MIS Report* 24.

John, A., and D. Gibbons. (1984). Policing the Police: The Portland Experience. *Journal of Police Science and Administration* 12: 315–322.

Kahn, R. (1975). Urban Reform and Police Accountability in New York City: 1950–1974. In *Urban Problems and Public Policy*, edited by R. Lineberry and L. Masotti. Lexington, Mass.: Lexington Books.

Kappler, V.; D. Carter; and A. Sapp. (1992). Police Officer Higher Education, Citizen Complaints and Departmental Rule Violation. *American Journal of Police* 11: 37–54.

Kerstetter, W. (1995). A "Procedural Justice" Perspective on Police and Citizen Satisfaction with Investigations of Police Use of Force: Finding a Common Ground of Fairness. In *And Justice For All: Understanding and Controlling Police Abuse of Force*, edited by W. Geller and H. Toch. Washington, D.C.: Police Executive Research Forum.

Kerstetter, W. (1985). Who Disciplines the Police? Who Should? in *Police Leadership in America: Crisis and Opportunity*, edited by W. Geller. Chicago: American Bar Foundation.

Kerstetter, W., and K. Rasinski. (1994). Opening a Window into Police Internal Affairs: Impact of Procedural Justice Reform on Third-Party Attitudes. *Social Justice Research* 7: 107–127.

Lenzi, M. (1974). Reviewing Civilian Complaints of Police Misconduct. *Temple Law Quarterly* 48: 89–125.

Letman, S. (1981). The Office of Professional Standards: Six Years Later. *Police Chief*, March, 44–46.

Letman, S. (1980). Chicago's Answer to Police Brutality: The Office of Professional Standards. *Police Chief*, January, 16–17.

Lewis, C. (1991). Police Complaints in Metropolitan Toronto: Perspectives of the Public Complaints Commissioner. In *Complaints against the Police: The Trend to External Review*, edited by A. Goldsmith. Oxford: Clarendon Press.

Littlejohn, E. (1981a). The Civilian Police Commission: A Deterrent of Police Misconduct. *University of Detroit Journal of Urban Law* 59: 5–62.

Littlejohn, E. (1981b). Civil Liability and the Police Officer: The Need for New Deterrents to Police Misconduct. *University of Detroit Journal of Urban Law* 58: 365–431.

Littlejohn, E. (1981c). The Cries of the Wounded: A History of Police Misconduct in Detroit. *University of Detroit Journal of Urban Law* 58: 173–219.

Loveday, B. (1988). Police Complaints in the USA. *Policing* 4: 172–193.

Luna, E. (1994). Accountability to the Community on the Use of Deadly Force. *Policing By Consent* 1: 4–6.

Lustgarten, L. (1986). Controlling Police Misconduct. In *The Governance of Police*. London: Sweet and Maxwell.

Maguire, M. (1991). Complaints against the Police: The British Experience. In *Complaints against the Police: The Trend to External Review*, edited by A. Goldsmith. Oxford: Clarendon Press.

Maguire, M., and C. Corbett. (1991). *A Study of the Police Complaints System*. London: Her Majesty's Stationery Office.

McMahon, M. (1988). Police Accountability: The Situation of Complaints in Toronto. *Contemporary Crises* 12: 301–327.

Muir, W., and D. Perez. (1995). Administrative Review of Alleged Police Brutality. In *And Justice For All: Understanding and Controlling Police Abuse of Force*, edited by W. Geller and H. Toch. Washington, D.C.: Police Executive Research Forum.

Naegele, T. (1967). Civilian Complaints against the Police in Los Angeles. *Criminology* 3: 7–35.

National Advisory Commission on Civil Disorders. (Kerner Commission). (1968). *Report*. New York: Bantam Books.

National Association for the Advancement of Colored People (NAACP). (1995). *Beyond the Rodney King Story: An Investigation of Police Misconduct in Minority Communities*. Boston: Northeastern University Press.

Neier, A. (1966). Civilian Review Boards—Another View. *Criminal Law Bulletin* 2: 10–18.

Nelson, P. (1986). Beyond the Blue Curtain: The Ombudsman's Role in Investigating Complaints against the Police in New South Wales. *Australian Journal of Public Administration* 45: 230–238.

New York City Civilian Complaint Investigative Bureau. (1992). *Survey of Civilian Complaint Systems*. New York: CCEB.

New York Civil Liberties Union (NYCLU). (1993). *Civilian Review Agencies: A Comparative Study*. New York: Author.

New York Civil Liberties Union (NYCLU). (1990). *Police Abuse: The Need for Civilian Investigation and Oversight*. New York: Author.

Pate, A., and L. Fridell. (1993). *Police Use of Force: Official Reports, Citizen Complaints and Legal Consequences*. Washington, D.C.: Police Foundation.

Paulsen, M. (1970). Securing Compliance with Constitutional Limitations: The Exclusionary Rule and Other Devices. In *Law and Order Reconsidered*, edited by J. Campbell. New York: Bantam Books.

Perez, D. (1994). *Common Sense about Police Review*. Philadelphia: Temple University Press.

Walker, S., and V. Bumphus. (1991). *Civilian Review of the Police: A National Survey of the 50 Largest Cities*. Omaha: University of Nebraska at Omaha.

Walker, S., and B. Wright. (1995a). Citizen Review of the Police, 1994: A National Survey. In *Fresh Perspectives*. Washington, D.C.: Police Executive Research Forum.

Walker, S., and B. Wright. (1995b). Citizen Review of the Police, 1995: An Analysis of Roles, Structures and Procedures. Presentation at the annual meeting of the Academy of Criminal Justice Sciences, March, Boston.

13

The Enemies Within: Reflections on Institutionalized Corruption

Robert Leuci

In 1995, the discussion of police corruption and physical abuse of citizens went from local print and TV coverage to the national media. All three TV networks, along with CNN, CNBC, and others, describing widespread police misconduct became routine TV fare. Public outcries from politicians and others over Mark Fuhrman and police scandals from New Orleans to Philadelphia occurred with numbing regularity. Common to all of these narratives of police abuse was the characterization of police as vessels of immorality and evil—a clan of rogues.

But while sensible people can agree that police corruption is to be utterly condemned, it was foolish, inaccurate, and unfair for many in the media to allow certain vested interest to paint the police with such a wide brush. The TV time given to the so-called "dream team attorneys" of the O. J. Simpson case was more than biased and unjust. It was insulting, not only to police professionals, but to the intelligence of the American public.

That said, the police dilemma in Atlanta, New York, Philadelphia, New Orleans, and Los Angeles raised the question: Has there been a national rise in police misconduct? Anyone who has traveled coast to coast, riding along with and speaking to police commanders and field officers in narcotics and public morals units, as I have, would say unquestionably that there has not been such an increase. Of course, as long as police officers are human beings, there will always be individual cases of police corruption. However, the systematized forms of corruption that infected big-city departments from the days of Prohibition through the 1970s no longer exists. The reason, it seems to me, that such institutionalized corruption has ceased to exist has been the deemphasizing of public morals units and the emphasizing of anti-street-crime units.

There was a time in New York City when thousands of police officers were involved in gambling and prostitution enforcement. These units were, in many cities, flea markets of corruption. Large and aggressive public morals units put the police in the untenable position of attempting to control public morality and enforce unenforceable laws. There is little public support for these units. Though remnants of these units remain, they have been severely downsized in cities like Chicago, Philadelphia, Detroit, Kansas City, and Boston. It makes much more sense for the police to be involved in hindering street violence than in chasing hookers and bookmakers.

Several years ago, I was sitting in the green room of a TV show, waiting to go on. Waiting with me was the police commissioner of a major East Coast city. The commissioner was deeply hurt. A number of his officers had been arrested in a federally run gambling probe. The commanding officer of the unit, an old friend of the commissioner, was one of those arrested. The commissioner did not know who I was, what I was about, or why I was asked to appear on the TV show with him. I told him I was not there to attack him or his department. I was, in fact, a fan of the police. I had been a policeman in New York City for twenty years. I knew a little something about how police officers can find themselves in real trouble—find themselves, in fact, behaving in ways that are foreign to their nature.

The commissioner felt shame. He hated being there, hated having to deal with the media. "They belong to another world and understand nothing of what it takes to be a policeman," he told me. He knew some of the arrested officers. They were good police officers, and he carried their arrests with him like a boulder in his stomach. "You understand," he said, "the most active officers, the ones with the highest records of arrests, are often the ones closest to the street." I asked him if he meant corrupt. He shrugged. I told him that, in my opinion, there is no such thing as a corrupt police officer. One is either a police officer, or corrupt. I explained to him that I knew from personal experience that you cannot have it both ways. I also told him that if he repeated to the TV audience what he just told me, it would not go easy for him. He smiled and said, "I'm not stupid."

Clearly there are exceptions to the rule, but it has been my experience that police—all police—reflect the moral standards, attitudes, history, and traditions of the departments they serve. In turn, departments are reflections of the cities they police. We do not recruit our police from Mars. They are us. They come from our communities, mirror our standards of what is admirable and what is inappropriate. If a community is racist, if their criminal justice system, politicians, courts, and DA's offices are rampant with corruption, it is impossible to have a police department that is not racist or corrupt.

We would like to think that police officers are people of honor by instinct, but that is drawing the line this side of candor. The fact is that most police officers will bend to the pressure of those they look up to and want to emulate. It is hard for outsiders to appreciate the uniqueness of the relationship of police officer to police officer, of supervisors to those they command. Police officers' behavior is often defined by the behavior of others: their partners, their immediate supervisors, the more experienced and streetwise officers within their units, and, most important, their commanding officers. There is no other profession where the value of role models is more consequential.

Historically, common notions of honor have played no role in the cop's world, with its secret protocols and class structure that make high tea with the British monarch seem informal and friendly. Superstar officers and detectives who are shoulder to shoulder with the street and who share the morality and mentality of the street can gain the kind of celebrity that we normally reserve for sports heroes. They are, in fact, a breed apart. And when that breed takes control, trouble is in the air.

For most people, honor and self-respect are two of the highest principles in life. They are preferable to misguided loyalty and this "stand-up guy" business. When I talk to police officers, I tell them that I have never been exactly sure what cops mean when they speak of a stand-up guy—though they sure were popular when I was a police officer. These are words that come straight from the dull mouths of Mafia members, not police officers. But I do know what is meant when we speak of honor and self-respect. A stand-up guy stands with those who stand up for what is right. It is not a complicated issue.

The public morals and narcotics units have always been, and continue to be, the most corrupt-prone commands. They are seductive and sensual places. They can change and distort police officers, turning good people into reflections of the people they police. There remains a small number of police officers who see assignment to such commands as winning some sort of lottery. And it is that small percentage of officers who are responsible for the vast majority of integrity problems. Police chiefs have a responsibility to staff sensitive commands with their best officers, officers who are streetwise and of unquestionable integrity. Popular notions aside, the two are not mutually exclusive.

The exercise of moral restraint remains an unrelenting question for police. Some exercise it, some do not. When those who do are supported and praised, those who do not will be condemned. The peer pressure on police officers is often overpowering. When there is determined pressure on officers to behave in ways that are honorable, without question, there are rarely integrity problems. It is now, and always has been, left to police commanders to make clear that certain practices cannot be understood nor tolerated.

The alternative is for police commanders to live between the hemispheres of light and darkness in the land of avoidance of truth—a dimly lit place between knowing and not knowing, a place where you can convince yourself that what you see before your eyes is either not happening or will sooner or later simply go away. An officer, a command, a precinct, or a department does not go bad overnight or in a vacuum. And once begun, misconduct does not disappear of its own volition, but multiplies and spreads like malignant cells.

There were ample warning signs in Los Angeles, New Orleans, Atlanta, New York, Philadelphia, and Washington, D.C. The problem was that good people looked, saw, turned away, and punted.

NOTE

Reprinted from *Subject to Debate* 10 (2) with permission of the Police Executive Research Forum. Copyright by Police Executive Research Forum.

III

The Impacts of Policing

14

Accomplishing Problem Solving in the Community: Reconciling the Concepts

Dennis Jay Kenney and T. Steuart Watson

Since 1979, when Herman Goldstein first proposed a problem-oriented approach to policing, the concept and its community-focused counterpart have gained nearly universal backing as the preferred means of policing for the future. Variations on these themes have been tried in locales as diverse as Madison, Wisconsin (Goldstein and Susmilch 1982), Baltimore County (Cordner 1985; Webster et al. 1989), and Newport News, Virginia (Eck and Spelman 1989), where project evaluators have each found their programs to be successful. In each case, those involved noted that specific community concerns had been addressed, overall reductions in crime had occurred, or community members had become less fearful as a result of the police-program interventions. In response to these apparent successes, the problem-focused approach has now been aggressively spread to focus on a diverse array of problems such as gangs (PERF 1993), drugs (Eck and Spelman 1989), school crime (Kenney and Watson 1996), and the management of police calls for service (Sherman 1989) in urban, suburban, and even rural communities (Diamond 1993). Despite the promise offered by these methods, however, many agencies are now discovering the application far more difficult than the concept, as frustration among officers and the potential for needless failure mounts.

THE CONCEPT AS INTENDED

As most are aware, the concept of problem-focused policing is the result of several decades of research into crime and the police response.

While much of the body of work that has contributed to the approach resulted from very different focuses, Spelman and Eck (1989) have observed three basic findings that were especially important:

1. Simply applying additional resources in response to individual crimes appears to have little real impact.
2. Few incidents, crimes, or criminals are isolated. Most are symptoms of underlying problems which means that many will recur predictably.
3. Since they are rooted to other issues, the most effective responses should be those that coordinate police, government, and private citizens and business.

Theorists and practitioners alike are now focusing aggressively on programs that involve citizens and the police in cooperative efforts at problem identification and solution. Though it often goes unrecognized as the focus is fixed on "quality of life" concerns, the overriding goal of the problem-focused approach is to produce better results against crime, fear, and disorder in our neighborhoods.

The Process

Actually, the problem-solving process is quite straightforward, though deceptively complex. During the initial scanning or problem-identification stage, officers are asked to identify various community concerns, determining which are to be considered problems appropriate for further work. Such scanning can be the result of the officer's own experience with the community, but will also typically include discussions with residents or workers who belong there coupled with crime analysis and other forms of official data. As a result, the issues of interest identified will often be as diverse as poor lighting, loitering youths, or damaged playgrounds or property. Obviously, this problem-identification stage is the most critical step in solving problems (Bergan and Tombari 1976; Hollister and Miller 1977; Lazarus 1976).

In the analysis stage, the officers set out to collect more detailed information about the problems they have identified. As proponents often note, the sources of information at use during this stage should include not only official police records but interviews, surveys, presentations, and outside opinions. The goal here is to gain an understanding of the scope and nature of the problem, which means that careful in-depth analysis of the factors that are contributing is especially important.

The analysis stage actually consists of four steps: (1) analyze the forces impinging on the problem, (2) brainstorm alternative strategies, (3) evaluate alternative strategies, and (4) specify the responsibilities of group members for each. Clearly, the analysis stage is where most decisions are made regarding action. In addition, during this stage of the process it is important that realistic goals be established for subsequent efforts. Using Goldstein's (1990) original model, a range of solution goals may include total elimination of the problem, substantially reducing the problem, reducing the harm(s) created by the problem, or devising better methods of dealing with the problem.

After analysis, the response stage has three objectives: develop a set of response options that are consistent with the information gathered, select a response, and implement it. Here, officers may call upon businesses, other government agencies, or local residents for assistance. In short, instead of relying upon traditional responses alone, anyone who can help should be invited to do so. In each case, the response options should be wideranging, with no approach being overlooked. A few of the possible options might be responses to do the following:

- Concentrate attention on those accounting for a disproportionate share of the problem. A relatively small number of individuals usually account for a disproportionate share of practically any problem, either by causing it, facilitating it, or suffering from it.

- Convey accurate information. Though one of the least used responses, this may be among the most effective options available. Conveying information can (1) reduce anxiety and fear, (2) enable those impacted to solve their own problems, (3) elicit conformity with rules not known or understood, (4) warn others about vulnerability and suggest protective steps, (5) demonstrate to others how they unwittingly contribute to problems, (6) develop support for solutions, and (7) acquaint all involved with the outcomes they can realistically expect.

- Alter the physical environment to reduce opportunities for a problem to recur.

- Alter or increase rules and policies that address conditions that contribute to a problem (Goldstein 1990).

Whatever approach is taken, problem solvers are encouraged to remember that their solution focus can be on the problem itself, the offender, the victim, or all three.

Regardless of the response option selected, it is important to guide the problem-solving group toward manageable goals. Psychologist Karl Weick (1984), who has studied problem-solving, points out that as people begin to look at social problems they do so on a massive scale. For example, they may look at eliminating all unemployment, homelessness, or crime. In doing so, they define these problems in such a way that they overpower all possible solutions that might be employed. The problem solvers then experience frustration, dashed excitement, and helplessness.

A more effective response, Weick (1984) argues, is to take large problems and break them into smaller ones. When done, a series of controllable problems of modest size are presented that allow for the development of specific responses that can succeed. These smaller wins may seem less important individually; however, when taken together they set an example that attracts support while reducing resistance to future efforts.

During the final stage, assessment or plan evaluation, the officers again collect data and evaluate the effectiveness of their responses. Officers and observers can compare the data regarding the problem prior to and during their interventions. Based on this evaluative review, the problem-solving officer can decide if his or her plan is working (based on the goal statement made during scanning) and make plans to solve other problems. If the plan is ineffective, the officers involved are expected to recycle through the problem-solving steps, beginning with scanning to determine if the problem was identified correctly (Eck and Spelman 1989).

The Problems with Problem-Oriented Policing

While the concept appears simple enough and proponents can provide plenty of anecdotal evidence of its success, in reality many agencies are finding implementation far more difficult than they had imagined. For example, some police managers now note that while most problem-solving projects are successful in meeting immediate objectives, long-lasting effects may not be taking place. This is so, they suggest, because of organizational cultures resistant to new expectations—especially when the emphasis is on noncrime problems. If this is so, then the short-term impacts of problem-solving efforts today probably are not appreciably different than the task forces that police have relied on for decades.

Other critics, however, have suggested more substantive concerns with the concept itself. After evaluating recent problem-solving programs in Baltimore County, evaluators noted the role played by supervision in achieving success. While many have discussed the need for a department's leadership to promote and support the philosophy of problem and community policing, Webster and her colleagues (1989) in Baltimore focused on more functional aspects of leadership. First, they found that, contrary to popular expectations, problem-solving activities could only be weakly related to the blocks of time when officers were available. While a majority of officers did indicate on before-and-after surveys that having sufficient time free was an issue, analysis of workloads showed that those same officers seldom spent more than 30 percent of on-duty time handling calls. Further, during face-to-face interviews officers seldom expressed the same concerns about time to handle their current problem-solving projects, although some did feel that the method as a routine might not be feasible. Similarly, most of the supervisors interviewed agreed that officer time could be blocked for worthwhile projects.

If it is more the perception of a heavy workload that impedes problem solving, then what explains the mixed results evaluators have observed? Clearly, Skolnick (1966) and others may be correct in their assertion that the police culture seems to support traditional responses even when they appear less promising (see also Rubinstein 1973; Sanders 1977; Skolnick and Bailey 1986). Still, in the Baltimore project Webster and colleagues (1989) note that considerable problem solving took place despite such cultural impediments. In fact, they explain, there was much evidence that precinct-specific influences were at work to stimulate the effort. Indeed, in two precincts officers frequently engaged residents and other agencies in resolving problems. What was different, they contend, was the consistency of leadership in the areas they observed.

At the top, the area with an enthusiastic captain assigned to the precinct throughout the study got off to an early start but paused noticeably while the captain was on a two-month leave of absence. The comparison area, however, began slowly, developing sustained problem-solving efforts only after a captain was permanently assigned. Similarly, the role of the lieutenants was considerable as well. In the comparison area, these middle managers appeared the most consistently supportive of problem solving, though they initiated little activity until the captain's arrival. Once they began, however, the evaluators note that all four officers assigned to the area provided oversight during problem identification and analysis, suggested outside resources when appropriate, and were complementary to officers who performed well.

From these observations, one could also conclude that organizational culture is less a problem than is lack of knowledge of how to proceed. While much has been made of the problem-solving approach during the past few years, most training and almost all of the written source materials feature anecdotal case studies prominently while offering little practical help as to how one actually does any of the four steps of the process. The San Diego department began to recognize this weakness by incorporating a basic worksheet for officers in their Problem Oriented Policing Training Guide (San Diego Police Department 1994). Even here, however, the support is vague, incomplete, and less a model for analysis than a plan for action. For example, the worksheets provided ask officers only to describe the problem and list the persons and/or groups that are affected by the problem during scanning. For analysis, officers are prompted to list the questions they have regarding the problems identified and describe the sources they should go to for answers. Though a start, such aids are unlikely to be of much help to officers unsure of how to proceed with problem solving in their on-street settings. For that, the department's guidelines fall back on a number of examples and a series of equally vague exercises. However, in light of recent research finding widely disparate cognitive skills in entry-level officers (suggesting that some are simply less able to perform the tasks of problem solving than others), we should hardly be surprised when officers wait for the kind of direction that was needed in Baltimore County. "Just tell me exactly what you want me to do," was how one Chicago officer recently explained his concerns in that city. What he may be asking, in fact, is less what to do than how he should do it.

Equally important are the growing concerns about who should do the problem solving in a community. Critics of the community focus worry that the focus expands the police function into public health areas that are beyond officers' expertise. Instead of policing, they suggest, our concern should be with community-oriented *government*. At the same time, however, others have begun to suggest that problem-solving efforts actually add little beyond a more systematic way for the police to deliver their traditional services. Officers, after all, remain responsible for identifying and analyzing community problems, creating solutions, and implementing changes. While citizens may be asked to participate—usually through surveys or door-to-door canvassing—their role remains limited; in many cases nearly nonexistent. As a result, while community participation in the process is often quite limited, officers find themselves pressed to become more and more involved in an ombudsman role for neighborhoods, addressing concerns with little clear association to crime, fear, or disorder. Frustration, cynicism, and a lack of meaningful commitment to their new roles of solving problems for the community have all too often been the result. Unfortunately, as such experiences become more common, it may be that the community and problem-oriented focuses will themselves grow increasingly at risk as many agencies and officers return to more traditional methods. In response to these concerns, some police agencies have begun to focus on both a more structured approach to problem solving in an effort to guide their officers in the mechanics of the process, as well as methods of mobilizing and facilitating neighborhood groups so that citizens can apply the problem-solving process to their own concerns. In effect, the police will themselves become trainers of problem solving to assist communities to develop self-sustaining efforts.

THE COLLABORATIVE MODEL

Essentially, there are two general models of problem solving: expert and collaborative. In the expert model, an outside person (expert) enters into the system or organization (community) where the problem

is occurring, identifies and analyzes the problem, and provides a solution for its remedy. In contrast, the collaborative model of problem
solving emphasizes shared responsibility between the expert and those
within the system, organization, or community. Using the expert as a
resource, in the collaborative model the community participants identify and analyze the problem, brainstorm possible solutions, select a
plan they view as appropriate, and undertake the implementation.
The expert's function is that of facilitator asking the right questions
and leading the other participants to the most tenable conclusions.

Contrary to the expectations of many, the traditional police approach
to problem solving remains almost exclusively an expert model. Given
some incentive, such as a crime-related problem, officers will arrive with
expectations that they possess the resources to create and provide some
needed response. While citizens may be invited to participate through
community meetings or some survey process, the responsibility for problem identification, analysis, solution formulation, and action remain with
the police. Even though officers are encouraged to engage the community and bring diverse information to bear on the problems being
addressed, given the pressures of other police responsibilities that often means little more than superficial input. As a result, the basic roles
of police and community remain unchanged. More important, however, is that such a process does little to enhance citizens' perceptions
of real control over the problems in their neighborhoods, fails to encourage grassroots empowerment since no proactive role for prevent-
ing or responding to crime problems is developed, and has little effect
on communications between police and citizens which might be helpful to the long-term benefit of the community.

Collaborative problem solving represents a different way in which
police can interact with their citizens. Instead of the role of expert,
these officers enter the community as knowledgeables who can mobilize neighborhoods to address concerns and enhance informal social
controls. Unlike the expert model, where the officer remains more central to the process than his or her citizen counterparts, the collaborative approach places the police on equal footing as coequals in the
problem-solving effort. That is, each participant, citizen and police
alike, brings skills and knowledge to contribute. Ideally, for problem
solving to be most effective a shared basis of power between the major participants is sought. Research indicates that most people prefer
the collaborative model of problem solving over the expert model
(Pryzwansky and White 1983) and that the more involved they actually become in the process, the more likely they are to successfully
implement plans and programs (Reinking, Livesay, and Kohl 1978).
Related educational research has shown that, as a result of interactions with skilled problem solvers, participants often report a greater
degree of control over problems (empowerment) and a greater degree

of satisfaction with both the process and outcomes (Gutkin and Ajchenbaum 1984). As a result, we propose that the focus of responsibility for community-based problem solving be moved from the police officer expert to neighborhood groups mobilized for collaborative action. To do so, the officers involved must be prepared to mobilize their communities to employ a four-stage problem-solving process structured more clearly than what is available today.

Mobilizing Collaborative Effort

The most difficult tasks facing any collaborative problem solver is the need to learn and use the model correctly, shed the expert role during the effort, and, seemingly the hardest, get citizens involved in active participation. As they accomplish each task, however, we believe that the expert role can be shed as groups of citizens with which to work are built.

Teaching officers to use the collaborative approach involves six distinct steps. In the first, didactic training in the philosophy and rationale of the model must occur. Much of the work in problem-solving training for the police has been focused here. To date, in fact, it is likely that few officers remain who are not aware of the general concept, its guiding principal that problems are better solved than repeatedly responded to, and the broad four-stage process to address problems. It is the second area, the need for direct training in the steps and substeps of the problem-solving model, where current training efforts have been weakest. As noted, problem-solving training today relies heavily on anecdotal examples rather than structured activities and tasks that can be taught and retaught to officers and citizens. As a result, the supervisory requirements discussed earlier remain central for officers who vary considerably in the skills and interest they bring to the process. Similarly, the third and fourth training needs require that officers and community problem solvers be well versed in the behaviors associated with success at each of the steps they employ, as well as with the verbal techniques to facilitate the process with others. Given the limited and unstructured nature of current problem-solving training, almost no attention is given to either of these areas.

Once officers are well prepared with the process, the fifth training need for collaborative problem solving involves skills building to enter and participate with community networks. If the responsibility for the actual problem-solving tasks is to rest with neighborhood groups, the participating officers (experts) must be prepared to facilitate the effort. One example of this approach are the community-mobilization efforts developed by the Chicago Alliance for Neighborhood Safety (CANS). CANS is a seven-year-old coalition of community organization that delivers a range of problem-solving services cooperatively with the Chicago Police Department to officers and citizens in all of the city's 279 beats. In addition, CANS staff now coordinate a 100-member community-based coalition, are active in the Community Policing Task Force, and supervise the anticrime organizing activities of twenty-one VISTA Volunteers. As part of their effort, CANS has recently developed its own crime analysis and mapping capabilities as well.

Finally, the sixth step of collaborative problem solving rests with the development of professional feedback to officers as they practice their problem-solving skills in the community.

Structuring the Problem-Solving Stages

Probably the most intensive task for a problem-solving facilitator is to address the difficulties expressed with the mechanics of the problem-solving process. As discussed, while the SARA method as currently taught makes extensive use of examples of problem solving, an officer's ability to translate that experience to his or her own environment is often difficult. Such training tells how problem solving can work but provides little real direction in how to actually make it work. The four stages of problem solving should be broken down into a series of manageable steps that offer guidance for application.

During the initial stage of scanning, for example, officers working with community groups should be prepared for the slowness and difficulty with which specific problems can be expected to emerge. As the neighborhood problem-solving groups begin their efforts, the first few attempts at problem identification will, in fact, usually produce a wide range of issues with little clear consensus about exact problems. Once ideas have been identified, however, successful problem solvers must go on to prioritize the available ideas using one of three approaches: from most to least serious, from easiest to most difficult to solve, or by identifying those problems that, if successfully addressed, might impact other related concerns. Only then should a broad goal statement be generated. Even here, however, the problem solvers should be able to give examples of where the problem occurs, which setting causes the most difficulty, how relevant information will be gathered and reported, and when that process should begin. While most officers are told that a multitude of information sources should be used during this stage, few are taught how to engage citizens in the process, how complex such involvement can be, or the varied methods by which relevant data can be collected. With that in mind, we were not surprised when Charlotte officers recently expressed that problem solving was seldom realistic since their department's crime-analysis section could not conduct sufficient surveys throughout the city. In their concern, at least, those officers were showing awareness that most variance associated with successful problem solving is directly attributable to correct problem identification.

Similarly, problem analysis should be viewed as a natural extension of problem identification, in that it begins with the target problem and focuses on establishing functional relationships with its environment. Questions about who, what, where, when, why, and under what conditions are all relevant at this stage to facilitate a better understanding of the problem. In other words, during the analysis stage the task of the neighborhood problem solvers (with officer support) is to gather and use data sufficient to provide specific problem clarity. Among the requirements of analysis are the following:

1. Determine first, with the data collected, if analysis should be continued or if the problem should be restated.
2. Identify problem antecedents. (What happens before the problem occurs?)
3. Identify sequential conditions of the problem. (What else is happening or not happening while the problem occurs?)
4. Identify consequences of the problem. (What happens after the problem has occurred?)
5. Identify the harm that results from the problem.
6. Determine the problem strength:
   - How often does the problem occur?
   - How long has this been a problem?
   - What is the duration of each occurrence of the problem?
7. Determine (once analysis has occurred) if the process should continue or if the problem needs restating.
8. Establish a hypothesis. (What conclusions can be reached about why the problem occurs?)
9. Establish a tentative definition of the goal. (What is desired instead of the problem?)
10. Identify the assets available to help solve the problem.
11. Identify the existing procedures or rules already established to address the problem.

As noted, once the analysis progresses, it is not unusual to return to problem identification to further refine the problem definition. As such, officers should understand and explain to others that while the four-stage problem-solving process is structured, it is also flexible in that one can always return to a previous step to correct or refine earlier information.

Next, during strategy formulation the two primary objectives are to select an appropriate intervention and implement it. Again, care should be taken not to rush through this stage since the procedural details—including the assignment of individuals to various roles, the supporting material to be gathered, and the training for individuals implementing the plan—are by now essential. Further, the preparation for intervention alone can often take weeks or more, depending upon how complex the problem is and how involved the neighborhood participants may be. In addition, possible plans should be brainstormed and evaluated on their likelihood of achieving the changes desired, while all details regarding preimplementation, implementation, and postimplementation should be discussed and assigned to individuals willing to accept responsibility for each detail. Plans must also be developed for procedures to be followed when the plan is not working or when the participants discover that implementation has gone poorly. Data collection continues during this stage, usually with the procedures developed earlier. In all, then, during this stage officers must be prepared to guide their citizens groups as they do the following:

1. Brainstorm possible interventions.
2. Consider the feasibility of each and choose among alternatives.
3. Determine what needs to be done before the plan is implemented.
4. Identify who will be responsible for these preliminary actions.
5. Outline the actual plan and who might be responsible for each part.
6. Clarify whether the plan is expected to accomplish all or only part of the goal selected earlier.
7. State the specific goals this plan will accomplish.
8. Specify what additional data might be needed and how it will be collected.
9. Anticipate the most likely problems with implementing the plan.
10. Select possible procedures to follow when the plan is not working or when it is not being implemented correctly.

The final stage, plan evaluation, is an ongoing process that begins immediately as the plan is implemented. The two questions that must be answered here involve the process (was the plan implemented as intended) and the outcome (was it effective). When plans are ineffective, the most fruitful strategy is to immediately return to problem identification to insure that the problem has been correctly identified. If it has not, the participants should repeat the previous steps in a sequential fashion to find possible errors or gaps in understanding or planning. For the effective strategy, meanwhile, determination of the impact of the plan's continuation, its removal, and other strategies that might enhance effectiveness should begin. Finally, methods to monitor future performance so that impact can be maintained should be determined. In all, during analysis, problem-solving officers should expect to provide guidance in determining the following:

1. If the plan was implemented.
2. What the goals were as specified in the strategy formulation.
3. If the goals were attained (how goal attainment can be determined).
4. What is likely to happen if the plan is removed.
5. What is likely to happen if the plan remains in place.
6. What new strategies might be available to increase the effectiveness of the plan.
7. How the plan can be monitored in the future.

IMPLEMENTING THE CHANGE

We believe that as officers become more proficient in the skills of problem solving, a natural by-product will be increased community involvement. A few issues of organizational readiness should be considered first, however.

Prior to implementation, each organization should first conduct a self-assessment of its readiness to begin problem solving. Supervisors will be responsible for coaching, training, and evaluating the work of their officers in problem solving. To do this, they must be committed to the process and its implementation. For example, what steps can they take to make sure that officers have time to engage in problem-solving activities?

Equally important is the discovery of departmental impediments that can hinder problem solving. Impediments can exist in policies and procedures, as well as in the manner in which officers are evaluated and disciplined. For the most part, current evaluation systems are based on numbers of arrests, tickets, and FIs that officers conduct. Schemes such as these send the message that these activities—and only these—are expected and valued. Though traditional responses can and should be included in the range of tools that officers use, officer evaluations should be changed to reflect problem-solving activities as well.

Organizational readiness also includes the abilities and willingness of officers. If supervisors do not recognize the differences that exist among their employees, they will lose the opportunity to provide training, coaching, or other support to officers who need it. Similarly, the department should also consider how ready its communities are to form partnerships with the police to solve problems. Some communities do not trust the police and may be unwilling at first to collaborate in problem solving. Others, however, will be enthusiastic from the start.

NOTE

Reprinted with permission from the Police Executive Research Forum. Copyright by Police Executive Research Forum.

BIBLIOGRAPHY

Anastasi, A. (1988). *Psychological Testing.* 6th ed. New York: Macmillan.
Bergan, J., and M. Tombari. (1976). Consultive Skill and Efficiency and the Implementation and Outcomes of Consultation. *Journal of School Psychology* 14: 3–14.
Berman, P., and M. McLaughlin. (1978). *Federal Programs Supporting Educational Change VIII: Implementing and Sustaining Innovations* (R-1589/8-HEW). Washington, D.C.: U.S. Government Printing Office.
Blalock, H. (1961). *Causal Influences in Nonexperimental Research.* Chapel Hill: University of North Carolina Press.
Campbell, D., and J. Stanley. (1966). *Experimental and Quasi-Experimental Design for Research.* Chicago: Rand McNally.
Cook, T., and D. Campbell. (1979). *Quasi-Experimentation.* Chicago: Rand McNally.
Cordner, G. (1985). *The Baltimore County Citizen Oriented Police Enforcement (COPE) Project: Final Evaluation.* Baltimore: University of Baltimore.
Diamond, D. (1993). *Community Policing and Regional Training for Small and Rural Jurisdictions.* Washington, D.C.: Police Executive Research Forum.
Eck, J. (1989). *Police and Drug Control.* Washington, D.C.: Police Executive Research Forum.
Eck, J., and W. Spelman. (1989). Who Ya Gonna Call? The Police As Problem-Busters. *Crime and Delinquency* 33: 31–52.
Goldstein, H. (1990). *Problem Oriented Policing.* New York: McGraw-Hill.
Goldstein, H. (1979). Improving Policing: A Problem-Oriented Approach. *Crime and Delinquency* 25.
Goldstein, H., and C. Susmilch. (1982). *Experimenting with the Problem-Oriented Approach to Improving Police Service: A Report and Some Reflections on Two Case Studies.* Vol. 4 of *Project on Development of a Problem-Oriented Approach to Improving Police Service.* Madison: University of Wisconsin Law School.
Greene, J., and S. Mastrofski, eds. (1988). *Community Policing: Rhetoric or Reality.* New York: Praeger.
Gutkin, T., and M. Ajchenbaum. (1984). Teachers Perceptions of Control and Preferences for Consultative Services. *Professional Psychology: Research and Practice* 15: 565–570.
Hollister, W., and F. Miller. (1977). Problem-Solving Strategies in Consultation. *American Journal of Orthopsychiatry* 47: 445–450.
Kenney, D., and S. Watson. (1996). Improving School Safety by Empowering Students. *The Educational Forum* 57: 50–62.
Kenney, D.; S. Watson; and D. Williams. (1994). *Improving School Safety by Empowering Students in the Educational Process: A Curriculum Guide for Problem-Solving Classes.* Washington, D.C.: Police Executive Research Forum.
Lazarus, A. (1976). *Multimodal Behavior Therapy.* New York: Springer.

Lewis, J. (1978). Some Views on Secondary Analysis or the Politics of Reanalysis from a Particular Perspective. In *Secondary Analysis of Social Program Evaluation*, edited by R. Baruch and P. Wortman. Thousand Oaks, Calif.: Sage.

Lobello, S. (1992). A Review of the Problem-Solving Inventory. In *The Eleventh Mental Measurements Yearbook*, edited by J. Kramer and J. Conoley. Lincoln, Neb.: Buros Institute of Mental Measurement.

Pate, A., and S. Annan. (1989). *The Baltimore Community Policing Experiment: Technical Report*. Washington, D.C.: National Institute of Justice.

Police Executive Research Forum (PERF). (1993). *Comprehensive Gang Initiative: Operations Manual for Implementing Local Gang Prevention and Control Programs*. Washington, D.C.: Author.

Pressman, J., and A. Wildavsky. (1973). A Critical View of the Uniform Crime Reports. *University of Michigan Law Review* 64: 121–130.

Pryzwansky, W., and G. White. (1983). The Influence of Consultee Characteristics on Preferences for Consultation Approaches. *Professional Psychology: Research and Practice* 14: 457–461.

Reinking, R.; G. Livesay; and M. Kohl. (1978). The Effects of Consultation Style on Consultee Productivity. *American Journal of Community Psychology* 6: 283–290.

Rossi, P.; H. Freeman; and S. Wright. (1979). *Evaluation: A Systematic Approach*. Beverly Hills: Sage.

Rubinstein, J. (1973). *City Police*. New York: Ballantine.

Sanders, W. (1977). *Detective Work: A Study of Criminal Investigations*. New York: The Free Press.

San Diego Police Department. (1994). *Problem Oriented Policing: Training Guide*. San Diego: Author.

Sherman, L. (1989). Repeat Calls for Service: Policing the "Hot Spots." In *Police and Policing: Contemporary Issues*, edited by D. Kenney. New York: Praeger.

Skolnick, J. (1966). *Justice without Trial*. New York: John Wiley and Sons.

Skolnick, J., and D. Bailey. (1986). *The New Blue Line: Innovation in Six American Cities*. New York: The Free Press.

Spelman, W., and J. Eck. (1989). Sitting Ducks, Ravenous Wolves, and Helping Hands: New Approaches to Urban Policing. *Comment* 35: 34–40.

Suchman, E. (1967). *Evaluative Research*. New York: Russell Sage Foundation.

Webster, B.; S. Wallace; J. McEwen; J. Eck; and D. Hill. (1989). *Evaluation of Community Crime/Problem Resolution through Police Directed Patrol: Executive Summary*. Alexandria, Va.: Institute for Law and Justice.

Weick, K. (1984). Small Wins: Redefining the Scale of Social Problems. *American Psychologist* 39: 40–49.

15

The Problems of Problem Solving: Resistance, Interdependencies, and Conflicting Interests

Michael E. Buerger

Fifteen years after it was first proposed, the concept of problem-oriented policing has a well-established foundation in the police practice of problem solving. Herman Goldstein (1979) first proposed problem-oriented policing as an alternative to the means-over-ends orientation of traditional reactive policing. To measure police performance in terms of outcomes rather than activities, Goldstein proposed the police abandon both their reliance on broad, legalistic categories that are essentially catch-alls, and their tendency to look at calls as episodic, unconnected events. He argued that the police need to go beyond the immediate dimensions of incidents in order to properly identify the real problems and devise realistic workable solutions.

Goldstein and Susmilch (1981, 1982a, 1982b, 1982c) went on to explore the possibilities of POP with the Madison, Wisconsin, Police Department in two studies of the drunk driver and the repeat sex offender. While the police provided valuable information, data collection and analysis were produced by the researchers, not by police officers (as true POP envisions). In Maryland in 1983, Goldstein helped Baltimore County's COPE (Citizen Oriented Police Enforcement) Team integrate problem solving into its fear-of-crime mandate (Cordner 1985). The Newport News, Virginia, Police Department engaged in a series of problem-solving initiatives in conjunction with the Police Executive Research Forum (Eck and Spelman 1987). Functional problem solving was an essential element of the Community Patrol Officer Program (CPOP), begun in New York City in 1984, even though CPOP is now promoted as "community policing" rather than as problem oriented (McElroy, Cosgrove, and Sadd 1993). Many departments across the country now use problem solving, even when it is not so identified by title, such as in the "Beat Health" program in Oakland, California (Green 1993), and major projects are underway elsewhere.

METHODOLOGY

This chapter is a qualitative analysis drawing on the author's participant observation of the Minneapolis RECAP experiment (from May 1987 through the end of the experiment in December 1987, and continuing during the following two years), and a content analysis of the original RECAP case files. Those files contained the officers' own written notes and analyses of their work at their assigned addresses, but, like many police reports, omitted many pertinent details. However, in early 1988 the RECAP officers wrote up their experiences for a casebook edited by the author (Buerger 1992), an interactive process which allowed for greater examination of the issues involved and the development of details not contained in the text files.

A SUMMARY OF THE RECAP EXPERIMENT

In December 1986, the Minneapolis Police Department inaugurated Repeat Call Address Policing. Devised by Lawrence Sherman (1987), the RECAP unit was a small team charged with developing problem-solving techniques that could be transferred to other elements of the department. It was both an experimental unit and a developmental process. Four handpicked patrol officers and a sergeant were detached from 9-1-1 response to work at reducing calls for police service at 250 of the most active addresses in Minneapolis. They were to devise and implement strategies to resolve the underlying problems that produced repeat calls for police service at their addresses. They had the latitude (informally granted by Chief of Police Bouza) to "do anything they wanted to solve the problems at their addresses, as long as it was legal, Constitutional, and ethical" (Sherman, Buerger, and Gartin 1988, 6).

Theoretically, the basis for the RECAP strategy lies in Cohen and Felson's (1979) Routine Activities Theory, which proposes that crime occurs during the intersection, in time and space, of motivated offenders and suitable victims (or targets), under circumstances of absent or inadequate guardianship—a crime triangle similar to the fire triangle of fuel, heat, and oxygen. Crime was presumed amenable to suppression if any of the three legs of the triangle was removed or neutralized. If RECAP officers could influence one or more human actors in the crime triangle to change their behavior—which for guardians might involve making changes in the physical environment—it could reduce the need for continued police intervention.

Operationally, RECAP sprang from the growing awareness that police administrators had all but surrendered the control and direction of patrol forces to the telephone. Through attrition and layoffs, the great hiring balloon of the late 1960s and early 1970s slowly shrank (Goldstein and Susmilch 1981, 24–25), forcing police to devote much more of their time to reactively answering calls and much less to proactive law-enforcement strategies (though Reiss [1971] and others have correctly noted that unassigned time and proactive law-enforcement activities are not synonymous). Police continued to devote the major portion of their resources to responding to mobilizations by citizens and dealing with incidents deemed serious by the citizenry. With their time dominated by the uncritical egocentric demands of "an oligarchy of chronic users" (Sherman 1987), the police could not work proactively on crime problems or those related to fear of crime (Wilson and Kelling 1982).

The RECAP Target-Identification Process

Target identification for prior experiments in problem-oriented policing was done on relatively subjective bases: the collective insight of a departmental task force in Madison, the input of citizens solicited for their concerns about crime in their Baltimore County neighborhoods, and a combination of a police task force and official crime statistics in Newport News. RECAP substituted an objective measure of problem seriousness: Any address that generated a high level of police responses was deemed to be a "problem" for the purposes of the experiment, regardless of factors such as population density or number of daily users. Excessive demand for police resources at a single address, rather than public perceptions of crime or deteriorating civility, became the standard by which "problems" were measured. RECAP thus preserved the Newport News definition of problem—"[a] group of incidents occurring in a community, that are similar in one or more ways, and that are of concern to the police and the public" (Eck and Spelman 1987)—but imposed geographical commonality instead of similarity of type of incident. Single addresses were to be the focus of the officers' attentions, to the exclusion of larger spatial units such as neighborhoods or even blocks.

RECAP began by identifying the chronic users of police services by addresses. A database of all known calls for police service for a twelve-month period was compiled from archived 9-1-1 tapes of the Minneapolis Emergency Communications Center (MECC). Addresses were divided into separate commercial and residential lists (because com-

mercial addresses dominated the top end of the list in terms of numbers of calls), and rank ordered according to the number of calls in the
baseline year. The top 250 addresses on each list were randomly assigned to either the experimental or the control group, each of which
was divided equally into 125 commercial and 125 residential addresses.
The addresses in the experimental group were then divided among
the four officers, who carried individual caseloads of approximately
sixty addresses through the experiment.

The program sought to identify as many types of problems, and
generate as many innovative police responses to them, as possible.
Because the only criterion for selection of an address was the number
of calls for police service it generated during the baseline year, RE-
CAP "featured a heterogeneous mix of the nature of the problems, of
tactics employed, and the level of effort applied across experimental
addresses" (Sherman, Buerger, and Gartin 1989, 1). RECAP target identification gave up the narrow range of police preferences in defining
problems for a definition which embraced the full range of citizen
definitions of problems. Instead of the glory assignments of "real police work"—visible and highly symbolic law-enforcement targets like
robberies and drug houses—the process embraced the broader spectrum of conditions which demanded (and got) police resources of time
and attention. This widening of the net had the effect of identifying
chronic problems instead of flare-ups (though the boundary between
those two conditions often is difficult to distinguish at any given moment in time), and established a substantive base distinct from those
employed elsewhere. Quantitative analysis of call data also provided
a means to objectively measure the effectiveness of the unit's work
across the wide range of problem types. Call data represented a wider
range of public concerns and a lower level of police gatekeeping than
official crime reports.

Statistical Results of the Experiment

Analysis of the calls to both groups during the experimental year
indicated that the RECAP unit failed to achieve its target goal to "prevent" as many calls as the officers would likely have answered had
they remained on active patrol service. That number was estimated at
1 thousand calls per officer, based on the number of calls and the number of officers assigned to patrol duties during that year. "Rather than
preventing 4,000 calls, [RECAP] was only able to prevent 475 within
the experimental design," while analysis of the prevalence of call reductions rather than frequency of calls showed "no statistically significant differences using a six-celled chi-square test" (Sherman,
Buerger, and Gartin 1989, 21).

In short, based on the criteria for statistical success established before the development of the strategies, RECAP was a failure in experimental terms. But even before the statistical results were known, the Minneapolis Police Department established RECAP as a permanent unit. Though the unit's successes were statistically overwhelmed by the effects of the case load (including addresses which became "turned around" late in the year, after early accumulation of large numbers of calls), the localized effects of the successes were obvious to observers. Though they could not "prevent their weight in calls," the RECAP officers paid for themselves in a different coin. In addition to some dramatically successful interventions at pernicious addresses (see Buerger 1992, 1–6, 133–139, 327–331), the unit helped streamline ineffective police responses like the shoplifting program (Buerger 1992, 308–318) and helped develop several plans for solutions to citywide problems.

Specific findings included the following, quoted verbatim (though presented in different form) from the RECAP Final Report:

- The residential locations, relative to the control group, showed a 21-percent reduction in assault, a 12-percent reduction in disturbances, and a 15-percent reduction in calls related to drunkenness.
- Commercial targets showed a 9-percent reduction in theft calls and a 21-percent reduction in shoplifting calls at seven stores participating in a special program.
- Residential burglaries were up 27 percent compared to controls.
- Calls for commercial predatory crime (criminal sexual conduct, robbery, and kidnapping combined) were up 28 percent at the experimental addresses relative to controls (Sherman, Buerger, and Gartin 1989, 23).

Overall, the experimenters concluded that these "mixed results . . . suggest that merely focusing police attention on chronic problems cannot guarantee their solution. . . . The results of a test with objective target selection seem far more modest than results of quasi-experiments using subjective target selection. . . . When the most troublesome addresses in a city are intentionally selected as targets, perhaps a more appropriate goal would be 'managing' rather than 'solving' (Eck and Spelman 1987) problems" (Sherman, Buerger, and Gartin 1989, 24).

The modest statistical outcomes were the result of the case assignments outstripping the resources which the unit could bring to bear on them, resulting in a large number of addresses remaining essentially static from the Time 1 to Time 2 measurement (Buerger 1993b). The cases upon which this analysis draws represent a smaller group of addresses, those "most troublesome" locations actively worked by RECAP, with persistent problems that defied easy solutions.

RECAP Tactics and Operations

The wide range of RECAP problems and tactics have been recorded elsewhere (Sherman 1987; Buerger 1992, 1993b). The officers received weekly printouts of the calls to each RECAP address during the previous week. They worked with the persons involved in the calls, or with the guardians of the address, as appropriate. The solutions which they devised included referrals to social services, law-enforcement actions, changes in the physical environment, informal counseling and cautioning in the traditional police manner, and occasionally more innovative responses, such as trying to arrange for a management takeover of a failing boarding house run by deeply religious but incapable guardians (Buerger 1992, 103–109).

The first commander of the unit, Sgt. Bud Emerson, analyzed RECAP's work as having three phases: cooperative, insistent, and coercive. Working from a nontraditional justification for target selection ("high demands for police service" rather than recognizable illegal activity) made "cooperation" a necessary first step for two reasons. First, the underlying problems were not always discernible from the call data alone, and the officers were to some degree dependent upon the formal guardians for information about the activity at the address (history, tenancy, external conditions which imposed on the address, etc.). Second, without a clear-cut criminal violation there were few coercive tools available to the officers in most cases.

This, plus the fact that they were an experimental unit testing uncharted waters, led to a tactical decision with both positive and negative consequences. The cooperative approach was more likely to secure compliance where the guardians or participants were genuinely interested in being good citizens, but it left the officers vulnerable to manipulations of the truth (lies, half-truths, lip service, and "redefinition") where the primary motivations were otherwise. The case loads were so great that considerable time could elapse before the officers learned that supposedly cooperative guardians were just paying lip service to RECAP requests (particularly in terms of longterm solutions, such as the use of tenant screening and the enforcement of "house rules"). Several addresses accumulated high numbers of calls before the officers shifted from cooperation and insistence to a more coercive aspect.

RECAP was an interactive process, one in which other actors had power equal to and sometimes exceeding that of the officers. This chapter addresses the actions (and inactions) of the other players, including problem-causing people, formal guardians, intermediaries, and nominal allies of the RECAP officers. The three main subsections examine the methods of resistance employed by address guardians and others, the problems RECAP faced in being dependent on others to implement their problem-solving ideas, and competing interests, chief among which was the Capitalist Imperative, which demands profits ahead of all other concerns. The latter was the most important element of resistance, and has the greatest implications for problem solving and problem-oriented policing.

CONFLICTING INTERESTS

One of the curious aspects of the RECAP cases was the degree to which a spirit of voluntarism pervaded the early efforts. Without stooping to the buzzwords of "coproduction" or "partnership" that infest policing publications today, RECAP nevertheless appealed to a presumed altruism on the part of the people with whom they interacted. Rational self-interest was not stinted, by any means, but the phrase "you can help" is a constant theme in the RECAP cases, so well rehearsed that there is little doubt but that it was the approach the officers took. Exchanges observed directly, during the persuasion phase and during attempts at coercion, all stressed the notion of individual and corporate responsibility to the larger units: the block, the neighborhood, the city. For example, fliers distributed by the team in the highrises in August carried the banner headline, "The Minneapolis Police need your help!"

In some cases, the officers' definition of altruism ran contrary to other visions of altruism, primarily in the social services areas. The manager of the downtown YMCA refused to cooperate with the RECAP officer's suggestions that a security system be installed to restrict access to the YMCA to residents after a certain hour (after analysis showed a concentration of latenight calls to remove drunk and disorderly "street people" from the lobby). The manager defined himself as "an ultra-liberal," furthering the YMCA's mission of being available to the street people, not restricting them (Buerger 1992, 78–83). The staff at the women's shelter were far more concerned with the well-being of their clients than with the small demands the shelter made on a public system that had otherwise failed their clients. Though profit was an issue in all of the RECAP dealings with the lodging and shelter facility which will be discussed, there was no doubt that the owner was sincerely dedicated to the welfare of his clients, however naïve his management may have been in some particulars.

Across the wider spectrum of resistant addresses, however, the appeal to altruism ran hard aground on the Capitalist Imperative: the desire to make the maximum profit from minimal expenditures. In one way or another, most of the resistance to RECAP interventions centered on financial matters, and RECAP had to find ways to make public safety and order competitive with the profit motive. Generally, among residential addresses their success was greater with the smaller landholders, for whom the two conditions were more closely linked, than those with larger holdings and greater experience (who had developed effective means of insulating themselves from the direct impact of their business practices). The unit's success with commercial properties was more mixed, as the corporate responses were not correlated with any known measure of corporate resources except possibly that of local ties.

Commercial Addresses

Shoplifting dominated the calls to the larger commercial addresses and was a significant problem in many of the smaller ones. RECAP began with the assumption that the stores would have a desire to curb their shoplifting losses, only to find that corporate hierarchies were much more concerned with the financial losses to lawsuits. A second theme, which runs through the officers' records of their initial contacts at various stores, is the stores' desire for help with employee pilferage, which was the cause of much greater losses than shoplifting. RECAP was ill-equipped to work on that type of problem, since it has traditionally been considered out of the realm of public crime and was not represented in the calls for police assistance that were their mandate and evaluation. In only one case, a downtown hotel, did RECAP deal with an internal matter, using a standard police technology of bait money soaked with dye to apprehend a housekeeping employee who was stealing from guests' rooms (Buerger 1992, 66–68).

Corporate Liability

An employee of one of the chain convenience stores put the matter in perspective when he observed, as quoted by the case officer, "When you're making sixty thousand dollars a month in profits, who cares if you lose three thousand to shoplifting?" (Buerger 1993b). Since awards in lawsuits could run into the millions, the shoplifting losses were essentially written off as an acceptable cost of doing business.

RECAP's interest in shoplifting activities was more localized, and incidentally shared by the employees of the stores, who were frustrated at not being able to take action against the predators. An "easy mark," such as a SuperAmerica convenience store, where corporate directives (since changed) allowed the criminally inclined to pilfer cigarettes and beer without challenge, bordered on being an attractive nuisance. Though the link between the uncontested crimes allowed by corporate policy (for all intents and purposes) and other criminal conduct in the area is only speculative, RECAP officers were inclined to see the disorder attracted by the stores as spilling over into the neighborhood, a "Broken Windows" type of situation (Wilson and Kelling 1982).

The Capitalist Imperative worked both ways in the case of the SuperAmerica stores: An employee (described by the regional officers as "disgruntled") filed a Workman's Compensation disability suit for stress related to the job. As a result of the case officer's work at the address, the employee had been aware of the RECAP statistics, and the case officer was deposed in the lawsuit on behalf of the plaintiff. Despite that, however, local franchise managers and the regional representatives refused to accept RECAP suggestions (and offers of free help) to restore a climate of order at the stores. They appealed to the higher authority of the parent company's Security Manual, which forbade employees to interfere with shoplifters because the law supposedly gave them no authority to do so (Minnesota law did, in fact, contain a Shopkeeper's Statute which permitted them to do so, but the financial ties of franchise management were stronger than RECAP's invocation of the law).

The turning point came with a shooting incident at the gas pumps of one of the inner-city SuperAmerica stores. The unit's commander sent a registered letter to the regional manager describing the store as a nuisance property and threatening to have the store's license revoked unless the company took more responsive action to deal with the disorder at their addresses. It is uncertain whether the connection could be sustained in court between the shoplifting and disorderly customer problems and an essentially random event like the shooting, but the letter restarted negotiations at a different level.

The SuperAmerica case was a difficult one for RECAP, as the regional representatives of the company resisted all of RECAP's initiatives. A direct appeal to the parent company, Ashland Oil, eventually broke the deadlock over the shoplifting policies, but the real gains that resulted may have been only peripherally the result of RECAP's actions. Over the summer, a series of early-morning armed robberies of SuperAmericas on the south side of Minneapolis may have provided the spur. An employee at one store advised the case officer that the company responded to the robberies by placing closed-circuit monitors at the counter: All customers entering the store could see themselves on the monitor, with the quiet but clear message that their features were now recorded somewhere on videotape. The employee observed that there seemed to be fewer problems at the store since that device was installed. At RECAP's urging, SuperAmerica did hire security guards at night, rotating guards among the stores in the inner core to deal with disorder problems, but the practice was instituted late in the year and probably had little impact on the call loads.

Occasionally, the Imperative worked in more subtle ways. When the unit first proposed to enforce the juvenile curfew, the officers worked to enlist the assistance of the twenty-four-hour convenience stores. The 7-Eleven stores balked at the proposal to exclude juveniles from the premises after curfew hours. Southland Corporation (the parent company of 7-Eleven) had tied the 7-Eleven stores to the national McGruff House child safety/crime prevention campaign, and the policy proposed by RECAP was in direct conflict with that initiative. This particular conflict was not resolved: The 7-Eleven stores were in the first commander's caseload, and the issue died quietly when he left for a year at Harvard's Kennedy School.

Impact on Good Customers

The case files for both SuperAmerica and a large independent grocery on the near north side contain notes indicating that the owners or managers claimed that a police presence on the premises, to deal with disorder and curb thievery at the former and to curb shoplifting and bar juveniles after hours at the latter, would offend their good customers. In both cases, the RECAP plan was put in force against the protests of the ownership: The parent company authorized the hiring of security guards in the SuperAmerica stores (under an existing contract with a national security company), and the RECAP case officer patrolled the grocery store aisles in uniform during peak shoplifting periods (to prove his point to the owner that it was better to deter than to catch). The case notes for both files contain notes that customers and employees made a point of thanking the officers, saying that they felt safer and expressing hope that the change would be permanent.

Interference by Police Officers

The Capitalist Imperative extended beyond those with proprietary interests to those who derived secondary benefits from employment at the stores. While regular employees of the establishments were appreciative of the unit's efforts, police officers who were part-time employees by virtue of their off-duty security jobs felt threatened by the shoplifting program. It was stridently opposed by several officers who feared it would lead to the termination of the off-duty jobs (though why it should have done so was not clear, since the officers did not process shoplifters and only stood near the front entrance like greeters; in fact, the institution of the shoplifting program did not lead to their termination). One officer, assigned to another specialty unit, reportedly was actively working against the case officer's plan for the northside independent grocery, for reasons which were never fully determined. And one officer in the Fourth Precinct went beyond his brief in opposing the hiring of a private security service at a large low-income housing complex, apparently because he had hoped to secure the security contract for off-duty Minneapolis officers. While these situations were more irritants than obstacles, they demonstrate the complexity that problem solving can encounter in police agencies.

Residential Addresses

A renters' market that prevailed in Minneapolis in 1987 was a driving force behind the Capitalist Imperative at residential addresses. Homeowners were moving or threatening to move to the suburbs, many rental units were vacant, and landlords struggled to get and keep paying tenants in order to meet mortgage or contract-for-deed payments. A bumper crop of abandoned properties was scattered throughout the city, providing squats for homeless men who declined to accept the regulations of shelters, and abandoned properties were part of the growing crack cocaine trade. It fell to the city to take the properties through legal action.

A change in the tax laws had encouraged the purchase of rental properties as investments, which brought new, inexperienced landlords into the business. Many would-be entrepreneurs, lacking sufficient capital to purchase buildings outright, negotiated contract-for-deed agreements with the titled owners of properties. The building's formal owner held the deed, and essentially acted as the financing agent. In return for privately negotiated down payments, the deed holder would turn the property over to the new "owner" who ran it, put whatever investments into it he or she wanted or could afford (which for the RECAP addresses often seemed to be "nothing"), and collected all the rental income from the property. The difference between the rents collected and the contract-for-deed payment was profit for the new owner, but the legal deed remained in the possession of the titled owner until the contract payments were all made—if they ever were.

Since most of the new-generation "investors" were looking for little more than ready cash income, improvements to the housing stock were rarely made and little attention was given to management practices, especially to tenant screening. If income dropped to an unacceptable level, or the hassles of landlording became too great, the owner of the moment had two choices: pass the property on to another investor through a second "balloon" contract for deed, or default on the contract, walking away from the property and letting it lapse back to the original owner. Both entailed potential costs, either continued expenditures or the loss of investment capital.

The practical consequence was that many landlords accepted any tenant who had the next month's rent in hand: empty apartments meant either no profit that month or perhaps a shortfall which took money out of the owner's pocket to make the mortgage or contract-for-deed payment. Some landlords accepted Section 8 tenants because it meant an automatic vendored rent payment each month, direct from the Welfare Department, without the usual hassles of collecting the rent moneys.

Because most landlords were absentee owners, they were insulated from the behavioral problems that their tenants brought with them. Newer, smaller landlords tended to be "on the line" more, both in collecting the rent, making repairs, and dealing with various complaints that more experienced property owners delegated to on-site caretakers or management companies. Many residential operations (both new and experienced) had neither leases nor house rules, and thus effectively had no means of imposing control over their tenants' behavior when the need arose. For the slumlords, who basically used the properties to warehouse people, behavioral problems were irrelevant unless and until they extended to physical damages which cut into the profit margin, at which point the tenant would be evicted.

When RECAP officers intruded, essentially demanding that house rules be instituted or prospective tenants screened for references, the financial house of cards was threatened. In the case of one medium-size apartment building, the property manager was dismayed to learn that the person he considered the best tenant in the building was a major drug dealer who the police wanted evicted. From the property manager's perspective, the low profile that the dealer used to protect his operation (never making demands, always paying the rent on time and in cash) made him an ideal, no-problem tenant. The eviction took place, but was rendered moot by the revocation of the dealer's parole (Buerger 1992, 275–278).

Addresses in transition felt the Capitalist Imperative even more keenly: Buildings with vacant apartments did not sell quickly, or as well, as those that were full. A property manager who could show a potential buyer a fully occupied building was peddling a commodity that was a "proven" maximum-income generator: The buyer could take ownership by paper or electronic transfer and immediately reap the benefits of ownership, both making the payments and making a profit. A buyer who took control of a partially empty building faced the necessity of filling it, which meant lower income, more work, and certainly more hassles.

The Capitalist Imperative very simply dictated the maximum profit for the minimum expenditure of capital, whether that capital be financial or the "sweat equity" variety. RECAP's requests and demands threatened the elegant simplicity of the equation for those who looked at their investments as short term, though the suggestions and assistance RECAP offered were frequently of great use to those whose generally more modest investments were directed toward the long term.

FORMS AND TACTICS OF RESISTANCE

Broadly, resistance to RECAP initiatives fell into three distinct categories, each specific to a target group. Owners and managers of commercial addresses felt the problems could be controlled if the patrol officers came around more often. Owners and managers of residential addresses claimed that problems at their buildings were a product of the surrounding neighborhood, both directly and indirectly (the former attributing the calls to neighborhood characters coming to the address, the latter taking the form of a claim that because of the neighborhood the building was in, the owner could not get any good tenants). Persons involved in disputes at the residential addresses either denied there was any problem at all or asserted that it was a private matter and so denied the legitimacy of RECAP intervention (despite the clear printed evidence that the dispute was in fact not private, but repeatedly required public resources in the form of police assistance).

The simplest way for an owner or manager to thwart RECAP was to stonewall, either by lying or by doing nothing at all. The caseload and time factors worked to their advantage. One store owner cloaked himself as a community activist dedicated to maintaining the neighborhood, until citizen protests and further investigation revealed that he was using the store as a front for an extensive drug distribution business (Buerger 1992, 5–52, 332–333). The owner of one of the worst residential properties on the RECAP list promised to institute all the recommendations of the case officer. As soon as the officer left, however, the owner instructed his on-site manager to ignore all the promises and to continue the prior business practices, renting to anyone with the rent money in hand (Buerger 1992, 143–149).

In some cases, an ambiguous or inconclusive diagnosis led to the creation of an exhortational action plan that was a "plan" only by courtesy of the title. In such instances, there was little that even a cooperative guardian could do, and resistant guardians were facile in finding excuses in imprecise recommendations or those which used supportive rather than directive language. That was due in part to the role that owners and managers played in the diagnosis itself, through which the RECAP officers were initially dependent upon them for preliminary information about the address. If given false or misleading information, the officers at first had no empirical or intuitive alternatives for the information provided by a resistant owner.

The same was true for participants in the 9-1-1 events. The process that turned 9-1-1 data into RECAP printouts took several days, and it was not unusual for the officers to learn of an event a week to ten days after it occurred. The resulting delay in their follow-up forfeited many advantages of timely intervention in interpersonal disputes, though it occasionally yielded new information which was not reflected in the call data. The time factor forced RECAP to be dependent upon patrol officers for either supportive action on calls at the RECAP addresses or timely notification of new events. Assistance of both types was rendered only sporadically.

Another tactic common to both commercial and residential owners was to insulate themselves from the RECAP officers by using intermediaries. It is essentially a "due process" dodge: If the owner is never informed about the problems, the owner incurs no obligation to do anything about them. Several of the residential case files contain stories about owners who were dedicated to not hearing about the problems at their addresses. RECAP officers overcame the difficulties of tracking down owners by a variety of tactics, including registered letters (e.g., Buerger 1992, 196–200) and, in at least one case, driving out to the owner's rural home to leave a written message. Employing incompetent intermediaries (chemically dependent, mentally slow, or mentally ill) accomplished the same end while giving the appearance of responsiveness. For commercial properties, the corporate structure provided a similar form of insulation. Refusals to return phone calls or keep appointments also served to keep RECAP officers at arm's length, at least temporarily.

Commercial Addresses

In all phases, the officers' first tool was information: the call data, supplemented at times by information from offense or arrest reports. Use of that type of information prompted a comparable tactic in rebuttal. Incriminating information supplied by the officers was countered with exculpatory information which supported the business perspective, though such information was often naked opinion unsupported by any empirical evidence or data. Within the information category were three primary countermeasures: (1) crying poverty, (2) attempting to redefine the problem, and (3) appealing to an alternate authority.

Crying Poverty

During the first year, the owner of a lodging facility (which served a mix of long-term residents and emergency shelter clients) consistently rejected the case officer's demands for better security and greater control over residents' behavior. The owner claimed that his business was operating so close to the margin that he could not afford to make the improvements being demanded or hire security guards or off-duty police officers recommended by the officer. He claimed that if Hennepin

County (the statutory provider of social services, and thus his funding source) upgraded its rating of his facility so that the facility was eligible for a higher per diem rate, he would be able to do so. The original case officer was stymied by the owner's refusal to show him the books to substantiate these claims (the officer suspected he was lying), and a year-long stalemate developed (Buerger 1992, 110–115).

In the unit's second year, another officer with better contacts in the Welfare Office took the case over and confirmed that the owner was trying to play RECAP off against the Welfare agency. The facility's operations were nowhere near to meeting the requirements for the higher rating, and the owner was attempting to manipulate the police definition of the problem in such a way that RECAP would broker his suit to the county. Once equipped with reliable information, the RECAP unit was able to move their tactics to the next level, at the threshold between persuasion and threat, which was moving to have the facility's contract with the County Welfare Office terminated (Buerger 1992, 334–335).

The boarding house and shelter was a special case. Because the establishment was a recipient of public funds, an alternate source of information existed about its financial health that was not available for privately held properties or corporations. The larger stores and national chains clearly had no cause to resort to this particular defense, but still balked at the expensive solutions proposed by RECAP (security cameras at a luxury hotel, security guards or off-duty police officers in convenience stores, etc. [Buerger 1992, 13–15, 18–20, 44–47]).

Redefining the Problem

Redefining the problem meant one of three things at the commercial properties. By far the most common response to RECAP's initial proposals were variations of, "This is what we pay so much in taxes for, to have you cops take care of the problem." It was fairly easy for RECAP officers to sweep aside the objection by pointing out that the address in question was using a disproportionate amount of resources compared to other addresses in the city. The second response was to attribute the high call levels to the failure of another entity or agency; scapegoating. The third was to acknowledge the problem, but to minimize it by asserting that other considerations were more worthy of the organization's resources.

Scapegoating. Frequently, the tax argument was intertwined with an indictment of the police department's operations, though this usually came from the smaller business owners. The most vivid example was the owner of a small corner grocery store who had a history of adversarial contacts with the police (Buerger 1992, 16–17). In addition to several outstanding lawsuits against patrol officers over their handling of problems at his store (which included arresting him for brandishing a pistol on the sidewalk as part of his "informal social control" measures against shoplifting), he had issued an edict to the Precinct Captain that no black officers were allowed to respond to calls at his store. Officers of larger corporations were sophisticated enough to understand the nature of the problems, and in any case the nature of their resources placed their dealings with RECAP on a much different footing than those of the smaller entrepreneur.

Almost everyone tried the gambit that the police were not doing their job: The excuse took on the aspect of a general, prophylactic, knee-jerk reaction to the news that an address was on RECAP's list. However, a few addresses had a well-developed list of particulars in that regard, and chief among them were the social service agencies. One of the case officer's greatest frustrations at a woman's shelter was their singleminded insistence on talking about the poor attitudes and nonresponsiveness of patrol officers who came to take domestic violence reports. The RECAP officer wanted to talk to them about their false alarms, and all the staff wanted to do was to lambaste the performance of his friends and former patrol colleagues (Buerger 1992, 86–88). The staff and people associated with a church-run shelter had similar complaints, though their relationship with another RECAP officer was more positive, based in part on the officer's better reaction to the criticism (Buerger 1992, 91–94).

Minimizing. Public agencies were the most likely to try to trivialize the problem, placing it lower on their list of priorities than the officers tried to make it. A senior corporate executive of the Minneapolis Public Library bluntly stated to the unit commander and the case officer assigned to a branch library address that the Library Board had to be concerned with personnel costs, long-term financing, and brick-and-mortar issues. While the fact that the librarians called upon the services of the Minneapolis Police Department some thirty-three times in 1986 was unfortunate, it was not important enough for the Library Board to divert resources away from other more pressing needs (Buerger 1992, 53–58).

Appeal to an Alternate Authority

The Minneapolis Community Development Authority (MCDA) administered the public housing addresses, including the several high-rise apartment buildings in the experiment. The middle- and upper-management levels of the MCDA simply appealed to higher authorities: those of HUD, which dictated that the vacancy rate be reduced, and of the courts, where recent case decisions had held that maintaining buildings exclusively for senior citizens was a discriminatory practice which denied equal access to public facilities. The MCDA's resort to HUD (which, like the corporate headquarters of SuperAmerica, was physically removed from the officers' jurisdiction) was the most obvious case of this tactic (Buerger 1992, 281–301).

Another example was provided by the branch library case: After the meeting with the senior library officials, RECAP received a follow-up note from them. The Library Board had contacted the Captain in charge of the precinct and had arranged to have a beat officer stop in periodically. The letter stated that they preferred that option rather than to implement RECAP's managerial suggestions, and basically told RECAP to stay out of their hair (Buerger 1992, 53–58).

When RECAP floated trial balloons about instituting an ordinance to require licenses for rental properties, one or more of the landlords with whom they were dealing called in a powerful ally: The Minnesota Multiple Housing Association (MMHA) called for a meeting with the unit commander (Buerger 1992). Though the meeting was entirely cordial and full of the language of mutual cooperation, the underlying message was clear: Any attempt to institute license provisions for rental housing would be met with well-organized, well-financed political opposition from the MMHA. While RECAP secured a promise of cooperation from MMHA to put "peer pressure" on resistant landlords and slumlords, it was clear that MMHA represented its members and was unlikely to put any pressure whatsoever on any member who the police might consider to be a slumlord.

The most obvious appeal to higher authority, going directly to the City Council member responsible for the ward, did not materialize during the experiment. RECAP officers anticipated it in dealing with the bar cases, particularly with Moby Dick's Bar, whose owners were reported to be well-connected politically by virtue of heavy campaign contributions to City Council members (Buerger 1992, 133–140). They prepared for such an eventuality, but did not encounter the problem.

Residential Addresses

Crying Poverty

Despite being an even more frequent reaction than at the commercial properties, the crying-poverty reaction was not always illegitimate at residential addresses (Buerger 1992, 232–236). Some landowners reacquired responsibility for an address they had once owned but sold, after the buyers defaulted on the contract-for-deed payment. In order to protect their investment (because as deed holders they were still obligated to make their own mortgage payments), the once-and-present owners had to resume management of the property, often inheriting a vastly different clientele and a neglected physical plant. These owners, however, were the most amenable to RECAP's suggestions, since the direct benefits of cooperating with RECAP were obvious, and since compliance brought with it some minimal police presence that could be inflated into a tacit threat when dealing with potential problems at the address.

Poverty was not a problem for slumlords who could easily make the physical changes mandated by the housing inspectors. Profitability was a greater concern for them, but their resistance to spending money that they had was as great an obstacle as the smaller holders' reluctance to incur debt spending money they did not have.

Redefining the Problem

The case files record very little use of the minimizing tactic at residential addresses—outright denial was more the rule, and it was easily defeated by the call printouts—but initial attempts to redefine the problems by scapegoating was close to universal. The neighborhood influence was a reasonable defense, since RECAP and control addresses were close to each other in many areas, especially in the neighborhoods with concentrations of social problems. However, in all instances there was evidence both of lackadaisical management practices particular to the address and of buildings in the same area that did not generate large numbers of calls for police assistance. The officers could reject that defense with relative ease.

A second type of scapegoating was to blame what was known locally as the "Gary Syndrome," claiming that an influx of welfare seekers from other states was making it impossible for the owners to get good tenants (Leinfelder 1988). The technique itself—trying to distract the officers from a specific problem by declaiming about a general one—failed, primarily because RECAP officers insisted on keeping the focus on the management of the buildings. However, in private statements the officers sometimes indicated that they were sympathetic to that analysis.

Appeal to an Alternate Authority

The invocation of the political power of the MMHA, as discussed, also constitutes one appeal to a higher political power. Aware of the City Council's concern for both suburban flight and the number of abandoned properties in the city, some landlords attempted to ward off RECAP attention with a threat to "walk away from" the address. The officers basically just ignored such threats, in part because, as one observed, an abandoned building could not be any worse for the neighborhood than it was in its current status. RECAP officers were aware of the larger problem and were concerned that their efforts not have a backfire effect in that way. Nevertheless, they counted on the Capitalist Imperative to minimize the amount of investment loss the owner would be willing to accept (in essence, reading the statement as a bluff, and calling it), and the nonresponse proved correct. No owner that RECAP dealt with just "walked away"; all found someone else to take over the property. Even when the formal guardianship changed hands properly, though, the instability of ownership required the officer to "go back to square one," in many cases forfeiting even the marginal gains that the officer had wrung from the resistant owner.

INTERDEPENDENCIES AND THE STRUGGLE FOR LEGITIMACY

As the several references presented indicate, RECAP's ability to identify the problems and devise appropriate plans to ameliorate them did not guarantee that the plans would be implemented. Some of their interventions were appropriate and effective because of the one-on-one relationships that the officers established and maintained with the individuals involved. Some, particularly the handful where CPTED tactics were appropriate, produced a long-term passive benefit once the initial plan was executed.

A few singular addresses required that the officers interact with specialty groups who held power that the unit did not have: The Mental Health Roundtable in the case of a halfway house in a suburban-character neighborhood (Buerger 1992, 75–77) and the anonymous Welfare Department sources of information about the financial situations of the boarding and shelter facility discussed are examples.

For residential addresses, the unit's work was in part hampered by the workload of the Hennepin County Sheriff's Office. By law, only the Sheriff could effect forcible evictions from a premises, even after the landlord properly obtained an Unlawful Detainer (eviction) notice from the courts. In several cases, landlords and the RECAP officers had to fight a holding action against tenants who had received an eviction order from the court—and therefore had nothing to lose by being destructive and belligerent—but refused to move until forcibly evicted. The Sheriff's office was at one point backlogged a full month with eviction orders, and would not change its schedule to accommodate the Minneapolis Police. (The sheriff is an elected office in Minnesota; jumping a RECAP case to the head of the list would benefit one voting landowner—if the landlord lived in the county—but might offend many more.)

For the most part, though, when individual persuasion failed to achieve the desired results and coercion was needed, the RECAP strategy depended on the assistance of four main groups: the City Attorney's office, the housing inspectors, police officers assigned to patrol duties, and the police administration.

The City Attorney's Office

The City Attorney's office was specifically needed for the shoplifting program, but deliberate inaction by that office ultimately eviscerated what might have been a promising solution to a widespread (if not overly serious) problem. Despite some reasonably good working relationships between RECAP officers and individual attorneys, all of the policies of the City Attorney's office were gatekeeping devices, and two practices were particularly galling. The office refused to prosecute any shoplifting case under a certain dollar amount, and changed that amount internally several times without any notice to RECAP. Their suggested alternative was that shopkeepers use a civil recovery process, which often cost more in filing fees than the original loss, and in any case was an unrealistic resort against welfare- and poverty-level suspects who were impervious to civil judgment out of simple inability to pay. Second, when RECAP arranged an alternative sanction, a nonpunitive decision-making course similar to the DWI schools used in some jurisdictions, the office refused to cooperate in sending a letter to the apprehended suspects telling them that attendance at the school was an alternative to prosecution. The office maintained that it was an extortionate threat: Since they had made an internal decision not to prosecute cases under a certain amount, there was no prosecution for the school to be an alternative to, even if the statute defined the offense as prosecutable under criminal law (Buerger 1992, 308–318).

Similarly, the officers had difficulty getting cooperation with any issues relating to the domestic assaults that were so frequent at RECAP residential addresses. Citing the overwhelming problem of lack of commitment on the part of domestic-violence victims, the City Attorney's office refused to commit resources to that area, even for the cases that RECAP officers were trying to shepherd through the system. Requiring victims to come to the City Attorney's office in the Hennepin County Government Center downtown in order to give a statement about the assault and to swear out a complaint was perceived by RECAP as a significant factor in victim reluctance (Buerger 1992, 174–176).

The conflicts with the City Attorney's office represented an interesting case of dueling managerial dictates. The City Attorney's office correctly decided that it could not deal on an individual level with every officer or unit of the Minneapolis Police Department who might have some new idea on how cases could be better handled. The police administration, in turn, was promoting bottom-up innovation, delegating a significant amount of authority to lower-level workers. As frequently happens in such instances, conflicts became personalized: RECAP officers saw themselves working past the old litany of "we can't" excuses in order to improve the quality of life in the city, and they could find no justification for the intransigence of the City Attorney's office. The impasse over the handling of domestic violence cases was temporarily broken when the Hennepin County Criminal Justice Coordinating Committee selected the domestic-violence issue as its first major project: RECAP was selected by the police administration to represent the Department on the Domestic Violence Task Force. The addition of other players with political power forced the representatives of the City Attorney's office into a more cooperative stance, at least temporarily (Buerger 1992, 319–324). Ultimately, the Task Force proved to be a classic case of suppressing action while appearing to take action: To the author's knowledge, nothing substantive was accomplished during the RECAP experiment, or in subsequent years, and the issue soon disappeared from the headlines.

Housing Inspectors

The housing inspectors were vital to the attempt to get the attention of certain stonewalling landlords, and the natural affinity of street-level workers provided for a solid alliance. Reliance on the housing inspectors ultimately ran afoul of the Inspections office's own bureaucratic mandates, however: At least one officer came to rely exclusively on the inspectors as a way to punish uncooperative landlords. He lost sight of the fact that the Inspections office was limited by its own procedural safeguards against abuses, and was subject to political control which the experienced slumlords had learned to manipulate. In the most resistant cases, the slumlords were as impervious to the relatively weak sanctions available to the housing inspectors as they were to the empty threats of the officer.

The Patrol Force

The patrol force was needed to put teeth into both the juvenile sweeps and the domestic-violence policy. The job of enforcing threats to arrest for domestic assault at 125 residential addresses was beyond the capacity of the unit, even if there had been a way around the four-hour limit for misdemeanor assault arrests. To have any deterrent effect at all, the domestic-violence policy had to be consistently applied, a job that had to be shouldered by the patrol force.

In order to quell the wide range of problems caused by unsupervised juveniles abroad at night, the unit needed to be able to transfer the responsibility for curfew enforcement to the patrol units. RECAP officers could not work both daytime hours to make their commercial contacts and nighttime hours to conduct juvenile sweeps. Even when they changed their work schedules in order to do sweeps, five officers in three cars were not enough to have a significant impact on a citywide problem. To be effective, juvenile curfew enforcement had to be done consistently by all patrol officers in all areas.

The patrol force, already critical of RECAP as a specialty unit, and more critical after a late August meeting in which the domestic-violence policy was reasserted, supported neither initiative (several individual exceptions to this only served to prove the rule). The case notes from the startup phase mirror the RECAP officers' confidence that they could obtain the assistance they needed by prevailing upon their former mates to help them on an individual basis. By late May, that confidence had begun to erode, and soon turned to frustration and resentment as officers who had agreed to follow RECAP's wishes continued to do nothing when they answered domestics at RECAP addresses.

In part, the resistance of the patrol force to RECAP initiatives was directly related to the amount and direction of change it meant for the officers' daily work life. The shoplifting program produced a positive change in an activity that patrol officers were already doing. Despite the usual "yeah, but" objections that were dredged up at the beginning of the program (while the details and unanticipated problems were being worked out of the system), patrol officers quickly recognized the change as an improvement in their work life. Most officers hated the toothless taxi service that the universal arrest policy had become. As soon as it became obvious that the squads were not being called to the stores as much, appreciation for the new procedures grew rapidly, and RECAP's stock with the patrol force rose a bit.

By contrast, the RECAP initiative for juvenile curfew enforcement was essentially a new activity for the patrol force, which had already convinced itself that it was overworked and understaffed. Though the curfew law had been on the books for years, it was a long-ignored regulation, and even the RECAP officers could not recall a time when it had been vigorously enforced. The domestic-violence policy was already despised, since its obligations ran counter to the local police culture's conclusion that "nothing could be done" about domestic violence. Being called upon to do more work, or to take more seriously an activity that they wished they could shed outright, did not improve the patrol officers' work lives, and they resisted (Buerger 1992).

Patrol officers had the power to avoid the domestic-violence policy in most cases by redefining the event: recoding it as an UNWANT

(Unwanted Person), handling the event as they saw fit and radioing that the abuser was GOA (Gone On Arrival) even when he was not, or simply clearing with a statement that the event did not meet the guidelines for invoking the department's preferred-arrest policy. Since officers worked in a low-visibility environment, and many supervisors were more sympathetic to their platoons than to RECAP or the department's policy changes, there was little the unit could do except to appeal up the chain of command for assistance.

The Police Administration

The police administration was needed to gain even the grudging cooperation of the patrol force, as well as that of external entities unused to dealing with requests from line police officers, such as the City Attorney's office, the YMCA board, or the higher echelons of the MCDA. The intercession of the administration was more effective with the independent entities than with the subordinate units nominally under its command.

RECAP was a bottom-up form of problem solving, and the unit frequently had to fight internal and interagency battles that do not seem to have been obstacles to the Newport News officers. RECAP was a small experimental project, given a free hand but minimal resources, and introduced by an outsider (Sherman) through personal lines of communication with the Chief of Police. The influence of the Chief of Police was used with outside interests, but sparingly, as the officers wanted to push the limits of what they (and other line officers) could accomplish by themselves. Within the department itself, the Chief's backing could be as much a liability as an asset: The Minneapolis department was still fighting the last rear-guard battles of a nine-year internal struggle for reform in which Chief Bouza was seen almost from the first as "The Enemy" by the unionized rank-and-file officers.

Chief Bouza was a reform chief, brought in by Mayor Don Frazer to stabilize and trim a politicized department that had grown top-heavy with rank. His primary adversaries at the time of the RECAP experiment were the civil-service Captains who commanded the four precincts and the various divisions within the investigative division. The embodiment of the conservative, thin-blue-line status quo, they commanded the allegiance of the line officers and supervisors who had come into the department with those expectations, and they vehemently opposed innovations (including RECAP) which stemmed from the Chief's office. Essentially, the Captains were the vestigial remains of the old politicized system, and they held the power of "No." They could not be removed from office because of civil-service rules. They provided both a rationale for continued resistance and a buffer against sanctions for nonperformance, which encouraged patrol officers to resist. At the same time, they obstructed as much as possible the administration's attempts to shine a brighter light on the patrol force's activities, effectively undermining discipline. To bypass the logjam, Chief Bouza had appointed the first untenured (non-civil service) inspector to command a precinct, a move which had been challenged by the Captains through a civil suit and was pending in the courts during the entire experiment.

With the resolution of the power struggle between the Chief's office and the Captains pending in the courts, change in the department was essentially in abeyance as everyone waited to see in which direction the future would be. The more progressive officers might be able to see a different future if the Chief's Inspectors plan prevailed, but those officers were for the time being under the command (and arguably at the mercy) of the Captains.

RECAP officers worked hard to overcome the patrol force's disdain of special units, a particularly difficult undertaking at a time when department staff levels were under authorized strength and the patrol force saw itself as being bled dry by transfers to new specialty units "taking bodies out of the precincts." In a corporate climate where "special unit" was synonymous with working-day shift Monday to Friday, RECAP won a measure of respect for working during the evenings and on weekends doing juvenile sweeps and other enforcement actions. Whenever they were on the air, they were available to assist patrol units as backup, and occasionally they took radio calls at their addresses, freeing patrol units for other work. And they worked hard to incorporate their work into that of the patrol force, sharing the lessons of problem solving in training sessions and providing 9-1-1 call information on troublesome buildings identified by district squads. (In the latter case, they were constrained by the scientific requirements of the experiment: They could not work on buildings outside of their assigned caseload, which occasionally generated some resentment.) Ultimately, their gains in this regard were modest, sufficient to retain their individual integrity but not enough to move the corporate mindset of the patrol division in a direction favorable to problem solving.

DISCUSSION

The issue of generalizability of results is important when evaluating the RECAP experience. At first glance, it would appear that the problems encountered by the unit were the particular product of the experiment and of the unusual method of determining problems to work on. The modest gains of RECAP seem dim against the firmament of published accounts of the successes of other programs with more traditionally "logical" targeting. Nevertheless, the lessons of the RECAP experiment may have greater utility for the field than first glance would indicate.

First, as police administrators have known for years, "every new program is successful." The professional magazines of police practitioners and the scholarly journals of their academic partners are filled with success stories, almost all of which have been told in the first flush of victory. Few recount the problems encountered along the way, except to triumphantly report that they were overcome, and few have the perspective of the year-long RECAP project. Those programs which do take a longer view report a decline in a variety of areas: officer satisfaction, citizen satisfaction, displacement of crime, or the return of crime to the "reclaimed" area (e.g., Schwartz and Clarren 1977; Wycoff 1988; for a review, see Buerger 1993a).

Second, though it is a minor footnote to the main point, the statistical failure of RECAP initiatives occurred within an experimental framework which included both the learning curve of the first half of the year and the more mature problem-solving efforts of the later months. The latter were frustrated by a lack of coercive tools and supportive resources, which contributed to the difficulties of doing realistic problem solving. The RECAP experiences highlighted to the civil authorities the need for more resources, and since the end of the experiment some have come into being and are facilitating current problem-solving efforts. RECAP officers lobbied long and hard for a city ordinance to license rental properties and for a "wethouse" facility to take inebriated persons who were not in need of medical detoxification for alcohol (the only resource available during the experiment was a medical facility run by the county). Both have since come into being, in part because of the documentation and groundwork provided by the unit.

Third, as the community-policing movement becomes more and more defined operationally as problem solving (regardless of the deployment scheme used) and police departments open up more of their prioritization to citizen input, they may well end up with problem addresses similar to those worked on by RECAP. The recent past has been dominated by the impact of the drug trade on city neighborhoods, particularly crack houses. As a problem, crack houses are amenable to resolution at the immediate local level by traditional law-enforcement tactics (though the issue of displacement continues to be a thorny one). However, a growing body of literature is beginning to document—almost haphazardly, in footnotes and academic asides—that the citizenry bring other types of problems to the police which are not so easily resolved (e.g., Guyot 1990).

The techniques of problem solving are not yet adequate to all the tasks brought to it, and the rhetoric of both the problem-solving advocates and the community-policing movement frequently oversells the possible gains to be had. Because both approaches require that the officers involved "buy in" to the premise, there is a strong emphasis on "celebrating the small successes" as a way of stimulating additional participation. Possible outcomes are promoted as if they were automatic, painless, and inevitable, when in fact they are not.

That is a double-edged sword: While the marketing of success may bring in new participants, it also sets them up for the failure of unfulfilled expectations. The unrealistic exhortations do not just fail to convince the "I'll just wait and see before I buy in" officers in a department. More dangerous, they can lead to the burnout and bail out of formerly committed officers whose enthusiasm is a critical element of the successes, small or otherwise (more recent, see the final report on the eight INOP projects sponsored by the Bureau of Justice Assistance [Sadd and Grink 1993]).

Naturally, not every department now faces the same combination of political and economic factors which attended the RECAP experiment, but many may conceivably face similar circumstances in the future. The lessons of the RECAP experience can help temper the unrealistic enthusiasm of the promotional industries that attend community- and problem-oriented policing (enthusiasm which is more or less falling on intentionally deaf ears anyway, at least in some quarters). Their inclusion in a training regimen, for instance, can help stimulate more realistic discussions of available resources, particularly those of information and political support. The prime benefit to others of the RECAP experience may well be to make the exercise of problem solving more real, and to more fully engage the participation of police officers who are grounded in what is, not what ought to be.

NOTES

Reprinted from *American Journal of Police* 13 (3), with permission from MCB University Press. Research for this article was supported in part by Grant #86-IJ-CX-0037 and a Graduate Research Fellowship, Grant #91-IJ-CX-0029, from the National Institute of Justice, whose support is gratefully acknowledged. The views expressed herein are those of the author alone, and neither represent nor purport to represent the official views of the United States Department of Justice, the Office of Justice Programs, the National Institute of Justice, the Crime Control Institute, the City of Minneapolis, or the Minneapolis Police Department. The access and encouragement provided by Lawrence W. Sherman is also greatly appreciated, as are the helpful comments of the anonymous reviewer.

BIBLIOGRAPHY

Buerger, M. (1993a). The Challenge of Reinventing Police and Community. In *Police Innovation and Control of the Police: Problems of Law, Order, and Community*, edited by D. Weisburd and C. Uchida. New York: Springer-Verlag.

Buerger, M. (1993b). Convincing the Recalcitrant: Reexamining the Minneapolis RECAP Experiment. Ph.D. diss. Ann Arbor, Mich.: University Microfilms.

Buerger, M., ed. (1992). *The Crime Prevention Casebook: Securing High Crime Locations*. Washington, D.C.: Crime Control Institute.

Buerger, M.; E. Cohn; and A. Petrosino. (1988) Defining the Hot Spots of Crime: Minneapolis. Crime Control Institute, internal memo (accepted for a forthcoming book edited by D. Weisburd and J. Eck), Maryland.

Cohen, L., and M. Felson. (1979). Social Change and Crime Rate Trends: A Routine Activity Approach. *American Sociological Review* 44: 588–608.

Cordner, G. (1985). The Baltimore County Citizen Oriented Police Enforcement (COPE) Project: Final Evaluation. Paper presented to the American Society of Criminology, November, San Diego, California.

Draper, N. (1993). "Welfare Magnet" Theory is Disputed. New Hennepin Arrivals Studied. *Minneapolis Star Tribune*, 21 December.

Eck, J., and W. Spelman. (1987). *Problem Solving: Problem-Oriented Policing in Newport News*. Washington, D.C.: National Institute of Justice.

Gainesville Police Department. (1986). *The Convenience Store Robberies in Gainesville, Florida: An Intervention Strategy by the Gainesville Police Department*. Gainsville, Fla.: Author.

Gilsinan, J. (1989). They Is Clowning Tough: 911 and the Social Construction of Reality. *Criminology* 27: 329–344.

Goldstein, H. (1990). *Problem-Oriented Policing*. Philadelphia: Temple University Press.

Goldstein, H. (1979). Improving Policing: A Problem-Oriented Approach. *Crime and Delinquency* 25: 236–258.

Goldstein, H., and C. Susmilch. (1982a). *The Drinking-Driver in Madison: A Study of the Problem and the Community's Response*. Madison: University of Wisconsin.

Goldstein, H., and C. Susmilch. (1982b). *The Problem-Oriented Approach to Improving Police Service: A Report and Some Reflections on Two Case Studies*. Madison: University of Wisconsin.

Goldstein, H., and C. Susmilch. (1982c). *The Repeat Sexual Offender in Madison: A Memorandum on the Problem and the Community's Response*. Madison: University of Wisconsin.

Goldstein, H., and C. Susmilch. (1981). *The Problem-Oriented Approach to Improving Police Service: A Description of the Project and an Elaboration of the Concept*. Madison, Wisconsin.

Green, L. (1993). *Treating Deviant Places: A Case Study Examination of the Beat Health Program in Oakland, California*. Ph.D. diss. Ann Arbor, Mich.: University Microfilms.

Greenwood, P.; J. Petersilia; and J. Chaiken. (1977). *The Criminal Investigation Process.* Lexington, Mass.: D. C. Heath.

Guyot, D. (1990). *Policing As Though People Matter.* Philadelphia: Temple University Press.

Hennessey, M., and D. Foster. (1990). *Minneapolis SAFE Program: Final Evaluation Report.* Minneapolis: City of Minneapolis.

Klockars, C. (1980). The Dirty Harry Problem. *The Annals* 452: 33–47. Reprinted in excerpt in *Thinking about Police: Contemporary Readings,* edited by C. Klockars and S. Mastrofski, 2d ed. New York: McGraw-Hill, 1991.

Klockars, C., and S. Mastrofski, eds. (1991). *Thinking about Police: Contemporary Readings.* 2d ed. New York: McGraw-Hill.

Leinfelder, J. (1988) The Gary Syndrome. *Minneapolis Twin Cities Reader,* 27 January, 10–12.

McElroy, J.; C. Cosgrove; and S. Sadd. (1993). *Community Policing: The CPOP in New York.* Newbury Park, Calif.: Sage.

Percy, S., and E. Scott. (1985). *Demand Processing and Performance in Public Service Agencies.* University: University of Alabama Press.

Petersilia, J. (1989) Implementing Randomized Experiments: Lessons from BJA's Intensive Supervision Project. *Evaluation Review* 13: 435–458.

Pierce, G.; S. Spaar; and L. Briggs, IV. (1984). *The Character of Police Work: Implications for Service Delivery.* Boston: Center for Applied Social Research, Northeastern University.

Reiss, A., Jr. (1971). *The Police and the Public.* New Haven: Yale University Press.

Reuss-Ianni, E. (1983). *Two Cultures of Policing: Street Cops and Management Cops.* New Brunswick, N.J.: Transaction Books.

Rosenbaum, D., ed. (1986). *Community Crime Prevention: Does It Work?* Sage Criminal Justice System Annuals, Vol. 22. Beverly Hills: Sage.

Sadd, S., and R. Grink. (1993). *Issues in Community Policing: An Evaluation of Eight Innovative Neighborhood-Oriented Policing Projects.* Vol. 1. New York: Vera Institute of Justice.

Schwartz, A., and S. Clarren. (1977). *The Cincinnati Team Policing Experiment: A Summary Report.* Washington, D.C.: Police Foundation.

Sherman, L. (1987). *Repeat Calls to Police in Minneapolis.* Washington, D.C.: Crime Control Institute.

Sherman, L.; M. Buerger; and P. Gartin. (1989). *Repeat Call Address Policing: The Minneapolis RECAP Experiment, Final Report to the National Institute of Justice.* Washington, D.C.: Crime Control Institute.

Sherman, L.; M. Buerger; and P. Gartin. (1988). *Policing Repeat Calls: The Minneapolis RECAP Experiment, Preliminary Report to the National Institute of Justice.* Washington, D.C.: Crime Control Institute.

Spelman, W. (1992) *Criminal Careers of Public Places, Final Report to the National Institute of Justice: Executive Summary.* Washington, D.C.: National Institute of Justice.

Wilson, J., and G. Kelling. (1982). Broken Windows: The Police and Neighborhood Safety. *The Atlantic Monthly,* March, 29–38.

Wycoff, M. (1988). The Benefits of Community Policing: Evidence and Conjecture. In *Community Policing: Rhetoric or Reality,* edited by J. Greene and S. Mastrofski. New York: Praeger.

16

Innovation in Policing Organizations: A National Study

Jihong Zhao, Quint Thurman, and Christopher Simon

American policing scholars and law-enforcement executives might agree that, by the 1970s, many police organizations had begun reassessing their basic organizational values and practices, much in the spirit of a paradigm shift. According to Trojanowicz and Bucqueroux (1990), the most commonly identifiable organizational change along these lines has been community policing.

Community policing reflects a set of new values which acknowledges the importance of the community in improving the general quality of life and the concept of the coproduction of order with, or a partnership between, the police and the community in planning and then implementing solutions (e.g., Wasserman and Moore 1988; Curtis, Thurman, and Nice 1991). Central to community policing is the goal of transforming police organizations from a bureaucratic model that emphasizes a paramilitary and hierarchical organizational climate to a more participative and innovative organization.

Lurigio and Skogan (1994) contend that, when applied, the community policing philosophy "translates into a variety of specific operations and practices" (p. 315; also see Wasserman and Moore 1988). In particular, policing scholars assert that both external and internal innovations are necessary to fully operationalize this concept (Kelling and Moore 1988; Trojanowicz and Bucqueroux 1990; Rosenbaum and Lurigio 1994).

Aside from recent results from the National Institute of Justice's National Assessment Program survey (McEwen 1994), which indicate that over 80 percent of the police chiefs surveyed say they have adopted community policing, Rosenbaum, Yah, and Wilkinson (1994) observe that the identification of key factors which affect the creation and implementation of community-policing innovations has eluded systematic study. This chapter is a step in that direction.

LITERATURE REVIEW

Skolnick and Bayley (1986) highlight several instances of community policing, offering a guide for "innovative ideas, strategies, and organizational reforms that might have some success in responding to city crime" (p. 1). Furthermore, their examples also might be used to explore organizational change and how community-policing innovations correlate with other police agency characteristics.

A review of the literature focusing on community-policing innovations suggests that two major dimensions of organizational change have been considered by American policing scholars (e.g., Kelling and Moore 1988; Goldstein 1990; Rosenbaum and Lurigio 1994). These two dimensions represent different domains of change, namely, *externally focused* innovations and those which are *internally focused* (see also Huber et al. 1993).

Externally focused innovations include the reorientation of police operations and crime-prevention activities in an effort to adjust an organization's influence and improve its relationship within the external environment. Different from the bureaucratic model that emphasizes the separation of police agencies from their external environment, community-policing innovations highlight the interactive role of the police in a complex and changing world.

Notable externally focused community-policing programs involving the reorientation of operations and prevention include foot patrol programs aimed at direct involvement with the community (Skolnick and Bayley 1986), special task-force units to address unique local problems (Goldstein 1990), storefront police stations, community crime-prevention newsletters (Brown and Wycoff 1987), the assignment of specially trained community-policing officers to schools and neighborhoods (Thurman, Bogen, and Giacomazzi 1993), and the deployment of police resources to promote crime prevention among specially targeted subpopulations, such as at-risk youth (Thurman, Bogen, and Giacomazzi 1993; Giacomazzi and Thurman 1995; Thurman et al. 1996).

In contrast, internally focused innovations primarily involve changes in police management. Central to this argument is that the bureaucratic style neglects the development of employee motivation and suppresses human potential in organizations (Argyris 1973; Sandler and Mintz 1974). In its place, community policing emphasizes cross-level communication and the empowerment of employees in an effort to deliver more valuable public services (Goldstein 1990).

Recent research has documented instances of internally focused organizational change. For example, Wycoff and Skogan's (1994, 379) three-year study of community-policing programs in Madison, Wisconsin, indicates that a participative and decentralized management style increases job satisfaction among community-policing officers (see also Lurigio and Skogan 1994; Rosenbaum, Yah, and Wilkinson 1994). Furthermore, community-policing administrative innovations aimed at changing a police department's paramilitary organizational structure are exemplified by innovations such as the creation of a master police officer rank, the institutionalization of management styles, and the increased hiring of civilian employees (Skolnick and Bayley 1986).

Linking Community-Policing Innovations with Organizational Structure and Other Intrinsic Factors

The literature contains at least two different schools of thought regarding the development of innovations. One perspective, which can be traced to the fields of business administration and management (e.g., Woodward 1965), focuses on the formal organizational structure as an important determinant of innovation. Alternatively, a less developed, second perspective emphasizes other intrinsic factors that affect innovations, particularly in police organizations.

Any discussion of organizational structure should begin with Max Weber, who posited the emergence of formal bureaucratic organizations as an inevitable consequence of social evolution (Ranson, Hinings, and Greenwood 1980; Kirton 1980). Weber, as translated by Gerth and Mills (1977), identified two essential dimensions of organizational structure. The vertical dimension concerns authority based upon positions within a hierarchical order and describes the relationship of people working in a formal organization as a firmly ordered system of super- and subordination, such as that which is observed among military personnel according to rank (e.g., generals, majors, captains, sergeants, etc.). In contrast, the horizontal dimension involves the distribution of special functions throughout an organization (Gerth and Mills 1977, 196–230), typically according to the variety of units and subunits that an organization maintains (e.g., in policing, we see patrol, traffic, and investigation units; subunits might include foot patrol, crime prevention, narcotics, etc.).

In terms of structure in particular, Hall (1964) identifies six dimensions from Weber's "ideal type" of bureaucracy. Hall's main argument is that structural variation affects organizational behavior (Hall 1964, 33–37). Following Hall and Pugh and colleagues (1968), Blau's (1970) differentiation of organizational structure theory offers additional insight into key dimensions of organizational structure in terms of occupational, functional, spatial, and hierarchical differentiation. Particularly relevant here, Blau's work, which has been widely tested and supported (see Kimberly 1976; James and Jones 1976, for excellent reviews), includes data analyses based on public organizations similar to police agencies (see also Blau and Schoenherr 1971).

Blau (1970) predicts occupational differentiation, also conceptualized as specialization, to covary with innovation, since (1) the internal demand for change likely is greater in an occupationally diverse organization, and (2) specialists are able to operate under less centralized administrative control than are other employees (Wilson 1966).

Hage and Aiken's (1965) study of public welfare agencies suggests that the number of occupational specialists in an organization is positively correlated with innovation (see also Aiken and Hage 1971). Hage (1965) asserts that an increase in the range of specialization results in reduced centralized control and facilitates both internal and external crossfacilitation of new ideas. Similarly, Damanpour's (1991) meta-analysis of published studies on innovations suggests that specialization is significantly associated with innovation, particularly in not-for-profit organizations such as public agencies. Based on these findings, we hypothesize that specialization is positively associated with innovation.

Blau (1970) identifies functional and spatial differentiation as the second and third dimensions of formal organizational structure, respectively. Both concepts refer to an organization's horizontal complexity. Similar to the proportion of specialists who comprise an organization, the extent of functional diversity (or number of distinct units) and spatial differentiation correlate with the presence of knowledge and experience necessary for innovation to occur.

Baldridge and Burham's (1975) study of 191 school districts in two states suggests that the presence of special educational units, as well as the amount of area that a school district covers, are both positively associated with innovation over time. They concluded, "As the number of differentiated subunits increases, the quantity of alternatives and solutions also increases in response to perceived unique problems" (p. 170). Accordingly, our second and third hypotheses, respectively, are as follows: Functional differentiation is positively correlated with innovation, and spatial differentiation is positively associated with innovation.

A fourth dimension of organizational structure recognized by Blau (1970) is hierarchical differentiation. According to Weber (Gerth and Mills 1977), positions which are arranged in hierarchical order and follow a clear chain of command are conducive to promoting efficiency; conversely, many scholars argue that hierarchical control impedes innovation. Recent studies generally support the assumption that a hierarchical organizational structure dampens innovation (Kimberly and Evanisko 1981; Damanpour 1991; Wycoff and Skogan 1994). It appears that the greater the number of hierarchical levels an organization possesses, the more rigidly bureaucratic it becomes. Consequently, the very nature of bureaucracy impedes innovation in an organization, particularly in policing. Thus, our fourth hypothesis is that hierarchical differentiation is negatively correlated with organizational innovation.

A final dimension of organizational structure also included in this analysis is the centralization of authority. We posit that the intensity of supervision—the proportion of an organization's workforce that is comprised of management and supervisory personnel—is positively correlated with centralization of authority, and, hence, negatively correlated with innovation.

Critics of a more traditional model of American policing point out that the inhibitory nature of a paramilitary organizational structure where strict ranks and firm managerial control delineate relationships among employees facilitates a climate where obedience is a special "virtue" (Sandler and Mintz 1974; Goldstein 1990). Trojanowicz and Bucqueroux (1990) argue that such a feature is contrary to a community-policing model which emphasizes substantial contributions from the rank-and-file officers to the development and attainment of organizational goals (see also Wycoff and Skogan 1994). Accordingly, our fifth hypothesis is that the concentration of authority is negatively correlated with organizational innovation.

In addition to the influence of bureaucratic structure, other intrinsic organizational factors have been identified by scholars of policing as important during a time of organizational change. These include the influence of top administrators, personnel diversity, and self-evaluation of previous performance. For example, Skolnick and Bayley (1986, 222) suggest that the police chief is a key figure who might prove instrumental in either promoting or blocking organizational innovation. Unfortunately, since the survey instrument that we employ in this study lacks an adequate measure of the depth of a chief's commitment to community policing, we use length of a chief's appointment as a proxy which might indicate how vested a chief is in an organization's culture. Hence, our sixth hypothesis is that a police chief's tenure is negatively associated with innovation.

Many policing scholars have commented that how a police chief is selected may be a crucial factor linked to innovation (e.g., Wilson 1968; Brown 1981). In particular, Wilson (1968) asserts that substantial organizational change usually occurs when the chief is appointed from outside of the department. Thus, we derive an additional hypothesis which is related to the role of the police chief in an organization: A chief recruited to his or her position from outside of the department which employs him or her will be more innovative than if he or she is promoted to the chief's position from within the organization.

Personnel diversity is another intrinsic factor that may affect community policing. Reiss (1992) notes that an important factor that challenges traditional organizational values in policing is the recruitment of minority and female officers. Since the passage of the Equal Employment Opportunity Act in 1972 which made Title VII of the Civil Rights Act of 1964 applicable to state and local government, police departments across the nation have been under tremendous pressure from both the government and federal courts to increase the rate of recruitment of minority and female officers (Warner, Steel, and Lovrich 1989). Therefore, our eighth hypothesis is that personnel diversity is positively associated with innovation.

Another important factor concerns the relationship between organizational learning and innovation. In "The Science of 'Muddling Through,'" Lindblom (1959) argues that organizational innovation is rarely guided by rational choice, and more often than not occurs piecemeal without a lot of deliberation. Evaluations of community policing innovations reported in Rosenbaum's recent book, *The Challenge of Community Policing*, are replete with examples of incremental change. It seems logical to expect that previous successful experiences of community-policing implementation will encourage, rather than discourage, police administrators to implement more community-policing innovations, leading to our ninth hypothesis: The more successful the experiences of community-policing implementation, the more innovations a police department is likely to endorse.

A control variable, city size, is also included in the analysis because of its close relationship with innovations and organizational structure. For example, Cole (1974) notes that municipal governments in cities with more than 100 thousand population are more likely than smaller cities to develop and then implement innovations that involved citizen participation in problem solving. Furthermore, other writers have noted a positive correlation between city size and the complexity of organizational structure as defined by the presence of multiple ranks and specialization (e.g., Blau 1970; Langworthy 1986). In fact, most of the available information concerning community-policing programs originates from larger cities (see also Skolnick and Bayley 1986).

METHODS AND MEASURES

A national mail survey of police chiefs provided the data for this study. The Division of Governmental Studies and Services at Washington State University has conducted a mail survey of a large sample of municipal police departments in continuous three-year intervals since 1978. The cities in the sample were selected from among those municipalities initially included in a representative sample of police chiefs in cities with more than 25 thousand population conducted by the International City Management Association in 1969. This sample includes 281 municipal police departments in forty-seven states, stratified by geographic region and city size. The data for the present study consist of responses from the sixth survey of municipal police departments conducted in 1993. A total of 228 departments returned completed questionnaires, for a response rate of 81 percent.

Either a police chief or an appointed representative was asked to identify from a prepared list the presence or absence of innovative programs and strategies implemented in the past three years in his or her agency. His or her responses were then used to gauge innovative organizational change as represented by scores from eighteen items. For the purpose of index construction, those police departments which had adopted more innovative programs or strategies were scored higher than those with a lesser number in operation. The two dimensions of organizational innovation were distinguished from the items appearing in the next section and in accordance with the previous discussion on external and internal foci of change.

Indices comprised of each set of items discussed served as dependent variables representing external and internal innovation, respectively. Scores for these indices ranged from zero for departments with no innovations to a maximum score of twelve for the external-innovations scale and six for the internal-innovations scale.

The five dimensions of organizational structure used as independent variables were operationalized primarily following Langworthy's (1986) application of Blau's (1970) theory to police organizations. Langworthy's research represents one of but a few studies available that focuses directly on police organizations.

Externally Focused Innovation:
Reorientation of Police Operation and Crime Prevention

1. Additional officers on foot, bicycle, or horse patrol.
2. Use of storefront police stations.
3. Use of special task units for solving special problems in targeted area.
4. Fixed assignment of officers to neighborhoods or schools.
5. Victim contact program.
6. Departmental sponsorship of community newsletter.
7. Crime education of the public.
8. Use of citizen survey to keep informed about local problems.

9. Neighborhood block watch program.
10. Business watch program.
11. Block meetings between agency staff and community participants.
12. Use of unpaid civilian volunteers who perform support and community liaison activities.

Internally Focused Innovation: Administrative Strategies

1. Increased hiring of civilians for non-law-enforcement tasks.
2. Adding the position of master police officer to increase rewards for line officers.
3. Reassigning some management positions from sworn to civilian personnel.
4. Authorizing crime-scene control to first officer at the scene.
5. Quality circles (problem solving among small groups of line personnel).
6. Reassessment of ranks and assignments.

Specialization or occupational differentiation was represented in the analysis by the proportion of civilian employees in a police department. Functional differentiation was measured by the number of divisions while spatial differentiation was gauged using the number of patrol beats in a police department. Hierarchical differentiation was depicted by the number of ranks separating patrol officers from the police chief. Finally, concentration of authority was represented by the proportion of sworn officers who rank lower than sergeant.

The top administrator's tenure was indexed as the number of years a chief had held this position in a department. Similarly, the top administrator's method of recruitment was measured using a single item that asked whether a chief was appointed from outside of the department or whether he or she was promoted from within. The recruitment of minority and female officers was gauged by the percentage of minority and female officers fully employed in a police department, and the experiences of community-policing implementation were measured by the subjective evaluation of community-policing programs or strategies ranging from responses that it was a waste of resources to those that indicated it was highly valuable. Finally, an affirmative-action variable (represented by three dummy variables) was included which indicated whether or not a diversity program existed as either an informal or formal program, or was one that was court ordered.

City size was measured by the four categories of city population depicted in *The Municipal Yearbook*: Cities with less than 100 thousand population, cities from 100,001 to 250 thousand, cities from 250,001 to 500 thousand, and cities with 500,001 and over. Univariate descriptive statistics for both indices and all of the independent variables used in the analysis appear in Table 16.1.

Two models were explored using ordinary least squares regression. Model I examined the impact of organizational structure on community-policing innovations, while Model II assessed the relationship between other intrinsic variables and innovation.

FINDINGS

Table 16.1 shows that police departments on average have adopted about nine of the twelve externally focused innovations. In contrast, the survey results for internally focused innovation depicted a mean adoption of only three of the six internal innovations possible. These findings suggest that community-policing innovations are relatively popular in police agencies across the country, much as survey data from the 1994 National Assessment Program indicated (McEwen 1994). Furthermore, the correlation between external innovations and internal innovations was significant and substantial ($r = 0.51$), suggesting that an increase in one dimension correlates with change in the other dimension.

Table 16.1
Univariate Descriptive Statistics

Variables	Description	Mean(SD)	N
Dependent Variables:			
EXTER	Externally focused innovation/index (0-12)	9.0 (2.1)	207
INTER	Internally focused innovation/index (0-6)	3.2 (1.5)	207
Independent Variables:			
Structural Variables			
CIVIL	Percentage of civilian employees	0.23 (0.16)	207
DIVIS	Number of divisions	7.37 (3.05)	207
BEATS	Number of patrol beats	19.5 (28.60)	192
RANK	Number of ranks	6.01 (1.61)	207
OFFICER	Percentage of line officers in dept.	0.76 (0.07)	196
Other Intrinsic Variables			
TENURE	Years of chief in office	4.97 (4.79)	183
RECRUIT	Chief's recruitment (0-1)	0.61 (0.49)	207
MI/FE	Percentage of minority and female officers	0.23 (0.16)	94
RATING	Subjective evaluation of COP programs (1-5)	4.63 (0.63)	207
AFFIR1	No affirmative action program	0.32 (0.47)	207
AFFIR2	Informal program	0.20 (0.40)	207
AFFIR3	Formal program voluntary/court order	0.39 (0.49)	207
Control Variable			
CITYSIZE	Population of city (0-1)	0.47 (0.50)	207

Community-Policing Innovation and Organizational Structure

Controlling for the effects of city size, the independent variables relevant for examining externally and internally focused innovation include the percentage of civilian employees, number of divisions, number of patrol beats, number of ranks, and the percentage of rank-and-file officers. Table 16.2 presents the findings for Model I, which includes the organizational structure variables.

Data from Table 16.2 are useful for examining the nine hypotheses stated earlier. Recall that the first hypothesis was that specialization differentiation, as represented by the percentage of civilian employees, is positively correlated with community-policing innovation. The analysis suggests that such a relationship is not statistically significant when externally focused innovation is the focus. However, it is significantly correlated with internally focused innovation. Thus, these data stand in contrast to Skolnick and Bayley's (1986) observation in six American cities that increased civilian hiring is closely linked with community-policing innovations, particularly external innovation.

The second and third hypotheses concern functional and spatial differentiation as measured by the number of departmental divisions and the number of patrol beats, respectively. The findings indicate that neither of these variables has any impact on externally or internally focused innovation.

The fourth hypothesis posited that hierarchical differentiation is negatively correlated with innovation. The results indicate that the number of officer ranks is not significantly related to either depen-

Table 16.2
Model I: Structural Variables as Determinants of Organizational Innovation

Variable	Externally Focused Innovation		Internally Focused Innovation	
	b	beta	b	beta
Civilians as % of Department	0.78	0.03	2.53*	0.15
Number of Divisions	0.04	0.07	0.02	0.04
Number of Patrol Beats	0.01	0.02	-0.01	-0.08
Number of Ranks	-0.09	-0.10	0.10	0.10
% of Line Officers	4.97*	0.15	1.98	0.08
City Size	1.25***	.30	0.54	0.18
	Adjust. R=0.14***		Adjust. R=0.06**	

Key: $*p < 0.05$; $**p < 0.01$; $***p < 0.001$.

dent variable. In contrast, the percentage of rank-and-file officers as a measure of centralization of authority, the fifth hypothesis, is a statistically significant predictor of external organizational innovation and in the direction predicted.

A final observation concerns the effect of the control variable. The results suggest that city size has a strong positive impact on externally focused innovation. As city size increases, so does the impetus for police departments to be responsive, and, hence, so does the number of externally focused innovations which are implemented.

Innovation and Other Intrinsic Organizational Factors

Table 16.3 reports the findings of other intrinsic factors (Model II) that might be relevant to organizational innovation. It was hypothesized that a police chief's length of service in the department was negatively correlated with organizational innovation. Furthermore, it was predicted that if a chief was recruited from outside, he or she would be more likely to support innovation. However, neither variable is significantly correlated with innovation.

Table 16.3
Model II: Both Structural and Intrinsic Variables as Determinants of Organizational Innovation

Variable	Externally Focused Innovation		Internally Focused Innovation	
	b	beta	b	beta
STRUCTURAL VARIABLES				
Civilians as a % of Department	-0.02	-0.00	1.92	0.11
Number of Divisions	-0.01	-0.01	0.01	0.11
Number of Patrol Beats	0.00	0.01	0.01	0.01
Number of Ranks	-0.12	-0.09	0.10	0.11
% of Line Officers	4.72*	0.15	2.11	0.09
INTRINSIC VARIABLES				
Tenure of Chief	-0.01	-0.01	-0.03	-0.10
Chief Appointment	-0.02	-0.01	-0.40	-0.13
% of Minority and Female Officers	0.58	0.05	-0.16	0.02
Rating of COP Value	1.12***	0.34	0.41*	0.17
Informal Affirmative Action	0.05	0.01	0.15	0.04
Formal Affirmative Action	0.91**	0.22	0.39	0.13
City Size	0.89*	0.22	0.34	0.11
	Adjust. R=0.27***		Adjust. R=0.10**	

Key: *p < 0.05; **p < 0.01; ***p < 0.001

The eighth hypothesis concerned the association between diversity of personnel and innovation. This indicator also fails to predict the extent of innovation in either model. In contrast, affirmative-action programs are shown to be significantly associated with innovations, at least in terms of those that are externally focused. While no differences are observed between police departments having no diversity programs or only informal programs, police agencies that have a formal program or are under court change orders are significantly more likely to manifest external innovations.

Concerning the ninth and final hypothesis, the relationship between the rating of the value of community policing and change was found to have a significant impact on both externally and internally focused innovation. This suggests that when the initial results from implementing innovations prove acceptable, a police department is more likely to continue supporting them.

In sum, the variables which were significant in the two models explained 27 percent of the variance for externally focused innovation and only 10 percent for internally focused innovation. The data collected from a representative national sample of over 200 police departments reflect the occurrence of innovations externally and internally and their relationship with organizational dimensions and related factors, controlling for city size.

Typically, innovations are more likely to be found in police departments that are located in larger cities, find themselves under court-ordered change, have a higher availability of rank-and-file officers (controlling for department size), and have had previous successful experiences with community-policing innovations. Further, these variables have more predictive power for externally focused innovation than internally focused innovation. Somewhat surprisingly, other key variables identified by previous research as theoretically important failed to further distinguish sufficient conditions for community-policing innovation.

Finally, both models performed poorly in explaining internally focused innovation. Except for the community-policing rating factor, all of the other variables failed to achieve statistical significance as predictors of the occurrence of internally focused community-policing innovation.

DISCUSSION AND CONCLUSION

Our examination of the effect of organizational structure on community-policing innovations suggests that this effect is extremely limited. Moreover, the findings suggest that community-policing innovations are primarily a reaction to external pressure rather than the result of a serious reform effort involving changes in structure and personnel, similar to the circumstances that produced the transition in American policing from a political model to a professional–legalistic model during the first half of this century. Since that time, a standardized form of organizational structure and recruitment procedures has remained intact and invariant. This may explain why organizational structure variables derived from widely tested management theories failed to predict the degree of community-policing innovation in police organizations. As a result, external innovations can be offered with greater frequency but with less overall investment in the outcome: when they are successful they are maintained, when they fail they are abandoned or replaced.

Similarly, our findings suggest that externally focused community-policing innovations are a response to external pressure as measured by larger city size, the presence of court-ordered change, previous "trial-and-error" experiences, and a relatively higher availability of rank-and-file officers relative to management personnel, although these variables have very limited explanatory power in predicting internally focused organizational innovation. Primarily, internal innovation in police departments nationally is occurring more slowly relative to external change since there is relatively less imminent pressure on the organization's internal structure for change to occur.

Recent research seems to support these conclusions (e.g., Sadd and Grinc 1994). Similarly, in an overview of community-policing innovations during the past twenty years, Rosenbaum, Yah, and Wilkinson (1994) observe that "Many of these outreach programs were not institutionalized as part of the police function (i.e., they were often specialized units, grafted onto the organization), and for this reason, often disappeared when the funding spigot was turned off" (p. 332). Based on their findings concerning police organizations, Rosenbaum, Yah, and Wilkinson conclude that "gains associated with community policing, however, should not be overplayed. The fact remains that the absence of change was the norm rather than the exception" (p. 349). In our view, the "absence of change" implies a lack of institutionalized community policing. Our findings suggest that implementation of internally focused change occurs at a slower pace than external innovation, and there are few variables that substantially contribute to internally focused change.

These findings have important policy implications with respect to the implementation of community-policing innovations. After nearly two decades since the introduction of the community-policing model, scholars and practitioners still have trouble reaching consensus concerning the definition of community policing and the extent of its development (e.g., Eck and Rosenbaum 1994). In our view, the lack of structural and other administrative changes is the primary weakness in the implementation of the community-policing philosophy.

NOTE

Used with permission from the Police Executive Research Forum. Copyright by Police Executive Research Forum. The authors wish to acknowledge the assistance and support of the Division of Governmental Studies and Services at Washington State University, and particularly Professor Brent Steel for permission to access the data source used in the preparation of this chapter.

BIBLIOGRAPHY

Aiken, M., and J. Hage. (1971). The Organic Organization and Innovation. *Sociology* 5: 63–82.

Angell, R. (1974). The Moral Integration of American Cities II. *American Journal of Sociology* 80: 607–629.

Argyris, C. (1973). Some Limits of Rational Man Organization Theory. *Public Administration Review* 33: 263–267.

Baldridge, J., and R. Burnham. (1975). Organizational Innovation: Industrial, Organizational and Environmental Impact. *Administrative Science Quarterly* 20: 165–176.

Blau, P. (1970). A Formal Theory of Differentiation in Organizations. *American Sociological Review* 35: 201–218.

Blau, P., and R. Schoenherr. (1971). *The Structure of Organizations*. New York: Basic Books.

Brown, L., and M. Wycoff. (1987). Policing Houston: Reducing Fear and Improving Service. *Crime & Delinquency* 33: 71–89.

Brown, M. (1981). *Working the Street: Police Discretion and the Dilemmas of Reform*. New York: Russell Sage.

Cole, R. (1974). *Citizen Participation and the Urban Policy Process*. Lexington, Mass.: Lexington Books.

Crank, J., and L. Wells. (1991). The Effects of Size and Urbanism on Structure among Illinois Police Departments. *Justice Quarterly* 8: 169–185.

Curtis, C.; Q. Thurman; and D. Nice. (1991). Improving Legal Compliance by Non-Coercive Means: Coproducing Order in Washington State. *Social Science Quarterly* 72: 645–660.

Damanpour, F. (1991). Organizational Innovation: A Meta-Analysis of Effects of Determinants and Moderators. *Academy of Management Journal* 34: 555–590.

Eck, J., and D. Rosenbaum. (1994). The New Police Order: Effectiveness, Equity, and Efficiency in Community Policing. In *The Challenge of Community Policing*, edited by D. Rosenbaum. Thousand Oaks, Calif.: Sage.

Eck, J., and W. Spelman. (1987). Who Ya Gonna Call? The Police As Problem-Busters. *Crime & Delinquency* 33: 31–52.

Gerth, H., and C. Mills, trans. (1977). *From Max Weber: Essays in Sociology*. 3d ed. New York: Oxford University Press.

Giacomazzi, A., and Q. Thurman. (1995). Cops and Kids Revisited: A Second Year Assessment of a Community Policing and Delinquency Prevention Innovation. *Police Studies* 17: 1–20.

Gibbs, J., and M. Erikson. (1976). Crime Rates of American Cities in an Ecological Context. *American Journal of Sociology* 80: 605–620.

Goldstein, H. (1990). *Problem-Oriented Policing*. New York: McGraw-Hill.

Guyot, D. (1979). Bending Granite: Attempts to Change the Rank Structure of American Police Departments. *Journal of Police Science and Administration* 7: 253–287.

Hage, F., and M. Aiken. (1965). Relationship of Centralization to Other Structure Properties. *Administrative Science Quarterly* 10: 72–92.

Hage, M. (1965). An Axiomatic Theory of Organizations. *Administrative Science Quarterly* 10: 289–320.

Hall, R. (1964). The Concept of Bureaucracy: An Empirical Assessment. *American Journal of Sociology* 69: 32–40.

Huber, G.; K. Sutcliffe; C. Miller; and W. Glick. (1993). Understanding and Predicting Organizational Change. In *Organizational Change and Redesign: Ideas and Insights for Improving Performance*, edited by G. Huber and W. Glick. New York: Oxford University Press.

Hull, F., and J. Hage. (1982). Organization for Innovation: Beyond Burns and Stalker's Organic Type. *Sociology* 16: 564–577.

James, L., and A. Jones. (1976). Organizational Structure: A Review of Structural Dimensions and Their Conceptual Relationships with Individual Attitudes and Behavior. *Organizational Behavior and Human Performance* 16: 74–113.

Kelling, G., and M. Moore. (1988). From Political Reform to Community: The Evolving Strategy of Police. In *Community Policing: Rhetoric or Reality?* edited by J. Greene and P. Mastrofski. New York: Praeger.

Kelling, G., and J. Stewart. (1989). Neighborhoods and Police: The Maintenance of Civil Authority. In *Perspectives on Policing*. No. 1. Washington, D.C.: National Institute of Justice.

Kimberly, J. (1976). Organizational Size and Structuralist Perspective: A Review of Critique and Proposal. *Administrative Science Quarterly* 21: 571–597.

Kimberly, J., and M. Evanisko. (1981). Organizational Innovation: The Influence of Individual, Organizational, and Contextual Factors on Hospital Adoption of Technological and Administrative Innovations. *Academy of Management Journal* 24: 689–713.

Kirton, M. (1980). Adapters and Innovators of Organizations. *Human Relations* 33: 213–224.

Langworthy, R. (1986). *The Structure of Police Organizations*. New York: Praeger.

Lawrence, P., and J. Lorsch. (1967). *Organization and Environment: Managing Differentiation and Integration*. Cambridge: Harvard University Press.

Lindblom, C. (1959). The Science of "Muddling Through." *Public Administration Review* 9: 79–88.

Lurigio, A., and W. Skogan. (1994). Winning the Hearts and Minds of Police Officers: An Assessment of Staff Perceptions of Community Policing in Chicago. *Crime & Delinquency* 40: 315–330.

McEwen, T. (1994). *National Assessment Program: 1994 Survey Results*. Washington, D.C.: National Institute of Justice.

Moore, M. (1992). Problem Solving and Community Policing. In *Criminal Justice: A Review of Research*, edited by M. Tonry and N. Morris. Chicago: University of Chicago Press.

Pugh, D.; D. Hickson; C. Hinings; and C. Turner. (1968). Dimensions of Organizational Structure. *Administrative Science Quarterly* 13: 65–105.

Ranson, S.; B. Hinings; and R. Greenwood. (1980). The Structuring of Organizational Structure. *Administrative Science Quarterly* 25: 1–17.

Reiss, A. (1992). Police Organization in the Twentieth Century. In *Criminal Justice: A Review of Research*, edited by M. Tonry and N. Morris. Chicago: University of Chicago Press.

Rosenbaum, D. (1995). *The Challenge of Community Policing*. Thousand Oaks, Calif.: Sage.

Rosenbaum, D., and A. Lurigio. (1994). An Inside Look at Community Policing Reform: Definitions, Organizational Changes, and Evaluation Findings. *Crime & Delinquency* 40: 299–314.

Rosenbaum, D.; S. Yah; and D. Wilkinson. (1994). The Effect of a Community Policing Management Style on Officers' Attitudes. *Crime & Delinquency* 40: 354–370.

Sadd, S., and R. Grinc. (1994). Innovative Neighborhood Oriented Policing: An Evaluation of Community Policing Programs in Eight Cities. In *The Challenge of Community Policing*, edited by D. Rosenbaum. Thousand Oaks, Calif.: Sage.

Sandler, G., and E. Mintz. (1974). Police Organizations: Their Changing Internal and External Relationship. *Journal of Police Science and Administration* 2: 458–463.

Shaw, C., and H. McKay. (1972). *Juvenile Delinquency and Urban Areas*. 3d ed. Chicago: University of Chicago Press.

Skolnick, J., and D. Bayley. (1986). *The New Blue Line: Police Innovations in Six American Cities*. New York: The Free Press.

Thurman, Q.; P. Bogen; and A. Giacomazzi. (1993). Program Monitoring and Community Policing: A Process Evaluation of Community Policing Officers in Spokane, Washington. *American Journal of Police* 12: 89–114.

Thurman, Q.; A. Giacomazzi; M. Reisig; and D. Mueller. (1996). Innovation in Gang Interventions: A Process Evaluation of the Neutral Zone. *Crime & Delinquency* 42: 279–295.

Thurman, Q.; A. Giacomazzi; and P. Bogen. (1993). Research Note: Cops, Kids, and Community Policing—An Assessment of a Community Policing Demonstration Project. *Crime & Delinquency* 39: 554–564.

Trojanowicz, R., and B. Bucqueroux. (1990). *Community Policing: A Contemporary Perspective*. Cincinnati: Anderson.

Warner, R.; B. Steel; and N. Lovrich. (1989). Conditions Associated with the Advent of Representative Bureaucracy: The Case of Women in Policing. *Social Science Quarterly* 70: 562–578.

Wasserman, R., and M. Moore. (1988). Values in Policing. In *Perspectives on Policing*. No. 8. Washington, D.C.: National Institute of Justice.

Wilson, J. (1968). *Varieties of Police Behavior: The Management of Law and Order in Eight Communities*. Cambridge: Harvard University Press.

Wilson, J. (1966). Innovation in Organization: Notes Toward a Theory. In *Approaches to Organizational Design*, edited by J. Thompson. Pittsburgh: University of Pittsburgh Press.

Woodward, J. (1965). *Industrial Organization: Theory and Practice*. London: Oxford University Press.

Wycoff, M., and W. Skogan. (1994). The Effects of a Community-Policing Management Style on Officers' Attitudes. *Crime & Delinquency* 40: 371–383.

17

Crime-Specific Policing

Larry T. Hoover

There is consistently accumulating evidence that focused police efforts to reduce particular crimes committed by particular offenders at particular times and places are effective. In this chapter, we refer to such approaches as crime-specific policing. Virtually every controlled experiment entailing crime-specific interventions has yielded positive results (i.e., crime went down). In other words, when the police concentrate resources on a particular crime, the incidence of that crime drops.

However, one of the most common misconceptions pervading modern criminology is that the police make no difference. Engendered by two early research studies on nondirective approaches, the Kansas City Preventive Patrol Experiment and the RAND Criminal Investigation Study, the axiom was born that nothing the police do has an appreciable effect on crime rates. Myths that have some basis in scientific fact die hard. And analyses of macro law-enforcement approaches indeed have indicated nominal police effectiveness. Bolstering the findings of the Kansas City and RAND studies is the fact that no correlation exists between police–citizen ratios in major U.S. cities and crime rates. Thus, if one tends to believe that the police make no difference, a quick glance at generic correlation between police staffing levels and overall crime rates can quickly confirm one's bias.

Research, however, refutes the axiom that the police make no difference. The research includes several well-known national studies. Over twenty years ago, the San Diego Field Interrogation Experiment (Boydstun 1975) demonstrated the efficacy of proactive stop-and-question techniques. Eck and Spelman's (1987) evaluation of problem-oriented techniques in Newport News, Virginia, launched an approach almost universally regarded as having the potential not only to reduce calls for service, but also to reduce crime. The Minneapolis Recap Experiment confirmed the short-term effect of problem-oriented approaches directed toward problem locations. More recently, the Kansas City Gun Reduction Experiment illustrated the effectiveness of focusing street enforcement on a specific problem.

There are other examples of the efficacy of crime-specific policing. In both Illinois and Texas, the creation of auto-theft task forces led to immediate and dramatic reductions in the incidence of that crime. Along the Texas border with Mexico, theft rates fell to one-third of their previous level in a year (nationally, auto-theft rates had decreased only slightly over the same time frame).

Perhaps more than any other research study, the 1993 Kansas City Gun Reduction Experiment demonstrates the very narrow effect of a particular police strategy (Sherman, Shaw, and Regan 1995). One might reasonably expect that with additional units aggressively patrolling target areas, overall crime in those areas would drop. But while there was a very dramatic effect on the targeted gun crimes, there was no measurable impact on other offenses. Police efforts targeted at particular offenders committing particular crimes produced results in the Kansas City Gun Reduction Experiment, as it did in Newport News, San Diego, and Texas. But unfocused strategies have produced few results. Directed patrol in Pontiac, Michigan, and New Haven, Connecticut, targeted various offenders committing a variety of various crimes at various times of the day, and no definitive results materialized. The same held true for the Wilmington Split-Force Patrol Experiment.

Nevertheless, we must be cautious about dismissing broad proactive arrest efforts. Dramatically increased enforcement activity in Houston and New York City recently produced considerable drops in crime. The most likely explanation is that the effectiveness of particular police strategies depends on environmental circumstances. When enforcement is lacking for long periods and there is a sudden and dramatic turnaround in general enforcement effort, results are measurable. At the same time, merely assigning added patrol units to an area apparently has little impact.

CRIME RATES IN THE 1990s

In the United States, we now find ourselves in the midst of a historically unprecedented drop in crime rates. For several years, virtually every type of crime has decreased. Granted, there is some unevenness. While crime is dropping precipitously in cities such as Houston and

New York, it has actually increased in a few others. But the exceptions are indeed few. There are five possible explanations for the decease:

- Social–Demographic Trends. Criminologists generally regard social–demographic trends as the strongest influence on crime rates, more important than structured social response (police–courts–corrections). A high proportion of fourteen- to twenty-five-year-olds equals a high overall crime rate. Factors such as migration patterns also influence crime. Mobile, disrupted groups tend to commit more crimes than settled, stable groups.
- Economic Conditions. The economy is recognized as influencing the rate of both violent and property crime. Extreme economic stress, for example, breeds social violence, particularly spouse abuse. Obviously, property crime is likewise influenced by changing economic conditions. However, the relationship is not necessarily a straightforward one. Property crime may increase in an improving economy, particularly if increases in wealth are unevenly distributed.
- Drug-Use Prevalence. Crime is linked in complicated ways to the supply of illicit drugs. Scarce supplies raise street prices, potentially increasing crime, but may also mean fewer users, thus decreasing crime. Drug supply and drug-use prevalence interact.
- Incarceration Rates. For the last ten years, most states have built new prisons at record rates. Incapacitation rates appear, at least on the surface, to offer one of the best explanations for decreasing street crime.
- Police Programs. Decreases in crime have not been evenly distributed. Where agencies have implemented aggressive intervention styles, crime has dropped precipitously. Clearly, the police make a difference.

There is no way to determine which of these factors is causing the current downward trend. However, one may certainly argue that of the five, two have had the greatest effect on incarceration rates and police programs. The others tend to have longer-term effects on crime rates. When crime drops in a particular city by 30 percent in one year, it is not likely that changes in demographics are the explanation. And indeed, there have been no dramatic shifts in the nation's demographics during the 1990s. The shifts that are occurring are, by and large, part of longer-term trends present for the last twenty-five years. Changes in economic conditions also do not appear to have had a dramatic effect. With the exception of two or three very mild recessions, the nation has experienced slow but steady economic growth since 1970. Unemployment rates have varied within a range of 2 percent. In fact, if one were to look to economics for any type of explanation, one might argue that changes in the distribution of wealth in the 1990s would beget more crime, not less. In addition, one cannot point to any dramatic economic changes in cities like Houston or New York that would account for the decreases in crime.

Like trends in demographics and economics, trends in drug use do not offer any apparent explanation for the decrease in crime. While the use of some drugs decreased in the late 1980s and early 1990s, the use of others remained steady. Further, in the mid-1990s drug experimentation surveys of high school students indicated increases in use, or at least in experimentation. Statistics on drug seizures indicate that trafficking continues unabated. The war on drugs has not caused the dramatic decreases in crime.

Unlike demographics, economics, and drug-use prevalence, incarceration rates should be considered as a possible explanation for the recent drop in crime. Over the past ten years, prison capacity has increased dramatically in some states. For example, in Texas prison capacity has tripled. Fed up with persistent high crime rates, the public has demanded that chronic offenders, particularly violent offenders, be locked up for long periods. Thus, a building boom has accompanied changes in sentencing laws.

Some cautionary notes are in order. In some states where incarceration has increased there has not been a dramatic decrease in crime. Further, it is unlikely that incarceration would have a sudden and dramatic effect on crime rates in individual large cities. To better understand the possible mixed effect of incarceration and police programming, Hoover and Caeti (1994) compared the sharp drop in crime in Houston in 1992 with the crime rate in other major Texas cities. While incarceration affected all of the state's major cities, a sudden and dramatic drop in crime occurred only in Houston. This drop correlated month by month with dramatically increased arrests.

The argument that most of the drop in crime in Houston was the product of police-agency productivity rather than offender incarceration was bolstered by a similar drop in New York City two years later. Like Houston, New York elected a new mayor who brought in a new police chief determined to use different approaches to crime. As in Houston, both the mayor and the police chief dismissed the fluff elements of community policing. Instead, they mandated that precinct commanders take personal responsibility for crime rates in their area. In turn, commanders ordered patrol officers to make arrests. Long-standing policies prohibiting patrol officers from enforcing vice and narcotic offenses were lifted (those policies were meant to control corruption at the beat level). Crime started dropping immediately.

College students are taught in their first research-methods class that correlation does not equal cause and effect. Indeed, instructors usually go out of their way to find historical accounts of the misinterpretation of correlation as cause and effect. The experimental design is, of course, offered as the ultimate solution to isolating cause and effect from correlation. Unfortunately, many criminologists who have spent their careers cautioning undergraduates about this phenomenon have allowed their own perspective to become distorted. They can no longer accept the obvious link between phenomena in the real world. Absent an experimental design, nothing should be accepted as causal. It is true that we can always find absurd examples of correlation. The viscosity of asphalt on a given day in a beach community correlates with the number of drownings. Obviously, there is no cause-and-effect linkage between these phenomena—more people swim on a warm day. But the link between increasing enforcement efforts and a drop in crime is not prima facie absurd; indeed, it is prima facie logical. And when several major cities dramatically increase enforcement efforts and the crime rate drops precipitously, it is illogical to dismiss the relationship as spurious.

An analogous international problem may be relevant here. The 1990s saw a different kind of violence in Bosnia. In an effort to stop the killing, U.N. troops were dispatched. However, commanders were hamstrung—ordered not to use force unless in immediate danger. The killing went on. Finally, fed up with the genocide, NATO took over dispatching troops with orders to shoot to stop the killing. And the killing stopped. It is perhaps stretching the point a long way, but the parallel between the crime in major U.S. cities and the situation in Bosnia is striking. When the police are merely present but passive, crime continues. When the police suddenly and decisively change their approach to one of proactive intervention, crime starts dropping.

OUR RESEARCH LEGACY: A BRIEF SYNOPSIS

Kansas City Preventive Patrol Experiment

The granddaddy of all police research is the Police Foundation's Kansas City Preventive Patrol Experiment (Kelling et al. 1974) conducted in Missouri from 1972 to 1973. The research is also the most frequently misinterpreted. To understand this misinterpretation, a quick review of the research design is necessary. The south patrol district contained fifteen beats. Five of these beats were designated as controls, where the level of routine preventive patrol for a year was to remain constant with past practice. Five of the beats were designated reactive. On these beats, patrol units would enter to handle calls for service, then immediately leave. In effect, routine preventive patrol was withdrawn. Five of the beats were designated proactive. The patrol units on the reactive beats were instructed to conduct routine preventive patrol in the proactive beats, in effect doubling the amount of patrol in these areas. Additional patrol officers were assigned to the south district, such that the patrol level on the proactive beats was two to three times what it had been. Everyone in the police field knows the results. Over the course of a year, no change was detected in reported crime, crime as measured by victimization surveys, citizen satisfaction with the police, or several other efficiency measures. Researchers, chief among them George Kelling, appropriately and conservatively concluded that routine preventive patrol as practiced in Kansas City, had no effect on crime (Kelling et al. 1974).

Unfortunately, the very conservative conclusions drawn were inappropriately and grossly overgeneralized in subsequent years. The conservative conclusion that "routine preventive patrol within the limits tested in Kansas City has no measurable effect on crime" became "the police don't make a difference." To fully appreciate just how wrong such an overgeneralization is, one must carefully consider what was tested in Kansas City. In 1972, routine preventive patrol was not a sharp, focused tactic. Typically, in urban areas, between 40 and 60 percent of patrol time is uncommitted (as opposed to committed to responding to calls for service). Analysis in several jurisdictions indicates that of the uncommitted patrol time, only about half is spent cruising through a beat. The other half is spent on administrative matters or breaks. Thus, for a typical beat, about two hours out of every eight are spent on nondirected cruising. This was the case in Kansas City.

There could not be a more generic approach to policing than routine preventive patrol. The patrol officer decides what merits attention. If an officer likes to engage in traffic enforcement, or is under pressure to do so, then that will occupy a substantial portion of routine preventive patrol time. If an officer is inclined to make a round of visiting on the beat, then that becomes routine preventive patrol. And so it goes. The individual patrol officer accounts for most of the variation in the specific activities conducted during routine patrol. However, patterns also vary by the nature of the beat, the time of the day, and the day of the week. No police strategy could be more diffuse. One must truly believe that the mere occasional presence of a patrol car cruising by deters crime to believe that routine patrol makes any difference.

Further, one must visualize the design of the Kansas City experiment (Kelling et al. 1974). On the one hand, the decision to concurrently test decreases in routine preventive patrol and increases in adjoining beats had its strengths, particularly in an era when there was virtually no research on police strategy. In withdrawing and increasing routine preventive patrol in the south district, the researchers assumed that citizens perceive the amount of preventive patrol, and react to it, within the confines of beat boundaries. In other words, someone living in a designated reactive beat would hypothetically conclude there was less preventive patrol based solely on the fact that there was less preventive patrol on that beat. Similarly, someone in an adjoining proactive beat would hypothetically conclude there was more preventive patrol based solely on the increase on that beat, ignoring adjacent beats. With rare exception, citizens do not know where the boundary lines are drawn. So our assumption is that most south district citizens would perceive more or less preventive patrol, and alter their behavior accordingly, within a living and working area bounded by a single beat.

However, someone residing in one beat and working and/or playing in another would in effect live in both a proactive and a reactive area. Indeed, any mobility at all would result in citizens experiencing all three levels of patrol. Thus, a necessary assumption is that most citizens would perceive variation, if it were to be perceived, independently and without overlap within the boundaries of the fifteen police beats. No one would propose that every citizen perceived the levels of preventive patrol exclusively within the boundaries of a single beat. Kansas City is a horizontal municipality. The south district contains a range of residential, business, and shopping and recreation areas. Everyone recognizes that a lot of citizens routinely crossed beat boundaries. The issue is perceptual effect. Would a lack of preventive patrol in a particular area, or an increase in another area, be perceived by enough people to change their behaviors?

From one perspective, that was the whole point of the experiment. It was designed to test such perception. But is it not possible that the perception of withdrawal was canceled by the perception of enhancement? In other words, is it possible that most citizens could not detect any difference in preventive patrol because, overall, in the south district there was no difference in the level?

This is not to suggest that the experiment was flawed. It was well conceived and carefully designed and monitored. The researchers drew conservative conclusions. The issue is overgeneralization of results. Like any good piece of research, the experimental variable in Kansas City was very narrowly drawn. It demonstrated that citizens did not perceive variation in routine preventive patrol across beats. It did not demonstrate that police activities directed at particular targets made no difference. It did not demonstrate that withdrawal of patrol across a broadly defined area made no difference. It did not demonstrate that increasing routine preventive patrol across a broad area made no difference. It says nothing about potential patrol saturation effect, regardless of the nature of the patrol activity (given the size of police beats in Kansas City's south district, two to three patrol units in one of those areas is hardly saturation). Most important, the Kansas City Preventive Patrol Experiment says nothing about the efficacy of planned, focused police field intervention. One must be very conservative drawing conclusions about police effectiveness from this study.

San Diego Field Interrogation Experiment

Following close on the heels of the Kansas City experiment is the San Diego Field Interrogation Experiment (Boydstun 1975). The contrast in results is striking, and it supports the principle that proactive patrol interventions reduce crime. To the extent that the Kansas City Preventive Patrol Experiment demonstrated that a passive police presence made no difference, the San Diego Field Interrogation Experiment demonstrated that an active police presence made a dramatic difference. Conducted in 1973, the experiment involved varying the intensity of police stop-and-question activities. Three areas in San Diego were compared. One group of beats was designated control, where field interrogations during the experimental period were maintained at the same intensity as before. In a second group of beats, officers were trained to conduct field interrogations with more courtesy (it was felt that an increase in the already high levels of field interrogations would infringe upon civil rights). A third group of beats was designated as "no field interrogations." Actually, field interrogations were allowed on these beats, but officers were to conduct them only when extreme suspicion existed. The level of field interrogations in the experimental beats dropped tremendously. Suppressible street crime was measured for seven months before the experiment, for nine months during which experimental conditions were maintained, and for five months as follow-up. Suppressible crime was defined as robbery, burglary, auto theft, street theft, street rape, other sex crimes, malicious mischief, and disorderly conduct.

There was no change in crime in the control beats and in those where officers were specially trained (Boydstun 1975). However, on the beats where field interrogations were withdrawn, the average number of suppressible crimes jumped from 75 to 104 per month. When field interrogations were reestablished, suppressible crime dropped down to 81 offenses per month. There was about a one-month lag time between the change in the number of field investigations and the change in crime rates.

While the passive police activity characterized as routine preventive patrol had no effect in Kansas City, the proactive activity characterized by field interrogation had a dramatic effect in San Diego. Interestingly, officers conduct most field interrogations after observing suspicious behavior while on routine preventive patrol. But some officers may engage in routine preventive patrol and never initiate a field interrogation. Thus, researchers must test these activities independently.

Directed Patrol in New Haven and Pontiac

As a result of the Kansas City Preventive Patrol Experiment, many agencies implemented directed patrol programs in the late 1970s. The idea was to use uncommitted patrol time to focus on particular problems (e.g., thefts from autos in shopping area parking lots). Evaluations of directed patrol efforts were conducted in New Haven and Pontiac (Cordner 1996). Little crime reduction was noted. However, it must be observed that the evaluators did not employ experimental designs. Further, the evaluators noted that implementing directed patrol was problematic.

Split-Force Patrol in Wilmington

Another effort to use uncommitted patrol time in a structured strategy was launched by the Wilmington, Delaware, Police Department in 1975 (Kenney 1992). The department divided its patrol division into a basic patrol force, about 70 percent of the officers, and a structured patrol force, about 30 percent of the officers. The structured patrol force was not to respond to calls for service except in emergencies, allowing them to conduct proactive crime-intervention activities. The structured patrol force spent their time on problem areas and initial follow-up investigations of all crime-in-progress calls. The patrol division's overall arrest rate increased by 4 percent, charges per arrest by 13 percent, and clearances by 105 percent. However, the detective division's clearance rate dropped by 61 percent, producing an overall drop of 28 percent for the department. The agency abandoned the split-force approach partially for the statistical reasons, and partially because of disillusionment in the patrol force. In particular, the officers in the basic patrol force deeply resented the freedom given the other officers.

Problem-Oriented Policing in Newport News

Nearly fifteen years after the Kansas City Preventive Patrol Experiment, the first truly innovative alternative use of uncommitted patrol time was developed in Newport News. Darrel Stephens, then chief of the police department, implemented problem-oriented policing. Refined by Herman Goldstein, the technique involves making patrol officers responsible for finding longer-term solutions to recurrent police problems. Eck and Spelman (1987) documented the success of problem-oriented policing in Newport News with regard to three issues: thefts from autos in the parking lots adjoining the shipyards, robberies associated with a deteriorating downtown area, and burglaries and other problems associated with the New Briarfield housing project. For all three problems, patrol officers attacked underlying conditions and substantially reduced crime rates. Problem-oriented policing is still one of the most popular patrol strategies.

Minneapolis Repeat Call Address Policing

In 1988, the city of Minneapolis determined that 3 percent of the city's 1,115 addresses accounted for 50 percent of police calls for service. Five percent of those addresses generated 64 percent of the calls and, during the time frame analyzed, nearly 60 percent of the city's addresses generated no calls. Minneapolis formed a special unit of five officers who were assigned 125 residential and 125 commercial addresses (Sherman 1990). They were to use problem-oriented techniques to reduce the calls for service coming from those addresses. After six months, the target addresses had 15-percent fewer calls for service (Sherman 1990). However, after one year, all the gains were erased; indeed, the residential addresses were actually producing more calls for service. The conclusion was reached that target rotation may be the best police strategy when dealing with problematic addresses.

Kansas City Gun Experiment

From July 1992 to January 1993, patrol overtime hours from 7 to 10 P.M. were directed at detecting concealed weapons in beat 144 of Kansas City. A total of 4,512 officer hours (2,256 patrol car hours) were concentrated in the beat during the six months. Typically, two extra patrol units were in the beat each evening. Beat 144 is an eight-by-ten-block area with a 1991 homicide rate of 177 per 100 thousand, about twenty times the national average. The beat is 92 percent nonwhite, and 66 percent own homes (Sherman, Shaw, and Regan 1995).

Police gun seizures in the target area increased by more than 65 percent, while gun crimes declined by 40 percent (Sherman, Shaw, and Regan 1995). Neither gun seizures nor gun crimes changed significantly in a similar beat several miles away, where directed patrol was not used. Further, there was no measurable displacement of gun crimes to patrol beats adjacent to the target area. While drive-by shootings dropped from seven to one in the target area, they doubled from six to twelve in the comparison area. Again, there was no displacement to areas adjacent to the target beat. Homicide showed a statistically significant reduction in the target area, but not in a comparison area. The investment of 4,512 police officer hours was associated with twenty-nine more guns seized and eighty-three fewer gun crimes, or about fifty-five patrol hours per gun crime and almost three gun crimes prevented per gun seized. Traffic stops were the most productive way to find guns, with an average of one gun found for every twenty-eight stops. Interestingly, two-thirds of the people arrested for carrying guns lived outside the target area. Only gun crimes were affected by directed patrols, with no changes in the number of calls for service or the total number of violent and nonviolent crimes reported.

The Unexplored Wilderness of Criminal Investigation

In a typical police department, 50 percent of personnel are assigned to patrol, 30 percent to investigative units, and the remaining 20 percent to traffic, records, custodial, planning and research, and various other functions. While from one perspective there is little research on the effectiveness of various patrol strategies, compared with research on the effectiveness of investigations the catalog of patrol research reports looks like a Library of Congress listing. There is almost no research on the relative efficacy of the strategies used by one-third of the personnel in a typical urban police agency (Greenwood and Petersillia 1975).

Like the patrol function, the criminal-investigations function suffers from an early macroanalysis with overgeneralized results. In 1975, the RAND Corporation tried to ascertain if any broad approaches to criminal investigation worked better than others by analyzing approaches used in major urban police departments (Greenwood and Petersillia 1975). A written questionnaire was sent to the 300 agencies employing more than 150 personnel that year, inquiring about investigative training, staffing, workload, and procedures. RAND received 153 responses. Researchers then made site visits to twenty-five of the responding agencies to gather more detailed information.

RAND (Greenwood and Petersillia 1975) concluded that the investigative division's organization and staffing could not be significantly related to variations in arrest or clearance rates as reported by participating police departments to the FBI Uniform Crime Reports (FBI 1995). The ancillary conclusions the researchers drew were perhaps as important as the primary one. They noted that (1) 65 percent of all serious crimes received no more than superficial attention from investigators; (2) the single most important factor in whether a case will be solved is the information the victim supplies to the responding patrol officer; (3) in cases that are solved, the investigator spends more time on postclearance processing than on identifying the perpetrator; and (4) of cases ultimately cleared in which a perpetrator was not identified during the initial police incident-reporting processes, almost all were solved as a result of "routine police procedures" (fingerprinting, obtaining tips from informants, etc.). The RAND study attacked the Sherlock Holmes image of investigators, implying that instead of super sleuths, detectives were, in effect, clerks for the district attorney, helping to prepare solved cases for courtroom presentation. For those inclined to believe that the police are by and large ineffective, the RAND report was music to their ears. While the preventive patrol experiment demonstrated that uniformed officers make no difference, the RAND study similarly demonstrated that plainclothes officers are equally useless.

The RAND study is a classic example of a piece of exploratory research being used as the definitive answer. It was, first of all, some of the first real research ever conducted on the investigative function. Although the RAND researchers had done precursory work in New York and Kansas City, the national survey was the first effort at using a quasi-experimental design (Eck 1996). There were shortcomings in identifying independent and dependent variables. The researchers simply looked for naturally occurring variation in investigative structure and workload, then compared what variation might exist with a very questionable dependent variable—agency reports on arrest and clearance rates. Both rates are subject to definitional ambiguity and manipulation. One would expect that a poorly run investigative unit would tend to inflate the numbers, while a well-run unit would be far more conservative in reporting arrests and clearances. To the extent that better-run investigative units would use more effective strategies, the use of conservative criteria for reporting arrest and clearance rates would conceal the efficacy of those efforts in any comparative analysis.

It is not that the RAND study was inherently flawed. Rather, we should not expect dramatic results from this type of research approach. At best, tentative conclusions might be reached; for example, specialization in investigations appears to, or does not appear to, result in higher clearance rates for the specific crimes. It is grossly inappropriate to assert that investigative units are useless.

Further, the study overdoes the "clerk for the district attorney" issue. Moving a case from a standard of probable cause to a standard of proof beyond a reasonable doubt is not a trivial task, and it certainly should not be characterized as the work of a clerk. Moreover, the fact that relatively few offenders are identified from super-sleuth techniques does not negate the importance of skilled investigative follow-up. The deterrent effect of such an approach may be enormous.

John Eck's (1983) insightful analysis of the criminal-investigations function stands in contrast to the overgeneralized conclusions often drawn from the RAND study. Eck examined burglary and robbery investigations in St. Petersburg, Florida, Dekalb County, Georgia, and Wichita, Kansas, and concluded that detective effort made a difference, but only if focused on particular cases.

The point is that police efforts must be analyzed in terms of focus. If all investigative follow-up is aggregated, it is impossible to tease out effective strategies. However, when we sort cases, a different picture emerges. In particular, when we rule out the majority of cases for which investigative follow-up is largely a waste of time, then analyze only the very small subset for which it is potentially fruitful, a very different picture emerges. Detectives do make a difference, indeed a dramatic difference, with regard to those cases. Given the fact that very few offenders commit only one crime, it is easy to understand why, if a detective makes a difference in only 5 percent of the cases, that 5 percent may be critical. An offender committing only one crime every three weeks will, on average, be caught annually. A single "cleared by arrest" by a skilled investigator can prevent scores of crimes over a few years (Eck 1983).

CONCLUSIONS FROM OUR RESEARCH LEGACY

Perhaps more than any other study, the 1993 Kansas City Gun Experiment demonstrates the very narrow effect of a particular police strategy. One might reasonably expect that with triple the number of patrol units in beat 144 conducting aggressive patrol in the evening, other crimes would drop as well. But while there was a very dramatic effect on the target gun crimes there was no measurable impact on other crimes. Police efforts targeted at particular offenders committing particular crimes produced results in Kansas City, as they did in Newport News and San Diego. And crackdowns conducted in situations previously lacking enforcement may produce results. But mere police presence does nothing. Further, defuse strategies without a sharp focus have produced little results. Directed patrol in Pontiac and New Haven consisted of targeting various crimes committed by various offenders at various times of the day and no definitive results materialized. The same held true for the Wilmington Split-Force Patrol Experiment. Likewise, research on the efficacy of investigations leads to precisely the same conclusion: It is focused police efforts that make a difference.

Among those who have been around since the 1960s, there is a universal fondness for pointing out to beginners that when we started out all the books in the field could fit on one standard bookcase shelf. Indeed, the literature has greatly increased. But there has not been an explosion in controlled experiments designed to ascertain which police strategies produce the best results. In fact, there are still only a few controlled experiments in policing. And, sadly, most of those were conducted twenty years ago during the golden era of the Police Foundation.

Controlled experiments are, of course, both complex and expensive. It is difficult to manipulate police field strategies. It is extraordinarily difficult to withdraw a service from a geographic area or clientele. It is a bit easier to differentially distribute new services (e.g., conduct saturation patrol in some beats but not in others). Even then, however, police managers face the dilemma of equity in distributing resources to the citizens they serve. If differential distribution might harm some citizens, ethical questions are obviously raised. In addition, the situations for which excess resources are available for differential distribution, though not rare, are not common either. Beyond these difficulties, for a field experiment to occur there must be a confluence of research expertise, a motivation to conduct the experiment, and a police administrator's willingness to take the risk involved. We can only hope that future years see more such experiments. First, however, we must be convinced that the police do make a difference.

BIBLIOGRAPHY

Boydstun, J. (1975). *San Diego Field Interrogation: Final Report*. Washington, D.C.: Police Foundation.

Cordner, G. (1996). Evaluating Tactical Patrol. In *Quantifying Quality in Policing*, edited by L. Hoover. Washington, D.C.: Police Executive Research Forum.

Cordner, G., and R. Trojanowicz. (1992). Patrol. In *What Works in Policing?* edited by G. Cordner and D. Hale. Cincinnati: Anderson.

Eck, J. (1996). Rethinking Detective Management. In *Quantifying Quality in Policing*, edited by L. Hoover. Washington, D.C.: Police Executive Research Forum.

Eck, J. (1983). *Solving Crimes: The Investigation of Burglary and Robbery*. Washington, D.C.: Police Executive Research Forum.

Eck, J., and W. Spelman. (1987). *Problem Solving: Problem-Oriented Policing in Newport News*. Washington, D.C.: Police Executive Research Forum.

Federal Bureau of Investigation (FBI). (1995). *Crime in the United States* (Uniform Crime Reports). Washington, D.C.: U.S. Government Printing Office.

Greenwood, P., and J. Petersilia. (1975). *The Criminal Investigation Process*. Vol. 1, *Summary and Policy Implications*. Santa Monica, Calif.: RAND Corp.

Hoover, L., and T. Caeti. (1994). *Crime-Specific Policing in Houston*. Texas Law Enforcement Management and Administrative Statistics (TELEMASP) Bulletin Series, vol. 1, no. 9.

Kelling, G.; T. Pate; D. Dieckman; and C. Brown. (1974). *The Kansas City Preventive Patrol Experiment: A Technical Report*. Washington, D.C.: Police Foundation.

Kenney, D. (1992). Strategic Approaches. In *Police Management: Issues and Perspectives*, edited by L. Hoover. Washington, D.C.: Police Executive Research Forum.

Sherman, L. (1990). Police Crackdowns: Initial and Residual Deterrence. In *Crime and Justice: A Review of Research*, edited by M. Tonry and N. Morris. Chicago: University of Chicago Press.

Sherman, L., and R. Berk. (1984). *The Minneapolis Domestic Violence Experiment*. Washington, D.C.: Police Foundation.

Sherman, L.; J. Shaw; and D. Regan. (1995). *The Kansas City Gun Experiment*. Washington, D.C.: National Institute of Justice.

Index

Testing bias, 29–31
Total institutions, 3–5
Total involvement, 47
Total quality management (TQM),
    46–47

Verification process, 71–73

Weber, Max, 267–269
Wechsler Adult Intelligence Scale
    (WAIS), 16, 18–21, 25, 27, 30–33

About the Editors and Contributors

Geoffrey P. Alpert is Professor of Criminal Justice at the University of South Carolina and Research Professor at the Institute of Public Affairs. For the past seventeen years his research and training have concentrated on the evaluation of high-risk police activities, including the use of force, deadly force, and pursuit driving. Dr. Alpert is working on a two-year study, funded by the National Institute of Justice, concerning the use of force to control suspects. He is author or coauthor of numerous books, monographs, and articles, including *Forces of Deviance, Police Use of Deadly Force: A Statistical Analysis of the Metro-Dade Police Department, The Force Factor: Measuring Police Use of Force Relative to Suspect Resistance,* and *Police Vehicles and Firearms: Instruments of Deadly Force.*

Michael E. Buerger is an Associate Professor at the College of Criminal Justice of Northeastern University. A former New Hampshire police officer, he has worked with police in numerous jurisdictions. He was Research Director for the Jersey City Police Department and on-site field director for the RECAP and Hot Spots experiments in Minneapolis. In addition to teaching, he is active in research and evaluation of community policing and problem solving.

Gary W. Cordner is Acting Dean of the College of Law Enforcement at Eastern Kentucky University, where he is also a Professor of Police

Studies and Director of the Regional Community Policing Institute. He received his doctorate from Michigan State University and served as a police officer and police chief in Maryland. Cordner is coauthor of textbooks on police administration and criminal justice planning and coeditor of *What Works in Policing?*, *Police Operations: Analysis and Evaluation*, *Managing Police Organizations*, *Managing Police Personnel*, and *Policing Perspectives: An Anthology*. He edited the *American Journal of Police* from 1987 to 1992, coedited *Police Computer Review* from 1992 to 1995, and now edits *Police Quarterly*. He is a consultant to Abt Associates on several national studies and a Senior Research Fellow with the Police Executive Research Forum. He served as President of the Academy of Criminal Justice Sciences during 1998–1999.

John E. Eck is an Associate Professor of Criminal Justice at the University of Cincinnati. He has been the Evaluation Coordinator for the Washington–Baltimore High Intensity Drug Trafficking Area, where he developed procedures for understanding the nature of regional drug trafficking. He has also been the Director of Research for the Police Executive Research Forum where he helped pioneer the development and testing of problem-oriented policing. His interests are in police effectiveness, the origins of crime problems and patterns, the study of crime places and hotspots, drug dealing, and problem analysis techniques. He has served as a consultant to the Office of Community Oriented Policing Services, the National Institute of Justice, the Police Foundation, the Police Executive Research Forum, the Royal Canadian Mounted Police, and the London Metropolitan Police. Dr. Eck earned his Ph.D. from the Department of Criminology of the University of Maryland. He also holds a Master of Public Policy degree from the University of Michigan.

Larry K. Gaines is a Professor and Chair of the Criminal Justice Department at California State University at San Bernardino. His research centers around policing and drugs. In addition to writing numerous articles, he is coauthor of a number of books, including *Police Supervision*, *Police Administration*, *Managing the Police Organization*, *Community Policing: A Contemporary Perspective*, *Policing Perspectives: An Anthology*, *Policing in America*, and *Drugs, Crime, and Justice*. His current research agenda concerns evaluating the effectiveness of police tactics in reducing problems and fitting within the community policing paradigm. He received a doctorate in criminal justice from Sam Houston State University. He has police experience with the Kentucky State Police and the Lexington, Kentucky, Police Department. He has also served as the Executive Director of the Kentucky Association of Chiefs of Police for fourteen years. He is a past president of the Academy of Criminal Justice Sciences.

Ronald W. Glensor is a Deputy Chief of the Reno, Nevada, Police Department. He is internationally recognized for his work in community policing and has provided training to more than a thousand agencies throughout the United States, Canada, Australia, and Great Britain. He is a featured speaker on such topics as community policing, problem-oriented policing, strategic planning, customer service, supervision and leadership. He has also assisted the British Home Office in London with research on repeat victimization. In 1996, he was one of ten U.S. public policy experts selected to receive an Atlantic Fellowship. He is also the recipient of the University of Nevada, Reno, Alumni Association's 1996 Outstanding Achievement Award and the Police Executive Research Forum's 1997 Gary P. Hayes Award. He received a Ph.D. in Political Science from the University of Nevada, Reno. He is the co-author of *Community Policing and Problem Solving: Strategies and Practices*, 2nd edition, and *Police Supervision*.

Larry T. Hoover has been on the Criminal Justice Faculty at Sam Houston State University, where he currently directs the Police Research Center, since 1977. In addition, he edits the Texas Law Enforcement Management and Administrative Statistics monthly bulletin series, teaches in the Bill Blackwood Law Enforcement Management Institute's Executive Issues Series, conducts research for the university's Community Policing Institute, and directs both a technology-transfer grant from the National Institute of Justice and a major information-systems development project (CRIMES). He is editor of *Police Management: Issues and Perspectives*, *Quantifying Quality in Policing*, and *Police Program Evaluation*. Holding a Ph.D. from the Michigan State University, he is past president of the Academy of Criminal Justice Sciences.

Thomas Kelley is an Associate Professor of Criminal Justice at Wayne State University. His current research interests include thought recognition, locus of control, and adolescent well-being with implications for delinquency prevention.

Dennis Jay Kenney is currently an Associate Director and Director of Research for the Police Executive Research Forum (PERF). He has more than twenty-eight years of experience in varied aspects of criminal justice—as a Florida police officer, as a director of research and planning in Savannah, as a project director for the Police Foundation, and as a university professor both at Western Connecticut State University and at the University of Nebraska at Omaha. He is the author or co-author of numerous articles and books including *Crime in the Schools* (1998), *A Conflict of Rights* (1998), *Organized Crime in America* (1995), *Crime, Fear and the New York City Subways* (1986), and *Police Pursuits:*

What We Know (1999). He has also provided consulting services to numerous police agencies and managed sponsored research and technical assistance projects. He is past editor of the *American Journal of Police* and a cofounder of *Police Quarterly*. At present, he is replicating his student problem-solving approach to addressing crime, fear, and disorder in several schools. He is also completing funded research projects on police performance evaluations, police fatigue and its impact on officer performance, and the nature and extent of abortion-related violence. Dr. Kenney holds a Ph.D. in criminal justice from Rutgers University.

Robert Leuci is a noted author and lecturer in the fields of law enforcement and criminal justice. He retired from the New York City Police Department in 1981 after twenty years of service, most of them spent in the areas of organized crime and narcotics enforcement. A portion of his career with the NYPD was the subject of the book and motion picture *Prince of the City*. Since retiring from active law enforcement, he has written numerous novels including *Doyle's Disciples, Odessa Beach, Captain Butterfly, The Snitch, Fence Jumpers*, and *Double Edge*. He is a member of the Writer's Guild, PEN America, and Mystery Writers of America.

Robert P. McNamara is currently an Assistant Professor of Sociology at Furman University. With varied research interests that include drug abuse, homelessness, education issues, urban redevelopment, gangs, AIDS, and policing, Dr. McNamara has assisted state, federal, and private agencies on a variety of social science topics. He is also the author of numerous books, including *The Times Square Hustler, Sex, Scams, and Street Life: The Sociology of New York City's Times Square, Social Gerontology, Perspectives in Social Problems, Beating the Odds: Crime, Poverty, and Life in the Inner City*, and *Crossing the Line: Interracial Couples in the South*. He holds a doctorate in Sociology from Yale University.

Timothy N. Oettmeier is a twenty-four-year veteran with the Houston Police department holding the rank of Assistant Chief. He acquired a Ph.D. in 1982 from Sam Houston State University. He has participated in national research and development projects involving fear reduction, performance evaluation, organization development, training, problem solving, and investigations. He has numerous publications in these areas and continues to work with departments throughout the country.

Kenneth J. Peak is Professor of Criminal Justice at the University of Nevada, Reno. He is author or coauthor of nine books and nearly fifty journal articles and book chapters. He is Chairman of the Police Section, Academy of Criminal Justice Sciences, and past president of the

Western and Pacific Association of Criminal Justice Educators. Prior to entering higher education, he was a municipal police officer, criminal justice planner, and university chief of police.

Christopher Simon received a doctorate from the Department of Political Science at Washington State University. He is currently an Assistant Professor at the University of Nevada, Reno. His research interests include public administration, political philosophy, and organizational change. His recent articles have appeared in *Policy Studies Journal* and the *American Review of Public Administration.*

Tara O'Connor Shelley, a PERF Research Associate, has five years experience in criminal justice research, training, and technical assistance. She serves as Deputy Project Director for BJA's National Guns First Training Program and is currently working on several projects regarding police early warning systems, uses of force, abortion related conflict, and violence. She is also conducting evaluations on gang units and the Texas Regional Community Policing Institute (TRCPI). In addition, she is the coeditor of *Problem-Oriented Policing: Crime Specific Problems, Critical Issues, and Making POP Work.* Before joining PERF, she worked for the Justice Research and Statistics Associationand the Bureau of Justice Assistance. She holds a Master of Science degree in Justice, Law and Society from the American University.

Steven Stack is Professor of Criminal Justice at Wayne State University. His current research interests include an assessment of Southern location on the odds of homicide victimization for blacks and whites. He is also working on a study of the relative impact of life sentences versus executions on homicide rates.

Erik Y. Taiji is a 1997 graduate of the University of California, Irvine. As an undergraduate, he conducted telephone surveys about police overtime practices while working with Dr. Bryan Vila. Since graduation, he has worked as a research assistant on a national study assessing the detrimental affects of fatigue on police officers' performance, health, and safety, as well as their relations with their families and the communities they serve.

Maria Tempenis is a doctoral student in Sociology at Vanderbilt University. Her areas of interest include criminology, education, religion, and sociological theory.

Quint Thurman is the director of the Midwest Criminal Justice Institute and a professor in the Hugo Wall School of Urban and Public

Affairs at Wichita State University. He holds an M.A. degree in Sociology from the University of Oklahoma and a Ph.D. from the University of Massachusetts. He has published in numerous journals and is currently completing several projects that focus on the assessment of criminal justice organizations.

Bryan Vila is Associate Professor of Political Science and Administration of Justice at the University of Wyoming. He is coprincipal investigator on a national study assessing the detrimental affects of fatigue on police officers' performance, health, and safety, as well as their relations with their families and the communities they serve. Prior to becoming an academic, Dr. Vila spent seventeen years in law enforcement, including nine years as an officer and supervisor with the Los Angeles County Sheriff's Department, six years as a police chief helping the emerging nations of Micronesia develop innovative law enforcement strategies, and two years in Washington, D.C., as a federal law enforcement officer working primarily on policy issues. His other interests include the application of geographic information systems technology to the study of gang activities and crime, as well as the development of comprehensive, long-term crime control strategies that emphasize attacking crime at its roots. Author of numerous articles, he is also coauthor of two recent books: *Capital Punishment in the United States: A Documentary History* and *The Role of Police in American Society: A Documentary History*.

T. Steuart Watson is currently Professor of School Psychology at Mississippi State University. He received a Ph.D. from the University of Nebraska in 1991. Included among his research interests are programs that focus on school safety, improving the academic and behavioral functioning of children, and enhancing the delivery of psychological services in schools. He is also actively involved in efforts to design maximally effective treatment procedures for a wide range of social, emotional, and behavioral problems evidenced by children. His most recent publications include *Crime in the Schools: Reducing Fear and Disorder through Student Problem Solving*, the *Handbook of Child Behavior Therapy*, and numerous journal articles. He is also the coeditor of the journal *Proven Practice: Prevention and Remediation Solutions for School*. The American Psychological Association chose Dr. Watson as the 1998 recipient of the Lightner Witmer Award for outstanding research by a young scholar.

Samuel Walker is Professor of Criminal Justice at the University of Nebraska at Omaha. He is the author or coauthor of several books on the police, criminal justice, and civil liberties, including *The Police in*

America, 2nd edition, *Sense and Nonsense about Crime*, 4th edition, and *The Color of Justice*. His is completing a book on citizen complaints and civilian oversight of the police entitled *Citizen Complaints and Police Accountability*. In addition, he is conducting a national evaluation of early warning systems for problem police officers.

Mary Ann Wycoff is a Senior Research Associate with the Police Executive Research Forum. From 1972 to 1995, she served as Project Director for the Police Foundation. In 1993, under a grant from NIJ, she completed a national survey on community policing. In addition, she has directed the Police Foundation's subcontract for the Weed and Seed evaluation, conducted an evaluation of the implementation of quality policing in Madison, Wisconsin, and conducted an evaluation of a personnel performance measurement system for Houston's community policing approach. She is now conducting a study of the integration of investigations with community policing and a followup study of community policing in Madison. She is also participating in a joint effort between PERF, Harvard's Kennedy School, and the Local Initiatives Support Corporation to promote community policing and community development in East New York. In partnership with Dr. Mark Moore of the Kennedy School and Dr. George Kelling of Rutgers University, Ms. Wycoff is also participating in a study of organizational change in policing. Her research interests include community policing, measurement techniques, organizational change, program implementation, and personnel and management issues.

Jihong Zhao is an Assistant Professor in the Department of Criminal Justice at the University of Nebraska, Omaha. He received a Ph.D. from Washington State University. His interests include organizational theories, police organizational change, and criminal justice planning. His research articles have appeared in a number of journals, including the *Journal of Criminal Justice, Social Science Research, American Journal of Police, Policing: An International Journal of Police Management*, and *Justice Quarterly*.